the Haunted Heroes of

Eugene O'Neill

Men still need their swords
to slash at ghosts in the
dark. Men, those haunted
heroes!

Lazarus Laughed, Act Three — Scene One

the Haunted Heroes of
Eugene O'Neill

EDWIN A. ENGEL

HARVARD UNIVERSITY PRESS

Cambridge, Massachusetts

1953

Distributed in Great Britain by
Geoffrey Cumberlege, Oxford University Press, London

The extracts from the plays of Eugene O'Neill
that are found in this volume have been quoted
with the kind permission of Random House

Library of Congress Catalog Card Number 53-5068
Printed in the United States of America

To Dorothy

Preface

"LET THE BEST WRITER cease to produce for a decade and he is as dead as mutton to the critical mind." So chides Van Wyck Brooks in his recent book, *The Writer in America*. A case in point is Eugene O'Neill who, says Brooks, has been "buried alive in oblivion, scarcely re-examined critically in fifteen years." To be sure, O'Neill may have stopped writing, but Brooks has exaggerated his need for disinterment. Except to the critic he has remained alive — neglected, perhaps, but never forgotten. His plays continue to be produced nearly every season both on and off Broadway; they seldom fail to be included in drama anthologies; they are vivid in the memory of everybody who attended the theatre between the two World Wars. But close to twenty years have passed since a new full-length study of O'Neill has been published in America.

Coming too late to vindicate the critic, the present book should at least escape the charge of prematurity. A much earlier attempt to follow the broad sweep of O'Neill's long career, to pass confident judgment upon his achievement, would have laid itself open to even more charges than it shall have to face at this late date. Tentative it is not, and therefore unlike so many recent critical studies of writers who are still midway in their productive life. And therefore, too, the faults with which it likely abounds — the misinterpretations, the erratic evaluations — are less excusable than I should like them to be. And alas, the reproval which I am certain to incur thereby cannot be shared with the already guilty profession of critics — or with anybody else.

Nobody is indifferent to O'Neill. He has had only enthusiastic supporters and energetic detractors, with the latter inclined to utter their opinion in the form of a "minority report." I have no illusions regarding the success with which I have tried to remain uninfluenced by members of either party. My method, however, has been always to focus rigidly upon the plays themselves, to keep peripheral not only the interpretations and opinions of other critics, but also such information as is contained in O'Neill's occasional statements of intention and in biographical articles. So far as possible I acquainted myself with this material subsequent to the close examination, the interpretation and evaluation, of the plays, and then used it sparingly.

Neither biographical nor bibliographical, the purpose of the study is critical. Nearly all of O'Neill's extant work has been included — referred to, if not discussed. O'Neill himself abrogated the early *Thirst* volume of short plays. I have felt it neither respectful nor necessary to criticize them. Likewise the unauthorized collection of the so called *Lost Plays*. Somewhat whimsically, perhaps, I have also chosen to omit entirely discussion of or reference to *The First Man*, a piece which should have been among the "lost" plays, but which is printed in the standard collected works — the three-volume Random House edition titled *The Plays of Eugene O'Neill*.

Although I have struggled to maintain critical independence I have been unable to dispense with the printed contributions of George Jean Nathan. Nathan remains either on stage or in the wings throughout most of the performance. Nor could I have done without Kenneth Macgowan who, for a while, plays the supporting role to O'Neill's lead. Or without Richard Dana Skinner whose book, *Eugene O'Neill: A Poet's Quest,* is now the most recent but one on O'Neill. To him I am indebted not only for his interesting interpretation but also for including in his book a chronology of the O'Neill Plays — as furnished by the playwright. And finally, Barrett H. Clark's *Eugene O'Neill* has been a most useful compendium of autobiographical, biographical, and historical information.

My self-sufficiency becomes even more illusory when I recall my indebtedness to friends, though teachers and colleagues: to Paul Mueschke for his patient and penetrating criticism; to Mary Needham for her never-flagging interest and faith; to Kenneth Rowe for his cogent suggestions; to Joe Lee Davis, Norman Nelson, Theophile Raphael, Allan Seager — all of whom read the book in manuscript and readily discussed it with me at my own convenience.

To my wife my debt has been continuous, pervasive, and large. About that I have never had any illusions.

June 1953   E. A. E.

CONTENTS

PART ONE

The Sea and The Jungle

The Theatre of Today

THE ROLE IN AMERICAN DRAMA which O'Neill began to play as he made his unheralded entrance at Provincetown in 1916 had been prepared by various hands: by the critics of our native culture, by exponents and producers in America of modern European drama, by the visionary founder and director of the Provincetown Players. The deficiencies of our drama were inherent in the national culture the precise characteristics of which had become increasingly apparent during the second decade of the twentieth century. In 1911 Santayana had observed that America "is a country with two mentalities," the sphere of one being "all aggressive enterprise," of the other "all genteel tradition." Forbidden by that tradition to confess that he is unhappy, the American, declared Santayana, is deprived of such higher things of the mind as "serious poetry and profound religion." Although Walt Whitman was the only American writer, according to Santayana, "who has left the genteel tradition entirely behind," William James, he was pleased to remark, had given it some "rude shocks." In 1912 John Macy had complained about the lack of vitality in American letters, observing that "our writers turn their backs on life, miss its intensities, its significance." They "have been high-minded," wrote Macy,

fine grained, eloquent in manner, in odd contrast to the real or reputed vigour and crudeness of the nation . . . Their physique is feminine; they are fanciful, dainty, reserved; they are literose, sophisticated in craftsmanship, but innocently unaware of the profound agitations of American life, or life everywhere.

Three years later Van Wyck Brooks had rebuked a literature which "in a more than usually difficult and sordid world . . . has applied its principal energies to being uncontaminated itself." Both Macy and Brooks had judged the American product by European standards; the former finding only two American writers, Edith Wharton and Dreiser, to compare favorably with ten British contemporaries; the latter accepting only the work of Whitman — and it with reservations — to set over against a European literature "which grows ever closer and denser and grapples to life more and more."

The year in which Santayana had pointed out the duality of the American character had seen the publication of *Ethan Frome,* of *Jennie Gerhardt,* and the re-issue of *Sister Carrie.* Before 1916, Mrs. Wharton had written two more novels; Dreiser, three. Meanwhile, in 1915, Edgar Lee Masters had emerged to take his stand against the genteel tradition beside the two writers of fiction. Appearing in the same year as *The Genius, The Spoon River Anthology* displayed a gratifying awareness "of the profound agitations of American life." Whereas the arts of fiction and of poetry had responded to the incitements of the critics the native drama continued to remain unmoved. For it had been retarded not only by what Brooks described as a "desiccated culture," but also by "stark utility." Plays by Ibsen, Shaw, Hauptmann had been produced sporadically in America since the 1890's; numerous translations of modern continental dramas were available — Tolstoy, Gorky, Andreyev, Strindberg, Wedekind, in addition to Ibsen and Hauptmann; and between 1912 and 1915 there had appeared in America a rash of books about the current European drama and theatre — books by Ashley Dukes, Huntley Carter, Hiram Motherwell, Archibald Henderson, Barrett Clark, Frank Chandler, Ludwig Lewisohn. In short, there had existed an abundance of examples to exhort the native playwright. But he had no theatre in which to experiment.

The eventual remedy for this condition had been introduced in Chicago in 1912. In that year, a quarter century after Antoine had founded the Théâtre Libre in Paris to begin a movement that spread throughout the Continent and the British Isles, Maurice Browne established America's first little theatre. In Chicago, George Cram Cook attended performances in Browne's theatre and was inspired by productions in that city of the touring Irish Players. "What he saw done for Irish life he wanted for American life — no stage conventions in the way of projecting with the humility of true feeling." Leaving Chicago, where he had associated with Sherwood Anderson, Floyd Dell, Theodore Dreiser, and Arthur Ficke, Cook went east. In New York, where "Broadway flourished almost unchallenged," he watched the newly organized Washington Square Players. Excited one night after seeing a production at the Neighborhood Playhouse, he went home and talked with Susan Glaspell, his wife, "of what the theatre might be. It is," he declared, "one of the mysterious and beautiful things of the world, if you are true to the things you feel, across gulfs of experience you find in another the thing he feels." At Provincetown in the summer of 1915, Cook's excitement had pervaded his group of friends, a collection of novelists, journalists, painters, sculptors, teachers and architects "drawn together by chance and a common sympathy." During an evening at the home of John Reed (or of Mary Heaton Vorse) conversation culminated in a decision by the group to put on their own plays. With Susan Glaspell, Cook had written a one-act comedy, *Suppressed Desires,* a satire on the faddish aspect of psychoanalysis, which even the little theatres had rejected on the ground that it was "too special." This play, together with another one-acter, was presented in a private home. A second performance was given in a fish-house at the end of the Mary Heaton Vorse wharf. Then, following a new bill, the first season closed. In preparation for a re-opening in spring 1916, the group "converted the fish-house into the Wharf Theater, a place where ninety people could see a play." Here the second season got under way with the presentation of a first bill, following which the group met at the home of George Cram Cook to read plays for a second. It was on this occasion that the Provincetown Players and O'Neill were brought together.

O'Neill was twenty-seven at this time and had been writing plays for the past three years, "the urge to write" having come to him while he was in a sanatorium recovering from pulmonary tuberculosis. Up to the time of his illness, in 1912–1913, he had lived, by most standards, a full and erratic life. Born in New York to parents who were devout Catholics, he lived his pre-school years among actors in the atmosphere of the stage. For he and his mother accompanied the father, James O'Neill, on the latter's "road tours in *Monte Cristo* and repertoire . . ." After attending Catholic and non-sectarian boarding schools, a preparatory school in Connecticut, he concluded his formal education abruptly, in 1907, when he was suspended from Princeton as he was about to complete his first year. The following five years of O'Neill's life were filled with an assortment of experiences — all of short duration and ranging in quality from dull and disappointing to downright distressing. He was employed briefly in a "mail-order business in which his father had an interest," he was married and divorced; he accompanied "a mining engineer on a gold prospecting trip to Spanish Honduras," returning at the end of six months with malarial fever and no gold; he served as assistant stage manager in his father's company; he shipped on a Norwegian barque from Boston to Buenos Aires, tended mules on a cattle steamer which sailed from Buenos Aires to South Africa and return, served as ordinary seaman on a British tramp which carried him to New York. Before sailing for New York in 1911 he had experienced "a lengthy period of complete destitution in Buenos Aires." "A bum on the docks," he had hung about the waterfront, making friends with sailors, stevedores, the down-and-outs. Resuming that existence in New York, he lived in a waterfront dive to which he returned after shipping to Southampton as able seaman on an ocean liner. His experiences as sailor and as outcast were involuntarily terminated when after a wild party he regained consciousness to find himself on a train bound for New Orleans where upon his arrival he discovered that his father was playing in the perennial *Monte Cristo.* O'Neill joined the troupe, played a minor part, and after touring the Far West retired to the family summer home in New London, Connecticut. Here he worked for nearly six months, until he fell ill, as cub reporter on the *New London Telegraph,* a daily, to which he also contributed verse.

In the sanatorium he had an opportunity to reflect, to consolidate and evaluate his experiences. Upon his discharge, during the period of convalescence, he began to write — plays, short and long; some verse. Fiction apparently appealed to him but little. Apart from a short story, "Tomorrow," printed in *The Seven Arts* in 1917 he published none whatever, and if he continued to have any lingering latent ambition to express himself in fiction he appears to have satisfied it in such long plays as *Strange Interlude* and *The Iceman Cometh,* both of which display aspects of the novel. As for verse writing, his efforts were never successful. Possessed of a poetic sensibility, he lacked a poetic talent — a judgment in which even his employer on the *Telegraph* had concurred when he suggested to the young man after reading some of his poems that "his forte was prose." O'Neill wrote verses, invariably banal, on a variety of subjects: journalistic, erotic, nautical, philosophical. On two occasions his poems pertained to the class struggle, one of which, "Fratricide," was published in 1914 in the *New York Call;* the other, "Submarine," appeared in *The Masses* in 1917. Most significant among his verses is one whose theme was to recur in the plays beginning about 1925 and continuing to the end of his career. Printed in the *New London Telegraph* in 1912, "The Lay of the Singer's Fall" concerned a happy, idealistic boy whose youthful certitude is subverted by the mocking Devil of Doubt. In succession the boy is bereft of faith, of heart, of soul, of life as he is persuaded respectively that there is no truth, that love is lust, that there is "nothing sure after death but death," that suicide is the "only logical thing" he knows. O'Neill's ineptitude as a poet is reflected not only in his verses, but also in the language of his tragedies. Yet the poetic impulse persisted, and although his ear was unattuned to poetry he contrived to satisfy the impulse in his plays. Piqued by the obtuseness of the critics who failed to perceive what he was trying to do in his tragedies, he complained in a letter to A. H. Quinn: "But where I feel myself most neglected is just where I set most store by myself — as a bit of a poet who has labored with the spoken word to evolve original rhythms of beauty where beauty isn't — ."

That O'Neill, once he had determined to become a writer, should have wished to write for the stage is comprehensible enough. For the twig had been bent: as an infant he had been nursed in the wings and in dressing rooms; during his early years he had known "only actors and the stage"; and as he grew up he watched performances from the other side of the footlights as well. "Even during his years of adventure and aimless wandering he often went to the theater: as a son of James O'Neill he could get free seats at almost any box office." His decision to become a playwright was not made out of deference for his father. If the elder O'Neill worried about his son and occasionally extended from above a helping hand, he seldom did so beyond the call of parental duty. Yet,

whether out of indulgence or desperation, he sent the young man
to Harvard in 1914 to take Professor Baker's course in playwriting,
and in the same year he guaranteed the publication cost of his
son's first plays. "He did believe in me — in a way," O'Neill has
said. But "he didn't see why I should write the kind of plays I did,
and he pointed out, quite properly, that there was no market for
them." "He didn't know how to handle me," recalled the son with
some bitterness, "he didn't 'get' what I was trying to do; he only
wanted me to settle down and make a living. He often used to
think I was just crazy." By achieving success O'Neill vindicated
himself. By achieving it in his father's domain he also appears to
have avenged himself. For he not only overshadowed the famous
parent, he was the ringleader in the rebellion against the theatrical
conventions and traditions of which James O'Neill was an embodiment. Even after his triumph, which had come about 1920,
O'Neill continually introduced in his plays the motif of discord
between son and father. If the rationale for such a recurrent tendency is to be found in contemporary psychological theory and in
prevailing literary practice it is also to be sought in the playwright's
own experiences and emotions. In short, the resemblance in the
plays of the omnipresent grim fathers to persons living or dead was,
we may surmise, not entirely coincidental.

Following the playwriting course at Harvard where he received
encouragement, if little else, O'Neill spent a winter in Greenwich
Village. There he consorted with "Radicals of the labor movement,
I.W.W.'s, anarchists," and with "the Negro and Italian inhabitants
of the quarter." Meanwhile the stage was being set at Provincetown for his arrival the following spring. Susan Glaspell has described the momentous entrance.

Two Irishmen, one old and one young, had arrived and taken a shack up
the street. 'Terry,' I said to the one not young, 'haven't you a play to read
to us?'

'No,' said Terry Carlin, 'I don't write, I just think, and sometimes talk.
But Mr. O'Neill has got a whole trunk full of plays,' he smiled.

That didn't sound too promising, but I said: 'Well, tell Mr. O'Neill to
come to our house at eight o'clock to-night, and bring some of his plays.'

So Gene took 'Bound East for Cardiff' from his trunk, and Freddie Burt
read it to us, Gene staying out in the dining-room while the reading went on.

He was not left alone in the dining-room when the reading had finished. Then we knew what we were for. We began in faith, and perhaps it is true when you do that 'all these things shall be added unto you.'

Bound East for Cardiff was performed, and when the curtain fell "the old wharf shook with applause."

If O'Neill henceforth provided the Players with their principal *raison d'être,* they stimulated him and gave him "a chance to work out [his] ideas in freedom." When the group moved to New York after the season of 1916 drew to a close they continued to be known as the Provincetown Players, but O'Neill suggested that they also call themselves the Playwrights' Theater. "One Thirty-Nine Mac-dougal Street was indeed the playwright's theater," members of the outfit have recalled. "The playwright was the god, and George Cram Cook was his prophet." For in contrast to commercial stage practice the author was expected to superintend the production of his play. Assessing his indebtedness to both prophet and priests, O'Neill declared to Barrett Clark that

Cook was the big man, the dominating and inspiring genius of the Players. Always enthusiastic, vital, impatient with everything that smacked of falsity or compromise, he represented the spirit of revolt against the old worn-out traditions, the commercial theater, the tawdry artificialities of the stage. I owe a tremendous lot to the Players — they encouraged me to write, and produced all my early and many of my later plays. But I can't honestly say I would not have gone on writing plays if it hadn't been for them. I had already gone too far ever to quit.

O'Neill's affiliation with the Provincetown Players, one of mutual benefit, continued beyond Cook's departure in 1922, a date which roughly marked the beginning of a renovation both in the organization and in O'Neill's playwriting. That phenomenon will be the concern of the second part of this study.

Meanwhile we shall observe the playwright's ascent to a position which might be characterized as the dramatic counterpart of that held by Wharton and Dreiser in fiction, Masters in poetry. Indeed, O'Neill's early plays seem to reflect at times the New England of *Ethan Frome,* the ponderous determinism and the "donkeyish solemnity" of certain Dreiser novels, the melancholy of *The Spoon River Anthology.* At other times, however — particularly in the

plays of the sea and of the jungle — they appear to have been inspired by Kipling, Conrad, and Jack London — all of whom O'Neill
had read.

The Sea-Weary Sailor

O'NEILL BEGAN and ended his career with plays that utilized
the experiences of his vagrant days, 1910–1912. Like the Emperor
Jones he traveled in a circle through the blackness of the Great
Forest and emerged where he had entered. For thirty years, from
1916 to 1946, he sought the truth through time and space, in the
outward and the inward worlds, in the pagan and the Christian,
only to return at last to his point of departure. There is a resemblance between the seamen's forecastle of the S.S. *Glencairn* and the
interior of Harry Hope's saloon, an affinity between the homeless
sailors of the early sea plays and the human derelicts of *The Iceman
Cometh,* an identity between the implied philsosophy of the first
and the expressed philosophy of the last play. Ship and saloon alike
are squalid refuges, cages without bars for creatures who have no
better place to go. Men of diverse nationalities, both the seafarers
and the bums are held together not by bonds of brotherhood but
by an animal-like gregariousness. They are, on the whole, doltish,
quarrelsome, even treacherous. Their sensibilities, already dull, are
further blunted by liquor. Their antics, like the ape's, provoke
laughter rather than pity. A member of the group but contrasted
with his fellows, both in the Glencairn pieces and in *The Iceman
Cometh,* is the man of feeling, a pensive figure with an acute consciousness, lonely and life-weary. O'Neill, shortly after he had first
created the character, professed to regard the type with disdain,
pointing out that "his gestures of self-pity," "his thin whine of
weakness," "his sentimental posing" are "much more out of harmony with truth, much less in tune with beauty, than the honest
vulgarity of his mates." He felt, in short, that the latter were in
accord with external nature, that the former was an anomaly. Yet
he later set about either to banish or to transform the mates and

to elevate the man of feeling, making him the perennial hero upon whom he was to bestow his attention, understanding and sympathy. But then, having devoted the greater part of his career to this effort, in *The Iceman Cometh* he recalled the original group and indicated again that they are in harmony with truth — with truth, that is, as he came to conceive it. Once again the man of feeling, filled with self-pity, and loathing himself this time, sits wretchedly by, unable to bring himself into harmony with "truth." Both early and late O'Neill demonstrated that the world belongs to the insensitive, unperceptive, unself-conscious brute.

Bound East for Cardiff was written in 1914, its three companion pieces in 1917. Each play was produced separately, and then in 1924 the group was presented on a single bill. Performed as an episodic unit, the plays were arranged in inverse order to that in which O'Neill wrote them, the curtain rising first on *The Moon of the Caribbees* whose dramatic situation, less particularized than that of the other plays, made it a logical choice for an introductory piece. The scene reveals *a forward section of the main deck of the British tramp steamer Glencairn, at anchor off an island in the West Indies.* In the light of the full moon the crew is discovered in various positions of repose on deck. *A melancholy Negro chant, faint and far off, drifts, crooning over the water.* The eternal note of sadness having been sounded it continues to reverberate for only one character, Smitty, a young Englishman with a blond mustache. He continues to sit and dream and sigh while his mates, unaffected by the distant music, impervious to sadness, transform the languorous, static scene into one of uproarious action. Twice the tumult reaches a climax, the first time as a group of native women board the ship, the second just before they depart. During the intervals of silence the melancholy song can be heard, and Smitty is provided the opportunity of voicing his complaint.

Uninterested in the women, he is eager enough to drink the rum which they have brought. This he does while the women are taken into the forecastle, leaving him alone with the old donkeyman and his own "beastly memories," a form of torment to which only the man of feeling is susceptive.

The Donkeyman. (*spitting placidly*) Queer things, mem'ries. I ain't ever been bothered much by 'em.

Smitty. (*looking at him fixedly for a moment — with quiet scorn*) No, you wouldn't be.

The Donkeyman. Not that I ain't had my share o' things goin' wrong; but I puts 'em out o' me mind, like, an fergets 'em.

Smitty. But suppose you couldn't put them out of your mind? Suppose they haunted you when you were awake and when you were asleep — what then?

The Donkeyman. (*quietly*) I'd get drunk, same's you're doin'.

Smitty. (*with a harsh laugh*) Good advice. (*He takes another drink.*) We're poor little lambs who have lost our way, eh, Donk? Damned from here to eternity, what? God have mercy on such as we!

To whom is Smitty referring? To the donkeyman and himself, or does he mean to include among the lost lambs the goats in the forecastle? Equally ambiguous is the genesis of Smitty's melancholy. As the donkeyman surmises, there is a girl "mixed up in it some place." But whether she threw Smitty over because he was drunk or whether he was drunk because she threw him over remains a mystery. Meanwhile he has gone on "thinking and — drinking to stop thinking." The quiet scene is terminated when the seamen and the girls reappear; the play itself shortly after the *drink-maddened* men get into a wholesale fight. Before the curtain falls there is silence once again, then the crooning music, Smitty's *sigh that is half a sob,* his weary response to the donkeyman's suggestion that he go into the fo'c'sle where the music cannot be heard, where there is more to drink. His exit is followed by a second or so of silence, *broken only by the haunted, saddened voice of the brooding music, faint and far-off, like the mood of the moonlight made audible.*

In other plays of the Glencairn series the sea functions as a force influencing the fate of the seafarers, but in *The Moon of the Caribbees* one is scarcely aware of its presence. Although it plays no discernible role O'Neill felt when he looked back upon his play that "the spirit of the sea — a big thing" is its hero. As for the central character, the sentimental Smitty, "a small thing," O'Neill disposed of him by recognizing his unheroic deficiencies. Yet nowhere in the context of the play is there any indication that Smitty's sentimentalism is out of harmony with the play's mood as O'Neill himself felt and created it. The discordant note is sounded by the rough seamen who, indifferent to "truth" and "beauty," violate the melancholy mood of the play. Indeed, Smitty suffers because he is too much a part of these gloomy elements. Despite O'Neill's contempt for his main character, his reluctance to regard him as hero, he created, as we have pointed out, similar protagonists in subsequent plays. For Smitty was made in the approximate image of the playwright himself. And self-contempt was only a temporary deterrent to O'Neill's overpowering compulsion to explore his own soul.

In *In the Zone,* another Glencairn play, Smitty is once again the central figure. Here in a mixture of farce and bathos the man of feeling suffers at the hands of his stupid and insensitive companions. His curious behavior on the ammunition-carrying Glencairn as it steams through the submarine zone in 1915 arouses the suspicion of the fearful sailors. While he is "out on the hatch starin' at the moon" they are gathered in the forecastle excitedly discussing the probability of his being a German agent. As their hysteria mounts they go so far as to consider choking "his rotten heart out" and throwing him over the side. "An' no one the wiser," declares one sailor. "He's the balmy kind what commits suicide." Their plans laid, upon Smitty's entrance they overpower him, seize a small tin box that he had been concealing and, fearing that the box contains an explosive, immerse it in a pail of water. Upon opening it they discover only love letters. Their suspicions are still unallayed. Convinced that the letters are in code they read them until, coming upon the one in which Smitty's fiancée dismissed him for preferring alcohol to love, they are persuaded of his innocence. As they finish reading *there is a deep silence, broken only by Smitty's muffled sobbing. The men cannot look at each other.* There follows a gratuitous touch which serves as added vindication of the rejected lover: "A bit av a dried-up flower — a rose, maybe" falls from the packet. Whereupon the crew withdraw in embarrassment. Smitty *covers his face* with his hands and *leans his head against the wall . . . ; his shoulders continue to heave spasmodically but he makes no further sound.* As the curtain falls his mates crawl quietly into their bunks.

"To me," wrote O'Neill, "*The Moon* works with truth . . . , while *In the Zone* substitutes theatrical sentimentalism." To be sure, the crooning music and the tropic moon are absent in the latter; but even without these Smitty remains unchanged, still an anomaly, still the victim of love and liquor — and also now of his mates' war hysteria. If in the second play the stupidity of the seamen is given more emphasis than their virility, the sailors have undergone no other alteration. Alcohol alone is now indicated as the original and sufficient cause for Smitty's catastrophe. The sea again plays no part, either as fate or as hero.

In the earliest of the Glencairn plays Smitty is an inconspicuous figure. Living and working with the other seamen he is scarcely distinguishable from them, sharing their suffering and their fate. In *Bound East for Cardiff* the sea is ominously present. The men, fearing and hating it, yearn vainly to escape from it; while in their midst their fate is concretely evident in the form of Yank, a fellow seaman, who lies in his bunk mortally injured in a fall aboard ship. During intervals when his pain subsides Yank mutters a seafarer's complaint in which he is joined by the others. They grumble about the lonely and dangerous life at sea, about the inadequacy of the ship's officers, the greed and indifference of the ship's owners who ride around in carriages while running a starvation ship. Throughout all this the blast of the steamer's whistle can be heard *at regular intervals of a minute or so,* for the ship is moving slowly through a fog in mid-Atlantic. The audible symbol of the lonely sea, of the oppressive fog, of approaching death, the whistle ceases as Yank dies.

Although the remaining play in the group, *The Long Voyage Home,* exemplifies how the sea holds one of the men who is determined to escape, in *Bound East for Cardiff* nobody tempts fate. Here, discontented though they are with their lot, the sailors make no effort either to escape from it or to improve it. They can only muse wistfully about a life of farming and domesticity and protest among themselves against a privileged class to whose selfishness they attribute much of the unpleasantness of seafaring. Their speech is tinctured by social radicalism, but they appear to be quite incapable of responding to such militant exhortations as O'Neill himself uttered in 1914 when, in *The Call,* he urged "all workers on the earth" to recognize their brotherhood and refuse to "bleed and groan for Guggenheim" or to "give their lives for Standard Oil."

Although Smitty and his mates were equally powerless to mitigate their own suffering, the quality of their pain differed. The latter, endowed with limited consciousness and dull sensibilities, were predisposed to suffer only physically; whereas Smitty, less fortunate in his natural gifts, was subject to mental agony as well. Such tendencies as remorse and self-pity were foreign to his companions but native to him. And the impermeability of their mental structure to haunting memories was an advantage which he had been denied. In short, he was a victim of his heritage. Not only a gentleman, he was an introvert, and predestined to endure the morbid mental and emotional states which that type of personality is heir to.

About a year after he had completed *The Moon of the Caribbees* O'Neill presented a second tender-minded hero, Robert Mayo, in *Beyond the Horizon.* Ostensibly a tragedy of circumstance and environment the play is actually one of character. O'Neill created a tragic situation wherein the protagonist, tricked by fate, becomes a farmer when all his life he had longed to go to sea. But it is evident that even had fate not intervened the hero was predestined to suffer interminably, to become, if not a frustrated farmer, a Werther of the whale's way like Smitty.

Robert Mayo is an incongruous figure among his own family much as Smitty was among his forecastle companions. *There is a touch of the poet about him expressed in his high forehead and wide, dark eyes. His features are delicate and refined, leaning to weakness in the mouth and chin.* His brother Andrew is *an opposite type — husky, sun bronzed, handsome in a large-featured, manly fashion — a son of the soil, intelligent in a shrewd way, but with nothing of the intellectual about him.* The father is Andrew *over again in body and face —* an Andrew *sixty-five years old with a short, square, white beard.* The uncle, Dick Scott, is a sea captain, *short and stocky, with a weather-beaten jovial face and a white mustache — a typical old salt, loud of voice and given to gesture.* Only the mother, Kate Mayo, exhibits qualities which distinguish her, as Robert is distinguished, from the elder son, the husband, the brother. But although she shares with Robert *a certain refinement of movement and expression,* she is a woman of no discernment and can offer him, therefore, only maternal solicitude — a bounty which Andrew shares equally. Since childhood Robert has been given to dreaming. An invalid, he "used to sit at the window, stare out over the fields to the hills, . . . and somehow after a time . . . forget any pain [he] was in" as he started to dream.

I knew the sea was over beyond those hills, — the folks had told me — and I used to wonder what the sea was like, and try to form a picture of it in my mind. . . . There was all the mystery in the world to me then about that — far-off sea — and there still is! It called to me then just as it does now.

"It's difficult to explain," he declared, "even to myself. Either you feel it, or you don't." And nobody does.

As the play opens Robert is about to respond to the call of the far-off sea. Captain Scott is to embark early the next morning and take his nephew "to sorta talk to and show things to, and teach, kinda." However, Andrew is "the boy," remarks the captain, "that would make a good, strong sea-farin' man — ." Startled, the father warns the uncle not to "put no such fool notions in Andy's head." "A born farmer, and a damn good one, too," Andy will "live and die right here on this farm." Then *with proud confidence* Mayo adds, "And he'll make this one of the slickest, best-payin' farms in the state, too, afore he gets through!" As for Robert, the father's attitude towards him is one of mild scorn verging on indifference. Andrew displays genuine affection for his brother, but he does not understand him. Practical-minded like his father, Andrew reminds Robert that "there's always a chance of a good thing coming your way in some of those foreign ports or other," and gently rebukes him for his indifference to the "practical side of it." And when Robert *pointing to the horizon — dreamily* explains to him that

it's just Beauty that's calling me, the beauty of the far off and unknown, the mystery and spell of the East which lures me in the books I've read, the need of the freedom of great wide spaces, the joy of wandering on and on — in quest of the secret which is hidden over there, beyond the horizon.

Andrew playfully asserts that his brother is "nutty" and admonishes him laughingly to say nothing "to Uncle Dick about spells and things" when he is on the ship lest the captain "chuck [him] over-board for a Jonah." And the mother, unconcerned with Robert's needs and wishes, is certain only that she wants him to stay home. He stays when Ruth Atkins, the girl from the neighboring farm whom Andrew was to marry, is *charmed by his low musical voice telling the dreams of his childhood*. She loves him for the dangers he has passed, but for no other apparent reason. Yet this is sufficient to keep him on the farm. Having notified his uncle that he is not going to sail with him — for he has found "a bigger dream" — he assures his parents that he is "not going to be a loafer on [their] hands any longer," that he intends "to settle right down and take a real interest in the farm, and do [his] share." His father is kindly but skeptical. As for the unoccupied berth on the uncle's ship, Captain Scott's only concern is for what his officers might think: "They're liable as not," says he, wiping *his perspiring brow in anguish at the thought*, "to suspicion it was a *woman* I'd planned to ship along, and that she gave me the go-by at the last moment!" He is delivered from an embarrassing situation when Andrew, overcome with anger and grief at being jilted, determines to sail in his brother's place. Furious with his son's decision the father cries prophetically: "You're runnin' against your own nature, and you're goin' to be a' mighty sorry for it if you do." A crucial pronouncement, its corollary is that Robert is "runnin' against" *his* nature by remaining on the farm.

The father's angry prophecy is fulfilled in the following two acts of the play. Designed to exhibit the tragic consequences of living contrary to one's true character they reveal primarily what was obvious from the early moments of the play: that "Robert was never cut out for a farmer." The effects of his ineptitude over a period of eight years upon property, family, and self is one of increasing deterioration. If we are mildly perturbed by the condition of the farm we are moved not at all by the plight of the family. For these, except for Robert's sickly and anemic-looking two-year-old daughter, are as disagreeable a lot as we are to encounter in all of O'Neill's plays. With the father dead and Andrew in foreign parts the mother, mother-in-law, and wife are in Robert's incapable hands — a situation to which they respond by contriving to avoid every quality that becomes a woman. Our sympathy for the hero is further excited by the death of the child, who was treated ten-

derly only by him; by the admission of Ruth, who has become
hard and spiteful, that she has never loved Robert — that she has
always loved Andrew; and by his illness — tuberculosis — to which
he succumbs before the end of the play.

Twice during the eight years Andrew returns to reveal the transformation that has been wrought upon this uprooted son of the
soil. In the second act it is apparent that his *old easy-going good-
nature* has *been partly lost in a breezy, business-like briskness of
voice and gesture.* He remains long enough to express his dislike
for the sea, for the East, to announce that he intends to go into
the grain business in Buenos Aires, to assure his brother that he
had never been in love with Ruth. When he reappears in the third
act Robert is dying. Having made a fortune, Andrew has lost most
of it speculating in wheat, "gambling with the thing [he] used to
love to create." For this crime he shall be punished, declares Robert,
who then insists that he marry Ruth — afterwards. This action
should serve the double end of rectifying the wrong done to Ruth
when Robert married her and of providing Andrew with the suffering that he needs for his own redemption.

Andrew's crime and Robert's sustained suffering owe their in-
evitability not to fateful circumstances in the action of the play
but to qualities inherent in the characters themselves. The tendencies which were to lead Andrew to sin in Argentina had been displayed before he left the farm. With opportunities to speculate in
wheat as accessible in America as in the Argentine there is no
reason why an acquisitive farm boy should have found them any
less irresistible than a world traveler. That Robert was as ill-fitted
to be a sailor as he was to be a farmer was evident from the outset.
Destined to suffer by sea if not by land he would merely have ex-
changed the companionship of the three harpies for that of the
tumultuous seamen with whom he would have had equally little
in common.

The Haunted

o'neill's temporarily ambivalent attitude towards the man of feeling led him to complicate the action of *Beyond the Horizon* and fail to illuminate the central tragic fact — the impingement of harsh objective reality upon the introverted hero. Unready as yet to erect a solid tragedy upon that foundation, he buttressed a superficial play with tragic trappings such as an external but irrelevant fate and a secondary hero of more powerful physical stature, whose actions lead to crime and subsequent retribution. In only one other play of this early period did O'Neill concern himself with the predicament of the man of delicate sensibility. Written in 1916, *Before Breakfast* is a short tour de force on the theme of mismating. Only the slovenly, scolding wife appears on stage while her husband, who "moons around all day writing silly poetry and stories that no one will buy," is off-stage shaving. His presence is apparent on one occasion as he reaches *a sensitive hand with slender fingers* into the room to grasp a bowl of hot water and on another as we hear the blood from his cut throat dripping upon the floor and the heavy crash of his falling body. The invisible hero is "the balmy kind what commits suicide."

Unbalanced if not balmy, a more common type of O'Neill hero before 1922 is the unprepossessing, insensitive creature whose indurated will drives him to disaster. Captain Keeney, the protagonist of the short play *Ile* which O'Neill wrote in 1917, is "as hard a man as ever sailed the sea." A study in mental rather than moral aberration, the captain is motivated neither by greed nor by pride. He is the victim of an obsessive compulsion. Like Melville's Ahab he is sailing "upon the present voyage with one only and all-engrossing object," "to git the ile" and stubbornly refusing to turn his ship for home although the crew are about to mutiny and his wife is going mad.

Ben. The ice is all broke up to s'uth'ard. They's clear water's far's you can see. He ain't got no excuse for not turnin' back for home, the men says.

The Steward. (*bitterly*) He won't look nowheres but no'th'ard where they's only the ice to see. He don't want to see no clear water. All he thinks on is gittin' the ile — 's if it was our fault he ain't had good luck with the whales. (*Shaking his head*) I think the man's mighty nigh losin' his senses.

Ben. (*awed*) D'you really think he's crazy?

The Steward. Aye, it's the punishment o' God on him. Did ye ever hear of a man who wasn't crazy do the things he does?

His wife, whom he normally regards with tender affection, pleads with him to abandon his quest insisting that there is no excuse now for refusing to turn back.

Keeney. (*harshly*) I can't, Annie.

Mrs. Keeney. Why can't you?

Keeney. A woman couldn't rightly understand my reason.

Mrs. Keeney. (*wildly*) Because it's a stupid, stubborn reason. Oh, I heard you talking with the second mate. You're afraid the other captains will sneer at you because you didn't come back with a full ship. You want to live up to your silly reputation even if you do have to beat and starve men and drive me mad to do it.

But Keeney's reply, inarticulate and cryptic, suggests that there is something more involved here than pride, something deeper interfused:

(*his jaw set stubbornly*) It ain't that, Annie. Them skippers would never dare sneer to my face. It ain't so much what anyone'd say — but — (*He hesitates, struggling to express his meaning*) You see — I've always done it — since my first voyage as skipper. I always come back — with a full ship — and — it don't seem right not to — somehow. I been always first whalin' skipper out o' Homeport, and — Don't you see my meanin', Annie? (*He glances at her. She is not looking at him but staring dully in front of her, not hearing a word he is saying*) Annie! (*She comes to herself with a start*) Best turn in, Annie, there's a good woman. You ain't well.

Mrs. Keeney. (*resisting his attempts to guide her to the door in rear*) David! Won't you please turn back?

Keeney. (*gently*) I can't, Annie — not yet awhile. You don't see my meanin'. I got to git the ile.

Mrs. Keeney. It'd be different if you needed the money, but you don't. You've got more than plenty.

Keeney. (*impatiently*) It ain't the money I'm thinkin' of. D'you think I'm as mean as that?

The Captain, clearly not moved by greed, nor yet by pride — if his own appraisal is valid — appears rather to be, as was Ahab, "gnawed within and scorched without with the infixed, unrelenting fangs of some incurable idea." He is driven by a compulsion to get the oil because he has always done so, an urge which is as irresistible and inscrutable as fate itself. Dimly aware of his obsession the inarticulate victim comprehends it not at all. In this early play O'Neill had not as yet achieved a facility for representing mental abnormality. Eventually he learned to use the conventional, convenient dramatic device of a confidant — a friend, a doctor — to explain to the character and to the audience the facts about the internal struggle which the helpless sufferer is incapable of grasping himself.

The dramatic conflict of *Ile* arises at the point in the play where Keeney's obsession is blocked by his normal feelings of affection and solicitude. The protagonist, a man of great physical strength, the weak and helpless victim of a mysterious inner force, is, in a sense, offered a tragic choice: he may accede to his wife's demands that he return home, thereby preserving her sanity at the cost of destroying himself (for he *became old* even as he considered this alternative), or he may succumb to the compulsive force. Fate intervenes as he struggles with the problem. The mate's announcement that the ice to the north is clearing brings him *out of a trance,* and, *dazedly collecting his thoughts,* he proceeds with grim determination to get his oil. Moved on with a push by his monomania, he is capable of giving little heed to any humane and normal inclinations. It is evident, after all, that he had no choice in the matter.

In *Where the Cross Is Made,* a one-act play written in 1918, O'Neill employed a theme similar to that of *Ile.* This time one character is completely lost from the start, the mad victim of an obsession; while a second, the son of the first, wages a losing struggle. Captain Isaiah Bartlett, now mad, had discovered two chests containing worthless Malay ornaments, but obsessed by the wish that the trinkets be precious, he and his three accomplices accept the fiction as fact, bury the "treasure," and make a map in order that it might be recovered in the future. But there is a special quality about Bartlett's obsession, for he is unwilling — not unable — to distinguish between fact and dream. His preference for dream over reality is a matter of free choice, Realizing that wish can be fulfilled only in dream, he refuses to accept two facts: that the paste and brass ornaments are not valuable jewels, that the ship which had sailed to recover the jewels has not been lost. He "knows — but he won't *believe*. He can't and keep on living." Thus the fiction sustains his life much as Captain Keeney's fierce determination to fulfill his purpose was a kind of afflatus, or life principle. At present he maintains a lonely lookout for the ship. His daughter, Sue, and his son, Nat, recognize his condition, and the latter has called in Doctor Higgins from the insane asylum. Nat's ostensible purpose for removing his father is to satisfy the demand of the man who holds a mortgage on the house, while his actual motive is to preserve his own sanity; for his father exerts an hypnotic effect upon him, the old man's dream threatening to take possession of the son. Already he has shown tendencies to seek refuge in the illusion:

Nat. (*wildly*) No! No! No! (*He takes the map from his pocket.*) Listen, Sue! For God's sake, listen to me! See! The map of the island. (*He spreads it out on the table*) And the treasure — where the cross is made. (*He gulps and his words pour out incoherently*) I've carried it about for years. Is that nothing? You don't know what it means. It stands between me and my book. It's stood between me and life — driving me mad. *He* taught me to wait and hope with him — wait and hope — day after day. He made me doubt my brain and give the lie to my eyes — when hope was dead — I knew it was all a dream — I couldn't kill it! (*His eyes starting from his head*) God forgive me, I still believe! And that's mad — mad do you hear?

Presently the Captain enters. *He bears a striking resemblance to his son,* although he is much stronger, and there is *an obsessed glare in his fierce dark eyes.* Accusing Nat of "turning traitor," of "mockin' at me" and "at himself, too, for bein' a fool to believe in dreams, as he calls 'em," he fixes his eyes *hypnotically on his son's,* and Nat responds with a *haunted, fascinated look in his eyes, which are fixed immovably on his father's.* Soon he falls completely under his father's sway, whereupon *his face is transfigured with the ecstasy of a dream come true.* Then father and son share the same vision: *A dense green glow floods slowly in rhythmic waves like a liquid into the room — as of great depths of the sea faintly penetrated by light.* There appear the phantom forms of the three men whom Bartlett had sent after the treasure; water drips from their clothes, seaweed mats their hair, their flesh is decomposed, their bodies sway *limply, nervelessly, rhythmically as if to the pulse of long swells of the deep sea.* The drowned men having returned, Bartlett's wish is fulfilled, and he departs with the dead trio, dead now himself. And the son assumes the father's place, to live the same mad dream.

The play reveals a merely tenuous connection with the idea of greed and, what is more, a dilute concern with formal psychopathology. For it is evident that O'Neill's convictions about abnormality are not quite identical with those of the psychiatrist who would diagnose the affliction of the two mad men as schizophrenia. Although O'Neill makes a distinction between dream and fact, his separation of abnormality from normality is only a nominal one. The conception of dream as wish-fulfillment is comforting, and this, together with its universal application, makes it difficult to regard as pathological. Even the doctor, when he picks up the paste and brass ornaments to examine them, does so *with eager curiosity,* a fact which does not escape Nat's attention, for he exclaims, "Ha-ha! You want to believe, too." Moreover, Bartlett's willingness to believe something that is clearly contrary to fact that he might satisfy a wish exercises a salubrious effect upon him in that it keeps him alive. In *Gold,* a longer play which reworks the same material, this phenomenon is called a "sustaining lie." Justification for what appears to be an excessive loyalty to morbidity is furnished in various philosophies which flourished around 1900 and in the drama itself. The pragmatism of William James accepted as true "whatever proves itself to be good in the way of belief." Proposing that there are "neuroses of health," Nietzsche suggested in *Ecce Homo* "that madness is not necessarily a symptom of degeneration, of decline, of a decadent culture." The pervasiveness and potency of fictions was demonstrated by Vaihinger in his *Philosophy of As If.* And Freud pointed out the wish-fulfillment content of dreams; explained reality in terms of pain-avoidance; revealed the universality of neurosis and psychosis which, although concealed, are nevertheless present in a quantitative sense — making normality a delicate, rare, and tenuous condition. In *The Wild Duck* Ibsen had Doctor Relling declare: "Rob the average man of his life-illusion, and you rob him of his happiness at the same stroke." Among more recent playwrights O'Neill's contemporary, Pirandello, applied himself most assiduously and continually to denying the existence of objective truth, to proclaiming the indistinguishableness of the world of fancy and the world of reality.

In *Where the Cross Is Made* the baleful aspects of psychopathology were attenuated by seeing in one of its common symptoms a comforting, even a life preserving, property. But in *Gold* (written 1920) O'Neill introduced such new material as to make mental morbidity identifiable as such to himself as well as to a psychiatrist. Where the short play analyzed the problem of dream, or hallucination, as a type of madness, with the dramatic conflict arising from the struggle of the protagonist to retain his sanity (a pointless struggle, since sanity was scarcely more attractive than insanity), the long play is concerned not only with the antithesis of dream and reality but also with the conflict between the "sustaining lie" and the moral conscience. The motif of wish-fulfillment, that compulsion to believe, the universal bulwark against the encroachments of the "reality principle," is present in *Gold* and serves a double function. It is the factor behind the motivation for murder; and once the murder has been committed it prevents the perpetrator from recognizing his guilt.

Captain Bartlett, rather than his son Nat, is the protagonist of *Gold*. Obsessed with the notion that the contents of the chest are of gold, he becomes morally responsible for the killing of his cook and his cabin boy that the secret of the valueless treasure may be kept when he gives his tacit approval of the act.

Cates. (*hoarsely*) Knife 'em — and be done with it — I say!

Bartlett. Or if they don't tell the schooner's skipper it'll only be because they're plannin' to come back themselves — before we kin — and dig it up. That cook — there's somethin' queer in his mind — somethin' he was hidin' — pretendin' not to believe. What d'ye think, Horne?

Horne. I think — time's gettin' short — and talkin' won't do no good. (*Insinuatingly*) They'd do for us soon enough if *they* was able.

Bartlett. Aye, murder was plain in his eyes when he looked at me.

Horne. (*Lowering his voice to a whisper*) Tell Jimmy — Captain Bartlett — is what I say!

Bartlett. It's agin the law, Silas Horne!

Horne. The law don't reach to this island.

Bartlett. (*monotonously*) It's agin the law a captain's sworn to swear wherever he sails. They ain't refused — nor mutinied.

Horne. Who'll know they ain't? They're tryin' to steal what's yours —

that's worse'n mutiny. (*As a final persuasion*) And Jimmy's a heathen and under no laws. And he's stronger'n you are. You couldn't stop 'im.

Bartlett. Aye — I couldn't prevent —

Jimmy. (*eagerly*) I fix um, Captain, they no tell! (Bartlett *doesn't answer, but stares at the treasure.* Horne *makes violent motions to* Jimmy *to go. The Islander stares at his master's face. Then, seeming to read the direct command there, he grunts with satisfaction, and pulling his knife from his sheath, he goes stealthily off left.*)

After the deed is done, Bartlett, uneasy, repeatedly reminds Horne and Jimmy that he had spoken no word. In Act Two the scene has moved from the barren coral island to the coast of California where, six months later, his conscience is tormenting him.

His hair has turned white. There are deep hollows under his cheek-bones. His jaw and tight-lipped mouth express defiant determination, as if he were fighting back some weakness inside himself, a weakness found in his eyes, which have something in them of fear, of a wishing to avoid other eyes.

He is less concerned about keeping the secret of the treasure than he is about concealing his crime which, as it preys upon his mind, he has been revealing in his sleep. Thus he is haunted now by ghosts in addition to his fixed idea. Struggling against his fears, he periodically gathers himself together in fits of *sudden defiant bravado,* boasting that "not all the ghosts out o' hell could keep me from a thing I've set my mind on," namely, to return for the gold. But the conflict between the "lie" and his conscience is intensified by the presence of his wife, Sarah, a person of equally fixed determination despite her physical decline subsequent to her hearing her husband's sleeping revelations. As fanatically obsessed by her rigid religious beliefs as Bartlett is by his will to believe in the fulfillment of a wish, she functions, in a sense, as an objectification of his religious conscience. She accuses him of trying to "fool with lies the conscience God put in him," whereupon he replies, once again with defiant bravado, that he is "strong enough to face anything, true or lie." As she points out to him that his guilty conscience is driving him mad, her eyes light up with religious fervor, and she implores him to confess his sin, "confess to God and men, and make your peace and take your punishment."

Bartlett. (*his face tortured by the inward struggle* — *as if the word strangled him*) Confess and let someone steal the gold! (*This thought destroys her influence over him in a second. His obsession regains possession*

of him instantly, filling him with rebellious strength. He laughs harshly.)
Ye'd make an old woman o' me, would ye, Sarah? — an old, Sunday go-to-meetin' woman snivelin' and prayin' to God for pardon? . . . What I've done I've done, and I've never asked pardon o' God or men for aught I've done, and never will. Confess, and give up the gold I've dreamed of all my life that I've found at last? By thunder, ye must think I'm crazed!

Although he is possessed once again he still must rely upon his wife, for to bring luck to his impending voyage, he wants her to christen the ship. This she unwillingly does, provided he will not take Nat with him and "drag him into sin." However, the daughter, Sue, contrives to have the schooner depart without either father or son, and as it sails out of sight Bartlett *shakes his clenched fist at the sky as if visualizing the fate he feels in all of this.* Then *in a tone of groping superstitious awe and bewildered fear* he says aloud to himself, "They be somethin' queer — somethin' wrong — they be a curse in this somewhere — ." To which his wife replies, *turning accusing eyes on him — with a sort of fanatical triumph:*

I'm glad to hear you confess that, Isaiah. Yes, there be a curse — God's curse on the wicked sinfulness o' men and I thank God He's saved you from the evil of that voyage, and I'll pray Him to visit His punishment and His curse on them three men on that craft you forced me to give my name — (*She has raised her hand as if calling down retribution on the schooner she can dimly see.*)

Whereupon, Bartlett starts *toward his wife with an insane yell of fury* screaming, "Stop it, I tell ye!" and towering *over her with upraised fist as if to crush her.* She asks with *a weak, frightened gasp,* "Would you murder me too, Isaiah?" The fourth, and last, act of the play is the point in the plot where the action of *Where the Cross Is Made* began. Bartlett's wife is dead; he himself, almost completely mad, awaits the return of the overdue schooner; Nat, hypnotically drawn by his father towards madness, lingers on the threshold; and a doctor — this time Doctor Berry, a family physician and friend (in place of Dr. Higgins of the insane asylum), *not the least of whose duties is to play father-confessor to his patients* (and, incidentally, to fulfill O'Neill's technical requirement of the confidant) — explains the old man's case:

Doctor. (*listening intently*) . . . There he goes pacing up and down, looking out to sea for that ship that will never come back! (*Shaking himself*) Brrr! This house of mad dreams!

Sue. Don't you think Pa'll come to realize the schooner is lost as time goes by and she doesn't come back?

Doctor. No, your father won't let himself look the facts in the face. If he did, probably the shock of it would kill him. That darn dream of his has become his life. No, Susan, as time goes on he'll believe in it harder and harder. . . . Send him to an asylum.

Sue. (*with a shudder*) No, Doctor.

Doctor. (*shaking his head*) You'll have to come to it in time. He's getting worse. No one can tell — he might get violent —

Sue. How can you say that? You know how gentle and sane he is with me.

Doctor. You're his one connecting link with things as they are — but that can't last.

Doctor Berry's prognosis turns out to be sound. Sue, her father's connecting link with reality (the personification of the "reality principle," a concept in contradistinction to the role of Mrs. Bartlett, who represented the conscience, which is the product of fanatical religion and therefore as mad as Bartlett's "lies"), succeeds in breaking through his veil of madness by pleading with him to save Nat from the fate which has engulfed himself. For Bartlett and his son had already begun to share the same mad dream of the ship's return, the former's face, in this play, being *transfigured by the ecstasy of a dream come true.*

Bartlett. (*letting his hands fall and staring at her haggardly — falteringly, as if reason were slowly filtering back into his brain*) Sue — ye said — drivin' him mad, *too!* Then ye think I be — ?

Finally, in an agony of conflict to get hold of his reason and, after *a tremendous struggle,* he lifts his tortured face to Nat's and confesses *in tones of despair* the three lies which had been sustaining him: that the ship is lost, that he had given the word — "in my mind — to kill them two. I murdered 'em in cold blood," and that the treasure was valueless: "I *had* to believe, I tell ye! I'd been dreamin' o' it all my days!"

Bartlett. (*uncovers his gray face on which there is now settling an expression of strange peace — stroking his daughter's hand*) Sue — don't think hard o' me. (*He takes the map*) An end to this! (*He slowly tears it into small pieces, seeming to grow weaker and weaker as he does so. Finally as he lets the fragments filter through his fingers, his whole frame suddenly relaxes.*)

As the doctor had predicted, looking the facts in the face has killed him. His death is the price that had to be paid for Nat's sanity (unlike *Where the Cross Is Made,* wherein the father's death gave Nat the opportunity to become the sole mad ruler). Whether Bartlett himself gained anything in the transaction is doubtful. To argue that the confession has won God's grace, that he has made his peace with God, as his wife had predicted, is to disregard Mrs. Bartlett's symbolic purport. The *expression of strange peace* which settled on Bartlett's face is the peace, rather, of one who has resolved his psychological conflicts, a consummation which differs in kind rather than in degree from what can be achieved in the *ecstasy of a dream come true*. The wife's religious fanaticism has no more to commend it than has her husband's wish to see gold where there is only junk. When she curses the departing ship she is indulging in precisely the same kind of superstitious behavior that her husband had displayed when, with groping superstitious awe and bewildered fear, he had felt "somethin' queer — somethin' wrong — . . . . a curse in this somewhere — ."

To see in *Gold* significant changes in O'Neill's spiritual attitude since the writing of *Where the Cross Is Made* is to misinterpret the play. Thus Richard Dana Skinner believes that "there are few episodes in the O'Neill saga so important as the change from nebulous despair in the short version to the final spiritual triumph in the complete play." Whereas the short play, according to Skinner, represented a mood, an early statement of a problem without a solution, the long play "shows the poet rising above this mood to achieve release through a cleansing of the soul — ." It is incorrect first of all to regard *Gold* as the completed form of *Where the Cross Is Made,* for they are two distinct plays, with different protagonists, different themes, different plots — in terms of emphasis and content as well as of quantity. To interpret the ending of the former, Bartlett's renunciation of his sinful illusions, as soul-cleansing is likewise erroneous. Evidence, internal and external, points to a divergent conclusion, one which converts the "final spiritual triumph" into a hollow victory. In the first place, by confessing he was following the advice of his wife whose religious ardor was obviously distasteful to O'Neill. In the second place, peace was purchased at the exorbitant price of death itself, a condition which the playwright shunned in nearly all of his plays. Moreover, the expression of peace which appeared upon Bartlett's face could be discerned only by the reader, since the phenomenon is mentioned in the acting directions alone. Sue's reaction to her father's death as the curtain fell was scarcely that of a person who had recognized the justice of God's ways or of one who regarded her father's newly attained condition as a consummation to be wished: she *tries with trembling hands to feel of her father's pulse, his heart — then begins to sob hysterically*. If the longer play is an improvement over the shorter one it is because of its greater degree of finality, an aesthetic rather than a spiritual achievement.

In the play *Diff'rent* (written 1920) O'Neill continued to display his preoccupation with mental aberration, with compulsive internal forces that drive their victims to catastrophe. Once again environmental factors are inconsequential; for although the action occurs in New England, a region which was almost invariably depicted in literary works as dark, narrow, and oppressive, the characters, except for their dialect, escape the customary blight. A similar unconcern with regional differences was apparent in *Where the Cross Is Made* and in *Gold* where California's bright expansiveness intruded not at all. The scene of *Diff'rent* is the parlor of the Crosby home in a seaport village of New England. The room is furnished with the appurtenances which one associates with such a locality — a bulky Bible with a brass clasp, photos of strained, stern-looking people — , but the people who inhabit the place are neither religious nor stern. Emma Crosby, the principal character, is a girl of twenty with a face which *in spite of its plain features gives an impression of prettiness, due to her large, soft blue eyes which have an incongruous quality of absent-minded romantic dreaminess about them*. The romantic dreaminess of her eyes is in ominous conflict with the *heavy, . . . self-willed stubbornness* suggested by her mouth and chin. When Emma gently censures her fiancé Caleb Williams for swearing, he reminds her that she ought "to be used to that part o' men's wickedness — with your Pa and Jack cussin' about the house all the time." To which she replies (*with a smile*):

Oh, I haven't no strict religious notions about it. I'm hardened in sin so far's they're concerned. Goodness me, how would Ma and me ever have lived in the same house with them two if we wasn't used to it? I don't

even notice their cussing no more. And I don't mind hearing it from the
other men, either. Being seafaring men, away from their women folks most
of the time, I know it just gets to be part of their natures and they ain't
responsible. (*Decisively*) But you're diff'rent. You just got to be diff'rent
from the rest.

No "stiff-necked one," Emma can tolerate the weaknesses of human
nature and sympathize with the need to deviate from an austere
moral code, but she is obsessed with the idea that the man she
marries must conform to an inhuman ideal of purity:

Emma. (*struggling to convey her meaning*) Why, Pa's all right. He's a
fine man — and Jack's all right, too. I wouldn't hear a bad word about them
for anything. And the others are all right in their way, too, I s'pose. Only
— don't you see what I mean? — I look on you as diff'rent from all of them.
I mean there's things that's all right for them to do that wouldn't be for
you — in my mind, anyway.
Caleb. (*puzzled and a bit uneasy*) Sailors ain't plaster saints, Emmer, —
not a darn one of 'em ain't!
Emma. (*hurt and disappointed*) Then you won't promise me to stay
diff'rent for my sake?

As for herself, she intends to conform to the same unattainable
ideal. She has it "fixed in her head" that she and Caleb ought to
make a married couple "diff'rent from the rest." It is obvious that
her eccentric and inexplicable pursuit of the absolute must lead to
isolation and spinsterhood, for the subtlest, most concealed gesture
might be construed as a violation of her goal of perfection. Thus
when it is revealed that Caleb, who is clearly a man of dog-like
fidelity, had been unable to avoid an affair with a native girl during
his recent voyage Emma announces *with quick resentful resolution*
that "there ain't going to be any wedding," although every member of Emma's family regarded Caleb's brief dalliance either as
amusing or as a natural and inevitable expression of animal spirits.
"There you go agen makin' a durned creepin'-Jesus out of him!
What d'you want to marry, anyhow — a man or a sky-pilot?"
chides her brother. Her father, Captain Crosby, an almost Fal-
staffian figure, expresses a similar sentiment:

Thunderin' Moses, what the hell d'you want Caleb to be — a durned, he-
virgin, sky-pilot? Caleb's a man wo'th ten o' most and, spite o' his bein'
on'y a boy yit, he's the smartest skipper out o' this port and you'd ought
to be proud you'd got him. And as for them islands, all whalin' men knows

'em. I've teched thar for water more'n once myself, and I know them brown females like a book. And I tells you, after a year or more aboard ship, a man'd have to be a goll-durned geldin' if he don't — . . . I knows Emmer ain't that crazy. If she ever got religion that bad, I'd ship her off as female missionary to the damned yellow Chinks. (*He laughs*)

And Emma's mother insists that "it'd be jest like goin' agen an act of Nature for you not to marry him." But nobody can prevail upon Emma to change her mind, for Caleb's behavior has made "him another person — not Caleb but someone just like all the others." Men may be men the world over and "if it was one of the rest . . . had done this I'd thought it was a joke, too. I ain't strict in judging 'em and you know it." Awaiting the entrance of Caleb she

stands for a while staring stonily before her. She sighs hopelessly, clasping and unclasping her hands, looking around the room as if she longed to escape from it. Finally she sits down helplessly and remains fixed in a strained attitude, her face betraying the conflict that is tormenting her. Slow steps sound from the path in front of the house. Emma *recognizes them and her face freezes into an expression of obstinate intolerance.*

The anguished and inarticulate heroine tries gropingly to explain her position. "I ain't got any hard feelings against you, Caleb — not now. It ain't plain jealousy — what I feel. It ain't even that I think you've done nothing terrible wrong." When Caleb, *with a glimmer of eager hope* asks, "Then — you'll forgive it, Emmer?" she replies,

Yes, I forgive it. But don't think that my forgiving is going to make any diff'rence — 'cause I ain't going to marry you, Caleb. That's final. (*After a pause — intensely*) Oh, I wish I could make you see — my reason. You don't. You never will, I expect. What you done is just what any other man would have done — and being like them is exactly what'll keep you from ever seeing my meaning. (*After a pause — in a last effort to make him understand*) Maybe it's my fault more'n your'n. It's like this, Caleb. Ever since we was little I guess I've always had the idea that you was — diff'rent. And when we growed up and got engaged I thought that more and more. And you was diff'rent, too! And that was why I loved you. And now you've proved you ain't. And so how can I love you any more? I don't, Caleb, and that's all there is to it. You've busted something way down inside me — and I can't love you no more.

Then, "things being what they be and me being what I am — I won't marry no man. I'll stay single. (*Forcing a smile*) I guess there's worse things than being an old maid." But if there are, the next act fails to name them.

In 1920 O'Neill was not yet prepared to participate in the current fashion of dealing harshly with the so-called neo-Puritan. Emma Crosby's curious revulsion against a natural, pagan way of life appears, on the surface, to suggest that O'Neill, like so many of his contemporaries, was writing a dramatic case study of the consequences of Puritan repression, an affliction, indeed, from which the entire nation was said to be suffering. Moreover, her peculiar, "self-willed stubbornness," a characteristic shared by Captain Keeney of *Ile* who, since he skippered a whaling ship, was presumably a New Englander, is a quality observed to be indigenous to that region. Mary E. Wilkins Freeman, for example, had written in the 1890's of that New England abnormality, the "deathless cramp of the will," which had been inherited from those "staunch old soldiers of the faith who landed on our inhospitable shores" and who "in spite of their godliness, and their noble adherence, in the face of obstacles to the dictates of their consciences," developed their wills "past the reasonable limits of nature."

O'Neill, however, has made it clear that Emma's decorousness and priggishness and her stubbornness are individual and special qualities which by no means obtain within her family or in the family circle. She could accept, as we have seen, cussing and animal sexuality in anybody but Caleb and herself. As for her "cramp of the will" — it might be regarded as an atavistic trait, but since it recurs only in this single instance, such an explanation is scarcely tenable. It appears, rather, that the New England setting is merely a coincidence, that O'Neill is depicting, instead of a Puritan maiden, the struggles of the daughter of a seafaring family — a family all of whose members are on the best of terms with nature and scornful of plaster saints — as she is caught in the toils of an obsessive force, an irrational compulsion to attain an inhuman ideal. If her aberration is psychologically unconvincing, it may well be because O'Neill was interested primarily in the philosophical implications of such a phenomenon, that is, in the discrepancy between the real and the ideal.

The contradiction in Emma Crosby's personality between what O'Neill called her romantic dreaminess and her self-willed stubbornness, one of the playwright's early examples of dissociation, has its effects in the second, and last, act. Her self-willed stubbornness, appearing in the form of a somewhat incredible type of monomania, has caused her to make the tragic choice of spinsterhood. Now her romantic dreaminess, after thirty years, is to assert itself to prove that it is a natural urge which must be satisfied, which cannot be forever repressed. Provided with no normal expression, frustrated by a strange compulsion, it expresses itself in a blatant, grotesque fashion.

The thirty years have transformed Emma into a withered scrawny woman. But there is something revoltingly incongruous about her, a pitiable sham, a too-apparent effort to cheat the years by appearances. The white dress she wears is too frilly, too youthful for her; so are the high-heeled pumps and clocked silk stockings. There is an absurd suggestion of rouge on her tight cheeks and thin lips, of penciled make-up about her eyes. The black of her hair is brazenly untruthful. Above all there is shown in her simpering, self-consciously coquettish manner that laughable — and at the same time irritating and disgusting — mockery of undignified age snatching greedily at the empty simulacra of youth.

She has formed an attachment for Caleb's nephew, Benny, a profligate youth of twenty-three recently home from the war. Inspired by Plutus rather than by Venus, the vicious and calculating Benny is at present exploiting Emma's affections for him with the expectation that he can extract more money from her than he can from his own "miserly" family. It soon becomes evident that Emma's present obsession, sex, has displaced the obsession of Act One, and that she is incapable of perceiving Benny's obvious intentions, even the revulsion he reveals for her. The climax of the action occurs with Emma's mounting desire; her manner which at first is coquettish, kittenish, roguish becomes morbidly intense, feverishly eager. And when the young man hits upon the diabolical scheme, which he hopes will serve the twofold purpose of revenge upon his family and profit by getting his hands on Emma's meager inheritance, Emma, *choking with emotion, dazed with joy,* accepts his proposal of marriage. At this point Caleb returns — Benny retires to the kitchen to overhear — to remind Emma that it is just thirty years ago today that he had promised to return and renew his offer of marriage. Partly because her original disappointment in Caleb still influences her feeling for him, but largely because she now expects to get some fun out of life while she is still in its prime, she flatly rejects Caleb's offer. Stunned and disgusted by Emma's disclosure of her intention to marry his dissolute nephew, Caleb is determined to prevent its consummation. Benny, having overheard his uncle's plan to bribe him with more money than he could get from Emma, re-enters as Caleb departs and frankly informs her that he intends to accept the better offer. Meanwhile Caleb had gone out to Emma's barn and hanged himself. And Emma, conscious at last of Benny's duplicity, *with a sudden outburst of wild grief,* calls, "Caleb!" *Then in a strange whisper,* "Wait, Caleb, I'm going down to the barn." Whereupon *she moves like a sleep-walker toward the door in the rear as the curtain falls.*

Thus the second act of *Diff'rent* exposes the consciousness of the spinster in whom the tendency towards romantic dreaminess has been frustrated. The antithesis in Emma's personality has not, however, become a conflict, for the two obsessions, the inhuman ideal and sex, are presented separately, one in the first act, the other in the second, with the unfortunate effect of destroying the unity of the play. In short, O'Neill has written two plays whose relation one to the other is fortuitous. In the first the theme is the compulsive force of an irrational idea; in the second it is the spinster's compulsion to fulfill her natural impulses. The first is simply a slight variation of the situation which Mary E. Wilkins Freeman had developed in 1891 in her short story "A New England Nun," wherein the heroine, Louisa Ellis, had been courted by her fiancé, Joe Dagget, for fifteen years. In the course of that long period she gradually "turned into a path so straight and unswerving that it could only meet a check at her grave, and so narrow that there was no room for any one at her side." "Serenity and placid narrowness" having become to her "as the birthright itself," it was with a sense of relief that she welcomed the opportunity to sever her affair with Joe and remain a spinster who could continue to sit peacefully, "prayerfully numbering her days like an uncloistered nun." Yet, even as Mrs. Freeman wrote, there existed psychologists who could have reminded her that her picture of the contented spinster consisted only of overtones, that a more penetrating look at the nun, cloistered or uncloistered, would have disclosed more than meets the eye. The "wonderful explorations by Binet, Janet,

Breuer, Freud, Mason, Prince, and others of the subliminal consciousness of patients with hysteria" were acclaimed by William James for their revelation of "whole systems of underground life." Scientific rationalists, men such as these had already cynically observed that Christ is regarded with affection by the "hysterical nun" because, starving for life, she has been led to accept an imaginary substitute for a more earthly object of affection. Thus nearly thirty years after Mrs. Freeman had published her story, O'Neill added a sequel in the second act that reflected theories of which neither he nor the short story writer had shown any awareness. Emma becomes a spinster whose unfulfilled desires result in hysteria. Unable to find tranquillity because of her willful behavior in Act One and incapable of discovering "an imaginary substitute for her 'affection,'" she is driven to a mad effort to satisfy her needs by direct means.

O'Neill's contemporary, Sherwood Anderson, likewise examined the consciousness of the small-town spinster in *Winesburg, Ohio* (1919) and exemplified the changes that had been wrought by the "new" psychology in the approach to the problem since the days of Mary E. Wilkins Freeman. In his story called "Adventure," Anderson's methods are more penetrating than Mrs. Freeman's, subtler than O'Neill's. In this tale, the heroine, instead of hanging herself in the barn, finally comes to terms with the "reality principle," but not so serenely as did Louisa Ellis. She had first to suffer the convulsions of unrequited love, the eruptions of instinctive desires. Where Louisa and Emma had for one reason or other dismissed their lovers, Alice Hindman, the heroine of "Adventure," was abandoned by hers. At the age of twenty-seven, hopelessly awaiting his return, she practised the devices common to lonely people, converting her prayers into whisperings to her absent lover, becoming attached to inanimate objects. As her desire grew vague, she wanted simply to be loved, "to have something answer the call that was growing louder and louder within her" until at last the pressure from within exploded into an overt and wildly irrational act. She was overcome by a mad desire to run naked through the streets and to feel the cold rain, thinking that it would have some creative and wonderful effect upon her body. Having released the energy, she regained control of herself and bravely faced the fact

"that many people must live and die alone, even in Winesburg."
O'Neill's play suffers in a comparison with Anderson's story. Crude
and confused in form and content, its perceptions, too, are less in-
cisive. But the drama is a difficult medium, *Diff'rent* an early play.
O'Neill slowly sharpened his perceptions and learned to convert
violence into power.

Women in Love

EMMA CROSBY WAS neither the first O'Neill heroine nor
the last. Followed eventually by Nina Leeds and Lavinia Mannon,
she was preceded by Eileen Carmody and Anna Christie. Eileen
appears in *The Straw,* a full-length play completed in 1919 about
love and death in a tuberculosis sanatorium. Unique among
O'Neill's tragic females, she is in possession of all the feminine
virtues — except charm — and possessed by none of the destructive
tendencies that made life so disagreeable for Emma, the later heroines, and the people with whom they were associated. She shares
Robert Mayo's physical affliction and like him she is at odds with
her family, particularly with her father; but unlike Robert she
is neither introverted nor schizophrenic. Eileen's predicament is
clearly defined; she is the innocent victim of a brutal parent, of
disease, of unrequited love.

In *The Straw* one is conscious of the absence of features which
in the other plays sometimes approached the sensational — not only
the major flaw, previously mentioned, of the central character, but
also the violent action and the haunting, brooding atmosphere. In
place of these O'Neill offered a detailed picture of life in a sanatorium, achieving an obtrusive verisimilitude by transferring to the
stage vivid recollections of his own experiences a half-dozen years
back.

Apart from these considerable divergencies the play exhibits no
other unfamiliar aspects. Thus, having previously been introduced
to a type of disreputable Irishman we meet him again in *The*

Straw. Paddy, *a squat, ugly Liverpool Irishman* appeared in the Glencairn plays. In *The Rope,* a crude one-act play that O'Neill wrote in 1918, a *sandy-haired Irishman* named Sweeney played a prominent part. Sweeney had a *bullet head* whose *bony face has a pressed-in appearance except for his heavy jaw, which sticks out pugnaciously*. About his mouth *there is an expression of mean cunning and cupidity*. A depraved character, he is given to drinking and to instinctively crossing himself. Bill Carmody of *The Straw,* father of the heroine, is as blatantly and exaggeratedly Irish as his two predecessors.

He is a man of fifty, heavy-set and round-shouldered, with long muscular arms and swollen-veined, hairy hands. His face is bony and ponderous; his nose, short and squat; his mouth large, thick-lipped and harsh; his complexion mottled — red, purple-streaked, and freckled; his hair, short and stubby with a bald spot on the crown. The expression of his small, blue eyes is one of selfish cunning.

Like Sweeney, *he crosses himself with pious unction* and drinks. Cruel to others, he constantly whines in self-pity. And he is stupidly scornful of people who read books. However, O'Neill distinguishes among Irishmen, for Eileen is of a contrasting and superior breed. Evidently a Cullen like her mother's people, she is of a type who, according to her contemptuous father, "always was dreamin' their lives out." Except for her *rather heavy Irish jaw* Eileen is as attractive as her father is repulsive. Her other features are delicate; her eyes *large and blue, confident in their compelling candor and sweetness; her lips, full and red, half-open, over strong even teeth, droop at the corner into an expression of wistful sadness;* . . . "Beautiful, sweet and good," she displays the virtue of maternal unselfishness. Such a demure female is rare in O'Neill's plays, but we shall soon become acquainted with another Irishman of the Cullen strain.

Familiar, too, is the concept of the "sustaining lie," a device that serves an important thematic function in *Gold*. Employed in *The Straw* it is a contrivance by which O'Neill brings about the denouement. No longer wishing to live, Eileen in the final act is dying of tuberculosis. Visiting at her bedside, the man whom she loves and whom she has assisted in a writing career is persuaded by the discerning superintendent of the infirmary to tell Eileen that he loves her. Although he has never "thought much of loving anyone — that

way," he is urged to "make her believe." "And you must ask her
to marry you," adds the superintendent.

If you're engaged it will give you the right in her eyes to take her away.
You can take her to some private San. There's a small place but a very good
one at White Lake. It's not too expensive, and it's a beautiful spot, out of
the world, and you can live and work near by. And she'll be happy to the
very last. Don't you think that's something you can give in return for
her love for you?

Having consented to lie to Eileen, the young man tiptoes to her
bedside, bends down, takes her in his arms, and kisses her. So
moved is he by her response — she is *in the seventh heaven* — that
he utters a muffled sob and begins to cry. Then the sustaining lie
is manifestly justified when he raises his face which is *alight with
a passionate awakening — a revelation*. "Oh, I do love you, Eileen!"
he cries. "I do! I love you, love you!" Suddenly he is horrified as
he remembers her doom. *For the first time Death confronts him
face to face as a menacing reality,* but the love which the lie revealed to him provides a straw of hope. ". . . we'll win together,"
he exclaims *fiercely as if defying* the superintendent. "We can! We
must! There are things doctors can't value — can't know the
strength of! (*Exultantly*) You'll see! I'll make Eileen get well, I
tell you! Happiness will cure! Love is stronger than —." *Taken
aback by his violence for a moment* the superintendent *finally bursts
into a laugh of helplessness which is close to tears* as she concedes
that the doctor, that no one, *knows* anything. "God bless you
both!" she mutters as, with handkerchief to eyes, *she hurries out to
the hallway without turning her head.*

 The Straw is clearly a maudlin, vapid piece; but it is, as Richard
Dana Skinner declared, one of O'Neill's most revealing plays. Without sharing Skinner's enthusiasm one can agree that *The Straw*
displays

a quality of simplicity and directness all too rare in many of his most
important works, and a quality of affirmation of life and faith in strong
contrast with the defeatism which has shadowed many of his moods.

The play is an early manifestation of O'Neill's religious sensibility,
of his desire for affirmation and faith. Yet Skinner over-estimated
the importance of the part it played at that time in the fulfillment

of the desire. Admiring "the power of O'Neill's ultimate assertion of free will," he overlooked the fact that the playwright evaded the problems which were implicitly posed in most of his other plays before 1922 — problems relating to the deterministic aspects of psychology and biology, to the ambiguity of truth and of reality. If *The Straw* discloses O'Neill's religious impulse, it also reveals a tendency, equally significant, referred to at the beginning of this paragraph. The sentimentality of this play, contrasting as it does with the predominantly hard-boiled quality of the other early plays, is particularly striking.

Anna Christie, however, is both hard-boiled and sentimental. And it displays, what is more, a negative religious impulse, becoming thereby a formidable barrier to the spiritual "progress" which Skinner was pleased to detect in the interior development of O'Neill's plays from *Beyond the Horizon* through *The Straw* to *Gold*. As a matter of fact the fluttering religious spirit, as we have seen, was extinguished before O'Neill got around to writing *Gold,* the play which, in order of composition, immediately precedes *Anna Christie.* In theme, tone, and even in characterization the latter recalls the Glencairn plays, especially *The Long Voyage Home.* Olson, the sea-weary, *middle-aged Swede* of that play, he who tried in vain to flee from the sea, is transformed into the sea-haunted sailor, Chris Christopherson, who also does all he can to escape from the evils of the sea. Yet, even as the play opens, it is evident that he is enjoying a false and temporary security as he foolishly rationalizes his choice of work, captain of a coal barge: "dis ain't real sailor yob. Dis ain't real boat on sea. She's yust ole tub — like piece of land with house on it dat float. Yob on her ain't sea yob." Working on the sea's edges at the start of the play, he will be drawn to its center at the end. Chris had long been pursued by the fury of the sea:

Ay don't know, Anna, why Ay never come home Sveden in ole year. Ay vant come home end of every voyage. Ay vant see your mo'der, your two bro'der before dey vas drowned, you ven you vas born — but — Ay — don't go. Ay sign on oder ships — go South America, go Australia, go China, go every port all over world many times — but Ay never go aboard ship sail for Sveden. Ven Ay gat money for passage home as passenger den — (*He bows his head guiltily*) Ay forgat and Ay spend all money. Ven Ay tank

again, it's too late. (*He sighs*) Ay don't know why but dat's vay with most
sailor fallar, Anna. Dat ole davil sea make dem crazy fools with her dirty
tricks. It's so.

Chris's family had suffered as well as he, although there is no
mention of hereditary evil or of retribution. The house of Christopherson is simply the inexplicable victim of fate — not a fickle fate,
nor a blind one, but a sinister one.

All men in our village on coast, Sveden, go to sea. Ain't nutting else for
dem to do. My fa'der die on board ship in Indian Ocean. He's buried at
sea. Ay don't never know him only little bit. Den my tree bro'der, older'n
me, dey go on ships. Den Ay go, too. Den my mo'der she's left all 'lone. Ve
vas all avay on voyage when she die. (*He pauses sadly*) Two my bro'der
dey gat lost on fishing boat same like your bro'ders vas drowned. My oder
bro'der, he save money, give up sea, den he die home in bed. He's only one
dat ole davil don't kill. (*Defiantly*) But me, Ay bet you Ay die ashore in
bed, too!

The action of the play concerns the discovery of an additional
victim of the "davil sea," Chris' daughter Anna, who, although she
was kept far inland, in Minnesota, was affected nevertheless by the
relentless evil force. And with the arrival of Anna from the Middle West a new episode in the Christopherson struggle begins, with
the sea inexorably drawing its prey to their doom. Chris had
thought that his daughter was safe on a farm, but the sailor's conception of rural life, wistfully expressed in the Glencairn plays, is
once again revealed to be completely erroneous. "Your bunk about
the farm being so fine!" Anna violently says to her father. "Didn't
I write you year after year how rotten it was and what a dirty
slave them cousins made of me?" Had Anna not been pursued by
the Christopherson fate she might have avoided the degradation
that came to her on her farm refuge where one of her cousins
"started me wrong. (*Loudly*) It wasn't none of my fault. I hated
him worse'n hell and he knew it. But he was big and strong — "

That was why I run away from the farm. That was what made me get
a yob as nurse girl in St. Paul. (*With a hard, mocking laugh*) And you
think that was a nice yob for a girl, too, don't you? (*Sarcastically*) With
all them nice inland fellers yust looking for a chance to marry me, I
s'pose. Marry me? What a chance! They wasn't looking for marrying . . .
I'm owning up to everything fair and square. I was caged in, I tell you —
yust like in yail — listening to 'em bawling and crying day and night —

when I wanted to be out — and I was lonesome — lonesome as hell! (*With a sudden weariness in her voice*) So I gave up finally. What was the use?

Whether or no this final step towards moral degradation is gratuitous is debatable. Given the initial impetus, fictitious females are known to have traveled the rest of the road to shame under their own power. But voluntarily to substitute prostitution for tending children on the ground that in the latter position one is "caged in" and "lonesome" is both novel and improbable. Like Smitty's addiction to drink, Anna's tragic choice appears to have been made as much out of consideration of O'Neill's needs as of her own.

Taking a divergent view from the creators of such fictitious harlots as Nana, Maggie, and Miss Thompson, O'Neill went even beyond Walt Whitman whose tender acceptance of the common prostitute was consistent with his faith in democracy, an attitude which O'Neill's skepticism and pessimism would appear to preclude. Whatever the playwright's attitude, his harlots are rarely common. Even Freda, in *The Long Voyage Home,* revealed singular sensibilities when Olson explained why he was eager to get home: "You know, Miss Freda, my mother get very old, and I want to see her. She might die and I would never — " Freda, *moved in spite of herself,* exclaimed, "Ow, don't talk like that! I jest 'ates to 'ear anyone speakin' abaht dyin'." And when Anna Christie and her colleagues were jailed for thirty days in St. Paul, the "others didn't seem to mind the cooler very much. Some of 'em was used to it. But me, I couldn't stand it. . . . I never could stand being caged up nowheres. I got good and sick and they had to send me to the hospital." It was not that she, unlike the others, was offended by the indignities of prison life; but that, like Ibsen's Ellida, she longed for the open sea. Nor is Anna merely an uncommon prostitute; she is, like Eileen, an uncommon O'Neill heroine, displaying unparalleled integrity, ingenuousness, and nobility of character.

When, early in the first act, Chris, Oedipus-like, angrily responds to the bartender's prophecy that Anna is destined to marry a sailor, the imminent conflict with fate becomes clearly defined. In the second act the spectator is prepared for the event when Anna exults in her sea environment, sensing somewhat mystically that she has been there before. Chris' grim foreboding that something is about to happen is confirmed, as is the prediction of the bartender, when the "davil sea" sends the shipwrecked sailor, Mat Burke, upon the scene. Burke, exhausted as he is, proceeds almost at once to make love to Anna, even proposing marriage. The act ends as Chris *turns suddenly and shakes his fist out at the sea* — [and] *with bitter hatred* says, "Dat's your dirty trick, damn ole davil, you! (*then in a frenzy of rage*) But, py God, you don't do dat! Not while Ay'm living! No, py God, you don't!"

In the third act occurs the struggle between the father and the sea-borne lover for possession of Anna. Burke's ardent love-making and passion for the sea overwhelm her. She *laughs helplessly,* and, *with a sudden joyous defiance,* confesses her love for him, assuring him that she has never loved a man in her life before, that he "can always believe that — no matter what happens." What does happen is that she refuses to marry him until she tells him about her sordid past. Although he had insisted that she is "the wan woman in the world for me, and I can't live without her now" and although he had dreamed of their having "a grand, beautiful life together" to the end of their days, he is overcome with revulsion upon her revelation and rushes off to drink "sloos of whiskey." It is obvious that by this time the distress of a whore, in love with an incredible Irish sailor, has displaced the somber theme of a family's struggle with fate. Burke possesses all of the exuberance, the pugnaciousness, and the boastfulness of the Playboy of the Western World and, in addition, a disposition to keen like the grief-stricken Maurya of *Riders to the Sea.* From a point two-thirds of the way through the third act up to the fourth speech from the end of the fourth and final act, the tempestuous love of Anna and Burke, mingled as it is with grief and rage, occupies all of the plot. After he is irresistibly drawn back to the barge after a two days' debauch, flashes of joy alternate with suspicions and doubts as the thought occurs to Burke that Anna might have resumed her evil ways ashore during his absence. In a rage, he has decided to "choke her dirty life out;" whereupon she enters with a revolver and points it at his chest. When he implores her to shoot and end the "rotten dog's life" he has lived the past two days, she is overcome and lets the *revolver drop to the floor, as if her fingers had no strength to hold it.* After a quantity of doleful dialogue Burke begins to resolve the conflict in an excess of faith.

Burke. (*after an inward struggle — tensely — forcing out the words with difficulty*) If I was believing — that you'd never had love for any other man in the world but me — I could be forgetting the rest, maybe.

Anna. (*with a cry of joy*) Mat!

Burke. (*slowly*) If 'tis truth you're after telling, I'd have a right, maybe, to believe you'd changed — and that I'd changed you myself 'til the thing you'd been all your life wouldn't be you any more at all.

Anna. (*hanging on his words — breathlessly*) Oh, Mat! that's what I been trying to tell you all along!

Then the final solution occurs to him. He takes from his pocket *a small, cheap old crucifix* which his mother had given him and challenges her "to swear an oath, now — a terrible, fearful oath would send your soul to the divils in hell if you was lying." Having sworn that he is the only man in the world "iver you felt love for" and that from this day she will be forgetting "all the badness you've done and never do the like of it again" she extracts from him a *stupendous sigh* and a profession of belief. This is followed by an anti-climax in which Burke is *appalled by some terrible doubt. With sudden fierce questioning:*

Is it Catholic ye are?

Anna. (*confused*) No. Why?

Burke. (*filled with a sort of bewildered foreboding*) Oh, God, help me! (*With a dark glance of suspicion at her*) There's some divil's trickery in it, to be swearing an oath on a Catholic cross and you wan of the others.

But after a brief interval:

Burke. (*suddenly holding her away from him and staring into her eyes as if to probe into her soul — slowly*) If your oath is no proper oath at all, I'll have to be taking your naked word for it and have you anyway, I'm thinking — I'm needing you that bad!

As *he crushes her to him and kisses her again* Chris appears in the doorway. The father's *old expression of hatred* is replaced by a *look of resignation and relief. His face lights up with a sudden happy thought. He turns back into the bedroom — reappears immediately with the tin can of beer in his hand — grinning.* With conflicts resolved and animosities removed, the play seems about

to end on a light-hearted note. Burke, who, as a superstitious and
backsliding Catholic, has contributed to the play an increasingly
comic spirit, appears to be confirming such a conclusion when once
again he *relapses into an attitude of gloomy thought* and then inquires of Chris,

Is it any religion at all you have, you and your Anna?
   Chris. (*surprised*) Vhy, yes. Ve vas Lutheran in ole country.
   Burke. (*horrified*) Luthers, is it? (*Then with a grim resignation, slowly,
aloud to himself*) Well, I'm damned then surely. Yerra, what's the difference? 'Tis the will of God, anyway.

At this point, shortly before the final curtain, the sub-plot ends and
the main plot is revived as Chris suddenly resumes his moody preoccupation and *speaks with somber premonition,*

It's funny. It's queer, yes — you and me shipping on same boat dat vay.
It ain't right. Ay don't know — it's dat funny vay ole davil sea do her vorst
dirty tricks, yes. It's so.

Burke nods his head in gloomy acquiescence, but Anna *forces a
laugh* and *with a determined gaiety* urges him to drink a toast to
the sea. He banishes his superstitious premonitions with a defiant
jerk of his head. Chris, however (*looking out into the night —
lost in his somber preoccupation — shakes his head and mutters*)
"Fog, fog, fog, all bloody time. You can't see vhere you vas going,
no. Only dat ole davil, sea — she knows!" (*The two stare at him.
From the harbor comes the muffled, mournful wail of steamers'
whistles.*)
   O'Neill himself expressed dissatisfaction with the ending. "It
seems," he wrote, "to have a false definiteness about it that is mis-
leading — a happy-ever-after which I did not intend."

I relied on the father's last speech of superstitious uncertainty to let my
theme flow through — and on . . . all of them at the end have a vague
foreboding that although they have had their moment, the decision rests with
the sea which has achieved the conquest of Anna.

The fault, it is evident by this time, is not in the ending — as the
playwright thought — but in the incongruous secondary plot. If the
theme does not "flow through — and on" as the author intended it
should, it is because it is dammed up by one complete act of melodramatic sensibility.

Thus the play was intended to be a single link in fate's endless chain which is relentlessly drawing the Christopherson family to their doom. If fate is whetting a sword for its victims, it is the sword of Damocles rather than of Justice, for no "disastrous history of dire offences" is charged against the family. They suffer because fate is inscrutable and ruthless: "It ain't your fault and it ain't mine . . ." says Anna, "We're all poor nuts and things happen, and we yust get mixed in wrong, that's all."

Since the "decision rests with the sea," and since the sea is not going to decide until after the final curtain has fallen, the protagonists are to continue to suffer, unlike the tragic heroine of Synge's *Riders to the Sea,* a play whose theme is identical to that of *Anna Christie.* In Synge's play finality is achieved when the sea has taken the last of the male members of the family, completing an emotional cycle. If pity and terror are not purged, they are, at least, definitely terminated.

The Hunted

ALTHOUGH MOST of O'Neill's early plays were concerned either with haunted sailors or with women in love, on two occasions they dealt with the American Negro, who neither sailed nor loved, but was both haunted and hunted. Before 1917 the stage Negro had almost invariably been "either of the white wool wig and kidney pain species . . . or of the species that was essentially a mere blacked-up Caucasian minstrel end man . . ." At best he was The Nigger in Edward Sheldon's play of that title. "Burnt-cork Sardou" as George Jean Nathan termed it, *The Nigger* as early as 1909 had discussed such topics as miscegenation and white supremacy. In 1917 there were produced in New York a group of plays that Ridgeley Torrence had written "for a Negro Theater" — plays which anticipated motifs and attitudes that were to appear in the dramas of O'Neill. Thus Granny Maumee's reversion during a paroxysm of anger and vengeance "from the love of Gawd back to that Affykin devil stuff," the sensational voodooism, the

criticism of the white man — "You didn't speck I'd steal too, like
a w'ite man did you?" asked Williams, the astute old Negro in
The Rider of Dreams — are familiar details to one who knows the
Negro plays of O'Neill.

The Dreamy Kid, a melodrama in one act which O'Neill wrote
in 1918, follows like so many of his plays of this period the traditional pattern of literary naturalism. Again the central character is
a man of physical strength, animal courage, small brain, who is
reduced to impotence by an intangible force, a brute brought to his
knees by a psychological mouse. His destruction is wrought by a
conflict of antithetical natural impulses; the instinct for self-preser-
vation is made ineffective by a recrudescence of childlike impulses.
Two events occurring simultaneously have produced this crisis in
the Dreamy Kid's life: the imminent death of his grandmother,
who has been a symbol of the complex of emotions which have
persisted since infancy; and the crime of murder — that of a white
man in self-protection — which he had committed the previous
night. Trailed by the police, he has come, against his better judgment, to the bedside of the dying Mammy. Now, beneath his hard,
efficient, snarling exterior there appears increasingly the soft and
dangerous tendencies which he has carried within him: the heaven
which had lain about him in his infancy, together with a subsequent emotional behavior pattern that had taken its impress from
the Southern Negro folkways. Superstition, affection, boyish bravado effect the disintegration of the adult Negro who was unfortunate enough to come of age in the sordid, alien, white man's environment of New York City. The shades of the prison-house have
begun to close upon him.

As Dreamy furtively enters the dark room wherein his Mammy
lies, he is nervous and uneasy, ready to flee. But the argument
which keeps him there is one whose transparently false logic reveals
his childlike mentality:

> Ceely. Yo' jest gotter stay wid her in her las' secon's on dis yearth when
> she's callin' ter yo'. (*With conviction as he hesitates*) Listen heah, yo'
> Dreamy! Yo' don' never git no bit er luck in dis worril ary agin', yo' leaves
> her now. Der perlice gon' ketch yo' shuah.
>   Dreamy. (*with superstitious fear*) Ssshh! Can dat bull, Ceely! (*Then
> boastfully*) I wasn't pinin' to beat it up here, git me? De boys was all per-
> suadin' me not ter take de chance. It's takin' my life in my hands, dat's what.

But when I heard it was ole Mammy croakin' and axin' ter see me, I says ter myse'f: 'Dreamy, you gotter make good wid ole Mammy no matter what come — or you don' never git a bit of luck in yo' life no mo'.' And I was game and come, wasn't I?

This ingenuous account of his purpose in coming is tempered by his display of genuine solicitude and tenderness:

> Dreamy. (*shudders in spite of himself as he realizes for the first time how far gone the old woman is — forcing a tone of joking reassurance*) What's dat foolishness I hears you talkin', Mammy? Wha' d'yuh mean pullin' dat bull 'bout croakin' on me? Shoo! Tryin' ter kid me, ain't yo? Shoo! You live ter plant de flowers on my grave, see if you don'.

Having always been considerate of his grandmother, he hopes now to collect the rewards of virtue, the avoidance of the curse which would befall him if he were now to be indifferent to her request. The play soon forsakes this penetrating analysis of the mind of primitive man; and, in place of a disquisition on the subject of "how natives think," we are provided with an explanation of how they act.

With the gratuitous intrusion of Irene, Dreamy's prostitute friend, the play swings into broad and violent action. Hysterical with joy at seeing her lover, she displays commendable forbearance in urging him to depart while he still can, for the police are on their way to Mammy's home. But he refuses to leave, and then, with an unexpected change of heart, he suddenly announces that the game is up, adding, *with gloomy fatalism,* "I s'pect it hatter be. Yes, suh. Dey'd git me in de long run anyway — and wid her curse de luck'd be agin me." This arbitrary surrender to fate is, however, difficult to reconcile with the rush of activity which immediately follows, when, *with sudden anger* Dreamy orders Irene to leave.

> You ain't aimin' ter git shot up too, is you? Ain't no sense in dat.
> Irene. (*fiercely*) I'se stayin' too, here wid you!
> Dreamy. No you isn't! None o' dat bull! You ain't got no mix in dis jam.
> Irene. Yes, I is! Ain't you my man?

Whereupon, in an access of devotion, he pushes her to the door, despite her vigorous pleas, and *hits her on the side of the face with all his might knocking her back against the wall where she sways as if about to fall. Then he opens the door and grabs her two arms from behind. . . . and pushes her into the hallway.* O'Neill's predilection and talent for melodrama is apparent in the conclusion of the play where Dreamy, the trapped animal whose instincts have betrayed him as they warred among themselves, barricades himself in the room with his nearly dead grandmother, while she, in semi-conscious retrospection, describes his babyhood and explains how he came to be called the Dreamy Kid. The juxtaposition of dissolute adulthood and innocent childhood, of violence and sensibility, makes the scene effectively melodramatic.

> Mammy. (*rambling . . . very feebly*) Does yo' know — I gives you dat name — w'en yo's des a baby — lyin' in my arms —
> Dreamy. Yes, Mammy.
> Mammy. Down by de crik — under de ole willow — whar I uster take yo' — wid yo' big eyes a-chasin' — de sun flitterin' froo de grass — an' out on de water —
> Dreamy. (*takes the revolver from his pocket and puts it on top of the chest of drawers*) Dey don't git de Dreamy alive — not for de chair! Lawd Jesus, no suh!
> Mammy. An' you was always — a-lookin' — an a-thinkin' ter yo'se'f — an yo' big eyes jest a-dreamin' an a-dreamin' — an' dat's w'en I gives yo' dat nickname — Dreamy — Dreamy —

The irony of the scene reaches its highest point at the curtain, as Dreamy repeats his determined pledge not to be caught alive. His Mammy, who by this time is gasping for breath, ironically misconstrues his blasphemous "Lawd Jesus, no suh" and, consoled by what she takes to be his piety, concludes the play with her own last words, "Dat's right — yo' pray — Lawd Jesus — Lawd Jesus — "

Had Dreamy enjoyed the good fortune ever to reach middle age he might have passed for Brutus Jones. To claim this distinction he would have had to remain unregenerate, to retain his capacity to act quickly and decisively, to study the ways of the white man in order to become more cynical, crafty, and unscrupulous. *The Emperor Jones,* written and produced in 1920, was the play that made the Provincetown Players famous and added to the fame which O'Neill had already attained in the Broadway presentation of *Beyond the Horizon.* If the character Jones is the middle-aged counterpart of the Dreamy Kid, the play itself anticipates *The Hairy Ape,* which O'Neill was to write one year hence, and which the Provincetown Players also produced. For when, in the latter play, the primitive stokers are described in the opening scene, and we are informed that *all the civilized white races are represented,* one must recall that the Negro had had a play to himself in *The Emperor Jones,* wherein his archaic past lay in the African Congo instead of in the Pleistocene age. Structurally, the two plays are similar, both being divided into eight episodic scenes with the evolutionary ladder figuratively occupying the center of the stage. Here the plays part company, for *The Emperor Jones* depicts the protagonist's descent of the ladder whereas *The Hairy Ape* reveals his thwarted effort to ascend. But the principal distinguishing feature exists not in terms of character or of technical devices, but rather in the end to which these are employed. *The Hairy Ape* transcends a representation of naturalism as an end in itself, moving beyond into speculation, as O'Neill begins to "dig at the roots of the sickness of today." *The Emperor Jones,* on the other hand, is a simple representation of psychological naturalism for its own sake, ingeniously contrived to a point where one must recognize the performance as a tour de force.

Yet, in the opening scene, O'Neill is clearly to be seen surveying the ground upon which he is to begin to dig in *The Hairy Ape.* Although the function of the scene is to prepare for the catastrophe which is to befall Jones in the subsequent seven scenes by providing a contrasting eminence to make his descent more violent and extreme, there are revealed unmistakable evidences of O'Neill's social consciousness. Brutus Jones, O'Neill sardonically informs us, is the emperor of an island in the West Indies which "is as yet not self-determined by White Marines." But it is in Jones himself that we are to observe sharp criticism of the civilization of the modern white man, for Jones is Negroid only in physical appearance and in speech in this scene. He is, rather, the American "success story" in black-face. *There is something decidedly distinctive about his face — an underlying strength of will, a hardy self-reliant confidence in himself that inspires respect. His eyes are alive with a keen, cunning intelligence. In manner he is shrewd, suspicious, evasive.* His rise to wealth and power, "from stowaway to Emperor in two years," had been achieved by virtue of his possession of none of the characteristics commonly associated with the Negro, such as shiftless laziness or lack of initiative. During the ten years in which he had served as Pullman car porter he had listened to the white quality — to George Babbitt, perhaps, as he traveled by Pullman to the Maine woods from Zenith — and adopted their ways. What he learned in those years was the white man's cynicism, shrewdness, efficiency, philosophy of self-interest. He had had explained to him, for example, the distinction between "little stealing" and "big stealing." "For de little stealin'," he informs the cockney Smithers, "dey gits you in jail soon or late. For de big stealin' dey makes you Emperor and puts you in de Hall o' Fame when you croaks." Having absorbed the ethic of the "white quality," he is quite as ready to exploit the natives as the white is to exploit the Negro:

You didn't s'pose I was holdin' down dis Emperor job for de glory in it, did you? Sho'! De fuss and glory part of it, dat's only to turn de heads o' de low flung, bush niggers dat's here. Dey wants de big circus for deir money. I gives it to 'em an' I gits de money. (*With a grin*) De long green, dat's me every time! (*Then rebukingly*) But you ain't got no kick agin me, Smithers. I'se paid you back all you done for me many times. Ain't I pertected you and winked at all de crooked tradin' you been doin' right out in de broad day? Sho' I has — and me makin' laws to stop it at de same time! (*He chuckles.*)

That Jones is the embodiment of white American materialism is further indicated by his reply to Smithers' contemptuous charge that Jones's actions are merely "Yankee bluff":

Ain't a man's talkin' big what makes him big — long as he makes folks believe it? Sho', I talks large when I ain't got nothin' to back it up, but I ain't talkin' wild just de same. I knows I kin fool 'em — I *knows* it — and dat's backin' enough fo' my game. And ain't I got to learn deir lingo and teach some of dem English befo' I kin talk to 'em? Ain't dat wuk? You ain't never learned any word fer it, Smithers, in de ten years you been heah, dough you know it's money in yo' pocket tradin' wid 'em if you does. But you'se too shiftless to take de trouble.

Paradoxically, it is the Negro, surging with Yankee enterprise, who berates the white man for his shiftlessness.

What is more, Jones shares with the white man, with the characters of O'Neill's plays whom we have already observed, a utilitarian attitude towards religion. Jones had been a "member in good standin' o' de Baptist Church," and in return the Church had protected him, he facetiously adds, by landing in hell all of the "pet devils and ghosts" which the natives had sent in pursuit of him. It had been part of his game to feign respect for the witch doctors while he has been on the island, since "it don't git me nothin' to do missionary work for de Baptist Church. I'se after de coin, an' I lays my Jesus on de shelf for de time bein'." How consistently O'Neill has adhered to this view of formal religion — sterile, vacuous, essentially un-Christian — becomes manifest when one recalls his assortment of hypocritical Catholics typified by Mat Burke who saw in his *cheap old crucifix* nothing more than a magic device whose purpose was to bring him luck; and fanatical Protestants represented by the religion-obsessed Mrs. Bartlett in *Gold,* whose God served her ends by punishing the persons whom she so designated.

Although he had climbed to the summit of success and power, Jones had never forgotten that fortune is fickle. He had, therefore, prepared for the inevitable descent — not, to be sure, the unpredictable one which he was to take. By his foresightedness, astuteness, singleness of purpose, he proved himself to be a wiser man than any other of O'Neill's heroes who rose to material success: Andrew Mayo spent eight years in the grain business running away from himself; the absurd Marco Polo foolishly chose to be a businessman instead of a poet; Sam Evans was simple-minded and immature. As for two other notable characters of fiction in the 1920's, Jones is patently the superior of the adolescent Babbitt, and of the Great Gatsby, who paid the "price of living too long with a single dream." Jones, to be sure, had no dreams, no illusions, no conflicts; he faced the facts of reality squarely, as no other O'Neill protagonist was to do. It would seem that he deserved a worthier adversary than abject terror. For in spite of his sagacious and resourceful plans — the silver bullet, and the caching of food in the forest along the path that leads to the French warship which would carry him to Martinique — Jones was to be the victim of a psychobiological force, the primitive past which the hysteria of fear dredges up. For the task of proving that instinct, emotion, necessity, must triumph over man's best laid plans, his free will, his reason, O'Neill employed the concepts of racial memory and of atavism.

If this was an old story to the reader of American fiction, it was a new and exciting one to the playgoer. And commonplace as it may have been as literature, it was most effective as melodrama. The services of the Negro actor, Charles Gilpin; the enthusiasm of the Provincetown Players, who drained their treasury to build a plaster cyclorama for the production; and the instinct of O'Neill for what is "good theatre" combined to make the performance a success, such a success, indeed, that the play moved uptown, and subsequently toured the country for two years. What made *The Emperor Jones* "good theatre" — and most of O'Neill's plays are — are its exploitation of the general preconception of the essentially primitive nature of the Negro, its structural perfection, and its ingenious employment of novel stage effects.

Although O'Neill had provided Jones with all the attributes of a white man, his sudden and rapid transformation to savagery was not in the least improbable, because the Negro's African past is relatively recent and therefore easily accessible. The literary naturalists had popularized a similar concept, as we shall observe in connection with *The Hairy Ape,* and applied it to the whites. If the cave man, or the Viking ancestor, lurks in the consciousness of the white man, ready to come charging out on the occasion of an emotional crisis, during drunkenness, or in a nightmare, why should the Negro's ancestor not deport himself in a similar disconcerting manner? Since there were currently in evidence such survivals of his African days as voodooism and superstition; a childlike temperament which was assumed to be a primitive heritage; and jazz music, which, by 1920, was becoming increasingly familiar, it was quite conceivable that Jones, particularly during a paroxysm of fear, should reveal equally primitive characteristics. These were to appear finally at the bottom of the shaft which had been sunk through the strata of his past and the past of his people, the individual Negro being a recapitulation of these pasts.

O'Neill achieved a remarkable concentration of dramatic power by means of several unifying effects. After the first scene, the action occurs between dusk of one afternoon and dawn of the following day in, or on the edge of, the Great Forest. The successive episodes are synchronized with Jones's revolver, the chamber of which contains approximately as many cartridges as there are scenes; as the gun is discharged the scene changes, approaching the point where

the sixth bullet, the silver one, coincides with the completed reversion to savagery. The beating tom-tom, like the steamer's whistle
in *Bound East for Cardiff,* also serves as an important unifying
factor, symbolizing as it does the pervasive and inescapable presence
of the primitive. Together with the revolver, it governs the inex-
orable movement towards the primeval, spatially and temporally.
For the tom-tom beats in the camp of the "bush niggers" to which
Jones is helplessly drawn, and it beats in Jones's body, representing
the primitive blood which charges through his arteries. Beginning
at a rate corresponding to the normal pulse beat and only faintly
heard, it becomes perceptibly louder and more rapid as Jones becomes increasingly terror-stricken, as his visions are regressively
aboriginal, as he approaches the camp of the "bush niggers." When
he is finally killed, with a silver bullet, the tom-tom instantly ceases.

An additional source of unity is to be found in the character of
the play itself throughout the six middle scenes, for here it becomes
a monodrama the action of which occurs within the infected mind
of the single character — reminding one not only of the appearance
of the three dead men in *Where the Cross Is Made,* but of the
grotesque dreams of Flaubert's St. Anthony, the visions of Hauptmann's febrile Hannele, Strindberg's "excruciating dream," the
hideous phantasms in Andreyev's *The Black Maskers.* The phantoms which torment the frenzied Jones exert upon him an inescapable and compulsive effect. As he impotently struggles against them
he fires the revolver, thereby obliterating the scene and releasing
himself from one nightmare experience only to move on to another.
In *The Emperor Jones* the objectification of the contents of the
character's haunted mind functions as a protracted symbol of fate
in the shape of the biological past. The madness of the fear-obsessed
Jones demonstrates that man is the sum not only of his own past
experiences but also those of his race, a notion that is based upon
the assumption of a psychical as well as a physical continuity between ancestor and descendant. For this conception O'Neill appears
to have been indebted to Jack London who, by means of "what
Weismann terms the 'germplasm,'" had found a way to account for
the existence of racial memories in his "atavistic brain," "memories
of the whole evolution of the race."

In *Before Adam* (1906) the racial memory of London's 20th century hero enabled him to describe his father in the "Younger World" as "half man, and half ape, and yet not ape, and not yet man." "It represented strength, that body of my father's," he added wistfully, "strength without beauty; ferocious, primordial strength, made to clutch and gripe and rend and destroy." Like his predecessor, Frank Norris, London explored in his novels the theme of the persistence in modern man of the brutish cave man, and pointed out the conflict and consequent "disassociation of personality" that this survival incurs. Also an heir of Darwin, and sharing their taste for red blood, Kipling had antedated Norris and London by more than a decade when he had observed that

> We are very slightly changed
> From the semi-apes who ranged
> India's prehistoric clay

and remarked that although new clothing was put on Neolithic man "of whiter, weaker flesh and bone more frail," a Christian age finds him "scuffling, squeaking, raging" still. Prior to *The Emperor Jones* O'Neill gave no consideration to his characters' biological past, yet without any primitivistic preconceptions he saw his common seamen, with a single exception, virtually as semi-apes; his powerful ship-captains as brutes with psychological distemper; his wild Irishmen and crafty Negroes as something less than human. After *The Emperor Jones* this brutalizing tendency crystallized. Having acquired a sense of the past, in 1921 he was prepared to call an ape an ape — but with neither the relish that Jack London had exhibited nor the seasoned admiration that he himself had once professed to feel.

Brought together again in *The Hairy Ape,* the crew of the *Glencairn* are now poor little apes who have lost their way and, clearly, are "damned from here to eternity." It is apparent at last that Smitty's doleful remark back in 1917 was directed at his mates as well as himself. Struck by the universality of Smitty's observation, O'Neill abstracted the seamen into "a symbol of man, who has lost his old harmony with nature, the harmony which he used to have as an animal and has not yet acquired in a spiritual way." While he respected Smitty's wisdom he was careful to avoid his "sentimental posing," and therefore cultivated for *The Hairy Ape* a tone of hard-boiled irony, subtitling the play "A comedy of ancient and modern life in eight scenes."

O'Neill saw no salvation for modern man, a brute who continues — redundantly — to be brutalized by machinery and industry. If man is essentially still an ape he has also become a machine and, in self-delusion, thinks that the elemental primitive force which he has retained and converted into steel can be an adequate end in itself. He enjoys a false sense of belonging to something, of being a part of steel and of machinery, whereas he is actually their slave. In those instances where he is not enslaved he has lost his vitality and become completely enervated — "a waste product in the Bessemer process," inheriting "the acquired trait of the by-product, wealth, but none of the energy, none of the strength of the steel that made it."

To Darwinian man O'Neill grafted Emerson's machine man "Metamorphosed into a thing"; the mechanic, according to Emerson, has become a machine, the victim of society in that degenerate state in which "the members have suffered amputation from the trunk." Upon London's mid-Pleistocene creature he superimposed contemporary conceptions of man-a-machine. In *The Coral* (1917), the first play of his *Gas* trilogy, Georg Kaiser depicted, as did O'Neill, the contrast aboard ship between the stokehole in which "men feed fire-belching holes" and the luxurious deck upon which the billionaire and his party enjoy the speed that has been bought at the expense of the men below. In *Gas — Part I* (1918) we hear of a workman's hand that, ceaselessly making the same movement at the machine, grew to be the whole man. "He never missed a stroke — the lever was always true — always exact. And he stood in front of it and served it like a dead man." The destructive, the dehumanizing effects of commerce and machines were dramatized in other plays — Toller's *The Machine Wreckers* (1922), Capek's *R.U.R.* (1922), Rice's *The Adding Machine* (1923). Whereas in most of these man saves himself through an act of will or an act of love, in *The Hairy Ape,* incapable of exercising such human prerogatives, he is forever damned, the victim of his own past.

O'Neill was convinced that the mass of men lead lives of clamorous desperation, their attitude being one of *bewildered, furious, baffled defiance.* Resembling both Neanderthal men and chained gorillas, they speak and act in unison, laugh as if they were barking, sooth themselves with whiskey, delude themselves with the thought that they "belong." The penalty one pays for defying his fate, for detaching himself from the primal horde and trying to rise above it, is inner conflict and self-destruction. Such a penalty is incurred by Yank, the group's *most highly developed individual — broader, fiercer, more truculent, more powerful, more sure of himself than the rest.* His doom is foreshadowed when, like Robert and Andrew Mayo, he determines to run against his own nature by trying to think, by becoming self-conscious — aware that he is an ape, by realizing that he does not "belong." Setting off on his quest Yank encounters most of the remedies for desperation that O'Neill himself had considered and, like O'Neill, rejects them. Principal among these is social reform. The brute mind, no more acute than it was in the Glencairn plays, is incapable of comprehending Socialist doctrine. This is evident as early as the first scene when Long jumps on a bench to harangue his mates:

We lives in 'ell, Comrades — and right enough we'll die in it. (*Raging*) And who's ter blame I arsks yer? We ain't. We wasn't born this rotten way. All men is born free and ekal. That's in the bleedin' Bible, maties. But what d'they care for the Bible — them lazy, bloated swine what travels first cabin? Them's the ones. They dragged us down 'til we're on'y wage slaves in the bowels of a bloody ship, sweatin', burnin' up, eatin' coal dust! Hit's them ter blame — the damned Capitalist clarss! (*There had been a gradual contemptuous resentment among the men until now he is interrupted by a storm of catcalls, hisses, boos, hard laughter.*)

Unmoved by the appeal to Christian principle and Socialist dogma, Yank stands up and glares at Long:

Sit down before I knock yuh down! . . . De Bible, huh? De Cap'tlist class, huh? Aw nix on dat Salvation Army-Socialist bull. Git a soapbox! Hire a hall! Come and be saved, huh? Jerk us to Jesus, huh? Aw g'wan! I've listened to lots of guys like you, see. Yuh're all wrong. Wanter know what I t'ink? You ain't no good for no one. Yuh're de bunk.

In Scene Four after the millionaire's daughter, Mildred Douglas, recoiled from the sight of Yank's abysmal brutality, his gorilla face, while Yank sits brooding and trying to think, Long tries once again to penetrate the primitive mentality, and again he fails. He touches a responsive chord only when he refers to his fellows as "bloody animals" on view below decks for the entertainment of the Capitalist's daughter. Yank, becoming increasingly conscious of his ape-like appearance, is obsessed with a frenzied desire for revenge against the girl rather than against her social class, as Long insists. Long's assurance that the law, the government, and God are all on the workers' side is swept away with *cynical mockery, abysmal contempt.* Scene Five finds Yank on Fifth Avenue accompanied by the Socialist, who still attempts to persuade his Neanderthal mate that his grievance is against a class not an individual; but the concept is too much for Yank to comprehend, and he continues to seek personal revenge. Long's figurative language and his sarcasm are meaningless to the dull mind. Indignant over the luxury on display in the jeweler's window: prices "more'n our 'ole bloody stoke-hole makes in ten voyages sweatin' in 'ell!" enough to "buy scoff for a starvin' family for a year," Long elicits from Yank only *naive admiration* for the jewelry: "Say, dem tings is pretty, huh?" But the sight of monkey's fur in the furrier's window — "Monkey fur — two t'ousand bucks!" — causes Yank to turn *pale with rage as if the skin in the window were a personal insult.* Resorting to violence, Yank attacks the procession of *gaudy marionettes,* symbols of the capitalist class, who emerge from church. Long urges him to come away, telling him "This wasn't what I meant." Whereupon Long is sent sprawling, after which he slinks off. Yank is clubbed to the pavement by the policemen. In jail in the following scene his simple and credulous mind fastens upon a single portion of a speech made by a Senator, a harangue against the I.W.W. which had been printed in the *Sunday Times:* "They plot with fire in one hand and dynamite in the other," said the demagogue. Yank responds *with a growl of fury:* "I got him. So dey blow up tings, do dey? Dey turn tings round, do dey?" Then, with the strength of an ape, he bends the bars of his cell. At the I.W.W. local a month later he is disappointed to find that the organization is nothing like the Senator had described it, that instead of violence its method is to "change the unequal conditions of society by legitimate direct action." Mistaken for "an agent provocator" and called a "brainless ape," he is thrown out into the street. There *he sits, brooding, in as near to the attitude of Rodin's "The Thinker" as he can get* and says *bitterly:*

So dem boids don't tink I belong, neider. Aw, to hell wit 'em! Dey're in de wrong pew — de same old bull — soap-boxes and Salvation Army — no guts! Cut out an hour offen de job a day and make me happy! Tree square a day, and cauliflowers in de front yard — ekal rights — a woman and kids — a lousy vote — and I'm all fixed for Jesus, huh? Aw, hell! What does dat get yuh? Dis ting's in your inside, but it ain't your belly. Feedin' your face — sinkers and coffee — dat don't touch it. It's way down — at de bottom. Yuh can't grab it, and yuh can't stop it. It moves, and everything moves. It stops and de whole woild stops. Dat's me now — I don't tick, see? — I'm a busted Ingersoll, dat's what. Steel was me, and I owned de woild. Now I ain't steel, and de woild owns me. Aw, hell! I can't see — it's all dark, get me? It's all wrong! (*He turns a bitter mocking face up like an ape gibbering at the moon*)

Modern man can be saved neither by the soap-box — socialism, anarchism — nor by the Salvation Army — Christianity. Doomed, he is nevertheless given a glimpse of paradise, a golden age when he was in harmony with nature, when he was part of a ship which was part of the sea — all merging to make One. Paddy, a weary, wistful, wise old Irishman, a superannuated Mat Burke, suggests what O'Neill had in mind.

Paddy. (*Who has been sitting in a blinking melancholy daze — suddenly cries out in a voice full of old sorrow*) We belong to this you're saying? Yerra then, that Almighty God have pity on us! (*His voice runs into the wail of a keen, he rocks back and forth on his bench. The men stare at him, startled and impressed in spite of themselves*) Oh, to be back in the fine days of my youth, ochone! Oh, there was fine beautiful ships them days — clippers wid tall masts touching the sky — fine strong men in them — men that was sons of the sea as if 'twas the mother that bore them . . . For the day that was, was enough, for we was free men — and I'm thinking 'tis only slaves do be giving heed to the day that's gone or the day to come — until they're old like me. (*With a sort of religious exaltation*) Oh, to be scudding south again wid the power of the Trade Wind driving her on steady through the nights and the days! Full sail on her! Nights and days! Nights when the foam of the wake would be flaming wid fire, when the sky'd be blazing and winking wid stars . . . And there was the days, too. A warm sun on the clean decks. Sun warming the blood of you, and wind over the miles of shiny green ocean like strong drink to your lungs. Work — aye, hard work — but who'd mind that at all? Sure, you worked under the sky and 'twas work wid skill and daring to it . . . (*His tone of exalta-*

tion ceases. He goes on mournfully) Yerra, what's the use of talking? 'Tis a dead man's whisper. 'Twas them days men belonged to ships, not now. 'Twas them days a ship was part of the sea, and a man was part of a ship, and the sea joined all together and made it one. (*Scornfully*) Is it one with this you'd be, Yank — black smoke from the funnels smudging the sea, smudging the decks — the bloody engines pounding and throbbing and shaking — wid divil a sight of sun or a breath of clean air — choking our lungs wid coal dust — breaking our backs and hearts in the hell of the stokehole — feeding the bloody furnace — feeding our lives along wid the coal, I'm thinking — caged in by steel from a sight of the sky like bloody apes in the zoo! (*With a harsh laugh*) Ho-ho, divil mend you! Is it to belong to that you're wishing? Is it a flesh and blood wheel of the engines you'd be?

Since the days which Paddy has described are irretrievable, he is resigned to "sittin' here at me ease, and drinking, and thinking, and dreaming dreams." Not only in the past were the virtues of nature apparent; they intensify the artificiality and sordidness of life today. In Scene Two, on the promenade deck, *the impression to be conveyed . . . is one of the beautiful vivid life of the sea all about — sunshine on the deck in a great flood, the fresh sea wind blowing across it. In the midst of this, these two incongruous, artificial figures, inert and disharmonious . . .* Similarly, in the scene on Fifth Avenue *the general effect is of a background of magnificence cheapened and made grotesque by commercialism, a background in tawdry disharmony with the clear light and sunshine on the street itself.* Acknowledging the benevolence of nature, Yank nevertheless is incurable:

De sun was warm, dey wasn't no clouds, and dere was a breeze blowin'. Sure, it was great stuff. I got it aw right — what Paddy said about dat bein' de right dope — on'y I couldn't get *in* it, see? I couldn't belong in dat. It was over my head.

The last scene of the play finds Yank in the monkey house at the zoo before the gorilla's cage. Here he perceives again what it really means to "belong," to be in complete harmony with nature. Addressing the gorilla, gropingly:

Youse can sit and dope dream in de past, green woods, de jungle and de rest of it. Den yuh belong and dey don't . . . But me — I ain't got no past to tink in, nor nothin' dat's comin', on'y what's now — and dat don't belong. Sure, you're de best off! You can't tink, can yuh? Yuh can't talk neider. But I can make a bluff at talkin' and tinkin' — a'most git away wit it —

a'most! — and dat's where de joker comes in (*He laughs*) I ain't on oith and I ain't in heaven, get me? I'm in de middle tryin' to separate 'em, takin' all de woist punches from bot' of 'em. Maybe dat's what dey call hell, huh? But you, yuh're at de bottom. You belong! Sure! Yuh're de on'y one in de woild dat does, yuh lucky stiff!

He opens the cage door, invites the gorilla to shake hands — a gesture which means, according to O'Neill, that Yank, unable to go forward, is now trying to go back. "But he can't go back to 'belonging' either." The animal, refusing to recognize him, crushes him to death.

A climactic play, *The Hairy Ape* culminates earlier tendencies, anticipates subsequent ones. O'Neill was ready now to abandon the Darwinian brute and the monomaniacal monster, whose limited tragic possibilities he exhausted, in favor of the man of feeling, with whom he felt a closer kinship, whose capacity for suffering is greater, and who is better equipped to be sent on a spiritual quest. For such a quest the allegorical and symbolical method, which he employed for the first time in the present play, will continue to be useful. And the tone of future plays will remain ironic — more bitter and mocking than comic.

PART TWO

Dream and Drunkenness

The Theatre of Tomorrow

BETWEEN 1920 AND 1922 O'Neill was rewarded with fame and success. *Beyond the Horizon* and *Anna Christie* won a Pulitzer Prize in consecutive years, *The Emperor Jones* received wide acclaim, *The Hairy Ape* confirmed much of what had been said in praise of its author not only in Greenwich Village but on Broadway; George Jean Nathan had become a friend as well as a critic. Yet even while he was being singled out as America's leading playwright, O'Neill was reflecting upon a plan for future work. As early as June 1920 he wrote to Nathan urging him to come up to Provincetown to hear about his new idea,

a scheme quite on a grand scale, and as far as my knowledge goes, an original plan in play writing. I do not mean by this that there is any heavy blank verse, soggy symbolism or bizarre innovations connected with it; but it is an idea which is so large in outline that, even having the temerity to grant one's ability for it, it will take some years of intensive and difficult labor to fill in. The question in my mind still is, is this thing as big as I think; is it worth the labor involved, and from a purely practicable standpoint, can it be done? So standing on the threshold, I would sure like to have your opinion.

Having mailed the letter he bought a copy of the July *Smart Set* and discovered an article by Nathan which affirmed O'Neill's position among American playwrights but which expressed serious doubt that he would ever ascend above second rating among the "first dramatists of present-day Europe." Fearing that the letter which he had just written would appear "in its too-aptness to have been inspired" by Nathan's appraisal, O'Neill, apparently irked by the "serious doubt," resentful, grateful, embarrassed, felt called upon to clarify his own attitude towards his status. Whereupon he sent another letter to inform his critic-friend that he was "familiar enough with the best modern drama of all countries to realize that, viewed from a true standard my work is as yet a mere groping. I rate myself as a beginner with prospects." Still young and determined to "grow," "to follow the dream and live for that alone," he was confident that his "real significant bit of truth, and the ability to express it, will be conquered in time — not tomorrow nor the next day nor any near, easily-attained period, but after the struggle has been long enough to merit victory." Thus, despite the reputation that he had earned, he exhibited — to Nathan at any rate — commendable humility, a virtue that was to be rewarded. For with few exceptions the critic was to regard O'Neill's future plays with increasing approbation.

Nathan had been encouraging the artistic revolt against the theatre of today on the grounds that it was trying to be "too perfect" — trying, that is, to compete with nature, to destroy illusion. He admired especially such rebels as Gordon Craig who brought back the "liquid beauty of theatrical artificiality," purging the theatre of its "mechanically perfect fol-de-rol, its amazing pretenses and realisms, its confusing encroachments upon life and reality." Although he felt that O'Neill was "the one writer for the native stage who gives promise of achieving a sound position for himself," the naturalistic plays could elicit from him only qualified admiration and the aforementioned "serious doubt." But now O'Neill, standing upon the threshold of the so-called theatre of tomorrow, was prepared to enter and fulfill not only his own dream but also the promise which Nathan saw in the early plays.

O'Neill had already turned his back upon the naturalistic drama in the form and method of *The Hairy Ape* — but not in the content. As yet he had found no way to penetrate the materialistic impasse which he himself had erected out of Darwinism and steel. Here Nathan was no help whatever. Choosing to absent himself from the harsh world rather than from felicity, he felt that life "is for the fortunate few — life with all its Chinese lanterns, and sudden lovely tunes, and gay sadness." Nathan was interested in the "surface of life," its "music and colour, its charm and ease, its humour and its loveliness. The great problems of the world — social, political, economic and theological — " did not concern him "in the slightest." If such problems had once concerned O'Neill, he came at last to feel that they were irrelevant. His rejection of them had been presaged not only in his plays but also in his extra-dramatic conduct. Thus Granville Hicks has related how O'Neill joined John Reed, his radical associate among the Provincetown Players, "in common abuse of the existing order," and how, more cynical than Reed, "O'Neill would sneer at the workers for failing to revolt, whereas Reed would cheer them on." Yet among literary radicals, as the 1920's approached, Reed's rather than O'Neill's became the exceptional attitude. In some instances the radical position was felt to be too perilous to maintain in the face of wartime drives against disloyalty and postwar investigations of subversive activity. In others it had been made untenable by psychoanalytic theory. Lincoln Steffens, for example, described the impact upon himself of the "new psychology," how, after he had been introduced "to the idea that the minds of men were distorted by unconscious suppressions, often quite irresponsible and incapable of reasoning or learning," he came to realize the absurdity of "his muckraker's descriptions of bad men and good men and the assumption that showing people facts and conditions would persuade them to alter them or their own conduct." In still other cases the literary radical was torn between literature and radicalism. Thus Floyd Dell and Max Eastman, editors of *The Masses* and members of the Provincetown Players, were loyal to Marx and at the same time devoted to their Muse. Dell in 1920 began to write a series of bourgeois novels, and Eastman before that had been given to indulging a lyrical poetic impulse. Both apologized for their inability to reconcile revolution and "life." But to friends who for some reason always expected him to involve his poetry "in tempests of social change" Eastman announced that "Life is older than liberty. It is greater than revolution. It burns in both camps. And life is what I love."

O'Neill, too, preferred life to revolution, although at times he seems to have made his choice by process of elimination. But having repudiated utterly and publicly his radical convictions, he at least was free to experiment with other faiths. Equally dissatisfied with a world they never made, other American literary artists at the turn of the decade dealt with the situation in various ways, all of which were congenial to O'Neill at one time or another during the next ten years. James Branch Cabell, antagonistic to realistic fiction, went beyond life into satirical allegory; Sherwood Anderson engaged in fumbling, dreamy mysticism; Sinclair Lewis resorted to realistic satire; Scott Fitzgerald exposed aspects of postwar reality that were far this side of paradise. The theatre, however, afforded advantages that were denied non-dramatic writers. When, in 1920, O'Neill began to dream about a new idea in playwriting he had been stimulated principally by tendencies that had come from abroad, tendencies that received their fullest artistic expression in the theatre. The following year, in *The Hairy Ape,* he cleared the way for a decade of experiments, aesthetic and religious.

In that play Yank, shortly before he was killed, had perceived that the gorilla was "de best off"; for he could dream, but he could not think. Yank, on the other hand, could think — only in rudimentary fashion, to be sure —, but having no past to dream in, he could not dream. And he ignored the admonition of his mates: "Drink, don't think!" If Yank "was a symbol of man who has lost his old harmony with nature," Paddy was a symbol of man's only hope. Although O'Neill relied to the end of his career on Paddy's formula, "dope-dream and drink," by transforming the ingredients into vision and rapture he saw a means to acquire harmony with nature "in a spiritual way." To "belong" is to achieve "oneness," union with nature in which God is immanent. How the theatre in the early 1920's encouraged and facilitated the representation of such spirituality is discussed in the pages which follow.

By 1922 O'Neill had not only won his Pulitzer awards, he had seen his plays open in Greenwich Village and then move uptown. In that year Arthur Hopkins, once assured of the success of *The Hairy Ape,* took over the production; and the Provincetown Players, becoming aware of their changing character, suspended operations for nearly a year and a half that they might discover their proper function in the theatrical world. Meanwhile, George Cram Cook departed for Greece. Apparently unimpressed by the excursions of his company to Broadway, he was convinced that the Provincetown Players had failed. Whereupon he abandoned hope of bringing "to birth in our commercial minded country a theater whose motive was spiritual," of creating "an oasis of living beauty" in the "dry heart" of his "great, chaotic, unhappy community." What he had dreamed of achieving in his little theatre of spiritual motive and living beauty was something essentially religious: the ultimate transformation of the theatre "into living Church." Failing, he preferred to live among ruins and ghosts in the land where the theatre had been "born of Primitive Dance" and had "hardened into Church."

Cook's was a collective dream, one that was shared by his successors: O'Neill, Kenneth Macgowan, and Robert Edmond Jones. Having offered Macgowan a dictatorship as director, O'Neill, then, along with Jones, became an associate director. "A happy combination of personalities," the critic, the playwright, and the scene designer "agreed in ideas and policies, choice of plays and actors." A prominent critic, Macgowan had published two books about the modern theatre: *The Theatre of Tomorrow,* in 1921, and, following a tour of European theatres in 1922, *Continental Stagecraft.* Jones had collaborated on the latter volume, for, like Macgowan, he had been excited by innovations on the foreign stage. As early as 1914 he had been acclaimed to be "perhaps the most imaginative of the young American designers." With Cleon Trockmorton, he had designed the settings for *The Hairy Ape,* and was attracted from Broadway because he was "eager for the wider scope afforded by a non-commercial theater." Nor was O'Neill himself out of touch with foreign developments in the drama, a fact of which he had apprised Nathan in 1920. Now, with the triumvirate in control of Cook's old organization, its name was changed to *Experimental Theater, Incorporated.* With the change in name went a change in character. It was significant that Jones should read to the players "from Stanislavski's 'Life in Art,'" that the programs imitated those of Reinhardt, becoming eight-page playbills containing "notes on the production and general theater news." There were more revolutionary transformations. Whereas the Provincetown under Cook had dedicated itself to the discovery and encouragement of native drama, the Experimental Theater exhibited more catholic interest, producing plays ranging from Congreve to Gilbert and Sullivan, from Strindberg to O'Neill. Whereas Cook's outfit had been a completely amateur one, under the new order it became increasingly professional. Whereas the Provincetown had been a so-called "playwright's" theatre, it now became a so-called "production" theatre. With two playhouses at their disposal — the Greenwich Village Theater in addition to the little theatre in Macdougal Street — the triumvirate proceeded to recover, even to surpass, the reputation that the organization had earned before 1920. Indeed, "to many a theatergoer the name Provincetown Playhouse still calls to mind the fine productions of the Macgowan-Jones-O'Neill regime." Yet, despite the transformation in means, the end which the directors sought to attain was essentially that for which their predecessor had striven. To find an expression of their creed one has only to consult Macgowan's book, published in 1921, *The Theatre of Tomorrow.* Written with remarkable prescience, the volume is also a useful compendium to many plays of O'Neill that were yet to appear.

"If some Martian," wrote Macgowan in *The Theatre of Tomorrow,* "were to see a performance in Athens or in Bankside placed beside a performance in the Belasco Theatre, would he guess for a moment that he had looked upon the same institution, the same instinctive expression of godhead?" Equally abashed by the prospect of a visit by a theatre-going man from Mars, Cook chose to be not at home. More optimistic, more resourceful, Macgowan had surveyed the new movements in the theatre and was confident that the American stage would shortly put on a show that would befuddle any visitor who tried to compare it with those he had witnessed in ancient Athens or in Elizabethan London. Although the modern theatre had been advancing along a single line, that of stagecraft, Macgowan was hopeful that the drama would soon catch up. To be sure, the situation had been reversed in Shakespeare's day: Inigo Jones had come "after the great days." But in 1921, it was reasonable to expect, another Jones — Robert Edmond — "may be coming before them." If any American playwright were capable of fulfilling Macgowan's expectations, surely it was O'Neill. And by 1921 O'Neill's intimations appeared to bear this out. His subsequent association with Jones and with Macgowan marked the arrival of the "great days," the synthesis of stagecraft and drama, the restoration of the theatre to its proper function: a place for the "instinctive expression of godhead."

The triumvirate agreed with Cook that the motive of the theatre must be spiritual. Like Cook, they were aware of the difficulty of bringing to birth such a theatre "in our commercial-minded country." In Europe Macgowan had visited churches and theatres and had watched drama performed in the church. Home once again, he decided that "the problem is to find a way for the religious spirit independent of the church," to make the theatre itself religious. At present, unfortunately,

America has no art and no religion which can make drama religious. America does not believe, in any deep sense. Science has shattered dogma, and formal religion has not been able to absorb an artistic or a philosophic spirit great enough to recreate the religious spirit in men.

It was a problem, he believed, which could be solved by the "artist of the theater," who, with the theatre as his "very extraordinary instrument," could "visualize with amazing intensity a religious spirit of which he has sensed only the faintest indications in life," who could "create a world which sings with exaltation and which seems — as it indeed is — a world of reality." Possessed by the concept "spiritual reality," Macgowan had an aversion for "reality of the flesh" and rejoiced over what he took to be the "twilight of realism."

Two-thirds of *The Theatre of Tomorrow* was devoted to stagecraft and theatre architecture, one-third to drama. In all three parts he celebrated the tendency towards "inner truth." He praised O'Neill at this early date — along with Ibsen — for occasionally going deeper in his realistic plays, for giving not only the "ephemeral exterior," but also certain "values which are, as near as we can measure them, eternal." *Rosmersholm* and *Beyond the Horizon* were cases in point. Yet "we are turning away even from their high realism," he explained, "because we are seeking an intense inner vision of spiritual reality which will push the selective process so far that to call the result realism will be an absurdity." He was convinced that "the significant thing in the theatre of today is the breakdown of realism in form and content, and the beginning of free, faint gropings towards a reality behind life." In the following chapters he described the form and content of the "drama of tomorrow."

The drama of tomorrow "will be free in form," Macgowan de-

clared. The Greeks obeyed conventions, "but these were all parts
of the religious ritual from which drama sprang." And if the
"Shakespearean form had its stock devices . . . , compared with
the intricate arrangements of the well-built three-act play it seems
almost formless." Macgowan believed that the play of the future
would contain a greater multiplicity of scenes. The "dialogue
[would] grow more condensed" and "seek less to imitate the
rambling uncertainties of natural speech." The "soliloquy will return again as a natural and proper revelation of the mind of a
character. Even the aside may redevelop as a deliberate piece of
theatricalism." To "reinforce dramatic expression" other mediums
will augment the word: "the dramatist of the future will think
more in terms of color, design, movement, music than he does
now, and less in words alone." But when he does think in words
he will think largely in prose, using verse in a variety of measures
as determined by the "emotion of the scene."

Having described the form of the future, Macgowan attempted
to guess its content. Of one thing he was certain. The play of
tomorrow

will attempt to transfer to dramatic art the illumination of those deep and
vigorous and eternal processes of the human soul which the psychology of
Freud and Jung has given us through study of the unconscious, striking to
the heart of emotion and linking our life today with the emanations of the
primitive racial mind.

That spiritual and beautiful drama which Cook had despaired of
finding, MacGowan had at last located. We had only to "recognize
the thing that, since Greek days, we had forgotten — the eternal
identity of you and me with the vast and unmanageable forces
which have played through every atom of life since the beginning."
Whereas Cook had perceived in psychoanalysis material for satirical comedy — having collaborated with Susan Glaspell on the popular one-act play, *Suppressed Desires* — Macgowan discovered in
Freudian psychology precisely what Cook had been searching for
in serious drama.

Psychoanalysis, tracing back our thoughts and actions into fundamental impulses, has done more than any one factor to make us recover the sense
of our unity with the dumb, mysterious processes of nature. We know now

through science what the Greeks and all primitive peoples knew through instinct. The task is to apply it to art and, in our case, to the drama.

It may be applied generally; it may give us a drama utterly apart from anything we have now, nearer perhaps to the Greek than to any other in spirit, yet wholly new in mechanism and method, mysteriously beautiful and visionary. The new sense of the significance of life, which we have won both through science and in spite of science, may take a dramatic form which springs straight from the life about us and requires no more trappings of mysterious beauty than does Kaiser's *From Morn to Midnight*. But whatever the form of the play, the content will have a spiritual quality that gives us this subliminal sense of mysterious age-old processes alive in us today.

Although he felt that Kaiser's play "is a bizarre piece" he admired it for getting past the surface of reality, "for penetrating the basic stratum of man's psyche." He was prepared to defend Expressionism, "narrow, neurotic, violent, and formless" though it was, "against the Realism of Augustus Thomas or even of John Galsworthy." But he would not "admit that it was the end of the reaction against resemblance." Indeed, he preferred to apply the term Expressionism "to the whole tendency against Realism," to regard it merely as a "way of escape," as a foreshadowing of the drama of tomorrow.

The form of that drama, as we have seen, was to be "free," the content spiritual, eternal, beautiful. Confronted next with the problem of attaining this dramatic perfection in a "commercial-minded country," Macgowan examined the social and economic forces that had conditioned the tastes of the American audience. Realism he found to be "the natural product of slavery to machines." But if its cause was "industrial capitalism," so also — for the present at least — was its cure. For the leisure class audience, he noted, was struggling to free themselves from the "obsessions of realism." An active group, they "sought deliberately for something beyond or apart from the literalness of life."

These men and women were a product of industrialism. They were members of a leisure class which it had created, a leisure class freed both from the absorption of money-getting and from the greater absorption of the search for the means of escaping the evils of money-getting. It was this class that supplied the sinews of the new art of the theatre.

Evidence that Macgowan's faith in the leisure class was well-placed came three years later while he was director of the Provincetown.

Seeking to raise $50,000 to take over the Greenwich Village Theater on a long-term lease, the supporters of the theater were gratified to see half the sinews supplied in a single week by Mrs. Willard Straight, Otto H. Kahn, Frank Crowninshield, and Mrs. August Belmont. Thus, while his bête noire, realism, was subdued, Macgowan found the situation in the theatre fairly tolerable. Yet he continued to dream of the theatre of tomorrow, a dream that was influenced by the actualities of the European stage. Impressed by Reinhardt's conception of the little theatre and the mammoth theatre — the Kammerspielhaus and the Grosses Schauspielhaus — Macgowan became a proponent of a similar idea, of the little theatre and the circus theatre. He foresaw, therefore, that the playwright would be faced with writing two types of drama for two different types of theatre. The little theatre, he thought, would be adapted to expressionistic plays like *From Morn to Midnight,* while the large theatre would exhibit such drama as Dunsany's *The Gods of the Mountain* or Rolland's *Danton.* Especially intrigued by the idea of a circus theatre he believed that it

opens up possibilities for the playwright that seem singularly broad and singularly pregnant with the spirit of the age. Such a theatre enables him to write in terms of movement as well as of words, to dramatize life upon varying levels of consciousness and of actuality, to reach ever closer to the life-giving vigor of vast audiences, to arouse in such mighty gatherings emotions which sweep in one gigantic swell to the players and are thrown back in still more majestic power to the audience again. In such a playhouse is born a sense of drama which transcends individual action.

In his dream of a circus theatre — a "mob theatre," a "theatre of crowds" — he included various dramatic innovations:

One can conceive of a drama of group-beings in which great individuals, around whom these groups coalesce, could be fitly presented only under the impersonal and eternal aspect of the mask; or, again, a drama in which the foil to the mob is the marionette who is thought to give it utterance. One can conceive as easily the mask and the marionette finding an inevitable use in intimate symbolic drama or in the expression of the unconscious.

"Such conceptions," he explained, "carry us far across tomorrow." To be sure, none of the elements which formed his vision was to be found in the leisure-class theatre of New York. Robert Edmond

Jones had employed the mask, but his conception of the "group-beings" had yet to reach the stage. Other elements were derived from foreign theory and practice: from Reinhardt; from Rolland, who had pleaded for a "People's Theatre" as early as 1903, and whose articles concerning the subject were translated and published by Barrett H. Clark in 1918; from Craig; from the social psychologists ranging from LeBon to McDougall. But the circus was not to be the ultimate theatre.

Macgowan dreamed also of the Theatre of Democracy and wrote about it in his last chapter. A "thing of the spirit," "a thing of the future," when democracy comes, he prophesied, "it will make over the theatre . . . And it will give it that deep spiritual sincerity, that religious content, in which great drama waxes." He discerned hopeful portents in the "new drama" that was abandoning realism, for its "spiritual elements"

go back to the emotional roots of instinctive racial drama even while they build on to conscious study and interpretation of instinct and intuition and in general the whole vast field of the unconscious mind of man. The content of the drama of tomorrow, cut off from realism, is clearly united with the content of primitive and democratic drama even while it goes ahead to a range of mental exploration that must be of gathering importance to a broadly democratic culture.

He expected the theatre of democracy to be a festival theatre,

in which the finest creative spirit of the community, exemplified in playwrights, artists and actors will labor. Under industrial imperialism or under revolutionary democracy such festival theatres, sheltered in exposition buildings or in natural valleys, may achieve as clear an expression of the spirit of democracy as they ever could under revolution.

One had only to await "the day when some fundamental change in our conception of life brings back something approaching the religious devotion that surrounded the Greek drama." We should then, at last, have a theatre to compare with "the great democratic theatres of Greece, of the Middle Ages and of Elizabethan England."

Impatient for that day to arrive, George Cram Cook, enchanted with the ancient Greeks, spent two happy years consorting with their descendants, contracted typhoid fever, and died in 1924. From the Temple of Apollo a stone was removed to place upon his grave.

As he looked at his book in retrospect, Macgowan was brought "up sharp against the sense of the dangers of apocalyptic fervors." But then he comforted himself with the thought that "it is impossible to deny a faith in the City of God" and added, to end the book: "There were once, you know, the Greeks." To him the Greek way of life was as compelling as it was to Cook; in the promise of American life and in the theatre of tomorrow he foresaw its resurrection.

If Macgowan's confession of faith failed to make any converts at the Provincetown, his presence there, together with his two brother apostles, rejuvenated the organization and made it solvent. Today the only enduring monuments that remain are the plays that O'Neill wrote, beginning with *The Hairy Ape* in 1921 and ending with *Lazarus Laughed* in 1926. In those plays, as we shall see, O'Neill embodied much of Macgowan's doctrine. To be sure, he was not entirely successful. Although he escaped from realism he did not — with the possible exception of *Lazarus* — free himself from the leisure-class theatre. His interest in crowds was confined to the stage and remained psychological and theatrical; for he appeared to share Nathan's scorn for the "popular, or mob, theatre," rather than Macgowan's optimistic democratic point of view. On the other hand, he was, like Macgowan, preoccupied with production — with stagecraft: with mobs, masks, and other innovations "short of the bizarre —"; and playwriting, unfortunately, was often overwhelmed. But above all, he sought to express spiritual reality rather than reality of the flesh, and did it largely according to the methods advocated by Macgowan. For he, too, was aware that "science has shattered dogma," that "formal religion has not been able to absorb an artistic or a philosophic spirit great enough to re-create the religious spirit in men," that the "problem is to find a way for the religious spirit independent of the church." Through his quest for "inner truth" he hoped to make the theatre religious. Neither Shaw's cynical suggestion that the "sensuous charms of the church service" be forced to subsidize the sterner virtue of the drama, nor T. S. Eliot's pious proposal that the drama "return to religious liturgy," to "a High Mass well performed," demanded a moment's serious consideration during that half-decade of faith and devotion.

"There were once, you know, the Greeks." Religious devotion had "surrounded the Greek drama." Cannot Dionysus be rejuvenated? If Pan is eternal, why not Dionysus? For a century and a half there had been a growing conviction that divinity is immanent in nature and in instinct, that eternal truth is revealed in the primordial, the archetypal, the mythical, and, finally, in the psychological. One recognizes the "mysterious age-old processes of nature" in the behavior of the pagan, the primitive, the child, the crowd. It was evident that Cook, in fleeing to Greece to make contact with ancient virtue, displayed a singular want of resourcefulness and imagination. He might, for example, have profited by the insights of his nineteenth-century forebears and stayed home. For Thoreau was a Greek whose paganism was "much earlier than Plato and never heard of Christ."

We read now-a-days [wrote Thoreau] of the ancient festivals, and processions of the Greeks and Etruscans, with a little incredulity, or at least with little sympathy; but how natural and irrepressible in every people is some hearty and palpable greeting of Nature. The Corybantes, the Bacchantes, the rude primitive tragedians with their procession and goat-song, and the whole Panathenaea, which appear so antiquated and peculiar, have their parallel now. The husbandman is always a better Greek than the scholar is prepared to appreciate, and the old custom still survives, while antiquarians and scholars grow gray in commemorating it. The farmers crowd to the fair to-day in obedience to the same ancient law which Solon or Lycurgus did not enact, as naturally as bees swarm and follow their queen.

It was comforting and exhilarating to Thoreau to discern that "the characteristics and pursuits of various ages and races of men are always existing in epitome in every neighborhood." Similarly, Thoreau's friend, Emerson, "could admire the Greek in an American ploughboy" as well as the Greek genius of Goethe, one of his Representative Men. "What new mythologies sail through his head!" exclaimed Emerson concerning the author of *Faust*. "In the menstruum of this man's wit, the past and the present ages, and their religions, politics and modes of thinking, are dissolved into archetypes and ideas." If not by Thoreau and Emerson, Cook might at least have been stimulated by Whitman who, by 1920, had surely become the most highly regarded American writer, who had been praised as early as 1890 by Havelock Ellis for bringing the "Greek spirit into art." Anticipating Macgowan, Whitman desired the

"divine literatus" to replace the "departing priest" and write "archetypal poems" for a democracy at whose core is the religious element.
"Nature, true Nature, and the true idea of Nature" must be restored, he declared. And by that he did not mean

the smooth walks, trimm'd hedges, poseys and nightingales of the English
poets, but the whole orb, with its geologic history, the kosmos, carrying fire
and snow, that rolls through the illimitable areas, light as a feather, though
weighing billions of tons.

Whitman was disparaging of the English poets, but even they
were aware of the virtues of pagan naturalism and preferred it at
times both to Christianity and to "getting and spending." Douglas
Bush has described the revival in England about 1800 of "poetry
inspired by a rich mythological symbolism," a revival that had been
made inevitable by "advancing Greek scholarship" and a "new
primitivistic conception of the imagination, of myth, of nature, and
of religion." But it was in Germany, as Emerson knew and as Bush
has pointed out, that "mythology of all kinds gained a new depth
and inwardness when it was seen as not only a primitive but a
permanently fruitful phase in the religious evolution of humanity."
Luther, having deprived the Germans of Roman Catholicism, destroyed at the same time "the mythological element of Christianity,
that poetical combination of beauty and truth for which they have
ever since been seeking in Greek or Nordic mythologies or by re-
verting to the Catholic faith." With the publication in 1755 of
Winckelmann's pamphlet, *Thoughts on the Imitation of Greek
Works in Painting and Sculpture,* the conflict in Germany between
paganism and Christianity began. It reached a crisis in 1872, the
year in which Nietzsche published *The Birth of Tragedy.*

Nietzsche, whose *Zarathustra,* as Paul Elmer More discerned, has
an affinity with *Leaves of Grass,* evoked as much admiration, exerted as profound an influence in America up to 1920 as did Whitman. In England his impact had been evident before 1900 in the
poetry of John Davidson and in the essays of Havelock Ellis. Shaw,
explaining his intent in *The Devil's Disciple,* asked, "Have they
[the critics] not heard the recent fuss about Nietzsche and his Good
and Evil Turned Inside Out?" "There never was a play," he continued, "more certain to be written than *The Devil's Disciple* at
the end of the nineteenth century." Elsewhere abroad Strindberg

had been displaying a temperament and a genius that was strikingly similar to Nietzsche's. Whatever the influence of one upon the other they engaged for a short time in correspondence of mutual admiration. A "one-sided Nietzsche," as Storm Jameson pointed out, "Strindberg was in savage revolt against the conditions of life. Unlike Nietzsche, he cannot laugh, he can only protest or seek oblivion in an allegorical dream." Among American poets and critics interest in Nietzsche was manifested early in the twentieth century. His spirit moved William Vaughn Moody as early as 1904. Huneker was an enthusiastic Nietzschean, as was H. L. Mencken, whose full-length book on Nietzsche appeared in 1906. Between that date and 1920, when he published his own translation of *The Antichrist,* Mencken extolled Zarathustra as ardently as he castigated the Neo-Puritan. As for Nathan, Mencken's associate and O'Neill's friend, he found the anti-herd element in Nietzsche to his taste, but he rejected Nietzsche's philosophy, "Be hard!" — preferring his own, which he epitomized as "Be indifferent." George Cram Cook did read Nietzsche — as early as 1912 — and was excited by his "vital, creative temperament." But he preferred to retain his faith in socialism, whose "spiritual significance was deeper." In the case of O'Neill the situation was reversed: his faith in Nietzsche outlived his faith in socialism. "Familiar with Nietzsche in translation before he went to Harvard" in 1914, while he was there, "with the help of a German grammar and dictionary, he read the whole of *Also Sprach Zarathustra* in the original." While he was at the Provincetown, before 1920, he engaged in a little proselyting for the German Messiah among the staff. And Barrett Clark has described how, some half-dozen years later, he went off to rehearsal of *The Great God Brown* at the Greenwich Village Theater with "a worn copy of Nietzsche's *Birth of Tragedy*" stuffed into his pocket.

Nietzsche's influence in America may not have been so powerful as it had been in Germany where he "appealed to something incommensurable and incalculable in the minds of his countrymen," but to those whose appetite for paganism had been stimulated by the *Rubaiyat,* and by the poems of Swinburne and of Whitman, Nietzsche furnished a rich, if rather indigestible, diet. He offered a religion and an aesthetic, a mythology and a psychology. To that most virulent form of Christianity, Calvinism, he provided an effective antidote. Not only did he castigate the ascetic and ridicule those who were tormented by a sense of sin, he had a formula for those who could accept neither Scripture nor Darwinism: substitute Dionysus for Christ, satyr for ape. He not only had anticipated Freud, he helped to clear the way for Freudianism by transvaluating — devaluating, Paul Elmer More insisted — values. His doctrine of the Will to Power gave hope to the Schopenhauerean pessimist. And his whole-hearted contempt for the herd, together with his concept of the Superman, encouraged those who refused to tolerate the idea of equalitarianism. To the artist who wished to "escape from realism" he lent support by criticizing attempts to copy thoughts and passions realistically, by disparaging the "naturalistic and inartistic tendency." For those who were unaware that Whitman had celebrated the phenomenon of death and rebirth, he offered his Heraclitean doctrine of Eternal Recurrence. And to those who suffered from a *Weltschmerz* induced by the chaos of modern life, he taught struggle in place of resignation, ecstasy in place of apathy, affirmation of life in place of denial. In short, he was the principal exponent of the Dionysian way of life. To Nietzsche the word "Dionysian" expressed:

a constraint to unity, a soaring above personality, the commonplace, society, reality, and above the abyss of the *ephemeral;* the passionately painful sensation of super-abundance, in darker, fuller, and more fluctuating conditions; an ecstatic saying of yea to the collective character of existence, as that which remains the same, and equally mighty and blissful throughout all change; the great pantheistic sympathy with pleasure and pain, which declares even the most terrible and most questionable qualities of existence good, and sanctifies them; the eternal will to procreation, to fruitfulness, and to recurrence; the feeling of unity in regard to the necessity of creating and annihilating.

In a world that was destitute of faith, of symbol and myth, the Dionysian element provided temporary relief, a stimulant, if not a cure.

As eternal as Emerson's Pan and much more vital, Dionysus had been Nietzsche's favorite deity ever since he wrote *The Birth of Tragedy*. In that work, published in 1872, Nietzsche perceived two forces operative in Greek tragedy before Euripides. The first of these he identified as Dionysian, its physiological analogue being the state of drunkenness. Antithetical to the Dionysian was the Apollonian, whose physiological analogue was dream. By means of these contrasting artistic energies he accounted for the perfection of Attic tragedy, which flourished while the duality was operative and declined with the appearance of a third element, Socratism — that is, conscious knowledge, reason and logic, intelligibility, "realism." Through the subjective Apollonian dream experience, Nietzsche explained, the Greeks revealed their "inner-most beings," their "common subconscious experiences," thereby arriving at the "higher truth" and achieving a calm repose. But with the awakening of the Dionysian emotions, the subjective vanished into complete self-forgetfulness, "Union between man and man is reaffirmed"; and "Nature which has become estranged, hostile, or subjugated, celebrates once more her reconciliation with her prodigal son, man." Thus intoxicated, man could enjoy the experience of "universal harmony" and could glimpse the "mysterious Primordial Unity." "In song and in dance [man] expresses himself as a member of a higher community; he has forgotten how to walk and speak; he is about to take a dancing flight into the air." When, according to Nietzsche, this primordial Dionysian element joined with Apollonian illusion, when the latter "begins to talk with Dionysian wisdom, and even denies itself and its Apollonian conspicuousness," the highest goal of tragedy and of art in general is attained. Emerson, too, it is interesting to note, was aware of the attraction for men of "dreams and drunkenness"; but, more prim than primitive, he warned against their dangers.

The tragic effect, Nietzsche insisted, must be explained on aesthetic rather than on moral grounds, and whether one be the "true aesthetic hearer" or merely "a Socratic-critical man" depended upon his ability to understand "*myth,* the concentrated picture of the world."

It is probable [suggested Nietzsche]

. . . that almost every one feels so broken up by the critico-historical spirit of our culture, that he can only make the former existence of myth credible to himself by learned means through intermediary abstractions. Without myth, however, every culture loses its healthy creative natural power: it is only a horizon encompassed with myths that rounds off to unity a social movement. It is only myth that frees all the powers of the imagination and of the Apollonian dream from their aimless wanderings.

Having sprung from the "Dionysian, with its primordial joy experienced in pain itself," tragic myth was ultimately destroyed by the emergence of Socratism. And "the ruin of tragedy," he regretfully announced, "was at the same time the ruin of myth."

But now Nietzsche was awaiting the rebirth of tragic myth from the spirit of music, whose source was also the Dionysian. His hope lay in Wagner in whom, so long as he remained loyal to pagan mythology, Nietzsche was pleased to discern an Hellenic analogy. Like Nietzsche, Wagner had foreseen that the "march of the Drama of the Future was towards Feeling, away from Understanding; towards the infallible receptive powers of the un-conscious, purely human Feeling," away from the "mechanism of logic." And he was in agreement with Nietzsche regarding the value of myth, insisting that the only task of the poet — who is "the knower of the unconscious, the aimful demonstrator of the instinctive" — is to expound myth. "The incomparable thing about the Mythos," he observed, "is that it is true for all time, and its content, how close soever its compression is inexhaustible throughout the ages." To be sure, this attitude towards myth was manifested throughout the century. Thomas Mann, descendant and admirer of both Nietzsche and Wagner, considers it to be the most conspicuous characteristic of "French impressionism, the English, French, and Russian novel, German science, German music." Mann has been struck by "the family likeness" of such antithetical figures as Zola and Wagner, by the similarity of such contrasting works as the *Rougon-Macquarts* and the *Ring des Nibelungens*. He finds that the

kinship of spirit, aims, and method is most striking. This lies not only in the ambition to achieve size, the propensity to the grandiose and the lavish; nor is it the Homeric leitmotiv alone that is common to them: it is first and foremost a special sort of Naturalism which develops into the mythical. For who would deny a mythical trend to Zola's epic, wherein the characters themselves are raised up to a plane above that of every day. And is that Astarte of the Second Empire, called Nana, not symbol and myth? Where does she get her name? It sounds like the babbling of primitive man in a moment of passion; Nana was a cognomen of the Babylonian Ishtar. Did Zola know this? So much the more remarkable and significant if he did not.

When Wagner betrayed the pagan way of life, abandoning Siegfried for Parsifal, Wotan for Christ, Nietzsche was bitterly disappointed. The composer, he sardonically remarked, atoned amply in his sad old days for his earlier sinful paganism. What Nietzsche had failed to perceive, Mann has pointed out; it was that "an art essentially sensuous, based on symbolic formulas . . . must lead back to church celebration," that "the secret longing and ultimate ambition of all theatre is to return to the bosom of the ritual out of which — in both the pagan and the Christian world — it sprang." In both Wagner and Nietzsche, Mann has discerned the same "complex of psychology, mythology, and music," the same "intuitive agreement with another typical son of the nineteenth century, the psychoanalyst Sigmund Freud," who also showed "an interest in the mythical, precultural, and primeval which is narrowly associated with the psychological."

Freud himself admitted that the "guesses and intuitions" of Nietzsche "often agree in the most astonishing way with the laborious findings of psychoanalysis." Wishing to keep his mind "unembarrassed," he avoided Nietzsche's philosophy for a long time on that account. Making his first important contribution in 1900, the year of Nietzsche's death, Freud came increasingly to the attention of the layman, particularly the Greenwich Villager and the colonist of Provincetown, after 1913 when the English translation of his *Traumdeutung* was published. Already known for his sensational theories pertaining to dream symbolism, sexual repression, the Oedipus complex, and the clinical procedure of free association, Freud published *Totem and Taboo,* a study of the origin of religion and morality, revealing therein to American readers in 1918 his interest in the mythical, precultural, primeval, as well as the psychological. Meanwhile it was evident that Freud's former disciple, Carl Jung, was displaying a similar preoccupation. For in 1917 *The Psychology of the Unconscious* was published in this country. By 1920 both psychologists had their adherents even outside the Village. Macgowan, the rare exception, seemed to find virtues in both Freud and Jung. O'Neill, although he preferred Jung, insisted that he was

no deep student of psychoanalysis. As far as I can remember, of all the books written by Freud, Jung, etc., I have read only four, and Jung is the only one of the lot who interests me. Some of his suggestions I find extraordinarily illuminating in the light of my own experience with hidden motives.

O'Neill, in short, protested that critics "read too damn much Freud into stuff that could very well have been written exactly as is before psychoanalysis was ever heard of," that "authors were psychologists . . . , and profound ones, before psychology was invented." Despite his disclaimer, the hidden motives which he revealed began, about 1923, to bear a curious resemblance to those which had been discovered not only in the work of Freud and of Jung, but also in that of Adler. Whatever his inspiration, he began, too deliberately perhaps, to write the "special sort of naturalism that develops into the mythical."

Pagan naturalism was a way of life that had appealed to Emerson, Thoreau, and Whitman; for they were aware that the great sea of nature washed civilized modern shores as it once had those of primitive Greece. They liked to immerse themselves, Whitman being the most intrepid, where the water was relatively shallow and clear. That part of the sea off the European coast was darker, deeper, more turbulent. It was not till after the turn of the century that the prodigious waves of Nietzschean doctrine reached the American shore. Arriving at last, with under-currents and ripples, they impressed upon O'Neill and his two associates the desirability, the feasibility, of the rebirth of tragedy from the Dionysian depths. The child had been "conceived in godhead," labor had been induced by Nietzsche and Wagner, standing by was Dr. Freud to demonstrate how the infant was to be nourished from the "mythical maternal bosom."

In Europe, drama and theatre alike had been permeated by the Dionysiac view of life, a view whose popularity had been stimulated by Nietzsche more than by any other single individual. Storm Jameson, for one, recognized this in her study of *Modern Drama in Europe* when she not only devoted her Foreword to an essay on "Nietzsche in Modern Drama," but also when she recurrently referred in the text to expressions of the Dionysian impulse. Strindberg, she felt, was the most complete embodiment of that impulse. In this, other critics have borne her out. Strindberg may not have been, as Edmund Gosse declared, "the most remarkable creative talent started by the philosophy of Nietzsche." But if he anticipated

Nietzschean doctrine, he was also affected by it. He was, as McGill observed, "one of the first men whom Zarathustra met on his downgoing." To Strindberg, Nietzsche appeared as "the herald of the decline of Europe and Christendom, . . . the one modern spirit

who has dared to preach the right of the strong, the wise, against the blockheads and midgets (the democrats), and I can understand the suffering of this great mind in the power of the host of petty ones, for this is a period in which everything is dominated by women and stupidity. I recognize in him the deliverer and as a teacher of the catechism, I conclude my letters to literary friends in the following way: read Nietzsche.

Nietzsche, in turn, as one might expect, approved of Strindberg's reaction against realism in drama.

O'Neill's opinion of Strindberg was expressed in the Provincetown Playbill printed for the first production of the Provincetown under the directorship of the "triumvirate." The play was *The Spook Sonata*. Its author, O'Neill declared, "was the precursor of all modernity in our present theater."

Strindberg knew and suffered [continued O'Neill] with our struggle years before many of us were born. He expressed it by intensifying the method of his time and by foreshadowing both in content and form the methods to come. All that is enduring in what we loosely call 'Expressionism' — all that is artistically valid and sound theater — can be clearly traced back through Wedekind to Strindberg's 'The Dream Play', 'There Are Crimes and Crimes', 'The Spook Sonata', etc.

Strindberg remains, O'Neill wrote, "the greatest interpreter in the theater of the characteristic spiritual conflicts which constitute the drama — the blood — of our lives today." In his "behind-life plays" he "carried Naturalism to a logical attainment of such poignant intensity" that they must be classified as "supernaturalism," asserted O'Neill, and placed in a class by themselves. The Playbill was issued in January 1924. If O'Neill's praise of Strindberg seemed inordinate, it must at least have been anticipated by anybody who had read the play *Welded* which O'Neill had completed the preceding winter. *Welded* represented flattery in its sincerest form.

Unlike Strindberg, O'Neill never descended into an Inferno. Unlike Wedekind, O'Neill never lived in the Dionysiac atmosphere of Munich to imbibe what Nietzsche called the "genuine witches' brew," that "horrible mixture of sensuality and cruelty." If his characters are seldom as frenzied and psychotic as Strindberg's, they are also less bestial, perverted, and diabolical than Wedekind's. O'Neill's animals are domesticated. His prostitutes are divine. Were one rash enough to seek evidence of Wedekind's influence he would find it, perhaps, in *Desire Under the Elms,* in *Strange Interlude,* in *Ah, Wilderness!* But the jungle beasts have become cows; the *Erdgeist,* Lulu, emerges as the civilized and sophisticated Nina; and *The Awakening of Spring* is scarcely recognizable in the bourgeois picture of a New England family.

Despite the similarity of his plays in both form and content to the drama of the German Expressionists, O'Neill persistently denied any influence. Although, as he told Nathan in 1920, he was familiar enough with the "best modern drama of all countries," he insisted that resemblances were coincidental. Even *The Hairy Ape* was not, strictly speaking, an Expressionistic play.

The first Expressionistic play that I ever saw [he replied to Barrett Clark who had inquired whether O'Neill "had consciously made use of the methods of Kaiser and the rest"] was Kaiser's *From Morn to Midnight,* produced in New York in 1922, after I'd written both *The Emperor Jones* and *The Hairy Ape.* I had read *From Morn to Midnight* before *The Hairy Ape* was written, but not before the idea for it was planned. The point is that *The Hairy Ape* is a direct descendant of *Jones,* written long before I had ever heard of Expressionism, and its form needs no explanation but this. As a matter of fact, I did not think much of *Morn to Midnight,* and still don't. It is too easy. It would not have influenced me.

Like Macgowan, O'Neill's attitude towards the Expressionistic drama was only less disdainful than it was towards the realistic play that concerned itself simply with the "banality of surfaces." Macgowan complained that it "requires all three Graces and a strong stomach" to "follow the banner of Expressionism in playwriting," that "the bizarre morbidity, the nauseating sexuality, the lack of any trace of joy or beauty . . . match Strindberg at his unhappiest, while the vigor with which they drive their ideas forth in speech far outdoes him." Apart from his feeling, with Macgowan, that Expressionistic drama was too bizarre — and, perhaps, too easy — O'Neill appeared to have no specific objection to it. If he did not consciously follow the "banner of Expressionism," it was not because of a weak stomach. He simply regarded his claim to the patrimony of Strindberg to be as legitimate as was that of the

Germans. The similarity of his drama to theirs may very well be a matter of parallel influence. For, as Barrett Clark has pointed out, the "three writers who most directly affected the dramatists of Young Germany" — Nietzsche, Strindberg, and Wedekind — "were among the most powerful influences on the youthful O'Neill" — "particularly the first two." That Strindberg was a precursor of the German Expressionists has been demonstrated most conclusively by C. E. W. L. Dahlstrom. That Nietzsche's "epoch-making work on *The Birth of Tragedy*" formed an "essential part of the Expressionist background," that "Expressionism in general was permeated by this Dionysiac view of life" has been confirmed by Samuel and Thomas in their study of *Expressionism in German Life, Literature and the Theater*. Despite O'Neill's disavowal, he has been identified as an Expressionist playwright, his relationship to the school being evident to its students even in such a late play as *Mourning Becomes Electra* with its "multiplicity of scene," its "preoccupation with elemental forces of life," its "treatment of individuals as types stripped of individual characteristics," its "background of ghost-like reality," its "themes of madness, passion, conflict, and relentless Fate." Moreover, his Hellenism has been, like that of his German counterparts, "intensely subjective, concerned with problems which ancient Greece never envisaged, with riddles of death Thebes never knew." This was a concept of Hellenism which Nietzsche had inspired.

At times, crowned though he was with vine leaves, the immortal and rejuvenate Dionysus also wore a hair shirt. Strindberg's *To Damascus*, O'Neill's *The Great God Brown*, the Expressionists' "Stationen" drama, their Mystery and Passion plays, their conception of "the passage of man and his soul through various changes," resemble in their formal aspect the religious drama of the Middle Ages more than the tragedy of ancient Greece. This dichotomy of Christian form and pagan content, the result in part of a desire to link the drama with primitive ritual, could be observed in the art of the theatre as well. Thus, Max Reinhardt produced *Everyman* as well as *Oedipus,* and by 1922 literally returned the theatre to the church when he gave performances — which Macgowan witnessed — in the Kollegienkirche of Salzburg. His dream at this time was of a Festival Theatre at Salzburg which would be "another and greater Oberammergau." Here he would produce Passion Plays that would be born "not of agony and renunciation" but of "music, song and beauty," religious masterpieces and music whose spirit would be that of paganism. Here the "gay science of Nietzsche" would "have a beautiful playground if not an altar or temple." Macgowan had paid his respects to Reinhardt and to the producers, artist-directors, and designers who "paralleled the progress of Reinhardt." For these, thought Macgowan, "had evolved a technique that applies to realistic plays as well as to plays of spiritual emphasis, plays of color, imagination, exaltation, inner truth." It was a technique, he felt, that could "perfect the old theatre as well as launch the new." After his return from Europe in 1922, he decided that "it is not a question of producing plays in cathedrals, but of producing the spirit of life in plays. It is not: Can religion make itself theatrical? But: Can the theater make itself — in a new sense — religious?" Within two years an answer was forthcoming. In 1924, about a year before O'Neill appears to have begun work on *Lazarus Laughed,* Reinhardt brought *The Miracle* to America — a religious pageant pervaded with a pagan spirit. So moving was the spectacle that even Nathan confessed that it deprived him of "a certain measure of cool sense," that his "critical penetration [was] considerably blunted."

All the elements that go into the life blood of drama [wrote Nathan] are here assembled into a series of aesthetic and emotional climaxes that are humbling in their force and loveliness. The shout of speech, the sweep of pantomime, the sob and march of orchestral music, the ebb and flow of song, the peal of cloister chimes, the brass clash of cymbals, the play of a thousand lights, the shuffle and rush of mobs, the rising of scene upon scene amid churning rapids of color, these directed by a master hand are what constitutes this superb psychical pageant brewed from an ancient and familiar legend and called now 'The Miracle'.

The theatre that we have known becomes lilliputian before such a phenomenon. The church itself becomes puny. No sermon has been sounded from any pulpit one-thousandth so eloquent as that which comes to life, in this playhouse transformed into a vast cathedral, under the necromancy that is Reinhardt.

All of this, and in a commercial playhouse! To create ecstasy — that, according to Macgowan, is the function of the "artist of the theater." Reinhardt succeeded.

For two decades before his appearance in America Reinhardt had been striving to achieve an identity of religion and theatre. His dream of a Festival Theatre at Salzburg had been preceded by the dream of a Theatre of the Five Thousand whose stage would echo the "tremendous changes which our entire mode of life is undergoing."

The technical revolution, the expansion of all dimensions, our electric existence, the discovery of society as a living organism, the re-awakened joy in the struggle to conquer the elements, the heightened consciousness of physical power, the love of nature and the cosmos, the growth of a new mythology — all these found singers and rhapsodists in Walt Whitman, Verhaeren, Johannes V. Jensen, Hamsun, Stefan George; and should nothing of this be expressed on the stage?

Here, in the Theatre of the Five Thousand, we have, I believe, the first attempt at such an expression. It arises, to my mind, from a similar feeling for our time, and the best of it is contained in the will to capture these manifestations of a new awakening and to set them reverberating. And it is perhaps not an accident that the belief in the myths of our time links itself to the belief in the myths of the ancients, as the really new is always strongly linked to the really old (or tradition).

This Dionysian regeneration of life was to be sought in a large theatre in which "the spectator feels and is impressed by the possibilities of space," in which the "effects are simplified and heightened according to the needs of monumentality."

Under the influence of these mighty spaces, these big severe lines, all that is small and petty disappears, and it becomes a matter of course to appeal to the hearts of great audiences with the strongest and deepest elements. The petty and unimportant — elements that are not eternal in us — cease to have effect. This theatre can only express the great eternal elemental passions and the problems of humanity. In it spectators cease to be mere spectators; they become the people; their emotions are simple and primitive, but great and powerful, as becomes the eternal human race.

To implement the Dionysian experience

the chorus arises and moves in the midst of the audience; the characters meet each other amid the spectators; from all sides the hearer is being impressed, so that gradually he becomes part of the whole, and is rapidly absorbed in the action, a member of the chorus, so to speak.

Far from being the thing, the play was only one of many means to Reinhardt's artistic end, an end which Nietzsche thought that the Greeks had attained: the "dissolution of the individual and his unification with primordial existence." More primitive, more important, than the action proper, declared Nietzsche, was the tragic chorus of the Greeks, "symbol of the collectively excited Dionysian throng." It was the chorus, he thought, the only reality, which "generated the vision of action and scene and celebrated it with the entire symbolism of dancing, music, and speech." As an "artist of the theater," Reinhardt sought to separate theatre and literature. By making the theatre, "which for a time, had become the exclusive domain of the art of speaking, once more the common property of *all* the arts," he not only satisfied Nietzsche's demands, but also proved himself to be "a direct follower of Richard Wagner" each of whose productions is a *Gesammtkunstwerk*.

The conception of the "artist of the theater" who obeyed only his Dionysian impulses and in whose theatre the drama was subvened or re-created, was shared, perhaps influenced, by Gordon Craig, who is said to have dreamed what Reinhardt lived. If Reinhardt shared the esteem around 1920 of the principal critics and workers of the American theatre, he shared it only with Craig. Deeply impressed with Craig's accomplishments, Macgowan declared his "genius to have been the greatest force in the theatre since Ibsen." George Jean Nathan had praised Craig as early as 1918, corresponded with him around 1920, and eulogized him after 1930:

He found a theatre absurd and pitiable in an ugliness born of lack of imagination and out of aesthetic darkness. He found a stage that was a disgrace to the beautiful drama it was occasionally called upon to harbour. He found a drama itself that cried out against its cruel and ignorant confinement in surroundings that cramped and distorted and vitiated it. These things, that other men seemed to be unaware of, this man found and saw. And out of a fancy, an inventiveness, a beauty and a skill of mind that had not been given to the theatre before him, he fashioned a theatre, a stage, and even a drama that we until his time had not known. A new theatre sprang into being. A new stage shone out before the world's eyes. And drama that had been bound in fetters of incomprehension was suddenly released and given wings. This man, alone and opposed by a theatre with eyes that could not see, accomplished against sneer, against blindness, against vituperation even, all this. His spirit is present on every stage today that makes any claim to resourcefulness, to dignity, and to grandeur.

If some of Craig's impulses were Dionysian, others had their origin in *fin de siècle* England. If his ideas were influenced by the work of Adolphe Appia, the Swiss designer and disciple of Wagner, they were also formed by the symbolists and by the decadents of the Eighteen Nineties. "Not only is Symbolism at the roots of all art," he declared, "it is at the roots of all life." Like the Symbolists, he found "a new delight," as Yeats expressed it, "in essences, in states of mind, in pure imagination, in all that comes to us most easily in elaborate music." As an artist of the theatre he was the counterpart of Verhaeren, Mallarmé, and Maeterlinck who, thought Yeats, foreshadowed "a new agreement among refined and studious men [that may give] birth to a new passion, and what seems litera-ture becomes religion." Craig revealed a kinship not only with Maeterlinck, but also with Wilde and Beardsley:

It is a pity that the Theatre is neither exquisite nor precious.
I want, in place of violent expression of violent emotions and ideas, more exquisite expression of more precious emotions and ideas.
In place of vulgar materials, such as prose, coarse wooden boards, canvas, paint, *papier-mâché* and powder, I would like more precious materials to be employed: Poetry, or even that far more precious Silence — ebony and ivory — silver and gold . . .

If, in the foregoing respects Craig diverged from orthodoxy in his worship of Dionysus, the core of faith was still present. Realism he continued to regard as original sin. Praying that "to-day's theatre [might] be to-morrow's church," he resurrected what he deemed to be the proper ceremonies, the so-called innovations that were to attract so many adherents in the twentieth century.

In 1919 Craig published a volume of essays and notes, *The Theatre — Advancing,* many of which had appeared before 1910. Here he lamented the deterioration of Dancing, Pantomime, Mari-onettes, Masks, "things so vital to the ancients, all essential parts of their respected Art of the Theatre at one time or another." Man's imagination, he complained, dulled by industrialism, has given up the idea of serious and beautiful dancing. Pantomime as "symbolic gesture" has disappeared. The Marionette, a participant in the "Feast of Bacchus when the Egyptians celebrated those rites," is now merely "a poor doll tied to a stick."

And then the Mask, that paramount means of dramatic expression, without which acting was bound to degenerate!

Used by the savages when making war at a time when war was looked upon as an art; used by the ancients in their ceremonies when faces were held to be too weak and disturbing an element; used by those artists of the theatre, Aeschylus, Sophocles and Euripides; found essential to their highest drama by the Japanese masters of the ninth and fourteenth centuries; rejected later on in the eighteenth century by the European actors, and relegated by them to the toy shop and the fancy-dress ball, the Mask has sunk to the level of the Dance, of Pantomime and of the Marionette. From being a work of art carved in wood or ivory and sometimes ornamented with precious metals or precious stones, and later made in leather, it has frittered itself away to a piece of paper, badly painted or covered with black satin.

Since "drama which is not trivial takes us *beyond reality*," Craig argued, it demands something less real than the "human face, the realest of all things to express all that." In place of the transitory — the fleeting expression of the actor's face — he wanted the eternal — the fixed and symbolic expression of the mask. In place of the many — the six hundred expressions of the face — he wanted the one, or, at most, the few — six masks. Nor was he motivated by an antiquarian impulse merely to copy the "old Greek masks and those of Japan and India, of Africa and America." He was obeying a creative urge, the wish to make the "world's mask."

If Craig was the most influential proponent of the mask he was not the only one. In 1917 Ernest Fenollosa and Ezra Pound published *'Noh' or Accomplishment, A Study of the Classical Stage of Japan* wherein they paid their respects to the use of masks. But more significant was the actual employment of the device by Yeats — also in 1917 — in his short play, *At the Hawk's Well.* This piece was included among *Four Plays for Dancers,* a group of plays, all of which require masks, which Yeats published in 1921. In his preface to the book, written 1920, he acknowledged his indebtedness to Mr. Edmond Dulac, who had taught "the value and beauty of the mask and rediscovered how to design and make it." As for himself, wrote Yeats,

. . . if I write plays and organize performances on any scale and with any system, I shall hope for a small number of typical masks, each capable of use in several plays. The face of the speaker should be as much a work of art as the lines that he speaks or the costume that he wears, that all may be as artificial as possible. Perhaps in the end one would write plays for certain masks . . . The mask, apart from its beauty, may suggest new situations at a moment when the old ones seem exhausted; 'The Only Jealousy of Emer' was written to find what dramatic effect one could get out of a mask, changed while the player remains upon the stage to suggest a change of personality.

In his last point, we might observe, Yeats anticipated by nearly a half dozen years the use to which O'Neill put the mask in *The Great God Brown.*

Although some of the foregoing theories had been familiar to American scene designers as early as 1914, their impact did not become manifest until the founding in 1916 of *Theatre Arts Magazine* under the editorship of Sheldon Cheney, who was joined in 1918 by Macgowan and two other editors. In 1923 Macgowan collaborated with the designer Herman Rosse, who had previously worked with masks, on a book called *Masks and Demons.* The volume was intended, Macgowan explained, "to tell the man who looks at a mask drawn by Craig or a mask made by Dulac, Stern, or Benda various facts that he should know about their ancestors, the holy masks of simpler men." The purpose of the book was

to bridge by just a little the gap that lies between the primitive man who puts a sort of idol on his face, and the Greek tragedian; between the Duk-Duk dancer who regulates morals and acquires riches in New Guinea, and some artist of the theatre who wishes to bring the mask back to the stage.

By means of photographic reproductions of masks from all parts of the world, together with explanatory material, Macgowan and Rosse tried to demonstrate that the mask had always been part of the ritual in religion and theatre alike, that the mask is as universal and eternal as Dionysus himself. They were aware that "with us the mask must come upon the stage shorn of the power of the religious spirit," yet they were not discouraged:

The mask may be amusingly novel to us. It may bring a grotesque comedy into our revues, or an aphrodisiac charm. But as a serious factor it suffers because mystical religion has gone out of our life taking its symbols with it. The task of the artist of the theatre may be to seek out new symbols — the symbols, perhaps, of beauty and pain, of exaltation and pathos —— and to make us feel them in one of the greatest of symbols, the ancient and mysterious mask.

Theory was accompanied by practice. In 1921, Robert Edmond Jones, who had long admired Craig, employed gigantic masks to symbolize the superhuman nature of the witches' power in Arthur Hopkins' production of *Macbeth*. Writing *The Hairy Ape* in that year, O'Neill appears to have come under Craig's influence when he described his Fifth Avenue capitalist-church-goers as "gaudy marionettes." Although masks were not mentioned in the text, they were used in the production in 1922, a production designed by Jones and Throckmorton. Masks were used in *The Spook Sonata*, 1924, the first joint production of the Provincetown Players under the direction of Macgowan, Jones and O'Neill. In the spring of that year the same group presented an arrangement that O'Neill had made of "The Ancient Mariner," in which "a masked chorus of seamen grouped and regrouped about the tall mast of the phantom ship." Before this, in 1922, O'Neill had called for *a pale mask with features indistinguishable* to be worn by the figure Death in *The Fountain*. Written the year in which *Masks and Demons* was published, *All God's Chillun Got Wings* required a Congo mask, the model for which could well have been the photograph facing page 57 in Macgowan and Rosse's book. In *Marco Millions,* completed in 1925, the chorus is adorned with masks, *the men with a male mask of grief, the women with a female*. Then, after giving the device its most emphatic statement in *The Great God Brown* and in *Lazarus Laughed,* O'Neill's enthusiasm waned. In *Days Without End,* having dispensed with the mask during the preceding half-decade, he used it once again — for the last time, and perfunctorily.

What O'Neill thought about the mask was not expressed until 1932, six years after *Lazarus*. Although by this time he appeared to be atoning for his "earlier sinful paganism," he published his "Memoranda on Masks." Engaged in retrospection that was wistful as well as regretful, he revived in the Memoranda some of the fervor that he had displayed a decade earlier. To be sure, it was a futile, even a pathetic, attempt to force the flowering, in the bleak and frosty 1930's, of a tradition that had long since languished. For he had not only ceased to use the mask in 1926: he was to refer disparagingly to the device as late as 1944, to the "obscuring over-load of masked pageantry" in *Lazarus*. What is more, he would consent to a production of that play "in a cut, condensed version with masks omitted." Yet, if the "Memoranda on Masks" are not to be taken at their face value, they remain the only evidence, outside the plays, of the playwright's intent.

Determined in 1920 to avoid bizarre innovations, O'Neill insisted in 1932 that masks are not to be regarded "as any 'stunty' resurrection of archaic props" and referred hopefully to the use of masks in "the new modern play, as yet only dimly foreshadowed in a few groping specimens, but which must inevitably be written in the future." Could he live through past productions of his plays, one thing he "most certainly would not change: the use of masks . . ." Indeed, he would "call for more masks in some of these productions and . . . use them in [others] where they were not used before." Even *Mourning Becomes Electra,* completed only the year before, he would now play with masks, now that he can free himself from a "Classical connotation" that had been too insistent while he was writing the trilogy. Without masks *Strange Interlude* had succeeded, he now felt, "in so far as it concerns only surfaces and their immediate sub-surfaces, but not where, occasionally, it tries to probe deeper." In the *Memoranda* O'Neill advocated masks "wherever a sense of impersonal, collective mob psychology is wanted," as in *Lazarus Laughed.* Since one of its principal values is psychological, he was convinced that the mask is

the freest solution of the modern dramatist's problem as to how — with the greatest possible dramatic clarity and economy of means — he can express those profound hidden conflicts of the mind which the probings of psychology continue to disclose to us. He must find some method to present this inner drama in his work, or confess himself incapable of portraying one of the most characteristic preoccupations and uniquely significant spiritual impulses of his time . . . A comprehensive expression is demanded here, a chance for eloquent presentation, a new form of drama projected from a fresh insight into the inner forces motivating the actions and reactions of men and women (a new and truer characterization, in other words) — a drama of souls, and the adventures of 'free wills,' with the masks that govern them and constitute their fates.

Like Gordon Craig, he felt that "the mask is the only right medium of portraying the expressions of the soul as shown through the expressions of the face." O'Neill regarded the mask as the symbol of "inner reality," the abstraction and projection of unconscious forces within the character, the objectification of a fate that resides in his soul. Because its values are psychological, mythical, and mystical, the mask possessed a larger symbolic significance, suggested by the universality of its function in the religion and drama of all peoples. The "mask *is* dramatic in itself," declared O'Neill, *"has always* been dramatic in itself." The modern actor, therefore, who is forced to wear it, far from being deprived of his greatest asset, would discover undeveloped possibilities of his art. "After all," O'Neill argued, "masks did not extinguish the Greek actor, nor have they kept the acting of the East from being an art." To be sure, the mask belongs only in the Imaginative Theatre, the theatre for which he had written *Lazarus Laughed,*

the one true theatre, the age-old theatre, the theatre of the Greeks and Elizabethans, a theatre that could dare to boast — without committing a farcical sacrilege — that it is a legitimate descendant of the first theatre that sprang, by virtue of man's imaginative interpretation of life, out of his worship of Dionysus. I mean a theatre returned to its highest and sole significant function as a Temple where the religion of a poetical and symbolical celebration of life is communicated to human beings, starved in spirit by their soul-stifling daily struggle to exist as masks among the masks of living!

O'Neill did not realize that the mask was also the symbol of his Yea-saying years, that period which began with his eager letter to Nathan in 1920 and ended with *Lazarus Laughed* — the period of his association with Macgowan and Jones. For a half decade he dramatized the conflict not only within man and between men, but within himself and between himself and other men, of the mystic dreamer and the destructive doer, of pagan and Christian, artist and Philistine, life and death. He resolved the conflicts in denouements of sudden insight into the "age-old processes of nature," of mystic ecstasy and throbbing exaltation. Then in 1927, having written seven plays for pagans, he found it impossible any longer to create ecstasy. The rhapsodic quality departed from his plays as the Nay-saying years set in. The dream of theatre as temple faded into the reality of the New York Theatre Guild. Dionysus died, the Bacchic reveller became a solitary drinker once again. O'Neill's religious sensibility remained as acute as ever, his personal problems as vexing. More grim, therefore, than exalted, he continued to fulfill the function to which he had dedicated himself since the beginning of the decade:

The playwright today must dig at the roots of the sickness of today as he feels it — the death of the old God and the failure of science and materialism to give any satisfying new One for the surviving primitive religious instinct to find a meaning for life in and to comfort its fears of death with. It seems to me that anyone trying to do big work nowadays must have this big subject behind all the little subjects of his plays or novels, or he is simply scribbling around on the surface of things and has no more real status than a parlor entertainer.

Beyond Beyond the Horizon

IF O'NEILL, in *The Hairy Ape,* stood upon the threshold of the theatre of tomorrow, he took his initial step inside in his next play, *The Fountain.* Completed in 1922, *The Fountain* "was first acquired by Arthur Hopkins and then by the Theatre Guild, but it was ultimately produced by Jones, Macgowan and O'Neill at the Greenwich Village Theatre in 1925." A poetic romantic tragedy "largely in prose," it "came as a surprise to nearly everyone who knew the work of O'Neill." The playwright, somewhat defensively, explained in a program note that "the idea of writing *The Fountain* came on finally from [his] interest in the recurrence in folklore of the beautiful legend of a healing spring of eternal youth."

Juan Ponce de Leon, in so far as I've been able to make him a human being, is wholly imaginary. I have simply filled in the bare outline of his career, as briefly reported in the Who's Who of the histories, with a conception of what could have been the truth behind his 'life sketch' if he had been the man it was romantically — and religiously — moving to me to believe he might have been! Therefore, I wish to take solemn oath right here and now that *The Fountain* is not morbid realism.

Neither morbid nor realistic, *The Fountain* exemplifies O'Neill's tentative effort to express his new idea in playwriting: to return the theatre to its "highest and sole significant function," to offer his audience an aesthetic-religious experience. So far had O'Neill's religious speculation advanced since *The Hairy Ape* that the playwright might have announced almost simultaneously with Bernard Shaw the discovery of a religion for the twentieth century, a faith "newly arisen from the ashes of pseudo-Christianity, of mere scepti-

cism, and of the soulless affirmations of the Mechanists and Neo-
Darwinians." Shaw was referring to Bergson's *Creative Evolution*,
a "religion" that had been the inspiration in 1921 of *Back to
Methuselah*. Inspired by a naturalistic pantheism — likewise an
optimistic vitalistic, mystical conception of reality — O'Neill found
a way to advance beyond the point at which he had been blocked
in *The Hairy Ape*. Former obstacles remain, but the hero can now
surmount them. The clamorous primal horde are still with us in
The Fountain, appearing not as Neanderthal men but as Spanish
rabble, soldiers, nobles, priests of about the year 1500. Brutes, they
are the product of perhaps the highest civilization of their day, but
a materialistic one. In contrast with these over-civilized creatures
are the American Indians, who, although more dignified and probably more virtuous than the gorilla, similarly illustrate what it
means to live in harmony with nature. Juan Ponce de Leon, the
hero, is the counterpart of Yank, for he too is a man in whose
bosom, alas, two souls dwell. Just as the aborigines are nobler than
the gorilla, Juan is nobler than Yank. Both of his souls are revolted
by the greed, cruelty, and fanaticism of his fellow Spaniards with
the consequence that he can not "belong" in his world of conquista-
dors and inquisitors. Intensifying the anguish of this feeling of isloa-
tion is Juan's awareness of the internal discord earlier mentioned.
Both Robert and Andrew Mayo reside within Juan. Thus in the early
scenes of the play Juan is governed by his "ambitious thinker"
personality. After a struggle, after he becomes older, sadder, wiser,
the other self, the "romantic dreamer," gains ascendancy. With the
assertion of this higher self the hero's motive is transformed from
conquest to quest. Now, again like Yank, he is confronted with a
persuasive argument — not of social reform but of Christianity.
For the first time O'Neill thrusts his hero into conflict with an accomplished Catholic adversary. After engaging in controversy with
this genuinely pious individual, after searching the more exalted of
his two souls, Juan emerges still destitute of faith. But his rejection
of Christian doctrine is justified at last when he experiences the
convulsions of ecstasy which attend sudden insight into the mystery
of life and death, when the human spirit finds complete harmony
with the transcendental order — that of pantheistic naturalism.

Juan finally demonstrates how man might acquire in a spiritual way his "old harmony with nature."

As an "ambitious thinker" Juan is noble but misguided. Contemptuous of his better self, he represses his love for Maria, a woman who loves and understands him, but who is the wife of another man. He mocks his friend, Luis de Alvaredo, a dissipated but attractive nobleman who is given to drinking and dreaming. Without conviction Juan argues that there is no profit in staking life for dreams. His ambition is to make Spain the "mistress of the world." When he hears a Moor tell about the "Great Khan, Cipango and Cathay and Cambuluc" he is deeply moved; for he hopes to see Spain surpass ancient Rome, if only "she will find leaders who will weld conquest to her," who "will dare to govern with tolerance." Accordingly, he plans to embark upon an expedition of conquest. Oddly enough, Luis, too, has dreamt of Cathay, a dream which coincided with the Moor's story. Paraphrasing the latter's verses Luis dreamily informs Juan that there is

in some far country of the East — Cathay, Cipango, who knows — a spot that Nature has set apart from men and blessed with peace. It is a sacred grove where all things live in the old harmony they knew before man came. Beauty resides there and is articulate. Each sound is music, and every sight a vision. The trees bear golden fruit. And in the center of the grove, there is a fountain — beautiful beyond human dreams, in whose rainbows all of life is mirrored. In that fountain's waters, young maidens play and sing and tend it everlastingly for very joy in being one with it. The wise men of that far-off land have known it many ages.

But Juan the warrior wishes that the Moor had "sung instead of the armies and power of the Great Khan." Yet Luis perceives that his friend sneers at beauty while his "heart calls him liar." And the audience infers that Juan's secret longing is not that of empire, but to sail beyond the horizon.

In Scene Two, which occurs a year later on board Columbus' flagship on the last day of the second voyage, other motives for the journey to what is expected to be Cathay are revealed. The aforementioned primal horde are possessed "by greedy longing, the lust for loot." Although he desires no wealth for himself, Columbus is equally reprehensible. *A commanding figure of noble presence* his

face is *full of the ardent, fixed enthusiasm of the religious devotee.*
Convinced that he is the chosen instrument of God, he needs the
power that wealth can give "for God's glory," not his own. Driven
by hatred for the infidel, he hopes to fit out an army for a last
Crusade. Juan's motive, also ill-advised, is that of benevolent imperialism. Essentially a good man, he abhors the adventurers who
loot and murder, the nobles with their "greedy visions of wealth,"
the monks who "torture useful subjects of the Crown into slaves
of the Church," Columbus who pillages to resurrect the Crusades.

Twenty years later, in Scene Three, the disenchanted Juan sits
in the *courtyard of the Governor's palace, Porto Rico, his face aged,
lined, drawn. His hair and beard are gray. His expression and attitude are full of great weariness. His eyes stare straight before him
blankly in a disillusioned dream. The lines about his mouth are
bitter.* It is apparent that the "ambitious thinker" has remained too
long in the evil external world, that the "romantic dreamer" must
soon take over. He therefore begins to dream of Cathay and of
the Fountain of Youth, the dream which his friend Luis has, in
the meantime, abandoned in favor of the Church. A Dominican
monk, Luis has found peace; for although *his face shows the years
. . . it has achieved a calm, peaceful expression as if he were at
last in harmony with himself.* Juan, growing old, facing death, seeks
spiritual comfort, but refuses to accept it upon the terms of the
Church. Of Luis he declares *with a mocking smile:* "My friend
here is growing impatient waiting for immortality in heaven and
would rather gain it here on earth —" Shocked and hurt, Luis
ejaculates, "Juan!" — precisely as an equally personable cleric responds to the cynical irreverence of John Loving in *Days Without
End* a decade hence. But Juan, convinced that the clergy is *ignorant
of and [despises] every first principle of real Christianity,* is unmoved even by his friend's persuasiveness. At its best the Church
is personified by Luis who explains that before he had become a
Dominican he had been an "aimless posing rake, neither poet nor
soldier, without place nor peace." "I had no meaning even to
myself," he continues, "until God awakened me to His Holy Will.
Now I live in truth. You must renounce in order to possess." However much Juan desires peace and harmony, he can neither forgive
the behavior of most clerics nor accept the doctrine of renunciation.

To Luis he replies: "The world would be stale indeed if that were true! (*After a pause — irritably*) I fight the battles; you monks steal the spoils! I seek to construct; you bind by hands and destroy!" Although Luis remonstrates that it is only the Franciscans who behave so abominably, Juan is not satisfied. Frowning, he answers Luis: "Whether you convert by clemency or . . . by cruelty, the result is the same. All this baptizing of Indians, this cramming the cross down their throats has proved a ruinous error. It crushes their spirits and weakens their bodies." Luis, holding his own, reminds Juan that "his army crushed them first." Conceding that this is true the "soldier of iron" insists that there he would have stopped. Then he irritably ends the controversy with an expression of fatalism: "God's blood, here we are arguing about the same issue — for the thousandth time! It is too late. Talk is useless. (*With a weary sigh*) We do what we must — and sand covers our bodies and our deeds." "Talk is useless" and thinking, too. The gorilla, it should be remembered, could neither talk nor think, and he was the "best off." Cast out materialism and fanaticism, reject the doctrine of renunciation, cease thinking and talking. Having repudiated these attributes and tendencies of Western civilization, Juan is free to dream his own dream, to pursue the myth of his own choice, to discover at last the meaning and the beauty of Universal Nature.

Evidence of Nature's holy plan is the Indian, Nano, who *is a tall, powerfully built creature. Although loaded down with chains, he carries himself erect with an air of aloof, stoical dignity.* When he enters he is accompanied, not only by his guards, but by Oviedo, a noble, and Friar Quesada, a Franciscan, personifications of corruption and evil in state and Church, and foils for the noble savage. Curiously enough, Nano can talk — under compulsion, to be sure, and only about the Spring of Life — and gives every indication of being able to think — as his carefully prepared plan to ambush the Spaniards attests. In Scene Seven we meet other Indians in addition to Nano. Children of Nature, they glide in and out of the shadow of the forest, not the sinister forest of *The Emperor Jones,* but one which is part of the surrounding natural beauty: the sand gleaming *a pallid white in the moonlight,* the *rhythmic ebb and flow of waves.* It is nature as it was represented in *The Hairy Ape,* vivid, beautiful, and harmonious, to contrast with the cheapness, grotesqueness, disharmony of civilization. The Medicine Man, a curious creature, is by no means the bizarre and terrifying witch-doctor of the Congo forest. He confers with the Chief and with Nano to arrange for the destruction of the white men, to discuss the depravity of their enemy. "What are Spaniards?" asks the mystified Chief. "Their winged canoes are like the boats of gods." The catechism continues:

Nano [replies] These are no gods. They are men who die from wounds. Their faces are white, but they are evil. They wear shirts that arrows cannot pierce. They have strange sticks that spit fire and kill. Their devils make them strong. But they are not true warriors. They are thieves and rapers of women.

Chief. Have they no God?

Nano. (*with scorn*) Their God is a thing of earth! It is this! (*He touches a gold ornament that the* Chief *wears*)

Medicine Man. (*mystified*) Gold? Gold is sacred to the Sun. It can be no god itself.

Nano. (*contemptuously*) They see only things, not the spirit behind things. Their hearts are muddy as a pool in which deer have trampled. Listen. Their Medicine Men tell of a God who came to them long ago in the form of a man. He taught them to scorn things. He taught them to look for the spirit behind things. In revenge, they killed him. They tortured him as a sacrifice to their Gold Devil. They crossed two big sticks. They drove little sticks through his hands and feet and pinned him on the others — thus. (*He illustrates. A murmur of horror and indignation goes up among them.*)

Medicine Man. To torture a God! How did they dare?

Nano. Their devils protected them. And now each place they go, they carry that figure of a dying God. They do this to strike fear. They command you to submit when you see how even a God who fought their evil was tortured.

Revolted by the un-Christian conduct of his countrymen, unable to accept Luis' ascetic doctrine of renunciation, Juan becomes increasingly obsessed by the myth of the Fountain of Youth. Here the Indians are expected to assist him; but unfortunately, through no fault of his own, he has earned their ill will. Humanitarian and "real" Christian that he is, he has shown the utmost compassion for them and has tried to protect them from the cruelty of the Spaniards. Yet, as a soldier of iron, he was compelled to use violence against them, to conquer them but never to harm them. He inquires of Nano whether he has heard of Cathay where there is "a fountain — a spring — in which old men bathe or drink and become young warriors again." Nano has heard of the Spring of Life, but only "those the Gods love can find it." Still a skeptical mocker, Juan exclaims *scornfully,*

Aha, that old trick of poets — evasion of facts! (*Turning to Luis*) Do you remember the Moor that night in Granada? 'Only to the chosen.' Here is the echo! Bah! What jugglery! (*Then thoughtfully*) But it is strange. Where there is so much smoke, there must be a spark of fire. The Moor traced his myth back to the East — Cathay — and now we discover it again — still in Cathay — circling the world —

Long eager to sail to Cathay for the glory of Spain, he now yearns to do so for his own spiritual fulfillment. While Columbus had sailed in search of "Bible-crazed chimeras" — the Garden of Eden, the mines of Solomon, Juan was forced to stay in Porto Rico to fight the Indians. Columbus is dead now, and Juan awaits a patent from the King to discover new lands. But having grown rusty the soldier of iron is despondent:

It is too late. Cathay is too far. I am too weary. I have fought small things so long that I am small. My spirit has rusted in chains for twenty years. Now it tends to accept them — to gain peace. (*With a passionate yearning*) If I could only feel again my old fire, my energy of heart and mind! If I could be once more the man who fought before Granada — ! But the fire smolders. It merely warms my will to dream of the past. It no longer catches flame in deeds. (*With a desolate smile of self-pity*) I begin to dread — another failure. I am too old to find Cathay.

The old fire is enkindled when Beatriz appears, *a beautiful young girl of eighteen or so, the personification of youthful vitality, charm and grace.* She is the daughter of Maria, the woman who loved Juan, and has been sent from Spain as Juan's ward, for her mother and father are dead. He first sees her through the fountain in the courtyard and *utters a stunned exclamation as if he saw a ghost.* Fascinated, he stares at her and then says, "I am bewitched! I thought you were the spirit of the fountain." From her mother Beatriz brings him "tenderness." *Deeply moved* he responds, "Tenderness? Do you bring me that, Beatriz? (*Then as if recalling himself*) No, do not — for it means weakness. Bring me the past instead. Give me back — the man your mother knew."

Having fallen in love with the girl, Juan now needs more desper-

ately than ever to find the Fountain of Youth. In the three months
which intervene between Scene Three and Scene Four he ages
greatly. *His hair and beard have grown perceptibly white. Beneath
the bitter, mocking mask there is an expression of deep, hidden conflict and suffering on his face as if he were at war with himself.*
Obsessed by the idea of the fountain he has not only neglected the
duties of a soldier, but he is reduced to torturing a helpless savage.
Nano is held captive in a circular dungeon of lofty cylindrical form
entered from a trap-door above.

*In the middle of the floor stands a soldier, thick-set, brutal-looking, his
sleeves rolled up over his muscular arms. He is blowing with a bellows on
a charcoal brazier, glowing red-hot, in which are thrust several irons. On
the wall in the rear, his toes barely touching the floor, Nano hangs with
his arms outstretched over his head, the wrists bound by chains to iron
sockets in the rock. His head hangs on one side as if he were in a state
of semi-consciousness. His body is thin and wasted.*

Juan pleads fiercely with Nano to tell him the way to the fountain,
but the Indian remains silent — his revenge, apparently, "for the
death of his wives and children." With a *furious cry* Juan rushes
to the brazier, takes a red-hot coal with the tongs. "Dog!" he cries.
"I will burn that scorn from your eyes! (*The Indian stares at the
hot iron immovably.* Juan *lets it fall to the floor with a desperate
groan of misery*) Pardon! Forgiveness in Christ's name! It is you
who torture me! Nano, I burn to hell! I love!" Nano is unimpressed. Registering neither sympathy for the tormented Juan nor
fear of death, he is watching for a chance to return to his own
people, an opportunity which arises immediately. Juan asks him
to guide the ships to the land of the fountain. Suspicious, Nano
asks how he can trust the Spaniard's word. "I take my sacred oath,"
replies Juan, taking it, as he raises his hand. "Your God is a God
of lies," Nano observes. Whereupon, Juan, who has been having his
own doubts about God, wildly exclaims, "By your God then —
since mine has forsaken me!"

Here then is O'Neill's hero growing old in an evil world, longing
for youth, love, tenderness, faith. Forsaken by the Christian God,
he seeks God in nature. Defending his growing faith in non-
Christian myth, to Luis he asserts, "I believe in Nature. Nature is
part of God. She can perform miracles." That the Fountain of

Youth is a universal myth is hopeful evidence that it has a basis in truth. "But this evidence is merely fable, legend, the dream of poets!" Luis protests, *pityingly*. To which Juan furiously replies, "Have praying and fasting made you an imbecile? What evidence had Columbus? And you — you believe Christ lived and died. Well, have you talked with men who saw Him in the manger, or on the Cross?" When Luis warns that this is blasphemous, Juan answers *with bitter despair,* "Then let it be! I have prayed to Him in vain." After which he adds, *with all the power of his will in the words,* "Let me be damned forever if Nature will only grant me youth upon this earth again! . . . There is no God but Love — no heaven but youth!" Forsaken by God, contemptuous of the world, recoiling from encroaching death Juan blindly follows Nano to the "fountain of youth," a spring in the forest. Here the Indians plan to kill him. Hesitating to drink for fear of being disappointed once again, he bends over the water and sees his own image. "The dead eyes of a corpse stare back" into his eyes. Kneeling, he feels the impulse to pray and does so — to the "Spirit of Eternal Youth," to Beatriz. Having prayed he drinks, discovers Nano's deception, and turns upon the Indian in a frenzy of rage. The ambushed Indians shoot him.

Now begins the mystic vision. As Juan regains consciousness *a tall woman's figure* appears to him. *The face is a pale mask with features indistinguishable save for the eyes that stare straight ahead with a stony penetration that sees through and beyond things.* Guessing that he sees a personification of Death, *in passionate invocation* he calls for Beatriz, for Youth. Beatriz sings from the darkness the song which Luis had sung in Granada:

> Love is a flower
> Forever blooming
> Life is a fountain
> Forever leaping
> Upward to catch the golden sunlight
> Upward to reach the azure of heaven
> Failing, falling,
> Ever returning,
> To kiss the earth that the flower may live.

Then Beatriz *appears within as if rising from the spring. She dances in ecstasy — the personified spirit of the fountain.* She disappears and is replaced by the *form of a Chinese poet, a venerable old man with the mild face of a dreamer and scholar.* The Moor back in Granada had mentioned him. Following the poet comes the Moor, and then Luis. The three join hands, symbolizing the unity of East and West, the universality of the myth. Beatriz adds her voice to theirs, and they sing a quartet, the song which we have just heard with the concluding three lines altered to:

> Born of God but
> Ever returning
> To merge with earth that the field may live.

The figures disappear. Juan is alone with Death trying to solve the riddle. "What is left when Death makes the hand powerless?" he asks. The figures return, the Chinese poet now as a Buddhist priest, the Moorish minstrel as a priest of Islam, Luis the Dominican monk, and, in addition, the Medicine Man of Scene Eight. It occurs to Juan that "all faiths — they vanish — are one and equal — within — ." The Fountain he now realizes is "that from which all life springs and to which it must return — God!" "Death," Beatriz' voice informs him, "is a mist veiling sunrise." Age and Youth "are the same rhythm of eternal life." The Figure, Death, slowly *vanishes in the fountain.* "Death is no more," Juan announces. Whereupon the Figure materializes, like the Cheshire cat, within the fountain, but this time without a mask. The face is that of Beatriz,

her form grown tall, majestic, vibrant with power. Her arms are raised above her head. Her whole body soars upward. A radiant dancing fire, proceeding from the source of the fountain, floods over and envelops her until her figure is like the heart of its flame. Juan *stares at this vision for a moment, then sinks on his knees — exultantly*) I see! Fountain Everlasting, time without end! Soaring flame of the spirit transfiguring Death! All is within! All things dissolve, flow on eternally! O aspiring fire of life, sweep the dark soul of man! Let us burn in thy unity!

Sobbing with happiness, Juan cries, "O God, Fountain of Eternity, Thou art the All in One, the One in All — the Eternal Becoming which is Beauty!" Unconscious again, he is discovered by Luis and a brother Dominican. As the curtain falls upon Scene Ten, Luis informs Juan that "it is the dawn." "The dawn!" exclaims Juan *exultantly.*

In the next scene, the final scene of the play, the authoritativeness of the mystical experience is verified by objective, external events. Some months later, in a Dominican monastery in Cuba, Juan sits in the courtyard where there is a fountain — *a crude little home-made* fountain. *Beyond the wall nature can be seen and felt — vivid, colorful, burgeoning with the manifold, compelling life of the tropics. Juan is pale and emaciated but his wasted countenance has gained an entirely new quality, the calm of a deep spiritual serenity.* With him is a portly monk whose *large eyes have the opaque calm of a ruminating cow's.* Beatriz enters accompanied by Juan's nephew whom she loves. It is soon made evident that the nephew, who is unnamed, is Juan's counterpart, the double which he had mentioned earlier and which he himself had hoped to be. Thus youth returns, and "life flows on eternally." Juan makes his last speech in a *ringing voice:*

One must accept, absorb, give back, become oneself a symbol! Juan Ponce de Leon is past! He is resolved into the thousand moods of beauty that make up happiness — colors of the sunset, of tomorrow's dawn, breath of the great Trade Wind — sunlight on grass, an insect's song, the rustle of leaves, an ant's ambitions. (*In an ecstasy*) Oh, Luis, I begin to know eternal youth! I have found my Fountain! O Fountain of Eternity, take back this drop, my soul! (*He dies. Luis bows his head and weeps.*)

Before the curtain falls, the voices of Beatriz and the Nephew *rise to an exultant pitch* in the fountain song, and the *chant of the monks swells out deep and vibrant. For a moment the two strains blend into harmony, fill the air in an all-comprehending hymn of the mystery of life . . .*

It is evident that Juan "belongs." He has fulfilled the longing of the Hairy Ape, and he is better off than Paddy. Superior to both torpid drunkenness and ruminating dope-dream, the romantic dream pays off when it culminates in that resplendent vision wherein one achieves mystic union with God, "the All in One, the One in All — the Eternal Becoming which is Beauty!" Juan is more fortunate, too, than an earlier romantic dreamer: Robert Mayo, released by death, finally embarked on his voyage beyond the horizon. It was "just Beauty" that had been calling him, "the mystery and spell of the East," a vague "freedom of great wide spaces . . ." At last the dreamer-poet was free to respond to the call. That was about as much as O'Neill, with his currently materialistic point of view, could do for his hero. Created four years later, Juan is a character of religious rather than aesthetic sensibility. Yet, in gratifying his craving for peace, harmony, love, and eternity he also discovers beauty and happiness. Like Robert, he is attracted by the "mystery and spell of the East," sensing that there is a secret which is hidden over there, beyond the horizon. Although he comes no nearer to the East than had Robert, Juan penetrates the mystery, experiences the spell, learns the secret. For East and West are one, as are man and nature. The faith which Juan's mystical experience reveals to him is that of a dynamic pantheism; a vitalistic Becoming rather than a static Being; an eternal, glorious continuum of birth and rebirth. For life, like Shelley's Cloud, changes, but it cannot die. Divine Immanence is apparent everywhere. God is the vital force, its impulsion and its receptor, its source and its goal. He resembles Emerson's "Brahma" who reminds the slayer who thinks he slays and the slain who thinks he is slain that

> They know not well the subtle ways
> I keep, and pass, and turn again.

He is like Whitman's Earth which "renews with such unwitting looks its prodigal, annual, sumptuous crops . . ." As in Nietzsche's conception of Dionysian eternal recurrence He is energy "which does not consume itself," which returns

from multifariousness to uniformity, from the play of contradictions back into the delight of consonance, saying yea unto itself, even in this homogeneity of its courses and ages, for ever blessing itself as something which recurs for all eternity, . . .

O'Neill's spiritual achievement was, unfortunately but inevitably, a dramatic and a financial failure. After two weeks *The Fountain* closed. George Jean Nathan in his review of the play overlooked the ineptitude of its romantic elements: the hero and the bombastic language out of seventeenth-century heroic tragedy, the Indians out of Cooper, the dungeon scene out of Gothic romance. Nathan commented upon the "periodic triteness," the "intermittent bravery of mind," the "uncommonly lovely scenes." Yet he failed to perceive the rhapsodic spirituality of the climactic vision scene, characterizing it instead as "little more than a John Murray Anderson Music

Box Revue number played behind a sequin-embellished scrim."
O'Neill wrote three more plays (*Welded, All God's Chillun . . . ,
Desire Under the Elms*) before *The Fountain* was produced, but
not until the second and the third of these was he able to bring his
new idea in playwriting under control. The play which followed
The Fountain in order of composition was, like its predecessor, a
fiasco. Not even Nathan could find anything extenuating to say
about it.

Married Love

THE FAILURE of *Welded,* as Nathan saw it, was the consequence of O'Neill's futile attempt "to duplicate the technic of such
a drama as 'The Father,'" of misjudging the Strindberg method,
which "is the intensification of a theme from within." O'Neill,
remarked the critic, "intensifies his theme from without." This is
penetrating criticism so far as it goes, and it applies admirably to
other O'Neill plays as well. But in disregarding the nature of
Welded's theme it neglects to account in this instance for the major
cause of failure. For in *Welded* although O'Neill again floundered
artistically, he continued his advance along the Mystic Way from
the material realm to the spiritual. And the floundering was the
result largely of his inability to communicate the mystical experience. Never distinguished for his articulateness, he now set himself
the task of expressing the inexpressible. Whereas the theme of *The
Father* is the eternal antagonism of the sexes, that of *Welded* is
the eternal mystical craving of heart for heart. Considering his
theme, O'Neill erred less in misjudging Strindberg's method than
in attempting to duplicate it at all. The power of Strindberg's
play is derived, as Nathan observed, "from the sparks that fly
upward from a prodigious and deafening pounding on the anvil."
But "all one gets in O'Neill's case," he added, "is the prodigious
and deafening pounding. The sparks simply will not come out."
O'Neill had not yet discovered that the fugitive mystic feeling
cannot be evoked by violent exertion.

Unlike Juan Ponce de Leon, the hero of *Welded* is a mystic from the start. Like his predecessor he attains salvation by insight at the end. Michael Cape

is thirty-five, tall and dark. His unusual face is a harrowed battlefield of supersensitiveness, the features at war with one another — the forehead of a thinker, the eyes of a dreamer, the nose and mouth of a sensualist. One feels a powerful imagination tinged with somber sadness — a driving force which can be sympathetic and cruel at the same time. There is something tortured about him — a passionate tension, a self-protecting, arrogant defiance of life and his own weakness, a deep need for love as a faith in which to relax.

Obviously a man of feeling, Michael displays an affinity not only with the older Juan, but also with Smitty and with Robert Mayo about whom, we may remember, there was a *touch of the poet expressed in his high forehead and wide dark eyes. Delicate and refined,* Robert's features leaned *to weakness in the mouth and chin.* If Michael resembles the earlier characters he also has much in common with O'Neill himself. For Michael, too, is a playwright and approximately O'Neill's age in 1922. Reputed to have been hard-boiled and whimsical, brutal and tender, O'Neill appears to have projected these antithetical aspects of his personality upon his hero. And if the marriage problem which Michael must solve had been suggested by Strindberg, it also represented the situation which confronted O'Neill at the time. Married for a second time in 1918, he was divorced in 1928. In *Welded* he appears to have been trying to work out imaginatively his own marital difficulties. That he was not averse to representing himself on the stage is demonstrated by the play *Exorcism.* Produced in 1920 but never published, this play was based upon an incident of O'Neill's "vagrant days," his attempt at suicide by poison, his rescue by two drunken companions.

Welded tells the story of the playwright Michael Cape and his actress wife Eleanor who, although they are in love, are out of harmony with themselves and with each other. The action progresses through vibrations of attraction and repulsion, flowing movements of merging and separation, conflicts between cosmic-consciousness and self-consciousness. Eleanor *is a woman of thirty. Her figure is tall. Her face, with its high prominent cheek-bones, lacks harmony. It is dominated by passionate, blue-gray eyes, restrained by a high forehead from which the mass of her dark brown hair is combed straight back. The first impression of her whole personality is one of charm, partly innate, partly imposed by years of self-discipline.*

The discord between husband and wife arises partly from the fact that the latter is more realistic and practical than the former, less sensitive, less imaginative, less spiritual; and partly from their possession of strong egos. Thus they frequently quarrel.

But on this night they hope to forget that they are actress and playwright. "Let's just be us — lovers," suggests Michael. Unfortunately they are inclined to think too much, particularly about each other's previous love affairs. Overcoming this tendency, they turn instead to dreaming, dreaming with each other in their past "to find there — a new faith." For having lost faith in everything, they have been saved by love. Their present faith is epitomized by an almost unattainable ideal — as Michael reminds his wife:

We swore to have a true sacrament — or nothing! Our marriage must be a consummation demanding and combining the best in each of us! Hard, difficult, guarded from the commonplace, kept sacred as the outward form of our inner harmony! (*With an awkward sense of having become rhetorical he adds self-mockingly*) We'd tend our flame on an altar, not in a kitchen range! (*He forces a grin — then abruptly changing again, with a sudden fierce pleading*) It has been what we dreamed, hasn't it, Nelly?

But Nelly is not so sure. More practical-minded than her husband, she fears that their ideal might be too difficult. For after they surrender everything to each other there would still be something left, and then as usual they would fight. Conceding that this might be so, Cape nevertheless adheres to the sacramental concept of love and marriage. Like Walt Whitman he "aches with amorous love" and, longing "to drink the mystic deliria deeper than any other man," he chants the following Adamic song:

Then let's be proud of our fight! It began with the splitting of a cell a hundred million years ago into you and me, leaving an eternal yearning to become one life again . . . You and I — year after year — together — forms of our bodies merging into one form; rhythm of our lives beating against each other, forming slowly the one rhythm — the life of Us! — created by us! — beyond us, above us! (*With sudden furious anger*) God, what I feel of the truth of this — the beauty! — but how can I express it?

Kissing him, Eleanor says simply, without a trace of sarcasm, "I understand." Captivated by Michael's rapturous impetuosity, she is prepared to share his "mystical feeling of enlargement, union, and emancipation." He strains *her to him with fierce passion* crying, "Oh, my own, my own — and I your own — to the end of time!" "I love you!" Eleanor declares. Then Cape, *with passionate exultance:*

Why do you regret our first days? Their fire still burns in us — deeper! Don't you feel that? (*Kissing her again and again*) I've become you! You've become me! One heart! One blood! Ours! (*He pulls her to her feet*) My wife! Come!

Almost swooning in his arms, she gasps, "My lover — yes — My lover — " "Come," says Michael. *With his arms around her he leads her to the stairway.* But then as they start to float up the "steep stairway of love" upon their oceanic feeling, there is a noise in the hall. Eleanor *hears it, starts, seems suddenly brought back to herself. Cape is oblivious and continues up the stairs. She stands swaying, holding on to the bannister as if in a daze.* Reaching the top of the stairs, Cape suddenly is aware that Eleanor is not with him. *He looks down passionately, stretching out his arms, his eyes glowing* and exclaims, "Come!" A knock on the door, Eleanor sways irresolutely, Cape stammers in a fierce whisper, "No! Don't go!" *Without looking at him,* she says mechanically, "I must." Frantically he cries,

They'll go away. Nelly, don't! Don't! (*Again she stops irresolutely like a hypnotized person torn by two conflicting suggestions. The knock is repeated, this time with authority, assurance. Her body reacts as if she were throwing off a load.*)

Cape reaches the bottom of the stairs *as she opens the door. He stands there fixed, disorganized, trembling all over.*

The visitor who is responsible for frustrating the mystic union is John, a theatrical producer, an old friend, one who has adored Eleanor for many years. A perceptive person, he quickly *becomes aware of the disharmonious atmosphere his appearance has created* and soon finds a pretext for leaving. Alone once again, Michael reproaches Eleanor because she was not "oblivious to everything."

He sinks down on a chair, his head in his hands, and says *with bitter despondency:*

Ruined now — gone — a rare moment of beauty! It seems as if some jealous demon of the commonplace were mocking us. (*With a violent gesture of loathing*) Oh, how intolerably insulting life can be! (*Then brokenly*) Nelly, why did you?

Nelly does not know. She asks Michael's forgiveness, but there is now a barrier between them. In a scene which anticipates the technique of *Strange Interlude,* the couple sit in chairs *side by side, each facing front . . . , stare straight ahead* and *remain motionless. They speak ostensibly to the other, but showing by their tone it is a thinking aloud to oneself, and neither appears to hear what the other has said.* Explaining that she feels crushed when Michael tries to possess her soul as well as her body, she points out logically enough that if she is destroyed there will be nothing left with which to love him, nothing left for him to love. Then the two halves of the cell drift farther apart as each, enveloped in its own ego, asserts itself. The playwright and the actress emerge once again, and the rest of the act becomes a scene out of Strindberg. Harmony is shattered by sexual and professional jealousy, *abysmal self-loathing, frightful hatred,* even violence. Seizing the wife *about the throat with both hands* the husband *chokes her,* forcing her *down to her knees.* He *rushes out of the door as if furies were pursuing him,* swearing that he will destroy their love. Glad to be free, Eleanor, too, departs.

Determined to liberate herself from her thralldom to Michael, Eleanor goes to John in search of comfort and revenge. After making two attempts to go upstairs to John's bed she realizes that she still loves her husband, that he has "trained her too well in his ideal." *Fatalistically* she says, "It's broken me. I'm no longer anything. So what does it matter how weak I am?" Then, *after a slight pause:* "I begin to know — something. (*With a sudden queer, exultant pride*) My love for him is my own, not his! That he can never possess! It's my own. It's my life!" Fortified by this insight, she goes home.

Meanwhile Michael also has been trying to "murder love." Scorning both alcohol and suicide, he seeks instead a third variety of degradation, a prostitute. In Act Two, Scene Two, he has accompanied her to her room.

The woman is fairly young. Her face, rouged, powdered, penciled, is broad and stupid. Her small eyes have a glazed look. Yet she is not ugly — rather pretty for her bovine, stolid type — and her figure is still attractive although its movements just now are those of a tired scrubwoman.

Like most of O'Neill's heroes who find themselves in a similar situation, Cape does not use the whore after her kind. The mystic, cruelly wrenched from his trance, is not to be placated by carnal love. Throughout the scene his condition verges upon hysteria — as O'Neill's directions indicate. Thus, when Cape enters *he is bareheaded, his hair disheveled, his eyes wild, his face has a feverish, mad expression* . . . then, *with a frightened puzzled glance* . . . *He starts, passes a trembling hand through his hair bewilderedly* . . . *with a start — evidently answering some train of thought in his mind — with a wild laugh* . . . *swallowing hard several times as if he were striving to get control of his voice — finally blurts out in a tone of desperation* . . . *with a sudden burst of wild laughter* . . . *jerkily* . . . *wildly* . . . *He stops shuddering* . . . *He presses his hands to his forehead* . . . *with unnatural intensity* . . . *with a strange, wild exultance, leaps to his feet* . . . *Making a tremendous visible effort he kisses her on the lips, then shrinks back with a shudder and forces a harsh laugh* . . . *starting — with wild scorn* . . . *dully, with no meaning to his question — like an automaton* . . . *again staring at her with strange intensity — suddenly with a queer laugh* . . . *with a wild laugh* . . . *laughing sardonically* . . . *startled — then with bitter mockery* . . . *staring at her intently — suddenly deeply moved* . . . *with unnatural intensity* . . . *Then he beats his head with both clenched hands — distractedly* . . . *He flings himself on the chair in a violent outburst of dry sobbing* . . . *controlling hysterical laughter — huskily* . . . *Then his bitter memories rush back agonizingly. He stammers wildly* . . . *He kisses her again and again frenziedly* . . . *Finally with a groan he pushes her away, shuddering with loathing, and sinks back on the chair* . . . *with dull impotent rage* . . . *startled — with a forced laugh* . . . *He laughs harshly* . . . *in anguish* . . . *rebelliously* . . . *very pale — stammering* . . . *with great pity* . . . *He kneels before her, looking up into her face* . . . *gets up and takes her face between his hands and stares into her eyes — then kisses her on the fore-head . . . in the same gentle tone . . . Then with a tremulous smile . . . impressed again . . . he smiles back at her affectionately . . . He goes out, closing the door after him.* The foregoing directions reveal the range of Cape's emotions from frenzy to the tranquillity which follows illumination. Intent upon "murdering love" and "satisfying hate," he makes two efforts, as we have just seen, to commit adultery. Midway through the scene he experiences an insight. "Do you know what you are?" he asks the Woman.

You're a symbol. You're all the tortures man inflicts on woman — and you're the revenge of woman! You're love revenging itself upon itself! You're the suicide of love — of my love — of all love since the world began!

Symbol though she be, when he suddenly recalls his bitter experience with Eleanor, he *clutches* the Woman *fiercely in his arms* and pleads, "Save me, you! Help me to kill! Help me to gain peace!" "You're the perfect death," he tells her, " — but I'm too strong, or weak — and I can't, you understand — can't! So, good-by." As he starts to leave, he announces that he is going to "go on in the dark." Now begins the change of heart. The Woman advises him to "beat it home," to return to his wife, adding *cynically,* "Aw, I'm wise. Stick to her, see? You'll get over it. You can get used to anything, take it from me!" Anguished, Cape replies, "Don't! But it's true — it's the insult we all swallow at the price of life." And the Woman, *with a sort of forlorn chuckle,* observes,

Oh, you'll go back aw right! Don't kid yourself. You'll go back no matter what, and you'll loin to like it. Don't I know? You love her, don't you? Well, then! There's no use buckin' that game. Go home. Kiss and make up. Forget it. It's easy to ferget — when you got to!

Whereupon Cape experiences a second insight. As he stares at the Woman, *an expression comes as if he were seeing her for the first time.* He speaks: "So — it still survives in you. They haven't killed it — that lonely life of one's own which suffers in solitude. (*Shamefacedly*) I should have known. Can you forgive me?" It had evidently never occurred to Cape that a measure of stoicism might be helpful. Yet before he takes his leave the Woman teaches him a way to improve even upon that philosophy.

Woman. I was thinkin' of the whole game. It's funny, ain't it?

Cape. (*slowly*) You mean — life?

Woman. Sure. You got to laugh, ain't you? You got to loin to like it!

Cape. (*this makes an intense impression on him. He nods his head several times.*) Yes! That's it! That's exactly it! That goes deeper than wisdom. To learn to love life — to accept it and be exalted — that's the one faith left to us! (*Then with a tremulous smile*) Good-by. I've joined your church. I'm going home.

Woman. (*with a grin that is queerly affectionate*) Sure. That's the stuff. Close your eyes and your feet'll take you there.

Cape. (*impressed again*) Yes! Yes! Of course they would! They've been walking there for thousands of years — blindly. However, now, I'll keep my eyes open — (*he smiles back at her affectionately*) — and learn to like it!

In Act Three, virtue intact, the Capes return to their apartment. Apprehensive, uncertain, they scrutinize each other. *When they come close, they instinctively reach out their hands in a strange conflicting gesture of a protective warding off and at the same time a seeking possession.* Eleanor says, penitently, "Michael!" Cape responds, humbly, "Nelly!"

They smile with a queer understanding, their arms move about each other, their lips meet. They seem in a forgetful, happy trance at finding each other again. They touch each other testingly as if each cannot believe the other is really there. They act for the moment like two persons of different races, deeply in love but separated by a barrier of language.

Returning to self-consciousness they quickly lose the harmony which they had just grasped. *Finally Cape exclaims with a dull resentment directed not at her but at life,* "What is — it?" *He makes a gesture of repulsing something before him.*

Eleanor. (*in his tone*) I don't know.

Cape. (*harshly*) A moment ago — there — (*He indicates where they had stood in an embrace*) We knew everything. We understood!

Eleanor. (*eagerly*) Oh, yes!

Cape. (*bitterly*) Now — we must begin to think — to continue going on, getting lost —

Eleanor. (*sadly*) It was happy to forget. Let's not think — yet.

Cape. (*grimly*) We've begun. (*Then with a harsh laugh*) Thinking explains. It eliminates the unexplainable — by which we live.

Eleanor. (*warningly*) By which we love. Sssh!

They have recognized, as did Juan Ponce de Leon, the relative value of thinking and of dreaming, but as yet they are incapable of making a choice. Meanwhile Eleanor *with a certain exultance* suggests, "Now — we know peace." Cape rejects the suggestion, saying *slowly,* "Peace isn't our meaning." Then they relate their experiences of the evening, enlarging the cleavage. Although each suffers, each struggles to understand. "I will believe!" Michael exclaims. Then, recalling what he had learned from the Woman, he continues: "But what difference does it make — believing or not believing? I've changed, I tell you! I accept!" Eleanor confesses that she had been unable to free herself from Michael because of "something stronger." "Love!" cries Michael *with a passionate triumph.* Recalling the revelation that she had experienced at John's apartment, she insists: "No! I didn't come back to you! It conquered me, not you! Something in me — mine — not you!" After further bickering, matters reach a climax, and Eleanor starts once again for the door. Cape, loyal to his new philosophy, says, "Well — I accept! Go — if you want to!" Once her hand is on the knob *he can stand it no longer.* He *jumps toward the door with a pleading cry,* "Nelly!"

Suddenly the elusive harmony which they had felt at the beginning of the scene is restored.

They stare into each other's eyes. It is as if now by a sudden flash from within they recognized themselves, shorn of all the ideas, attitudes, cheating gestures which constitute the vanity of personality. Everything, for this second, becomes simple for them — serenely unquestionable. It becomes impossible that they should ever deny life, through each other, again.

That condition for which they have been striving has been attained: they have simultaneously annihilated the self. A mystical phenomenon, it is an aspect of the Dionysian way of life, as is their determination to affirm the goodness of the "most terrible and most questionable qualities of existence." "And we'll torture and tear, and clutch for each other's souls! — ," cries Cape exultantly, "fight — fail and hate again — (*he raises his voice in aggressive triumph*) but! — fail *with pride* — with joy!" Eleanor, *exalted by his exultation rather than by his words,* says, "Yes!" "*Our* life," Cape continues, "is to bear together our burden which is our goal — on and up! Above the world, beyond its vision — our meaning!" *Her eyes fixed on him,* Eleanor *dreamily* exclaims, "Your dream!" The ineffable quality of Cape's experience is apparent when he half-sobs

as the intensity of his passion breaks the spell of his exultation, and
he cries, "Oh, Nelly, Nelly, I want to say so much what I feel but
I can only stutter like an idiot!" *He has fallen on his knees before
her.* Then, *straining passionately for expression,* he describes the
unitive life to which they have just ascended:

Listen! Often I wake up in the night — in a black world, alone in a hundred million years of darkness. I feel like crying out to God for mercy
because life lives! Then instinctively I seek you — my hand touches you!
You are there — beside me — alive — with you I become a whole, a truth!
Life guides me back through the hundred million years to you. It reveals
a beginning in unity that I may have faith in the unity of the end!

Eleanor, this time, is the first to reach the top of the stairs. Looking
down at her husband, she *stretches out her arms,* and *with a passionate, tender gesture,* says, "Come!"

> Cape. (*leaping to his feet — intensely*) My own!
> Eleanor. (*with deep, passionate tenderness*) My lover!
> Cape. My wife! (*His eyes fixed on her he ascends. As he does so her
> arms move back until they are stretched out straight to right and left, form-
> ing a cross.* Cape *stops two steps below her — in a low, wondering tone*)
> Why do you stand like that?
> Eleanor. (*her head thrown back, her eyes shut — slowly, dreamily*) Per-
> haps I'm praying. I don't know. I love.

As the final curtain descends, Cape joins her, and *as their hands
touch they form together one cross.* Mysticism being the essence of
religion, it has led the Capes to the faith which they have craved.
Prayer and love are, as they should be, identical. Even the cross has
been given a new significance, a fresh sanctity.

Only God's Chillun Got Wings

THE ZEAL with which O'Neill set about to spiritualize his
drama led him in *The Fountain* and in *Welded* to over-estimate
the strains and stresses that the themes of those plays could bear.
To grow old is not disastrous, nor is it calamitous to be interrupted
in the ceremony of concupiscence. Even by other, higher sounding,

names — immortal longing, eternal love — O'Neill's themes were too slight to support a ponderous tone of high seriousness or to justify the tragic demeanor of the heroes — their extreme anguish, their violent behavior. But O'Neill avoided this basic blunder in *All God's Chillun Got Wings,* a tragedy of the Negro in general, of a supersensitive member of the race in particular. Here the potentialities of a manifestly tragic theme — that of racial injustice — are actually increased by making the protagonist at once a "good" man and a man of feeling.

Throughout the play the spiritual part of Jim Harris's nature is given a preponderance over its animal cravings and impulses, so that, although Jim is the victim of biological, social, and psychological forces, he benefits in the end in a way that was denied to both the Dreamy Kid and Brutus Jones. Having reproached God for cruelly subjecting him to undeserved, ever-increasing agony, he experiences sudden mystical illumination before the final curtain falls. Still affected by his racial past the Negro now, however, owing to the revision of O'Neill's primitivistic theories, is spared the fate which befell his predecessors of the earlier plays. The concept of atavism has been discarded and with it the Negro's frightful, savage ancestors. Now he can boast of a rich, primitive racial heritage. Having progressed along anthropological lines O'Neill's thought moved also into the psychological milieu of the 1920's. Motivation of the principal characters of *All God's Chillun* . . . was influenced by the teachings of Alfred Adler who, incidentally, was less inclined than Freud to emphasize man's animal tendencies.

The protagonist's losing battle with fate begins in childhood, that period in which the emotional difficulties of the adult are said to have their genesis, and ends after some seventeen years. By the end of the first scene the source of Jim Harris's anguish is clearly indicated by his reaction to the fact of racial differences. Although the children, black or white, freely accept one another the characteristics of each race are sharply differentiated on an emotional as well as a physical basis. Thus, the Negroes frankly participate *in the spirit of Spring, the whites laugh constrainedly, awkward in natural emotion.* Jim already suffers from a feeling of inferiority, having endured, as even a very young Negro must, the derision of the whites, for he had shrunk from the appellations "Crow," "Chocolate," "Smoke," "nigger." To escape such ignominy he has drunk chalk and water, because he had been told that it would make him white. Nine years hence, in the second scene, the effect of his early sense of inferiority is apparent in his quiet manner, his *queerly baffled, sensitive face* and, above all, in his determination to succeed in a white man's profession. It is this ambition which intensifies the cleavage between the two races, which arouses the contempt of his fellow Negroes. The black world as well as the white is alien to the introverted protagonist. He is accused of "aimin to buy white." When Ella Downey, the blond white girl who had been tolerant and affectionate in the first scene, abandons him in favor of one Mickey, a *vicious natural bully,* Jim's sense of isolation is complete. Other consequences of his mental state become manifest, for it is evident that there exists a psychological obstacle which thwarts his plans to become a lawyer. He has been able to accomplish in five years of study what he should have achieved in two. Since his mental capacity is adequate and his health sound, one must surmise that he is suffering from some emotional difficulty:

Jim. . . . I can't explain — just — but it hurts like fire. It brands me in my pride. I swear I know more'n any member of my class. I ought to, I study harder. I work like the devil. It's all in my head — all fine and correct to a T. Then when I'm called on — I stand up — all the white faces looking at me — and I can feel their eyes — I hear my own voice sounding funny, trembling — and all of a sudden it's all gone in my head — there's nothing remembered — and I hear myself stuttering — and give up — sit down — They don't laugh, hardly ever. They're kind. They're good people. (*In a frenzy*) They're considerate, damn them! But I feel branded!

In the written examination the results are equally discouraging:

For weeks before I study all night. I can't sleep anyway. I learn it all, I see it, I understand it. They give me the paper in the exam room. I look it over, I know each answer — perfectly. I take up my pen. On all sides are white men starting to write. They're so sure — even the ones that I know know nothing. But I know it all — but I can't remember any more — it fades — it goes — it's gone. There's a blank in my head — stupidity — I sit like a fool fighting to remember a little bit here, a little bit there — not enough to pass — not enough for anything — when I know it all!

Neither the Dreamy Kid nor Brutus Jones would remotely have comprehended the nature of Jim's suffering, nor would the sea-captains whose compulsive drives and haunted minds represented psychological abnormalities of a quite different order — less subtle, less convincing, and antiquated. Jim, in short, is the victim of a neurosis, the origin of which lay, not in the conflict between "ego and sexuality," that is, between civilization and man's ineradicable animal nature, which is Freud's theory, but within the ego itself, which is the theory of Adler, one of Freud's dissident disciples. Emphasizing the ego rather than the "libido," Adler insisted that the well-spring of human behavior is not that of sexual energy, but rather of a force akin to Nietzsche's will to power. Through the positing of fictitious goals whose purpose is to satisfy the egoistic will, life is rendered bearable. But when, as in the case of Jim Harris, the normal expression of the will to power is threatened by a feeling of racial inferiority, trouble may be anticipated. This consciousness of the weak point, Adler explained, dominates the neurotic to

such a degree that often without knowing it he begins to construct with all his might the protecting super-structure. Along with this his sensitiveness becomes more acute, he learns to pay attention to relationships which still escape others, he exaggerates his cautiousness, begins to anticipate all sorts of disagreeable consequences in starting out to do something . . .

Having lost the peace of mind which guarantees mental health, the victim, mistrusting himself, may turn either to maliciousness and envy, or to obedience, submission and humility, the latter being the course which Jim's neurotic behavior takes. Thus, in the third scene, he welcomes Ella back, despite the fact that she had cruelly discarded him five years before and that, cast aside now herself, she is faced with the gloomy choice of destroying herself or becoming a prostitute. More than this, he humbles himself before her in a fashion which suggests something in addition to the love and gratitude that he says he feels:

I don't ask you to love me — I don't dare to hope nothing like that! I don't want nothing — only to wait — to know you like me — to be near you — to keep harm away — to make up for the past — to never let you suffer any more — to serve you — to lie at your feet like a dog that loves you — to kneel by your bed like a nurse that watches over you sleeping — to preserve and protect and shield you from evil and sorrow — to give my life and my blood and all the strength that's in me to give you peace and joy — to become your slave! — yes, be your slave — your black slave that

adores you as sacred! (*He has sunk to his knees. In a frenzy of self-abne-
gation, as he says the last words he beats his head on the flagstones.*)

It is evident that the roots of Jim's "inferiority complex," are
nourished by the American experiences of his ancestors. This survival of ancestral habits — the recrudescence of servility, the persistence of the doglike devotion of slave for master — predestines
him to fail in his quest for equality and justice, a quest which he
pursues down a double path. For he not only continues to study
law, he also is to be married to a white woman. Outside the church
after the marriage ceremony, aware of the unconventionality of the
step which he has just taken, conscious too, perhaps, of the fact that
he has challenged his fate, *he is on the verge of collapse, his face
twitching, his eyes staring.* Trying to comfort himself, as well as
Ella, an *hysteric quality of ecstasy . . . breaks into his voice:*

. . . Hope! That's for us, Honey. All those blessings in the sky! What's it
the Bible says? Falls on just and unjust alike? No, that's the sweet rain.
Pshaw, what am I saying? All mixed up. There's no unjust about it. We're
all the same — equally just — under the sky — under the sun — under God
— sailing over the sea — to the other side of the world — the side where
Christ was born — the kind side that takes count of the soul — over the
sea —

The discrepancy between God's promise of equal justice and the
impossibility of its fulfillment is the ultimate source of Jim's anguish and the tragic theme of the play. His imminent emotional
collapse is indication of his feeling of hopelessness with respect to
the prospects of resolving the contradiction. Yet he refuses to re-
sign himself to fate. Returning to New York after two years in
France, he resumes his studies only to continue to fail in his efforts
to pass the bar examinations. In the final scene he again receives
word of his failure:

Pass? Pass? (*He begins to chuckle and laugh between sentences and phrases,
rich, Negro laughter, but heart-breaking in its mocking grief*) Good Lord,
child, how come you can ever imagine such a crazy idea? Pass? Me? Jim
Crow Harris? Nigger Jim Harris — become a full-fledged Member of the
Bar! Why the mere notion of it is enough to kill you with laughing! It'd
be against all natural laws, all human right and justice. It'd be miraculous,
there'd be earthquakes and catastrophes, the seven Plagues'd come again
and locusts'd devour all the money in the banks, the second Flood'd come
roaring and Noah'd fall overboard, the sun'd drop out of the sky like a

ripe fig, and the Devil'd perform miracles, and God'd be tipped head first right out of the Judgment seat! (*He laughs, maudlinly uproarious.*)

And presently he is *giggling and gasping idiotically,* overtaken by the psychosis which attacks such individuals as set for themselves an unattainable ideal, an impossible "life goal."

The case of Ella Downey may also be explained in part by Adler's "individual psychology." Her madness, which developed before the close of the play into a "murderous mania," had its genesis, like Jim's, in the race "deep down in her." Despite the desperate situation from which Jim had rescued her; despite her fatuity; despite her realization that Jim is the "only white man in the world," whereas her white associates were all "black to the heart"; she is compelled to assert her superiority to the Negro. Racial pride is the only means available to her by which her egoistic will to power can express itself. When, therefore, she finds herself married to a Negro, living in a colored household, completely dependent upon members of an inferior race, she is driven to extricate herself somehow from this intolerable position. This she does by displaying an attitude of "indifferent superiority" to Jim's sister, Hattie, a woman who excels her in every respect. Then, by way of exemplifying the alternative course which the behavior of the victim of the "inferiority complex" may take, she becomes malicious and envious — in contrast to Jim's obedience, submission, and humility. Unable to surpass her Negro husband, she becomes aggressively determined that he shall not surpass her. Consequently she tries to dissuade him from studying law; but Jim, in most circumstances a perceptive and intelligent man, is curiously obtuse in this matter, and fails to realize what Ella is attempting to do. Meanwhile, she goes into a decline; she becomes pale, and there is a *strange, haunted expression in her eyes* as she frantically tries to *shake off her obsession.* By the second scene of the second act she has acquired the disconcerting habit of entering the room, in which Jim is studying, wearing *a red dressing-gown over her night-dress,* bare-foot, and carrying a carving-knife in her right hand. Such goings-on are not conducive to study, and, even without his "inferiority complex," Jim conceivably might have failed to pass his examinations. Fortunately for Jim, Ella's deep hatred is concentrated upon the Congo mask which Hattie gave him as a wedding present and which has become for Ella a symbol of that threat to her superiority which is presented by the Negro race. For, in the last scene, she plunges the knife, not into Jim, but into his surrogate, the mask, an act which she triumphantly makes upon being informed of her husband's final failure. The evil spirit that had haunted her has been exorcised:

It's dead. The devil's dead. See! It couldn't live — unless you passed. If you'd passed it would have lived in you. Then I'd have had to kill you, Jim, don't you see? — or it would have killed me. But now I've killed it. (*She pats his hand*) So you needn't ever be afraid any more, Jim.

But the peace which she finds at last has been won at the cost of adulthood and of sanity, even of life itself — for she has intimations of impending death. Fleeing from a reality which provided her with no opportunity to satisfy her egoistic will, she took refuge first in neurosis and finally in a return to childhood. She reveals only a vague sense of having done anything wrong when she asks, *like a child*, "Will God forgive me, Jim?"

The psychology of the two main characters, obliquely influenced as it appears to be by the theories of Adler, succeeds in avoiding those animal cravings and impulses which appeared in *The Emperor Jones* and in *The Hairy Ape,* but it furnished no opportunity to pay heed to the spiritual part of the characters' natures. To find a place for the heart in his anatomy of love would seem to be an insoluble problem for O'Neill in *All God's Chillun,* for neither the love of Jim for Ella nor of her for him has its source in anything more sublime than personal need. Jim's emotional attachment stems from an internal necessity, being a recrudescence of a racial habit, that characteristic inherited from days of slavery when the Negro adored, preserved, and protected his white master, or mistress. And Ella "loves" Jim through external necessity. Whatever affection she revealed for Jim at the time she consented to marry him was motivated by gratitude: he had been "the only one in the world who had stood by her." When he declared his love for her, she, despondent as she was, could find in her heart nothing more than a moderate "I like you, Jim — better than anyone else in the world." Considering that her only other extant friend was Shorty, a pimp, her mild affection for the Negro was not particularly flattering. Yet, in spite of the sordid origins of Ella's attitude towards Jim,

O'Neill, by some curious alchemical process transmuted her commonplace feelings into "genuine love." When Hattie expresses
justifiable skepticism — which, unfortunately, the audience shares
— after Jim relates the facts of his first year of marriage — how he
and Ella had lived like friends, like a brother and sister — her
doubts are too easily dispelled by Jim's insistence that Ella would
not be suffering were she not in love with him. That she is suffering is abundantly evident, but that she loves Jim is less evident,
despite O'Neill's protestations. Indeed, the best case that he can
establish for the depth and integrity of Ella's love appears in the
second scene of the second act, when Jim explains to Hattie why he
cannot leave his deranged wife:

I can't leave her. She can't leave me. And there's a million little reasons
combining to make one big reason why we can't. (*A pause*) For her sake —
if it'd do her good — I'd go — I'd leave — I'd do anything — because I
love her. I'd kill myself even — jump out of the window this second — I've
thought it over, too — but that'd only make matters worse for her. I'm
all she's got in the world! Yes, that isn't bragging or fooling myself. I know
that for a fact! Don't you know that's true?

Hattie's reply is a *non sequitur:* "Yes, I know she loves you, Jim. I
know that now." Tawdry and unconvincing as Ella's passion is, it
facilitates the shifting of the tragedy from an exclusively naturalistic level to a somewhat more spiritual plane. Her disintegration
becomes, therefore, the end-result of a struggle more dignified than
that of a thoroughly vapid and vulgar creature. It becomes the
tragic consequence of the conflict within her soul of the powerful
emotions of love and hate.

It is a simpler matter to transmute the naturalistic compulsions
that attach Jim to Ella into motives sufficiently noble to deserve the
euphemistic term, love. For, whatever their origin, the qualities of
self-denial, tenderness, and faithfulness still may be passed for virtues despite the skepticism of the scientist and the scorn of the
Nietzschean. And these "virtues" Jim possesses in excess. One is
permitted to forget, as the play progresses, that they are merely
symptoms of an "inferiority complex," the effects of years that a
race had spent in slavery. Since, in his anatomy of love, O'Neill
ignored the matter of sex, and since he made no subsequent reference to the etiology of Jim's aberration, we may surmise that he

intended to find a place for the heart, that he wished to transform the internal and the external necessities, of which the love of Ella and Jim is compounded, into the heart's need.

This dubious triumph over the "animal cravings and impulses" of the hero and heroine was accompanied, as we have already intimated, by a rejection of the idea of atavism as it was employed in *The Emperor Jones*. A journey down the subterranean stream of their racial past no longer brings the Negroes to voodooism and bestiality, but to something far more fair indeed. The hideous Congo witch doctor is transfigured into an image of beauty, the symbol of which is the Negro primitive mask from the Congo that adorns the Harris flat. To Ella, the mask is the embodiment of her fear and hatred of the Negro, since it symbolizes for her the threat to her feeling of "white superiority." O'Neill describes it as a *grotesque face, inspiring obscure, dim connotations in one's mind, but beautifully done, conceived in a true religious spirit.* When Hattie explains the mask to Ella as one "which used to be worn in religious ceremonies by my people in Africa," declaring that "it's beautifully made, a work of Art by a real artist — as real in his way as your Michael Angelo," Ella can only reply that it looks ugly and stupid to her. The intrinsic value of the Negro's primitive culture in terms of aesthetic impulse and religious spirit is recognized only by Hattie, a recognition which is objectified in the furnishings of the flat. In the room, there is conveyed a contrast between what is *cheaply ornate, naively, childishly gaudy* — the taste, that is, of the Negro who "aims to buy white" — and what is new and *severe to a point of somberness* — the product of Hattie's affirmation of the worth of her race's culture. Thus the symbol of the folly of "buying white" is the portrait of the elderly Negro who has an *able, shrewd face,* but who is clothed *in an out-landish lodge regalia, a get-up adorned with medals, sashes, a cocked hat with frills,* illustrating the vulgar practices of the American "joiner." Whereas the primitive mask is "a work of Art by a real artist," not a weird savage, a real artist who never had occasion to be contaminated by white American civilization.

Although O'Neill glorified the primitive, his hero finds salvation in the child. Jim has met defeat on every side: Ella's hatred and evil design have become apparent to him; he has proved incapable of "shielding her from evil and sorrow"; he has failed with finality to pass the examinations; above all, he has had to admit the futility of realizing on earth the ideals of equality and justice. At last he is prepared to acknowledge the presence in the universe of over-whelming evil. When Ella asks, *like a child,* whether God will forgive her, Jim replies, "Maybe He can forgive what you've done to me; and maybe He can forgive what I've done to you; but I don't see how He's going to forgive — Himself." Having uttered the blasphemy, Jim sobs pitifully and then is beyond tears. Where-upon the child-like Ella says *brightly:*

Well, it's all over, Jim. Everything'll be all right now. (*Chattering along*) I'll be just your little girl, Jim — and you'll be my little boy — just as we used to be, remember, when we were beaux; and I'll put shoe-blacking on my face and pretend you're white just as we used to do — and we can play marbles — only you mustn't all the time be a boy. Sometimes you must be my old kind Uncle Jim who's been with us for years and years. Will you, Jim?

Jim is utterly resigned, until Ella reminds him that he is all she has in the world and that she loves him. When she *kisses his hand as a child might, tenderly and gratefully,* he is deeply touched. He

suddenly throws himself on his knees and raises his shining eyes, his trans-figured face [and cries] Forgive me, God — and make me worthy! Now I see Your Light again! Now I hear Your Voice! (*He begins to weep in an ecstasy of religious humility*) Forgive me, God, for blaspheming You! Let this fire of burning suffering purify me of selfishness and make me worthy of the child You send me for the woman You take away!

Ella calls him to come and play. Jim, *still deeply exalted,* re-sponds, "Honey, Honey, I'll play right up to the gates of Heaven with you!" The curtain falls.

Out of the hopeless and horrifying spectacle of the broken mind, out of the psychologically convincing fact of Ella's regression to childhood, O'Neill abstracted the religious experience. Jim has not only consummated his mystical union with God, he has, by im-plication, recognized the truth of the Gospels: "Except ye be con-verted and become as little children, ye shall not enter the kingdom of heaven." When he offers to play right up to the gates of heaven with his child wife he is confident that she will be admitted. It is unlikely that even an apocalyptic fervor could have obscured from O'Neill, as it did from Jim, the irony of the situation, the implication that madness is a qualification for admission to heaven. But if the truth eluded him at the time, he compensated for the oversight two years later in *The Great God Brown*.

Children of Adam

RETURNING TO HARLEM in *All God's Chillun Got Wings*, O'Neill observed aspects of life among its inhabitants that could not have been apparent to him five years earlier at the time he wrote *The Dreamy Kid*. And when he revisited the New England farm in *Desire Under the Elms*, his sharpened perceptiveness disclosed to him a pulsating reality beneath appearances of rural life that he had depicted in *Beyond the Horizon*. In both instances his second look led to trouble with the censor, a New York District Attorney who tried unsuccessfully to stop the performance of both plays. Having objected to the representation on the stage of miscegenation — technically unconsummated though the deed was in O'Neill's play — he disapproved six months later of the assorted passions and crimes that he witnessed in *Desire Under the Elms*.

Going back to New England days when Thoreau and Emerson saw Paphlagonians in woodchoppers, Greeks in ploughboys, O'Neill perceived pagans in farmers. With a profounder "pantheistic sympathy" than that of the Concord pair, he recorded "the most terrible and most questionable qualities" of New England rural life — greed, lechery, incest, adultery, revenge, murder — declared them good, and sanctified them. *Desire Under the Elms* celebrates the divinity of nature, the triumph of pagan naturalism over indurated religion, the victory of mother and son over the father. All of the principal characters in the play "belong," for their unity with what Macgowan called "the dumb, mysterious processes of nature" is clearly established. Their relationship to the earth is more than reciprocal. Owning it, they are owned by it. Flowing and uniting with all natural objects, they display a process of merging that would have delighted Whitman. Reduced to animals, they possess a harmony with nature that would have been the envy of Yank, the enraged and frustrated anthropoid.

Neither self-conscious nor cosmic-conscious, the Cabots, father and sons, are animal-conscious. Like animals, much of the time they are "placid and self-contained." In the peaceful, final scene of *The Fountain* O'Neill introduced a portly monk whose *eyes* [had] *the opaque calm of a ruminating cow's.* In *Welded* he presented a stolid, bovine Woman who imparted wisdom and peace to the frenzied hero. And in plays subsequent to *Desire Under the Elms* he continued to represent attractive aspects of bovinity. In the present drama Eben Cabot, tormented, has the eyes of a wild animal in captivity. But at other times his behavior is that of a domesticated quadruped. Describing his experience with Min, "the Scarlet Woman," he proudly tells his two brothers how he "begun to beller like a calf." And that pair, as they go off to eat, make their exit by turning, *shouldering each other, their bodies bumping and rubbing together as they hurry clumsily to their food, like two friendly oxen toward their evening meal.* Their eating is as naturally unrestrained as that of *beasts of the field.* This is, perhaps, why "the cows knows us" "an' likes us," "an' the hosses, an' pigs, an' chickens." "They knows us like brothers — an' likes us," and why, after eighteen years, Simeon's memory of his dead wife is of her hair, "long's a hoss' tail — an yaller like gold." Although the father's relationship with his bovine sons is far from cordial, he is on the best of terms with the other livestock, whom he takes pleasure in visiting because "it's nice smellin' an' warm" with them, because in their company he finds rest and peace and understanding. One of the kindest remarks he makes to Eben is that, like the cows, Eben is queer. Seized by a desire to make love to his new wife, Ephraim, the father, borrows his metaphors from the Song of Solomon: "yer eyes air doves," he tells her, "yer two breasts air like two fawns."

Not only do the Cabots have an affinity and an identity with the animal kingdom, they are part of the earth. Simeon and Peter wear *thick-soled boots caked with earth. Their clothes, their faces, hands, bare arms and throats are earth-stained. They smell of earth.* Simeon *stamps his foot on the earth and addresses it desperately,* "Waal — ye've thirty year o'me buried in ye — spread out over ye

— blood an' bone an' sweat — rotted away — fertilizin' ye — richin' yer soul — prime manure, by God, that's what I been t'ye!" Narcissistically they remark that the scene about them is "Purty." Similarly, Ephraim is involved:

> When I came here fifty odd year ago — I was jest twenty an' the strongest an' hardest ye ever seen — ten times as strong an' fifty times as hard as Eben. Waal — this place was nothin' but fields o' stones. Folks laughed when I tuk it. They couldn't know what I knowed. When ye kin make corn sprout out o' stones, God's livin' in yew! They wa'n't strong enuf fur that! They reckoned God was easy. They laughed. They don't laugh no more. Some died here abouts. Some went West an' died. They're all under ground — fur hollerin' arter an easy God. God hain't easy. (*He shakes his head slowly*) An' I growed hard. Folks kept allus sayin' he's a hard man like 'twas sinful t' be hard, so's at last I said back at 'em: Waal then, by thunder, ye'll git me hard an' see how ye like it! . . . God's hard, not easy! God's in the stones! Build my church on a rock — out o' stones! an' I'll be in them! That's what he meant t' Peter! (*He sighs heavily — a pause*) Stones. I picked 'em up an' piled 'em into walls. Ye kin read the years of my life in them walls, every day a hefted stone, climbin' over the hills up and down, fencin' in the fields that was mine, whar I'd made thin's grow out o' nothin' — like the will o' God, like the servant o' His hand. It wa'n't easy. It was hard an' He made me hard for it.

Contented to be animals and creatures of earth, the sons are nevertheless resentful, because of the way in which their father drives them. He had slaved to death his second wife, Eben's "Maw," and, says Peter, "He's slaved himself t' death. He's slaved Sim 'n' me 'n' yew t' death — " "It's somethin' — drivin' him — t' drive us!" observes Simeon. They resent, moreover, the way in which Ephraim has fenced them in. With *sardonic bitterness* Peter complains: "Here — it's stones atop o' the ground — stones atop o' stones — makin' stone walls — year atop o' year — him 'n' yew 'n' me 'n' then Eben — makin' "stone walls fur him to fence us in!" "Stone atop o' stone," adds Eben, "makin' walls till yer heart's a stone ye heft up out o' the way o' growth onto a stone wall in yer heart!" "Something there is that doesn't love a wall." The sons' dislike at being driven, their hostility to walls of stone are aspects of their antagonism to the Old Testament God. The hard God is in the stones and in the father. Both are inimical to a free and peaceful animal existence.

To aggravate matters, the sons have discerned behind Ephraim's religious ardor his essentially animal nature. Simeon, *imitating his father's voice,* says, "I'm ridin' out t' learn God's message t' me in the spring like the prophets done," and then adds, "I'll bet right then an' thar he knew plumb well he was goin' whorin', the stinkin' old hypocrite!" Whatever the outward form of the old man's faith, his lasciviousness betrays him. He is more satyr than saint. Having "hitched up an druv off into the West," Ephraim remains away from the farm for two months. He returns from his sexual quest with his young third wife, Abbie, who, it soon becomes apparent, is the embodiment of a force that is more pervasive and potent than that which Jehovah exerts. Abbie, the incarnation of fertility and love is, like the Cabot men, part of the earth. Whereas Jehovah's symbol is the stones, that of Abbie is the elms — the tree being the primordial symbol of fecundity and maternity. We recognize the potency of her powers when she directs them at Eben:

> Abbie. Ye look all slicked up like a prize bull.
> Eben. (with a sneer) Waal — ye hain't so durned purty yerself, be ye? (*They stare into each other's eyes, his held by hers in spite of himself, hers glowingly possessive. Their physical attraction becomes a palpable force quivering in the hot air.*)
> Abbie. (*softly*) Ye don't mean that, Eben. Ye may think ye mean it, mebbe, but ye don't. Ye can't. It's agin nature, Eben. Ye been fightin' yer nature ever since the day I come — tryin' t' tell yerself I hain't purty t' ye. (*She laughs a low humid laugh without taking her eyes from his. A pause — her body squirms desirously — she murmurs languorously*) Hain't the sun strong an' hot? Ye kin feel it burnin' into the earth — Nature — makin' thin's grow — bigger 'n' bigger — burnin' inside ye — makin' ye want t' grow — into somethin' else — till ye're jined with it — an' it's your'n — but it owns ye, too — an' makes ye grow bigger — like a tree — like them elums — (*She laughs again softly, holding his eyes. He takes a step towards her, compelled against his will*) Nature'll beat ye, Eben. Ye might's well own up t' it fust 's last.

The irresistible Abbie is to be the means of Eben's liberation from a mother complex on the one hand and a tyrannical father on the other.

For if Ephraim is the embodiment of harsh paternity, if the cows talk to Cabot and Cabot talks to God, Eben is the victim of a sinister maternity and therefore talks to his mother although she is dead. He hates his father and prays for him to die. He is possessed by the memory of his mother. Abbie is to displace both parents and to satisfy all of Eben's biological and spiritual needs. Something of an earth spirit herself, she possesses the attributes which Eben admires in Min the prostitute, who is "like t' night . . . soft 'n' wa'm, her eyes kin wink like a star, her mouth's wa'm, her arms're wa'm, she smells like a wa'm plowed field . . ." Abbie is all this and more. She is not only a whore, she is the tender mother. To Ephraim she is the farm for which he has such deep affection: "Sometimes ye air the farm an' sometimes the farm be yew. That's why I clove t' ye in my lonesomeness . . . Me an' the farm has got t' beget a son!" But the son which she begets is Eben's whose possessiveness includes all of the property. By gaining possession of Abbie, Eben ensures his possession of the farm as well, the rights to the land having been previously asserted by his mother. In Part Two, Scene Three, the convergence of sex, tenderness, and acquisitiveness occurs:

Abbie. When I fust come in — in the dark — they seemed somethin' here.
Eben. (*simply*) Maw.
Abbie. I kin still feel — somethin'. . . .
Eben. It's Maw.
Abbie. At fust I was feered o' it. I wanted t' yell an' run. Now — since yew come — seems like it's growin' soft an' kind t' me. (*Addressing the air — queerly*) Thank yew.
Eben. Maw allus loved me.
Abbie. Mebbe it knows I love yew, too. Mebbe that makes it kind t' me.
Eben. (*dully*) I dunno. I should think she'd hate ye.
Abbie. (*with certainty*) No. I kin feel it don't — not no more.
Eben. Hate ye fur stealin' her place — here in her hum — settin' in her parlor whar she was laid — (*He suddenly stops, staring stupidly before him.*)
Abbie. What is it, Eben?
Eben. (*in a whisper*) Seems like Maw didn't want me t' remind ye.
Abbie. (*excitedly*) I knowed, Eben! It's kind t' me! It don't b'ar me no grudges fur what I never knowed an' couldn't help!
Eben. Maw b'ars him a grudge.
Abbie. Waal, so does all o' us.
Eben. Ay-eh. (*With passion*) I does, by God!
Abbie. (*taking one of his hands in hers and patting it*) Thar! Don't git riled thinkin' o' him. Think o' yer Maw who's kind t' us. Tell me about yer Maw, Eben.
Eben. They hain't nothin' much. She was kind. She was good.
Abbie. (*putting one arm over his shoulder. He does not seem to notice — passionately*) I'll be kind an' good t' ye.
Eben. Sometimes she used t' sing fur me.

Abbie. I'll sing fur ye!

Eben. This was her hum. This was her farm.

Abbie. This is my hum. This is my farm.

Eben. He married her t' steal 'em. She was soft an' easy. He couldn't 'preciate her.

Abbie. He can't 'preciate me!

Eben. He murdered her with his hardness.

Abbie. He's murderin' me!

Eben. She died (*A pause*) Sometimes she used to sing fur me. (*He bursts into a fit of sobbing.*)

Abbie. (*both her arms around him — with wild passion*) I'll sing fur ye! I'll die fur ye! (*In spite of her overwhelming desire for him, there is a sincere maternal love in her manner and voice — a horribly frank mixture of lust and mother love*) Don't cry, Eben! I'll take yer Maw's place! I'll be everythin' she was t' ye — an' ye kin kiss me back 's if yew was my son — my boy — sayin' good-night t' me. Kiss me, Eben.

Then the restrained kissing of mother and son gives way to lustful wild passion, and Abbie pleadingly explains to Eben, who is stricken with terror, that "lovin' like a Maw hain't enuf." To be happy they must love "much more — a hundred times more." Whereupon he dutifully inquires of his mother, whose presence he feels in the room, what he should do about this imminent usurpation of her position. His face suddenly lights up *with a fierce triumphant grin,* and he cries, "I see it! I see why. It's her vengeance on him — so's she kin rest quiet in her grave!" The next morning he announces *with a strange look,* "Maw's gone back t' her grave. She kin sleep now." And Eben, too, should be at peace now, having released his "libidinal desires from his mother." But it is ironical that in freeing himself from his Oedipus complex he should have transferred his love to his stepmother. The father still threatens him.

When Ephraim persuades Eben that Abbie has betrayed him, that she had the child in order to inherit the farm, the son grapples with the father in a *murderous struggle* and is thrown to the earth. *Between sobs and gasps* he accuses Abbie of being "a damn trickin' whore," threatens to go to California and to get his revenge by praying "t' Maw t' come back t' help me — t' put her curse on yew an' him!" But when Abbie vindicates herself by smothering the baby, Eben, moved by this evidence of her love, selflessly insists upon sharing her guilt — a gesture which elicits grudging admira-

tion even from the father. "Purty good — fur yew!" declares
Ephraim. Having loved not wisely but too well, the lovers must pay
a penalty, their crime being infanticide. As for adultery and incest,
these offenses they refuse to recognize. "I don't repent that sin!"
cries Abbie, *lifting her head as if defying God*. "I hain't askin' God
t' fergive that!" "Nor me — " adds Eben. As they are led off to jail
they stop to kiss, to reaffirm their love, to admire the sunrise, and
then, as the curtain falls, to look up *raptly in attitudes aloof and
devout*. Thus, ecstatic yea-saying has transformed their rapacious-
ness, cunning, violence into rapturous and unquestioning devotion.
Burning with desire, panting like two animals, Eben and Abbie,
once their passion is consummated, are converted into self-sacri-
ficing lover and tender, forbearing mistress.

On the surface O'Neill's tragedy resembles certain other plays
modern and ancient. Sidney Howard's *They Knew What They
Wanted,* produced in 1924, dramatized the situation of a younger
woman married to an older man, and the consequences: adultery,
an illegitimate child, regeneration, forgiveness. In 1920 the Theatre
Guild had staged *The Power of Darkness*. Written in 1886, Tolstoy's play contained motifs of adultery, incest, homicide, infanticide — a tragic situation that was resolved by confession and
repentance. *Desire Under the Elms,* with its symbolism and its
non-Christian ethic, differs radically from both of the foregoing
plays. Similar qualities distinguish it from *The Hippolytus* of
Euripides wherein the over-powering love of the heroine for her
step-son was not only unreciprocated, but was as abhorrent to her
as it was to him. And if O'Neill's play has a kinship with *Oedipus,*
it is with the complex rather than *Rex*.

Before 1924, familial relationships in the dramas of O'Neill were
seldom cordial or affectionate, but the usual variety of family discord was that which obtained between husband and wife. In
Desire Under the Elms appears for the first time an example of
the bitter hatred that exists between father and son, an enmity
which persisted until *Ah, Wilderness!* That this relationship had
appeared in literature before Freud had called attention to it, is,
of course, recognized, but never in pre-Freudian days had the
motif appeared with such grim regularity as it had since about

1910, when Freud was beginning to receive the attention of the layman as well as of the psychiatrist. It is impossible to determine whether O'Neill's inhibitions were suddenly removed so that he dared to hold the mirror up to his own inner life; whether he picked up the idea directly from Freud's works; whether it reached him circuitously through such foreign novels as *Sons and Lovers* (1913) or from the German Expressionistic drama which ran its course between 1910 and 1924 and wherein the father-son motif "plays a specially important role"; or whether, like many persons of the 1920's, he simply soaked up such psychological commonplaces.

To anyone who was concerned, as O'Neill surely was, with Greek tragedy and the nature of religion, the theories of both Freud and Jung should have been of inestimable interest. In *Totem and Taboo* — published 1912, translated 1918 — Freud speculated on the origins of religion and morality. Reconstructing the conditions of the primal horde, he described a rebellion of the sons against the violent primal father who stood in the way of their sexual demands and of their desire for power. It was evident to Freud that after the idea of god appeared he was "in every case modelled after the father and that our personal relation to god is dependent upon our relation to our physical father, fluctuating and changing with him, and that god at bottom is nothing but an exalted father." The revolt was not Satan's but the son's, that is, Christ's. For he was related to earlier conceptions of gods who had "enjoyed the favours of maternal deities and committed incest with the mother in defiance of the father, finally murdering the latter. But the slaying of the father left its mark, and here is where religion and morality began." Hating their father, the sons also loved and admired him. O'Neill, dramatizing the hostility of sons for fathers, saw no evidence of ambivalent feeling and therefore no cause for remorse, guilt, redemption. Indeed, the Cabot boys never even kill the father; but their resentment, their threats, their overt acts are those of the primal horde. They detest him for his power, for his demonstrable priority in conquest of women, threatening to rape his "new woman." They wish him dead, a desire that for an instant appears to be fulfilled when Abbie informs Eben that she has killed "him." Under a misapprehension, Eben *savagely* cries, "An' serves him right!" But like the stones, the father, as O'Neill saw it, is indestructible. And he is to haunt the heroes and heroines of most of the plays to come.

Eben Cabot's repeated plaintive appeal to his Maw is the earliest indication that O'Neill was to enlist the services of the Mother in the struggle against the Father and against God. In this project Jung, among others, seems to have been especially helpful. If the Swiss psychiatrist incurred the deep displeasure of Freud, he earned the gratitude of such people as assert the coexistence, if not the pre-eminence, of the spirit. Instinct and spirit he found equally mysterious and expressed their ineffableness in symbol, in allegorical language. For these reasons in general his theories were perhaps attractive to O'Neill; but his assignment of the predominant role in the instinctual and spiritual world to the mother rather than to the father should have been particularly appealing. "The most immediate primordial image," Jung declared, "is the mother,"

for she is in every way the nearest and most powerful experience; and the one moreover that occurs in the most impressionable period of a man's life. Since the conscious is as yet only weakly developed in childhood, one cannot speak of an individual experience at all. The mother, however, is an archetypal experience; she is known by the more or less unconscious child not as a definite, individual feminine personality, but as the mother, an archetype loaded with significant possibilities. As life proceeds the primordial image fades, and is replaced by a conscious, relatively individual image, which is assumed to be the only mother-image we have. In the unconscious, on the contrary, the mother always remains a powerful primordial image, determining and colouring in the individual conscious life our relation to woman, to society, and to the world of feeling and fact, yet in so subtle a way that, as a rule, there is no conscious perception of the process.

The dementia praecox patient who "seeks to leave the world and to regain the subjectivity of childhood," the universal "secret longing for the maternal depths," the "childish longing for the food-giving mother," the marrying of a woman who resembles the mother, personifications like Mother Germania, mother earth, mother nature, *mater ecclesia* — these are all signs to Jung of the presence of a universal wish to enter the mother's womb a second time and be born again.

Life of a Salesman

HAVING SOJOURNED in the Dionysian depths in *Desire Under the Elms,* O'Neill emerged, never to find the way back again — a misfortune which he lamented in *The Great God Brown* and *Lazarus Laughed.* Meanwhile, however, he wrote *Marco Millions* wherein he chronicled the tragic defeat of another variety of paganism. Conceived even before he had written *The Fountain, Marco Millions* was completed in 1925, the year in which the former was produced. The Theatre Guild, having turned down *The Fountain,* undertook the production in 1928 of *Marco Millions,* an equally costly enterprise but a slightly better risk. The play was inspired, according to George Jean Nathan, by Otto Kahn who had asked O'Neill to write a work that glorified the American businessman. "His answer," reported Nathan, "was to write *Marco Millions,* the sourest and most magnificent poke in the jaw that American big business and the American business man have ever got." While accepting the legend, one may reject the verdict. Sharper blows had been landed by Lewis in *Babbitt,* by Kaufman and Connelly in *Beggar on Horseback.* Bristling with moral indignation, armed with irony, O'Neill dissipated the force of his attack by persisting to gratify tendencies that are inimical to satire: sentimentalism, pathos, romance. Dedicated as he was to deal earnestly with religious matters, he encumbered the satire with excessive illustrations of Oriental wisdom and spirituality.

The ambiguity of *Marco Millions* might be attributed to shifting circumstances during the four years in which O'Neill appears intermittently to have worked on the play. Lured ever since 1918 by the "mystery and spell of the East," he provided Juan Ponce de Leon with the same susceptibility. After Juan finally acknowledged the vanity of empire and began to dread the encroachments of old age he longed for Cathay where there is "a spot that Nature has set apart from men and blessed with peace . . . a sacred grove where all things live in the old harmony they knew before man came."

Lusting for loot, Juan's fellow-travelers were eager to go to "Marco Polo's land," as they called it, because of the "golden cities." If the fifteenth-century Spaniard never reached China by sea, the thirteenth-century Venetian made it by land, his journey being recorded in *The Travels of Marco Polo*. Translated into English in 1818, *The Travels* was readily obtainable in Everyman's Library. Then Manuel Komroff, an habitué of the Provincetown Playhouse, feeling that a more readable and accurate text was needed, selected and adapted what he thought was best in two nineteenth-century translations of the work and published his edition of *The Travels of Marco Polo* in 1926. In the introduction Komroff pointed out that after death Marco Polo became for the incredulous Venetians the personification of exaggeration and falsehood and was represented as a comic figure at their carnivals, a clown known as "Marco of the Millions."

In 1921 Donn Byrne published his Sino-Celtic romance, *Messer Marco Polo,* a tender, sentimental love story, permeated by a gentle paganism, and widely read. There was no precedent in *The Travels* for Byrne's characterization of either his hero or his heroine or for the romantic plot. His Marco Polo is not only uninterested in barter, he gives up God and Venice for love. Having fallen in love with Golden Bells, daughter of the great Khan, he marries her. She, rather than Kogatin who is mentioned only briefly in *The Travels,* appears to have been the prototype of O'Neill's heroine, Kukachin. Marco Polo is loved by the princess in both novel and play but not in *The Travels*. As for O'Neill's Marco — a fool preoccupied only with trade, lusting for loot not love — he was conceived in the traveler's posthumous image.

Although Marco Polo's actual career was as inherently romantic and heroic as Juan Ponce de Leon's, O'Neill chose to emphasize the man's subsequent unjust reputation. Yet in other respects the play which he wrote about Marco resembles the one about Juan. He again depicted the antithetical ways of life, the evils of Western civilization as opposed to the virtues of paganism. Apart from the satire the tone once again is romantic, spiritual, tragic. And, as in *The Fountain,* he indulged his taste for voluptuous theatricalism: for pageantry, tableau, multiplicity of elaborate scene, crowds, songs, rhetorical language. All of which suggest that O'Neill originally

intended to make *Marco Millions* a sequel to *The Fountain;* that
he later introduced the incongruous satire either to diverge from
Byrne's novel or to respond negatively, perhaps impulsively, to
Otto Kahn's suggestion. Whatever the cause, *Marco Millions* is a
potpourri of *The Travels of Marco Polo, Messer Marco Polo, The
Fountain,* and even *Babbitt.*

Like the younger Juan Ponce de Leon, Marco Polo at fifteen —
when we first meet him — is endowed with two personalities. He,
too, is an ambitious thinker and a romantic dreamer, a rudimentary
businessman and a young poet-lover. Uncorrupted as yet by the
merchants of Venice, he is youthfully handsome, displaying a quality of adolescent charm that we are not to encounter again till
Ah, Wilderness! But unlike Juan's, Marco's two selves seldom clash.
Capable of tender love, he nevertheless is aware that marriage must
have a practical end. A dreamer, he is also "surprisingly quick at
figures." A poet, his verses abound with allusions to material
wealth. Soon the shades of the counting-house begin to close upon
the growing boy. Within three years, before the end of Act One,
Marco has lost his soul, whereas it took Juan twenty years to discover that he had one. After Marco's complete degradation the
dichotomy of dreamer-thinker, poet-businessman, spirit-flesh, is
maintained, not in terms of dissociated personalities, but in terms of
a divided world. O'Neill contrasted the spirituality of the Pope with
the crassness of the merchant, the beauty and wisdom of the East
with the sordidness and stupidity of the West, the perfection of
nature which obtains among pagans with the nastiness and greediness which has possessed civilized man.

By the time Marco reaches China his mortal soul has apparently
been completely destroyed by his acquisitive instinct, and with it
all impulses towards innocent love and the writing of poetry. His
soul's evanescence is depicted in three stylized travel scenes in
which he progressively approaches manhood and China. In the first
of these — Act One, Scene Three — the setting reveals a Mahometan mosque.

*Before the mosque is a throne on which sits a Mahometan ruler. On the
right, the inevitable warrior — on his left, the inevitable priest — the two de-
fenders of the State. At the ruler's feet his wives crouch like slaves. Every-*

thing is jewelled, high-colored, gorgeous in this background. Squatted against the side walls, forming a sort of semi-circle with the throne at center, counting from left to right consecutively, are a mother nursing a baby, two children playing a game, a young girl and a young man in a loving embrace, a middle-aged couple, an aged couple, a coffin. All these Mahometan figures remain motionless.

Full of curiosity and wonder, Marco detaches himself from his father and his uncle, who are engaged in exchanging traveling salesman jokes with some Mahometan merchants, and gazes at *this strange life*. It is a scene which symbolizes all of existence from the cradle to the grave, and the boy's response proves that his soul is not yet lost. For he smiles tenderly at the baby, he is fascinated and stirred by the lovers, curious about the aged couple, in awe of the coffin. With the entrance of the half-naked and alluring prostitute who *smiles at Marco enticingly* and offers herself to him without charge, we have further evidence that cynicism and acquisitiveness have not as yet possessed him entirely; for he rejects the woman's offer, neglecting to grasp a bargain when he sees one. Although the harlot is endowed with qualities of spirituality and wisdom, her virtues are not appreciated as were those of the Woman in *Welded*. Her function in *Marco Millions* is rather to emphasize the materialism and the obtuseness of the merchant class, which is blind to the simple truth that O'Neill has her utter: "Money isn't everything, not always."

In the next scene Marco is seventeen and has lost some of the *freshness of youth*. Glancing about *with a forced scorn* at the scene which *is the exact duplicate of the last except that here the locale is Indian,* he looks at the people *with the casual, indifferent attitude of the worldly-wise*. Towards the living he is contemptuous and impudent, but he *obviously averts his head from the coffin*. Some sensibility remains. When the ubiquitous prostitute appears, he kisses her, but only to win a wager. Having done so he is *genuinely overcome by a sudden shame*. Moved to pity, he exclaims, "It's too bad she's — what she is." Whereupon his uncle advises him not to waste pity, reminds him that "Her kind are necessary evils," that "All of us are human." In contrast to this insensitive attitude is that of a Buddhist merchant who reveals the moral superiority of his religion:

The Buddha taught that one's loving-kindness should embrace all forms of life, that one's compassion should suffer with the suffering, that one's sympathy should understand all things, and last that one's judgment should regard all persons and things as of equal importance.

To which Maffeo Polo contemptuously replies, "They're all crazy, like the Mahometans. They're not responsible." But Marco is not so sure. He had watched a middle-aged couple eating a bowl of rice and had been struck with this *evidence of a humanity common with his*. As the scene ends he declares, "I saw two of them with a bowl of rice — ."

To lose these last traces of compassion requires only a year. Outside the Great Wall of China in the next scene Marco, nearly eighteen, is *a brash, self-confident young man, assertive and talky*. It is he now who exchanges dirty jokes with other merchants. And his relations with the prostitute are on a business-like basis. Not only has she got all of his money, she has stolen the locket which contains Donata's picture and the crumpled paper upon which he had written his poem three years earlier. She unfolds the paper, reads a stanza, and laughs, "Are you a poet, too?" *Abashed and furious,* he denies having written it. The woman exclaims:

You're lying. You must have. Why deny it? Don't sell your soul for nothing. That's bad business. (*She laughs, waving the poem in her upraised hand, staring mockingly*) Going! Going! Gone! (*She lets it fall and grinds it under her feet into the earth — laughing*) Your soul! Dead and buried! You strong man! (*She laughs*)

Symbol of the soulless West, he enters into China, into the palace of Kublai, the Great Kaan. Thenceforth the play depicts the two extremes of culture. Kublai

is a man of sixty but still in the full prime of his powers, his face proud and noble, his expression tinged with an ironic humor and bitterness yet full of a sympathetic humanity. In his person are combined the conquering indomitable force of a descendant of Chinghiz with the humanizing culture of the conquered Chinese who have already begun to absorb their conquerors.

But Marco is to be one conqueror whom they do not absorb. His presence among them is to prove catastrophic. For, during the succeeding fifteen years he brings tragedy to the royal family, turmoil to the nation. The Pope had foreseen these consequences but, in despair at stemming the rising tide of acquisitive and destructive materialism, stood by while it flowed over the Eastern world as it had over the Western. To him the Polos had conveyed the Kaan's request for a hundred wise men to argue with the latter's "Buddhists and Taoists and Confucians which religion in the world is best." Revealing a singularly defeated attitude, the Pope announced *sardonically* that he had "no hundred wise men — nor one! Tell the Great Kaan he must have been imposed upon by your patriotic lies, or he could never make such a request." Marco's presence, he decided with *a sudden whimsicality,* would be more instructive:

Let him set an example of virtuous Western manhood amid all the levities of paganism, shun the frailty of poetry, have a million to his credit, as he so beautifully phrased it, and I will wager a million of something or other myself that the Kaan will soon be driven to seek spiritual salvation somewhere! Mark my words, Marco will be worth a million wise men — in the cause of wisdom!

In his bitterness and helplessness His Holiness had expressed little indignation. Instead, he had been resigned, amused, sardonic, whimsical. This is precisely the attitude of Kublai Kaan and his adviser, Chu-Yin, after Marco arrives in China. Kublai, as wise as the Pope, quickly apprehends the Pope's motive in sending Marco in place of the wise men. "Did their Pope mean that a fool is a wiser study for a ruler than a hundred wise men could be?" he asks Chu-Yin. "This Marco touches me, as a child might, but at the same time there is something warped, deformed — Tell me, what shall I do with him?" When Chu-Yin suggests that Marco be permitted to "develop according to his own inclination," that he be observed in order that "at least, if he cannot learn, we shall," Kublai agrees, saying, "Yes. And be amused." This, to be sure, is foolish advice, and much too dear a price is to be paid for wisdom and amusement. Kublai has after all recognized Marco for what he is — an evil thing, not only a child, but "something warped and deformed." To anticipate entertainment from such a creature is to reveal a fundamental defect in his own character. But for the sake of the plot and of recorded history, Marco remains in China for fifteen years. Kublai — a wise man, a stern and efficient ruler — sits quietly by while the Venetian merchant destroys everything with which he comes in contact. As Kublai calmly observes the "nastiness and greediness of the sordid brute" he jeopardizes all that he holds dear. If the Pope, in his part of the world, was impotent to stop the vicious mischief, the Kaan in his is surely capable of preventing it. Never for an instant does he have any illusions about Marco. Tolerating his presence in China to facilitate O'Neill's bitter indictment of "our Christian civilization," Kublai functions as an exemplar of that perfection of nature which obtains among pagans, as detached commentator upon the behavior of the Western barbarian, as eventual victim of the tragic fate which he himself invited.

O'Neill's hatred and contempt for his native culture is conveyed through a paucity of wit but a wealth of ridicule and irony. He attacks first of all Marco's outrageous pride, his presumption in assuming that he is distinguishable from any other beast. "Well, I'm not an animal, am I?" he asks. "That's certainly plain enough. (*Then proudly*) No sir! I'm a man made by Almighty God in His Own Image for His Greater Glory!" "So you are the Image of God!" Kublai exclaims *ecstatically*. "There is certainly something about you, something complete and unanswerable — ." O'Neill suggested in the tableau scenes which depicted the journey to the East that Marco experienced intimations of mortality. He shuddered and shrank as he gazed upon the coffin. But his arrogance at last has overcome his squeamishness. Fortified by a false and foolish faith in the immortality of his soul, despite his possession of no soul whatever, he now cannot imagine his own death. Yet he trembles when Kublai threatens him with death, which is evidence enough to Kublai that Marco's "soul is a stupid invention of [his] fear," that when he dies he "will be dead as a dead dog is dead — "

After fifteen years in China it is still evident that Marco has no soul. In its place is "only an acquisitive instinct." At last Kublai has begun to weary of "his grotesque antics."

A jester inspires mirth [he observes] only so long as his deformity does not revolt one. Marco's spiritual hump begins to disgust me . . . We have given him every opportunity to learn. He has memorized everything and learned nothing. He has looked at everything and seen nothing. He has lusted for everything and loved nothing. He is only a shrewd and crafty greed. I shall send him home to his native wallow.

Chu-Yin relates how Marco has presumed to impose his tawdry culture upon one Chinese community:

I talked recently with a poet who had fled from [Yang-Chau, a city where Marco has been mayor] in horror. Yang-Chau used to have a soul, he said. Now it has a brand new Court House. And another, a man of wide culture, told me, our Christian mayor is exterminating our pleasures and our rats as if they were twin breeds of vermin!

Although Marco was born too soon to defend the evangelical church as did Babbitt, he still can join Lewis's hero in supporting the state, "domestic brightness and sound business." Like Babbitt he is a "hustler," a joiner, a booster, a political-economic-social reactionary. But unlike Lewis's character, he is the embodiment of vast and destructive evil. For he possesses power. A "child-actor," a "clown," wearer of *childishly fantastic regalia,* he personifies all that is bizarre and stupid among the American philistines. He displays at the same time the *manner and appearance* of a successful movie star at a *masquerade ball* and the *grave responsible expression of a Senator from the South of the United States of America.* The reforms which he has introduced are those which Babbitt would enthusiastically endorse: the removal of taxes upon excess profits, upon luxuries; the levying of taxes upon necessities; the passing of laws making interference with culture subject to fine, sending to jail anyone who is unhappy. Citizens in the community who complain, he calls radicals, malcontents, and prohibits all free expression of opinion as treasonous. He appoints hundreds of committees to carry on his work, that he might "retire confident that with the system [he has] instituted everything will go on automatically and brains are no longer needed." Having described his political and administrative innovations, Marco then announces his two supreme contributions to Eastern culture, the most diabolical of all: paper money and cannon. "You conquer the world with this — and you pay for it with this. You become the bringer of peace on earth and good-will to men, and it doesn't cost you a yen hardly."

Gradually O'Neill transforms his Babbitt-like creature, his child-actor, his clown, into a personification of the corruption and depravity of the human race. Marco, no longer a mere merchant of Venice, symbol of middle-class America, becomes the misanthropic embodiment of O'Neill's utter contempt for his fellow man, a Yahoo among Houyhnhnms. Differing from Swift's vile animal chiefly in pretending to the practice of Christian virtues, rather than to reason, Marco shares with the Yahoo the ultimate vice, pride. Like Gulliver, when Kublai beholds a "lump of deformity . . . smitten with pride, it immediately breaks all the measures of his patience." For the noble Kaan, "endowed by nature with a general disposition to all virtues" — particularly that of humility —, never forgets Marco's proud boast that he was made in the image of God. Now, fifteen years later, after the Venetian has demonstrated his innovations and contributions, Kublai solemnly reminds him, "You haven't yet proved you have an immortal soul!" "It doesn't need proving," Marco replies; but when pressed to bring forward one reliable witness, he suggests his father and his uncle. These the Chinese rejects, for "their evidence is prejudiced." *Worried now,* Marco looks *hopefully* at Chu-Yin for support. But the sage only smiles and says cryptically, "I believe that what can be proven cannot be true." Wherefore Marco *stands puzzled, irritated, looking stubborn, frightened and foolish.*

At precisely this point O'Neill's play shifts its emphasis from moral satire to romantic tragedy. It is ironically tragic that Kukachin, the Kaan's granddaughter should fall in love with perhaps the most disagreeable character in all of O'Neill's plays. *A beautiful young girl of twenty, pale and delicate,* she has loved Marco for a long time — not for the dangers he had passed, but because he has been a "strange, mysterious dream-knight from the exotic West, an enigma with something about him of a likable boy who brought her home each time a humble, foolish, touching little gift!" Incredulous, Kublai asks Chu-Yin how one can "deal seriously with such a child-actor." To which the adviser replies, "Most women, including Kukachin, love children — and all women must take acting seriously in order to love at all." Chu-Yin, long suspecting the girl's infatuation for the "dolt," has been reconciled, because he felt some good might come of it. "An enchanted moment" for the princess, it would "remain," he thought, "a poignant memory to recompense her when she is no longer a girl but merely a Queen." As for Marco, some day he "may see into her eyes and his soul may be born." Now, blinded and deceived by romantic love, Kukachin

is convinced that, contrary to her grandfather's and Chu-Yin's conviction, Marco has a soul. She speaks up as he stands helplessly
before the court. "How can you know, Princess?" asks Kublai. And
she replies:

Because I have seen it — once, when he bound up my dog's leg, once when
he played with a slave's baby, once when he listened to music over water and
I heard him sigh, once when he looked at sunrise, another time at sunset,
another at the stars, another at the moon, and each time he said that Nature
was wonderful. And all the while, whenever he has been with me I have
always felt — something strange and different — and that something must
be His Honor's soul, must it not?

With wondering bitterness Kublai says, "The eye sees only its own
sight," and adds mockingly but sadly, "I cannot contest the profound intuitions of virgins and mystics." Nor, apparently, can
O'Neill. For, despite the unalterable case made against him on all
sides, Marco is still unaccountably endowed with certain virtues.
These appear incongruously and unexpectedly for the purpose, presumably, of developing the episodes of romantic love. Chu-Yin, to
be sure, had hoped that Marco's soul might be born as he looked
into Kukachin's eyes. And as she bears witness that he has a soul,
Chu-Yin observes that "a woman may feel life in the unborn."
Thus, Marco can still be moved by poetry — although he feels foolish for being moved. More than this, he displays clear signs of
being an heroic figure. Not only is he a competent sailor, but, like
Juan Ponce de Leon, he is a brave warrior. When pirates attack,
his "brave sword warded off their curved knives from [Kukachin's]
breast and struck them dead at [her] feet." What is more, when
she is swept from the deck of the royal junk during a typhoon,
Marco rescues her. Tenderness, too, seems now to be one of his
virtues. He tends the Princess night and day as the fever wastes
her, and brews medicines that bring her back to life. If all of this
has been accomplished through devotion to duty rather than for
love, still Marco's increasing stature cannot be reconciled with his
earlier vile and groveling condition. At last satire and tragedy clash
in a burlesque episode. Kukachin, having expressed a longing to
die, solicits Marco's concern.

Marco. (*worriedly, suddenly reaches out and takes her hand*) Here now,
young lady! Don't start getting morbid!

Kukachin. (*with a thrill of love*) Marco!

Marco. I believe you're feverish. Let me feel your pulse!

Kukachin. (*violently*) No! (*She draws her hand from his as if she had been stung.*)

Marco. (*worriedly*) Please don't be unreasonable. There'd be the devil to pay if you should suffer a relapse of that fever after I sweated blood to pull you through once already! Do you feel hot?

Kukachin. (*wildly*) No! Yes! On fire!

Marco. Are your feet cold?

Kukachin. No! Yes! I don't know! (*Gravely Marco kneels, removes a slipper, and feels the sole of her foot — then pats her foot playfully.*)

Marco. No. They're all right. (*He gets up — professionally*) Any cramps?

Kukachin. You fool! No! Yes! My heart feels as if it were bursting!

Marco. It burns?

Kukachin. Like a red ember flaring up for the last time before it chills into gray ash forever!

Marco. Then something must have disagreed with you. Will you let me see your tongue?

Kukachin. (*In a queer hysterical state where she delights in self-humiliation*) Yes! Yes! Anything! I am a Princess of the Imperial blood of Chinghiz and you are a dog! Anything! (*She sticks out her tongue, the tears streaming down her face as he looks at it.*)

Then she strives *pitifully to arouse his jealousy* by reminding Marco that she is soon to marry the ruler of Persia. "He shall look into my eyes and see that I am a woman and beautiful!" she says tauntingly. But Marco only replies, "That's a husband's privilege." "Or a man's — a man who has a soul!" continues Kukachin scornfully. Recalling now Chu-Yin's direction to Marco to look daily into her eyes and note what he sees there, she orders him now to fulfill the task. "See my eyes as those of a woman and not a Princess! Look deeply! I will die if you do not see what is there! (*She finishes hysterically and beseechingly.*)

Look! See! [she cries] (*She throws her head back, her arms outstretched. He bends over and looks into her eyes. She raises her hands slowly above his head as if she were going to pull it down to hers. Her lips part, her whole being strains out to him. He looks for a moment critically, then he grows tense, his face moves hypnotically toward hers, their lips seem about to meet in a kiss. She murmurs*) Marco!

Marco. (*his voice thrilling for this second with oblivious passion*) Kukachin!

The incredible birth of Marco's soul is aborted by Maffeo, who *suddenly slaps a stack of coins into the chest with a resounding clank* and calls "One million!" The spell is broken. Delivering Kukachin to the Khan of Persia, Marco sails on for Venice. In the following scene Kublai receives a message from the Princess announcing that "Death woos" her. She is to die "for love of a fool."

   Although Marco's soul had been "dead and buried when he was eighteen, although the notion that he differed from any other animal was regarded with the utmost scorn, although his condition was clearly that of a sheep and a swine, and although the woman who loved him finally admitted that he had no soul, O'Neill still felt impelled to incise the moral satire and probe the consciousness of his hero to see whether after all the soul whose death he had announced was really quite dead. He found evidence that it was not. For he continued to reveal glimpses of it in Marco's occasional flashes of sensibility and in his responsiveness to Nature. And the power of woman's love almost gave it a rebirth. The foregoing scene, with its distasteful mixture of pathos and low comedy, represents a point in O'Neill's drift away from naturalism to "supernaturalism," a drift which had begun in *The Hairy Ape*. Within the brute-hero of that play was an unfathomable region which O'Neill never quite dignified with the term soul. Discriminating among beasts, O'Neill saw that the hero of *Desire Under the Elms,* who was more of an ox than a human being, fared better in a spiritual way than either the ape or the swine. Because he lived in complete harmony with Nature, the existence of Eben Cabot's soul was never questioned. But the romantic love which Eben experienced must surely have refined and improved the soul which was tacitly there. If there is something to be said for O'Neill's concept from a theological point of view, there is much to be said against it from a literary and dramatic. The dissociation of dreamer and thinker had in itself caused little difficulty even as it moved from a psychological to a theological preoccupation. But to seek a reconciliation of the soul and the flesh, of the God-like and the beast-like in a play whose dominating tone is that of savage satire is to solve Swift's problem by suggesting that the Houyhnhnms intermarry with the Yahoos. On the other hand, if the play is not predominantly satire, then O'Neill erred in making his hero so swinish.

   To be sure, *Marco Millions* could just as well be regarded as tragedy, in which case Kublai Kaan, rather than Marco, would be the hero. Kublai, who elicits our sympathy, is a man of wisdom and dignity. Suffering as a tragic hero should, he utters frequent cries of affliction as befits his function, ponders the inscrutability of existence, capitulates to an evil fate which takes the form of Marco Polo, finds metaphysical and religious comfort at the end. Indeed, the play is as much concerned with his suffering as it is with Marco's folly. It opens with an elaborate prologue showing Kukachin's coffin being transported over the plains of Persia by thirty slaves. If the five first scenes and a portion of the fifth of Act One are Marco's, the first scene of Act Two establishes the tragic influence which Marco is to exert upon Kublai and his grand-daughter. In this scene, which occurs at *Xanadu, the City of Peace,* Kublai and Kukachin sadly discuss the unfortunate necessity of her coming departure from China to become Queen of Persia. His expression is *masklike, full of philosophic calm. Her air is grief-stricken.* In the garden is a flute player *playing a melancholy air* to which Kukachin recites a disconsolate verse in a low tone. *With deep emotion* Kublai informs her:

You have been a golden bird singing beside a black river. You took your mother's place in my heart when she died. I was younger then. The river was not so black — the river of man's life so deep and silent — flowing with an insane obsession — whither? — and why? (*Then suddenly forcing a smile*) Your poem has made me melancholy. And I am too old, if not too wise, to afford anything but optimism! (*Then sadly*) But now you in your turn must leave me, the river seems black indeed! (*Then after a pause — tenderly*) If it will make you unhappy, you need not marry Arghun Khan.

But Kukachin realizes that a refusal "might mean war." Anyway "Arghun is as acceptable as any other." At this point the touching scene is interrupted by the intrusion of the court fool, Marco. And after Kukachin reveals her fondness for the jester, the play resumes its satirical tone. The scene ends as Kukachin prevails upon her grandfather to permit Marco to command the fleet on her voyage to Persia. To Kublai now it is obvious that Kukachin has designs upon Marco. Wherefore, as the curtain falls he stares at them *with weary amazement* and utters a philosophical observation that is neither profound nor poetic: "Life is so stupid, it is mysterious!"

In the next scene, Act Two, Scene Two, Kublai and Kukachin again dominate the action as the curtain rises. Their separation is imminent and tearful. Kublai is willing to refuse her hand to Arghun even if it means war, and is capable, moreover, of keeping Marco in China if she wishes. *With calm sadness* she replies, "Do I want a slave?" Then *dreamily*, "I desire a captain of my ship on a long voyage in dangerous, enchanted seas." Seeing his grand-daughter thus beguiled of herself, Kublai cries *with a fierce defiance of fate*, "I am the Great Kaan! I shall have him killed!" Chu-Yin, who always remains close by and whose function is to expound Oriental truisms, exerts a soothing influence upon the wrathful protagonist who is thus vainly rebelling against fate. "The noble man ignores self," Chu-Yin *recites*, "The wise man ignores action. His truth acts without deeds. His knowledge venerates the unknowable. To him birth is not the beginning, nor is death the end." Hearing his adviser advocate a philosophy of passive resist-ance against fate, Kublai bends his head *in submission. Tenderly* he bids farewell to the Princess. "Live," he says. "There is no other advice possible from one human being to another." "Live — and love!" Kukachin adds. Kublai departs, but Chu-Yin remains to soothe Kukachin as he has Kublai with his wisdom. "A little sleep, Princess, and you will be beautiful," he teases. "The old dream passes. Sleep and awake in the new. Life is perhaps most wisely regarded as a bad dream between two awakenings, and every day is a life in miniature." *Wearily and drowsily* she says, "Your wis-dom makes me sleep." Whereupon she sleeps. Chu-Yin, after a pause, calls softly, "Kukachin! (*He sees she is asleep — chuckles*) I have won a convert. (*Then speculatively*) Youth needs so much sleep and age so little. Is that not a proof that from birth to death one grows steadily closer to complete life? Hum." (*He ponders on this*) Now the Polos sweep in, disrupting the peace of Kukachin's sleep and Chu-Yin's contemplation, symbolizing the disharmonious effect that their type has had upon a superior culture. In the fol-lowing scene Kukachin again holds the center of the stage, her personal tragedy being the central fact of the action. Her face is that *of a woman who has known real sorrow and suffering*. Rein-forcing the tragic effect is the chorus of sailors and of women who chant about the rigors of the sea voyage, of sorrow, marriage, and death. While this has been going on, the two elder Polos have been squatting in the foreground counting their gold coins, indifferent to the universalities of existence. As the chant ends, Kukachin *bows her head in resignation,* a stage direction that has a singular irrelevancy considering her hysterical behavior, her unabashed and persistent pursuit of the man she loves. Although O'Neill continually emphasizes her attitude of "resignation," of "fatalistic acceptance," of "submission," of "renunciation," seldom has a woman clung so tenaciously to a foolish hope, or rebelled so preposterously against her destiny.

In the third act the tragic resolution occurs. Kublai's evil destiny, the "greedy hypocrisy" of the West, is manifesting itself first in the corruption of Chinese morality — exemplified by the emergence of a warlike spirit that is motivated by imperialistic ambitions and promoted by means of patriotic cant — and second in the tragic disillusionment of both Kublai and his granddaughter. "What good are wise writings to fight stupidity?" Kublai asks. "One must have stupid writings that men can understand. In order to live even wisdom must be stupid." And Kukachin, convinced at last that Marco has no soul, is already possessed by Death. Learning of Kukachin's fate, Kublai, enraged, is determined to avenge her until Chu-Yin soothes him with wisdom. *His anger passing* Kublai says *wearily and bitterly:*

Rise, my old friend, it is I who should be at your feet, not you at mine! (*He sinks dejectedly on his throne again. After a pause, sadly*) She will die. Why is this? What purpose can it serve? My hideous suspicion is that God is only an infinite insane energy which creates and destroys without other purpose than to pass eternity in avoiding thought. Then the stupid man becomes the Perfect Incarnation of Omnipotence and the Polos are the true children of God! (*He laughs bitterly*) Ha! How long before we shall be permitted to die, my friend? I begin to resent life as the insult of an ignoble inferior with whom it is a degradation to fight!

He then gazes into his crystal, and on the forestage we watch the festivities in Venice which celebrate the return of the Polos, the "true children of God," of Marco, the "true ruler of the world." Having gazed *with fascinated disgust,* he turns away *with a shudder of loathing — and, in spite of himself, a shadow of a smile.* As the curtain falls he speaks *with a pitying scorn:* "The Word became their flesh, they say. Now all is flesh! And can their flesh become the Word again?"

The Pope's two-fold prediction, made on the eve of the Polos' departure for the East, has been fulfilled. The Kaan has been "driven to seek spiritual salvation somewhere." And Marco has been "worth a million wise men — in the cause of wisdom!" Arriving at Xanadu, Marco confidently proclaimed that he was made in the image of God, an absurdity which provoked in Kublai condescending amusement. But irony changed to pessimism as Kublai became wiser; for he has realized at last that Marco was right. The mad world which God created — without purpose and meaning, in which evil is rewarded, virtue and wisdom punished — is evidence that God is only an "infinite insane energy." Marco, indeed, reflects His image. Burdened now with *weariness and disbelief,* Kublai seeks spiritual salvation in the last scene of the play — and finds it in a profusion of light and color, sound and smell, of song, dance, prayer, and masks — a lavish spectacle whose pretext is the funeral of Kukachin. Intended to represent a great up-welling of the religious spirit, it reveals instead precisely that taste for gaudy display which the "substantial bourgeois" exhibited in Venice upon the homecoming of the newly rich Polos. Kukachin's return to her people is marked by a voluptuousness — sad though it is meant to be — which destroys much of the contrast that O'Neill wished to emphasize between the two homecoming scenes. This elaborate solemnity is his method of celebrating a great awakening, of driving home the truth of a newly discovered non-Christian conception.

Appropriately enough, the theme of the pageantry is death, the continual apprehension of which is to be responsible for an increasing depression of spirit in most of O'Neill's tragedies from now on. Like Juan Ponce de Leon, Kublai is concerned with the question of "what is left when Death makes the hand powerless." And, as in *The Fountain,* four priests, symbolizing four great religions, are summoned and dismissed to indicate that all other faiths vanish in the presence of the larger and deeper truth that O'Neill found. Kublai asks the four priests — Taoist, Confucianist, Buddhist, Islamic — whether they have discovered how to conquer death. Sadly, submissively, fatalistically, each in turn can only reply that "Death is." Dissatisfied with this response, Kublai rises to his feet and, *with overstressed arrogance,* cries:

I am the Great Kaan!

(*Everyone in the room rises with one motion of assertion*)

Chorus. (*accompanied by a clangor of brass from the musicians — recite with discordant vigor*)

> Greatest of the Great!
> Son of Heaven!
> Lord of Earth!
> Sovereign of the World!
> Ruler over Life and Death!

Kublai. (*silences them by an imperious gesture — and now even the great palace bell is stilled — halfmockingly but assertively*) The Son of Heaven? Then I should know a prayer. Sovereign of the World? Then I command the World to pray! (*With one motion all sink to the position of prayer*) In silence! Prayer is beyond words! Contemplate the eternal life of Life! Pray thus! (*He himself sinks to the position of prayer — a pause — then slowly*) In silence — for one concentrated moment — be proud of life! Know in your heart that the living of life can be noble! Know that the dying of death can be noble! Be exalted by life! Be inspired by death. Be humbly proud! Be proudly grateful! Be immortal because life is immortal. Contain the harmony of womb and grave within you! Possess life as a lover — then sleep requited in the arms of death! If you awake, love again! If you sleep on, rest in peace! Who knows which? What does it matter! It is nobler not to know!

A "Mongol Chronicler" then comes forward to chant the *official lament for the dead. He declaims in a high wailing voice accompanied by the musicians and by the Chorus who sway rhythmically and hum a rising and falling mourning accompaniment.* Concluding his lament he reiterates the theme: "Against Death all Gods are powerless."

Since God has revealed neither strength nor purpose — impotent as He is to do anything about death, incapable as He is of creating a universe with any apparent design — O'Neill's protagonists have taken matters into their own hands. They imprecate and depose the old God, solve the problem of death, discern design in a universe that had appeared to be only a monster of energy. "Death is no more," announced Juan Ponce de Leon. "Life lives!" cried Michael Cape. "Contemplate the eternal life of Life," commands Kublai. The rhythmic rise and fall of the fountain's waters symbolized for Juan the rhythmic eternal return of life. Perception of the cell's unity inspired Cape with "faith in the unity of the end." Kublai discovers a harmony in extremes. Yea-sayers, all three.

After the elaborate ritual has ended and the curtain has fallen upon *Marco Millions,* O'Neill reminded us in an epilogue of his play's satirical intent. Dressed as a thirteenth century merchant still, Marco has been sitting in the audience. The tired businessman looks *a bit sleepy, a trifle puzzled, and not a little irritated as his thoughts, in spite of himself, cling for a passing moment to the play just ended.* But by the time he reaches the lobby *his face begins to clear of all disturbing memories of what had happened on the stage.* Once again his bearing becomes *stolid with the dignity of one who is sure of his place in the world.* Implicit in O'Neill's words is a bitter irony. That such a man should be sure of his place in the world is too much to endure. Ironically apotheosized as the Great God Brown, Marco shall suffer excruciatingly. O'Neill saw to that.

Saint and Satan

NEVER QUESTIONING or denying, never railing, Eben Cabot alone among O'Neill's heroes of this period was in harmony with life. Juan Ponce de Leon was dismayed by its transitoriness; Michael Cape found it insulting, Jim Harris baffling, Kublai Kaan stupid. Ultimately all accepted it and were exalted. Happily they were caught at last in a violent uprush of subliminal intuitions and learned to "say yea to contradiction and strife," to life and death. In each instance access of mystical affirmation climaxed a struggle with life-denying tendencies: Christian renunciation, bigotry, fanaticism, cruelty, even Oriental resignation and submission. These forces, augmented by destructive materialism, became increasingly formidable. How they destroyed the peace and harmony of the pagan world was illustrated in *Marco Millions.* Their devastating effect upon the creative life is ostensibly the theme of *The Great God Brown.*

By 1920 it had become apparent that the so-called genteel tradition had reverted to its Calvinist source and in so doing had recovered its original vitality; that, moreover, it had joined forces with aggressive enterprise to cast a blight upon the free creative spirit. Seeking to discover the cause of the poverty of American letters, Van Wyck Brooks in 1918 suggested that the "creative impulses of men are always at war with their possessive impulses," that "poetry springs from brooding on just those aspects of experience that most retard the swift advance of the acquisitive mind." Since the acquisitive life "has lost the sanction of necessity which the age of pioneering gave it," he looked forward hopefully to the new age just begun in which the nation was already calling for the creative life. Yet, four years hence he was still to find that "the creative will in this country is a very weak and sickly plant." Other critics — H. L. Mencken, Randolph Bourne, Waldo Frank — joined Brooks in an effort to hold up the languishing creative spirit. Unanimous in blaming the neo-Puritan, they converged on the problem from various directions. Mencken theorized that the Puritan was driven by a "will to power," that with the evangelization of the nation, business methods came to be applied to religion which, "heavily capitalized and astutely manned," then began to wage organized drives on "immorality." In such manner the Puritan-Philistine was destroying the creative will. Bourne, too, believed that the Puritan was motivated by a will to power. Supplementing Nietzsche with Freud, he argued that the "primitive currents of life [in the Puritan] are not blocked and turned back on their sources, but are directed into powerful and usually devastating channels." Frank, who acknowledged himself a disciple of Brooks and a follower of Mencken, composed variations upon the foregoing themes. He referred not only to the repressed psychic life of the pioneer but also — invoking Jung — to his "passionate extraversion." To both Brooks and Frank, Mark Twain was the personification of the artist destroyed by the Puritan, extraverted, acquisitive society in which he lived. Thus, wrote Frank,

The generic Clemens was a tender and dreaming and avid spirit, in love with beauty, in love with love. But he was born in the ranks of a hurling and sweating army. He forced himself to move with it at its own pace. He forced himself to take on its measures of success: to take on that distrust of life and love which so well defended the principal business of its march. For this betrayal of his soul, his soul brought him bitterness, and the mass of his works are failures.

And Brooks:

His unconscious desire was to be an artist, but this implied an assertion of individuality that was a sin in the eyes of his mother [who was a Calvinist] and a shame in the eyes of society. On the other hand, society and his mother wanted him to be a business man, and for this he could not summon up the necessary powers in himself. The eternal dilemma of every American writer. It was the dilemma which . . . Mark Twain solved by becoming a humorist.

Such was the current conception of the artist's predicament. By 1925 O'Neill was prepared to offer his version of the situation. As we shall see, the dilemma of Dion Anthony, a painter-poet, coincides in many respects with that of Mark Twain; in others it diverges startlingly and significantly.

Produced by Macgowan, Jones, and O'Neill in January 1926, *The Great God Brown* remained on display for nearly a year. Before it had run a month O'Neill wrote a letter to the *Evening Post* containing a key to the allegory. Tracing "the mystical pattern which manifests itself as an overtone in *The Great God Brown,* dimly behind and beyond the words and actions of the characters," he explained that Dion Anthony represents Dionysus and St. Anthony —

the creative pagan acceptance of life, fighting eternal war with the masochistic, life-denying spirit of Christianity as represented by St. Anthony — the whole struggle resulting in this modern day in mutual exhaustion — creative joy in life for life's sake frustrated, rendered abortive, distorted by morality from Pan into Satan, into a Mephistopheles mocking himself in order to feel alive; Christianity, once heroic in martyrs for its intense faith now pleading weakly for intense belief in anything, even Godhead itself.

After explaining the symbolic purport of the other three principal figures, O'Neill continued with the hero's story:

Dion's mask of Pan which he puts on as a boy is not only a defense against the world for the super-sensitive painter-poet underneath it, but also an integral part of his character as an artist. The world is not only blind to the man beneath, but it also sneers at and condemns the Pan-mask it sees. After that Dion's inner self retrogresses along the line of Christian resignation until it partakes of the nature of the Saint while at the same time the outer Pan is slowly transformed by the struggle with reality into Mephistopheles. It is as Mephistopheles he falls stricken at Brown's feet after having condemned Brown to destruction by willing him his mask, but, this mask falling off as he dies, it is the Saint who kisses Brown's feet in abject contrition and pleads as a little boy to a big brother to tell him a prayer.

If *The Great God Brown* represents the predicament of the American creative artist, it appears also to be a personal allegory depicting the ordeal of Eugene O'Neill. Dion Anthony is a recurrent type of O'Neill hero — shy, lonely, misunderstood; unhappy in his relationship with his parents — with his father in particular — and with his wife. Transformed into an inebriate not only by unfulfilled love but also by a frustrated yearning for religious faith, he seeks a solution in pagan naturalism. Like Nietzsche, O'Neill was a disciple of Dionysus and would "sooner be a satyr than a saint." And like Nietzsche, who had insisted that Christianity is the product of man's "will for self-torture," he was repelled by its masochistic tendencies. Yet at times he seems to have agreed with Nathan that Nietzsche was too "hard" and proceeded to temper his harshness with tender love, with compassion — an essentially Christian element which Nietzsche had denounced as a "depressant," as that which "preserves whatever is ripe for destruction." Thus, in *The Great God Brown,* Dionysus is the symbol not only of affirmation and regeneration of life, but also of love. In Dion Anthony's scorn for Christianity, in his expressions of irreverence, there is frequently a quality of bravado. He is both attracted and repelled by the Gospels; and despite his avowed preference for the satyr, he is continually tempted by the saint. A similar polarity exerted its effect upon O'Neill. Introducing the religious debate in *The Fountain,* he appeared to have resolved the conflict in *Desire Under the Elms,* wherein paganism was triumphant. But the mocking irony and life-weariness of *Marco Millions* suggested that the triumph was short lived. And in *The Great God Brown* he deplored this turn of events, while tracing the cause to his own spiritual struggle. The play symbolizes, in the first place, the conflict between his aesthetic and his religious impulses, between unfettered creativity and Catholic, not Calvinistic, faith; and in the second place, his sense of isolation in an antagonistic bourgeois culture.

Nietzsche was the principal inspiration for *The Great God Brown,* but in addition the play perhaps owes something to *The Temptation of St. Anthony,* both for Dion's name and for the grotesque quality of his suffering. And to *Faust* there is more than a casual resemblance. Like Goethe's hero, Dion is self-torturing. Both figures engage in a compulsive quest — Faust for knowledge,

a desire to grasp infinite Nature; Dion for faith, the recovery of
lost spiritual comfort and protection. Both are "guilty" of the pantheistic heresy; each has his Mephistopheles and his Margaret; and
in the end both characters are redeemed — Faust in heaven, Dion
in heaven on earth. That O'Neill was interested in Goethe's tragedy
is indicated by his note in the "Memoranda on Masks":

> Consider Goethe's 'Faust,' which, psychologically speaking, should be the
> closest to us of all the Classics. In producing this play, I would have Mephi-
> stopheles wearing the Mephistophelean mask of the face of Faust. For is not
> the whole of Goethe's truth *for our time* just that Mephistopheles and Faust
> are one and the same — are Faust?

In *The Great God Brown* O'Neill followed his own suggestion:
Mephistopheles and the Faustian Dion "are one and the same."
Dion, however, wears his own Mephistophelean mask. If O'Neill
was influenced by Nietzsche, Flaubert, and Goethe, he was also
inspired, perhaps, by Strindberg, as he had been previously in
Welded. Indeed, the Inferno-like experiences of Dion recall the
anguish of Michael Cape.

Creative artists both, Dion and Michael are brothers under their
thin skin, sharing the conviction that "life is intolerably insulting,"
craving a faith to comfort themselves. The more searching study in
sensibility, Dion draws his breath in pain not for a single evening,
like Cape, but for 18 years. During this extended period he is at
odds with himself, with God, with all the manifestations of a materialistic culture, with society's unnatural laws, with father, wife,
sons. So preoccupied is he with introspecting, self-pity, complaining,
mocking, drinking, dying that, although he is an artist, he never
gets around to painting anything.

The Great God Brown is concerned with William Brown as well
as with Dion Anthony. Structurally it consists of two somewhat
distinct cycles of action. The first, depicting the tragedy of Dion
Anthony, is completed at the end of Act Two. The second, that of
William Brown, is concluded at the end of Act Four. Anthony's
tragedy is precipitated by Brown; Brown's is induced by Anthony's
revenge. A prologue and an epilogue bind the two cycles into a unit.
In the prologue the adolescent Dion is *shrinking, shy and gentle,
full of a deep sadness. With a suffering bewilderment* he exposes
his soul:

Why am I afraid to dance, I who love music and rhythm and grace and song and laughter? Why am I afraid to live, I who love life and the beauty of flesh and the living colors of earth and sky and sea? Why am I afraid of love, I who love love? Why am I afraid, I who am not afraid? Why must I pretend to scorn in order to pity? Why must I hide myself in self-contempt in order to understand? Why must I be so ashamed of my strength, so proud of my weakness? Why must I live in a cage like a criminal, defying and hating, I who love peace and friendship?

Given a personality like Dion's, a traumatic experience at pre-school age can condition one's entire life. Such an experience was provided by Brown. "Listen!" Dion confides to Billy,

One day when I was four years old a boy sneaked up behind me when I was drawing a picture in the sand he couldn't draw and hit me on the head with a stick and kicked out my picture and laughed when I cried. It wasn't what he'd done that made me cry, but him! I had loved and trusted him and suddenly the good God was disproved in his person and the evil and injustice of Man was born! Everyone called me cry-baby, so I became silent and designed a mask of the Bad Boy Pan in which to live and rebel against that other boy's God and protect myself from His cruelty. And that other boy, secretly he felt ashamed but he couldn't acknowledge it; so from that day he instinctively developed into the good boy, the good friend, the good man, William Brown!

Thus, at the impressionable age of four, when less sensitive and precocious children innocently believe in Santa Claus and the Easter bunny, Dion experienced the sudden shocking awareness that God is to be neither loved nor trusted. Humble, meek, and pure in heart, the little child discovered not the kingdom of heaven, but a world of evil and injustice. Far from inheriting the earth, he was driven by his meekness to wear a mask in self-defense. Pure in heart, he still could not see God. Beneath the mask, the man without a skin never forgets the promise of the Gospels. The painful revelation of early childhood possesses him entirely, and he cannot rest until the promise is somehow fulfilled. In short, Christianity not only betrays the devout and those who most require its comfort and protection; it becomes a compulsive obsession which distorts and destroys one's life.

The protection that should have been forthcoming from God is furnished instead by the mask of Pan and by the Mother. By the time the play opens the Pan mask is already being transformed into a Mephistophelean mask, but in the prologue, seven years

earlier, it is *mocking, reckless, defiant, gayly scoffing and sensual.*
Dion's real face at this time is *dark, spiritual, poetic, passionately
supersensitive, helplessly unprotected in its childlike, religious faith
in life.* Between mask and face there is no marked disharmony as
yet; for the mask, O'Neill tells us, *is a fixed forcing* of the face.
Before his parents, who reflect the bourgeois culture of which Brown
is the main symbol, Dion wears his mask. He mocks his father
who "imagines he is God the Father." With *intense bitterness* he
utters cryptic remarks, prompting his father to ask the mother with
bitter hopelessness, "Who is he? You bore him!" And, Pan-like, he
suddenly cuts grotesque capers, *laughing with forced abandon.* If
the abandon is forced, it is because Pan is merely a mask. Speaking
through the mask to Margaret, Dion reveals the advantages of a
paganism now lost:

I love, you love, we love! Come! Rest! Relax! Let go your clutch on the
world! Dim and dimmer! Fading out in the past behind! Gone! Death!
Now! Be born! Awake! Live! Dissolve into dew — into silence — into night
— into earth — into space — into peace — into meaning — into joy — into
God — into the Great God Pan!

But the reality of the present has destroyed the possibilities of attaining the ecstatic primordial unity. Dion continues: "Wake up! Time
to get up! Time to exist! Time for school! Time to learn! Learn to
pretend! Cover your nakedness! Learn to lie! Learn to keep step!
Join the procession! Great Pan is dead! Be ashamed!"

Pan is dead, but his mask is retained for rebellion and protection
against his successor, the Great God Brown. If divinity, immanent
in Nature, is diffused everywhere, it is concentrated in the Mother,
who is not only the source of life, but also the means of making
life endurable. Through her the promise of the Gospels is fulfilled.
In her the supersensitive Dion finds protection against God the
Father, Brown's cruel God. After his parents are dead, Dion reveals
another source of his misery. He recalls first his ill-feeling for his
father, who appeared briefly on stage as a bewildered and pitifully
insignificant figure:

What aliens we were to each other! When he lay dead, his face looked
so familiar that I wondered where I had met that man before. Only at the
second of my conception. After that we grew hostile with concealed shame.

If his hatred for his father was less intense than was Eben Cabot's for Ephraim, his love for his mother surpassed in tenderness and pathos that of Eben for his dead mother. Dion continues:

And my mother? I remember a sweet strange girl, with affectionate, bewildered eyes as if God had locked her in a dark closet without any explanation. I was the sole doll our ogre, her husband, allowed her and she played mother and child with me for many years in that house until at last through two tears I watched her die with the shy pride of one who has lengthened her dress and put up her hair. And I felt like a forsaken toy and cried to be buried with her, because her hands alone had caressed without clawing. She lived long and aged greatly in the two days before they closed her coffin. The last time I looked, her purity had forgotten me, she was stainless and imperishable, and I knew my sobs were ugly and meaningless to her virginity; so I shrank away, back into life, with naked nerves jumping like fleas, and in due course of nature another girl called me her boy in the moon and married me and became three mothers in one person, while I got paint on my paws in an endeavor to see God! (*He laughs wildly — claps on his mask*) But that Ancient Humorist had given me weak eyes, so now I'll have to foreswear my quest for Him and go in for the Omnipresent Successful Serious One, the Great God Mr. Brown, instead!

Although Dion was forsaken by his mother when she died, he had hoped to find in Margaret a more than adequate substitute. But in the prologue we witness another of his overwhelming disappointments, his traumatic disillusionments. Margaret loves Dion, for he is "so different from all the others. He can paint beautifully and write poetry, and he plays and sings and dances so marvelously. But he's sad and shy, too, just like a baby sometimes, and he understands what I'm really like inside — " At first she is "Dion's little girl." But *more and more strongly and assertively . . . she is a wife and a mother:* "And I'll be Mrs. Dion — Dion's wife — and he'll be my Dion — my own Dion — my little boy — my baby! The moon is drowned in the tides of my heart, and peace sinks deep through the sea!" (*She disappears off left, her upturned unmasked face like that of a rapturous visionary.*) Dion responds to Margaret's "passion," for "underneath" he loves love. He had always believed that "girls only allow themselves to look at what is seen," that Margaret loves not him but his mask. Now when he learns that she is waiting for him, love triumphs over fear, and *he slowly removes his mask. His face is torn and transfigured by joy. He stares at the sky raptly* and speaks:

O God in the moon, did you hear? She loves me! I am not afraid! I am strong! I can love! She protects me! She is warmly around me! She is my skin! She is my armor! Now I am born — I — the I! — one and indivisible — I who love Margaret! (*He glances at his mask triumphantly — in tones of deliverance*) You are outgrown! I am beyond you! (*He stretches out his arms to the sky*) O God, now I believe!

Anticipating the ecstatic mystical experience of being born again, Dion is bitterly frustrated when the rebirth miscarries. For Margaret, when she re-enters, is terrified as she is confronted by the man without a mask. The "eternal girl-woman with a virtuous simplicity of instinct, properly oblivious to everything but the means to her end of maintaining the race," Margaret is not the sort to peer behind masks or to accept what she sees there. She may be the divine source of life, but she is unfortunately not the refuge which Dion has frantically been seeking. In a *passionate agony* he cries that he loves her, but she remains frightened. Whereupon he *puts on his mask again* and says, *quietly and bitterly:* "All's well. I'll never let you see again . . . By proxy, I love you." The wretched Dion marries her even though he must keep the mask.

This, then, is the situation as the curtain rises on Act One — Scene One. "Born without a skin," "with ghosts in [his] eyes," the supersensitive Dion experienced the series of crushing shocks that have been described in the foregoing paragraphs. During the seven years which intervene between prologue and Act One, Dion quit his study of architecture, which he had chosen to pursue partly at his parents' instigation, partly because it sounded "less laborious"; and, like Jim Harris and Ella, went abroad with Margaret where he enjoyed a few years of peace and happiness. Home again, having "spent" all that his father had "spun," he faces an impossible reality. His wife cannot understand him; his sons are strangers, his home reflects the offensive bourgeois tastes of a nation which worships the Great God Brown:

The sitting room of Mrs. Dion Anthony's *half of a two-family house in the homes section of the town — one of those one-design districts that daze the eye with multiplied ugliness. The four pieces shown are in keeping . . . the background is a backdrop on which the rear wall is painted with the intolerable lifeless realistic detail of the stereotyped paintings which usually adorn the sitting rooms of such houses.*

Most bitter and ironical of all, he must not only make a living, he must ask Brown to employ him. Meanwhile the mask of Pan, which Dion has worn to spare himself from the reality which Brown has created, has been losing its former serviceability. *It is older, more defiant and mocking, its sneer more forced and bitter, its Pan quality becoming Mephistophelean.* It had once been not only a "defense against the world for the supersensitive painter-poet underneath it," but also "an integral part of his character as the artist," a symbol, that is, of the Dionysian impulse of "creative joy in life for life's sake." Frustrated by the "masochistic, life-denying spirit of Christianity," sneered at and condemned by a society of Philistines, the creative pagan impulse is being transformed into a destructive force. As the mask becomes Satanic, the face becomes ascetic. It has *aged greatly, grown more strained and tortured, but at the same time, in some queer way, more selfless . . . , more fixed in its resolute withdrawal from life.* With his soul torn between a desperate skepticism and a compulsive, irresolute faith, Dion faces the world at the beginning of Act One. Discovered, when the curtain goes up, sitting in Mrs. Dion Anthony's ugly middle-class home, he

(*suddenly reaches out and* [like Faust] *takes up a copy of the New Testament which is on the table and, putting a finger in at random, opens and reads aloud the text at which it points*) 'Come unto me all ye who are heavy laden and I will give you rest.' (*He stares before him in a sort of trance, his face lighted up from within but painfully confused — in an uncertain whisper*) I will come — but where are you, Savior? (*The noise of the outer door shutting is heard.* Dion *starts and claps the mocking mask on his face again. He tosses the Testament aside contemptuously*) Blah! Fixation on old Mama Christianity! You infant blubbering in the dark, you! (*He laughs, with a bitter self-contempt*)

Margaret enters, gently chides her husband for sleeping in the afternoon, for being indifferent to the children:

Margaret. (*squeezing his hand — with possessive tenderness*) Play with them. You're a bigger kid than they are — underneath.

Dion. (*self-mockingly — flipping the Bible*) Underneath — I'm becoming downright infantile! 'Suffer these little ones!'

Margaret. (*keeping to her certainty*) You're my oldest.

Dion. (*with mocking appreciation*) She puts the Kingdom of Heaven in its place!

She reproves him for drinking and gambling, vices which began when he "realized it wasn't in [him] to be an artist." Like his mother before her, Margaret is convinced that Dion *"can* paint— beautifully." Then, having reminded him that he has dissipated his inheritance, she obliquely moves to her point. She had met Billy Brown on the street. Brown had said that Dion would have "made a good architect if [he'd] stuck to it," and had asked why Dion has "never been in to see him." Continuing to speak through his mask, Dion's irony is as infantile as the faith against which it is directed. In this inverted universe, men such as Brown are "heaven-bent for success," for it is the "will of Mammon." Brown's career testifies to design in the universe: It is "one of God's mud pies!" Pride is a virtue, "the pride which came after man's fall — by which he laughs as a creator at his self-defeats!" "Pride without which the Gods are worms!" But the urgency of the situation, his love for Margaret, his Christian impulses, force the masked Dion to yield. "Pride is dy- ing!" he exclaims *in a trembling expiring voice.* Then, as if he *were suffocating, he pulls the mask from his resigned, pale, suffering face. He prays like a Saint in the desert, exorcizing a demon.* "Pride is dead! Blessed are the meek! Blessed are the poor in spirit!" Hav- ing yielded, Dion claps on his mask again and resumes his ironical utterances: "Blessed are the meek for they shall inherit graves! Blessed are the poor in spirit for they are blind!"

While Margaret is in Billy Brown's office late that afternoon, Dion is getting drunk. Brown, who wears no mask, is *a fine-look- ing, well-dressed, capable, college-bred American business man, boyish still and with . . .* [an] *engaging personality.* Margaret's *face is concealed behind the mask of the pretty young matron, still hardly a woman, who cultivates a naively innocent and bravely hopeful attitude toward things and acknowledges no wound to the world.* She speaks defensively of Dion, refuses to understand or to accept Brown's offer to help him. But when Brown tactfully revises his proposal to make it appear that the generosity would be Dion's, she eagerly accepts, assuring Billy that "Dion will be so glad to help an old friend."

With no God in which he can believe, with no mother to protect him, with Saint and Satan struggling for possession of his soul, Dion finds refuge in drunkenness. But in Act One–Scene Three his redemption begins — in Cybel's parlor. Incarnation of the Earth Mother, Cybel is a descendant of the uncommon prostitutes of the naturalistic plays. Anna Christie, having been abstracted into a symbol as the Woman in *Welded,* had picked up in *Desire Under the Elms* the characteristics of both Abbie, the wanton mother, and Min the whore who was "warm like the earth," and now makes her re-entrance in *The Great God Brown* as the mythical Cybele, Mother of the Gods and great Asiatic goddess of fertility. She is more substantial than the Pelasgian Mothers of *Faust,* less carnal than Zola's "Astarte of the Second Empire"; less immaterial than the Cybele whom Flaubert's Saint encountered briefly in his vision. She is quite the opposite of Wedekind's "Erdgeist," Lulu, incarnation of Eve who incited men to sin. She is not at all like Joyce's Bella Cohen — Circe the sorceress in whose brothel men were turned into beasts; or like Molly Bloom — Penelope — bawdy, eternal-maternal feminine. O'Neill's Cybel is precisely what the wretched Dion has been craving: a satisfactory deity and a tender, maternal protectress. From the moment that he awakes from his drunken sleep upon her couch he becomes the recipient of therapeutic benefits that surpass those offered by the psychoanalyst. Unmoral, unjudging, unintimidated by society's unnatural laws, Cybel accepts Dion at his face value. During his contacts with her, which extend over a period of seven years, he learns to endure the reality of William Brown's world, to transfer his "fixation on Mama Christianity" to Mama Earth, to be comfortable in her presence without his mask, to calm his fear of death. However, he continues to suffer from the dissociation of his personality: his Mephistophelean mask becomes more demonic, his face more saintlike and ascetic. But under Cybel's influence his face begins to reflect a new quality, the ultimate spiritual values of love and peace.

The divine prostitute has a mask which she wears only before the unnatural world: it is the *rouged and eye-blackened countenance of the hardened prostitute.* At such times she speaks in *a coarse, harsh voice.* Her home expresses a similar duality. Cheap and squalid, like a brothel — *dirty gilt second-hand sofa, bald-spotted crimson plush chair* — it contains also symbols of her divinity: a player-piano *groggily banging out a sentimental medley of 'Mother-Mammy' tunes, cheap wallpaper of a dull yellow-brown, resembling*

a blurred impression of a fallow field in early spring. Consistent
with these expressionistic symbols of the Earth Mother is the
description of Cybel herself:

*She is a strong, calm, sensual blonde girl of twenty or so, her complexion
fresh and healthy, her figure full-breasted and wide-hipped, her movements
slow and solidly languorous like an animal's, her large eyes dreamy with the
reflected stirring of profound instincts. She chews gum like a sacred cow
forgetting time with an eternal end. Her eyes are fixed, incuriously, on Dion's
pale face.*

Sprawled on his back, fast asleep on the sofa, Dion has been placed
there by Cybel who had found him on her steps. Not wanting "to
run any risk getting into more trouble with the cops," those symbols
of man's unnatural laws, she had taken him in "to sleep it off."
As Dion awakes, the old conflict is immediately apparent. Scarcely
conscious, mask on chest, he *stirs, sighs and murmurs dreamily,*
" 'And He laid his hands on them and healed them.' " *Then with
a start he opens his eyes and, half sitting up, stares at* [Cybel] *bewilderedly, . . . reaches for his mask and claps it on defensively.*
But unlike Margaret, Cybel prefers man without a mask. Whereupon Dion slowly removes it and humbly apologizes. For he begins
to respect the prostitute, as Michael Cape, equally distraught,
scoffing and blasphemous, came to acknowledge the wisdom of the
bovine Woman, the masked Cybel's counterpart. Unmasked, however, Cybel is the Mother. A little slow to perceive this, Dion suggests that they be friends, since he has sensed that she too "is lost
in blind alleys." *With a strange sternness* [she] *searches his face*
and asks, "And never nothing more?" *With a strange smile* he replies, "Let's say never anything less!" Billy Brown appears at the
door, and masks go on. Bored, Cybel is about to leave the two men
alone. *She starts to go — then, as if reminded of something,* says to
Dion, "Life's all right if you let it alone." These words remain the
gist of Cybel's comforting wisdom. Although Dion is incapable of
heeding her advice, he is evidently impressed by it; for he continues
to patronize her.

Thus, seven years later, in Act Two–Scene One, he is discovered
in her parlor, *about sunset in spring. The arrangement of furniture
is the same but the chair and sofa are new, bright colored costly
pieces,* for the Successful Mr. Brown has also been visiting the pros-

titute. Yet the symbols of Cybel's divinity have not been substantially affected by the materialistic, visionless Brown. The piano is still present, although he hates it. The wallpaper is new, but its motif is unchanged. Suggesting the eternal processes of nature, the lifeless fallow field in early spring of the preceding scene is now a brilliant, stunning profusion of *crimson and purple flowers and fruits* [which] *tumble over one another in a riotously profane lack of any apparent design.* Cybel *has grown stouter and more voluptuous, but her face is still unmarked and fresh, her calm more profound. She is like an unmoved idol of Mother Earth.* Dion's *face is that of an ascetic, a martyr, furrowed by pain and self-torture,* but it is now *lighted from within by a spiritual calm and human kindliness.* For he is learning to "accept life." As the *piano is whining out its same old sentimental medley,* Cybel says *musingly,* "I love those rotten old sob tunes. They make me wise to people. That's what's inside them — what makes them love and murder their neighbor — crying jags set to music!" "Every song is a hymn," observes Dion *compassionately.* "They keep trying to find the Word in the Beginning." The wise Cybel, knowing how disastrous that Faustian tendency can be, remarks, "They try to know too much. It makes them weak." Consistent with the Earth Mother's admonition, "Life's all right if you let it alone," is her observation regarding love. One should accept love as he accepts life, for "It's just one of a lot of things you do to keep life living." Moreover, "It takes all kinds of love to make a world!" Which is to say that the agony of the individual love affair must be viewed in the right perspective. If love is a natural concomitant of life, so also is jealousy; but here again one must remember that it too is natural. "I don't blame your being jealous of Mr. Brown sometimes," Cybel says, and then confesses, "I'm jealous of your wife, even though I know you do love her." By the process of free association O'Neill at last brings Cybel to the point where she can reveal her philosophy of death as well as of life. Thus, Dion remarks, "I love Margaret. I don't know who my wife is," an utterance which means, apparently, that he loves the individual beneath her mask, that the wife mask is a stranger to him. Touched by Dion's misery — symbol of universal wretchedness — the Earth Mother exclaims, *with a queer broken laugh:*

Oh, God, sometimes the truth hits me such a sock between the eyes I can see the stars! — and then I'm so damn sorry for the lot of you, every damn mother's son-of-a-gun of you, that I'd like to run out naked into the street and love the whole mob to death like I was bringing you all a new brand of dope that'd make you forget everything that ever was for good! (*Then, with a twisted smile*) But they wouldn't see me, any more than they see each other. And they keep right on moving along and dying without my help anyway.

If the generality of men are too much without vision and too self-torturing to avail themselves of Nature's Nepenthean advantages, of her capacity to comfort their fear of death, Dion is to be an exception. "You've given me strength to die," he says *sadly*. And Cybel replies, "You may be important but your life's not. There's millions of it born every second. Life can cost too much even for a sucker to afford it — like everything else. And it's not sacred — only the you inside is. The rest is earth." Cybel's philosophy is a synthesis of Heraclitean and Platonic doctrine. Life, love, and death, she has been saying, are natural cyclic processes and should therefore be accepted as casually as one regards the earth itself of which they are a part — now fallow, now teeming. On the other hand, the individual soul, the spirit, is not subject to these temporal conditions. Yet, despite the Earth Mother's comforting explanation, Dion is terrified at the thought of death. He *gets to his knees and with clasped hands looks up raptly and prays with an ascetic fervor:* " 'Into thy hands, O Lord,' . . ." (*Then suddenly, with a look of horror*) "Nothing! To feel one's life blown out like the flame of a cheap match . . . !" Unable to endure such prospects, he seeks the protection of his mask. Clapping it on his face, he *laughs harshly* and exclaims: "To fall asleep and know you'll never, never be called to get on the job of existence again! 'Swift be thine approaching flight! Come soon — soon!' " (*He quotes this last with a mocking longing*) Cybel *pats his head maternally* and tries to reassure him: "There, don't be scared. It's born in the blood. When the time comes, you'll find it easy." As a matter of fact, Dion has had not only intimations of mortality but a warning from his doctor to stop drinking, a warning which he refuses to heed. Cybel, too, through her *profound instincts* shares the same foreknowledge. As he is about to leave her, she *suddenly starts and calls with deep grief,*

Dion! (*He looks at her. A pause. He comes slowly back. She speaks strangely in a deep, far-off voice — and yet like a mother talking to her little son*) You mustn't forget to kiss me before you go, Dion. (*She removes his mask*) Haven't I told you to take off your mask in the house? Look at me, Dion. I've — just — seen — something. I'm afraid you're going away a long, long ways. I'm afraid I won't see you again for a long, long time. So it's good-by, dear. (*She kisses him gently. He begins to sob. She hands him back his mask*) Here you are. Don't get hurt. Remember, it's all a game, and after you're asleep I'll tuck you in.

Dion utters a *choking, heart-broken cry,* "Mother!" *Then he claps on his mask with a terrible effort of will* and exclaims *mockingly,* "Go to the devil, you sentimental old pig! See you tomorrow!" *He goes, whistling, slamming the door.* And even Cybel is moved to question the ways of an inscrutable universe, the apparent senselessness of death-born-of-life. *Like an idol again,* she asks, "What's the good of bearing children? What's the use of giving birth to death?" *She sighs wearily, turns, puts a plug in the piano, which starts up its old sentimental tune.*

If the phenomenon of death has aroused even in the Earth Mother a weary sense of futility, Dion is not aware of it. Good mother that she is, Cybel has concealed her qualms from her child. In Act Two–Scene Two — his face *gentler, more spiritual, more saintlike and ascetic than ever before* — Dion *reads aloud from the 'Imitation of Christ' by Thomas à Kempis, like a priest, offering up prayers for the dying:*

'Quickly must thou be gone from hence, see them how matters stand with thee. Ah, fool — learn now to die to the world that thou mayst begin to live with Christ! Do now, beloved, do now all thou canst because thou knowst not when thou shalt die; nor dost thou know what shall befall thee after death. Keep thyself as a pilgrim, and a stranger upon earth, to whom the affairs of this world do not — belong! Keep thy heart free and raised upwards to God because thou hast not here a lasting abode. 'Because at what hour you know not the Son of Man will come!' Amen. (*He raises his hand over the mask as if he were blessing it, closes the book and puts it in his pocket. He raises the mask in his hands and stares at it with a pitying tenderness*) Peace, poor tortured one, brave pitiful pride of man, the hour of our deliverance comes. Tomorrow we may be with Him in Paradise!

As Margaret approaches, *he grabs up the mask in a sudden panic* and puts it on, that she need not look upon his face. Masked, the fear of death surges up in him again. *With sudden wildness —*

torturedly, sinking on his knees beside her, he cries, "Margaret! Margaret! I'm lonely! I'm frightened! I'm going away! I've got to say good-by!" She pats his hair and comforts him, "Poor boy! Poor Dion! Come home and sleep." But, in his mask Dion is not only ironical and blasphemous, he is proud. "No! I'm a man!" he shouts, "I'm a lonely man! I can't go back! I have conceived myself!" Beneath the mask he knows that this is not so; for, as his relationship with Cybel testifies, he longs to be a child again. Nor has he conceived himself; rather, he has conceived his mask. He continues, *with desperate mockery,* "Look at me, Mrs. Anthony! It's the last chance! Tomorrow I'll have moved on to the next hell! Behold your man — the sniveling, cringing, life-denying Christian slave you have so nobly ignored in the father of your sons! Look!" Whereupon *he tears the mask from his face, which is radiant with a great pure love for her and a great sympathy and tenderness.* Having found the Mother, Cybel, who has lavished upon him sympathy, tenderness, understanding, love, Dion has obliterated the effect of the disillusioning occurrences that had begun to twist his life in early childhood. Mother love has given him courage and strength, the capacity to forgive, to love, to remove his cruel mocking mask. He can accept the Gospels now, because he has recovered the faith and innocence of the infant. To Margaret he can now plead: "O woman — my love — that I have sinned against in my sick pride and cruelty — forgive my sins — forgive my solitude — forgive my sickness — forgive me!" *He kneels and kisses the hem of her dress.* Margaret, *who has been staring at him with terror,* cries, "Dion! Don't! I can't bear it! You're like a ghost! You're dead! Oh, my God! Help! Help!" She faints. Dion *looks at her — then takes her hand which holds her mask and looks at that face — gently* he says, "And now I am permitted to understand and love you, too!" *He kisses the mask first — then kisses her face, murmuring,* "And you, sweetheart! 'Blessed, thrice blessed are the meek!'" He has the capacity at last of loving Margaret without reservation, her mask as well as her face, Mrs. Anthony the wife as well as Margaret. He has become the personification of love. In the next scene, his last, the mask falls off as he is dying to reveal a *Christian Martyr's face at the point of death.* He dies without the mask, begging Brown to forgive him. "Bury me," he implores Billy, "hide me, forget me for your own happiness! May Margaret love you! May you design the Temple of Man's Soul! Blessed are the meek and the poor in spirit!" *He kisses Brown's feet — then more and more weakly and childishly:* "What was the prayer, Billy? I'm getting so sleepy . . ." Brown responds *in a trancelike tone:* " 'Our Father who art in Heaven.' " But Dion repeats drowsily only "Our Father . . ." and dies. For his devotion has been to the Mother into whose Kingdom of Heaven on earth — having become as a little child — he is now entering.

Billy Brown now becomes the protagonist as his tragedy gets under way. Brown, explained O'Neill in his letter to the *Post,*

is the visionless demi-god of our new materialistic myth — a Success — building his life of exterior things, inwardly empty and resourceless, an un-creative creature of superficial preordained social grooves, a by-product forced aside into slack waters by the deep main current of life-desire . . .

Brown has always envied the creative life force in Dion — what he himself lacks. When he steals Dion's mask of Mephistopheles he thinks he is gaining the power to live creatively, while in reality he is only stealing that creative power made self-destructive by complete frustration. This devil of mocking doubt makes short work of him. It enters him, rending him apart, torturing and transfiguring him until he is even forced to wear a mask of his Success, William A. Brown, before the world, as well as Dion's mask toward wife and children. Thus Billy Brown becomes not himself to anyone. And thus he partakes of Dion's anguish — more poignantly, for Dion has the Mother, Cybel — and in the end out of this anguish his soul is born, a tor-tured Christian soul such as the dying Dion's, begging for belief, and at the last finding it on the lips of Cybel.

Envy is obviously the cause of Brown's downfall. It is ironical that he should envy the very power for which he had been responsible in Dion's character. He had forced Dion to wear the mask of Pan in self-protection, giving Dion the "power to live creatively." Hitherto Brown had been stolid, like Marco Polo, who bore him-self "with the dignity of one who is sure of his place in the world." Insensitive, with *unquestioning faith in the finality of* [his] *achieve-ment,* Brown never suffered as Dion had, never needed a mask of any sort — much less that of Pan. The counterpart of Marco, he has been

merely a successful freak, the result of some snide neutralizing of life forces — a spineless cactus — a wild boar of the mountains altered into a packer's hog eating to become food — a Don Juan inspired to romance by a monkey's glands . . .

Yet he is to share in Dion's blessedness by atoning for his original sin — committed when he had hit the four-year-old Dion on the head and destroyed the sand picture, thereby giving birth to the "evil and injustice of Man."

Having hired Dion to work in his office, Brown still needs even the dead Dion "to reassure himself that he is alive." Whereas Dion had "loved, lusted, won and lost, [sung] and wept . . . been life's lover . . . fulfilled her will [when he had done all these things O'Neill never makes clear], Brown had been "neither creature nor creator." Thinking that he had engaged the creative Dion, Brown put him to work on "some cathedral plans." But Pan had long since been "forbidden the light and warmth of the sun," had grown "sensitive and self-conscious and proud and revengeful." Dion's dream of "painting wind on the sea and the skimming flight of cloud shadows over the tops of trees" was never realized. Instead, out of revenge, he designed for Brown a cathedral:

They've been accepted — Mr. Brown's designs! My designs really! . . . He hands me one mathematically correct barn after another and I doctor them up with cute allurements so that fools will desire to buy, sell, breed, sleep, love, hate, curse and pray in them! I do this with devilish cleverness to their entire delight!

The cathedral, "one vivid blasphemy from sidewalk to the tips of its spires," "will make Brown the most eminent architect in this state of God's country," Brown who "couldn't design a cathedral without it looking like the First Supernatural Bank!" For he believed "only in the immortality of the moral belly!" — in, that is, a Puritanical voraciousness; a righteous, bourgeois materialism. But life can only be creative. "It isn't enough," as Dion asserted, "to be her creature, you've got to create her or she requests you to destroy yourself." One must be "life's lover," "fulfill her will," and "dominate her in turn." Anything less than this, declared Dion, makes blasphemy seem like faith.

Embodiment of a culture that is destroying itself by satisfying the demands of its "moral belly" rather than those of life, William Brown, curiously enough, has in his blood "that germ which wriggles like a question mark of insecurity," "part of the creative life" which he had stolen from Dion. Envious, he also tried to steal the objects of Dion's love, Margaret and Cybel. Yet he not only envied Dion, he loved him, because Dion had "always possessed the power [Brown] needed for love, because [Dion was] love." Dying, Dion uttered his last will and testament: "I leave Dion Anthony to William Brown — for him to love and obey — for him to become me — then my Margaret will love me — my children will love me — Mr. and Mrs. Brown and sons, happily ever after!" Having bequeathed his satanic mask to Brown, the mask fell from his face, and Dion begged Brown's forgiveness. "He's dead — at last," pronounces Brown *dully.*

(He says this mechanically but the last two words awaken him —wonderingly) At last? (Then with triumph) At last! (He stares at Dion's real face contemptuously) So that's the poor weakling you really were! No wonder you hid! And I've always been afraid of you — yes, I'll confess it now, in awe of you! Paugh! (He picks up the mask from the floor) No, not of you! Of this! Say what you like, it's strong if it is bad! And this is what Margaret loved, not you! Not you! This man! — this man who willed himself to me! (Struck by an idea, he jumps to his feet) By God! (He slowly starts to put the mask on. A knocking comes on the street door. He starts guiltily, laying the mask on the table. Then he picks it up again quickly, takes the dead body and carries it off left . . .)

When Margaret enters, Brown reappears in Dion's clothes and mask. *She stares wonderingly at him and he at her; goes to him and puts an arm around him,* pleased that he looks stronger and better; she thinks that he has stopped drinking. "Give Mother a kiss," she says. *They kiss. A shudder passes through both of them. She breaks away laughing with aroused desire.* Delighted with Dion's transfiguration, the wife-mother throws *her mask away from her as if suddenly no longer needing it — the mask of the brave face she* [had put] *on before the world to hide her suffering and disillusionment.*

To the first half of the play, which ends at this point, the second half is tenuously appended by means of the transferred mask. The mystical background pattern repeats the theme of the first two acts, namely, that one must create, or be destroyed. As for the so-called "living drama" — interest in it is sustained through the use of two motifs, that of revenge and that of mistaken identity. The dramatic cycle, completed at the end of Act Two, is repeated in the next two acts when Brown assumes Dion's exterior personality to mock and rail, to suffer and redeem himself. Motivated by envy, Brown steals Dion's mask only to be haunted by its demonic power much as Ella Downey had been affected by the Congo mask in *All God's Chillun*. Its force is not only psychological, mystical and abstract, but magical as well.

Having appropriated Dion's mask, the insensitive Brown, the self-assured success, learns to feel what self-conscious, sensitive wretches feel. And the self-knowledge that he acquires fills him with "self-loathing and life-hatred." Inspired by Silenus, companion of Dionysus, Brown is convinced that the "best good is never to be born." At last he resolves to destroy himself, to "murder this God-damned disgusting Great God Brown." In Act Four–Scene Two, counterpart of Act Two–Scene Two, Brown offers up *prayers for the dying:*

On his knees beside the table [upon which the mask of Dion stands], *facing front, stripped naked except for a white cloth around his loins, is* Brown. *The clothes he has torn off in his agony are scattered on the floor. His eyes, his arms, his whole body strain upward, his muscles writhe with his lips as they pray silently in their agonized supplication. Finally a voice seems torn out of him.* Mercy, Compassionate Savior of Man! Out of my depths I cry to you! Mercy on thy poor clod, thy clod of unhallowed earth, thy clay, the Great God Brown! Mercy, Savior! (*He seems to wait for an answer — then leaping to his feet he puts out one hand to touch the mask like a frightened child reaching out for its nurse's hand — then with immediate mocking despair*) Bah! I am sorry, little children, but your kingdom is empty. God has become disgusted and moved away to some far ecstatic star where life is a dancing flame! We must die without him. (*Then — addressing the mask — harshly*) Together, my friend! You, too! Let Margaret suffer! Let the whole world suffer as I am suffering!

Possessed by Dion's spirit, Brown at last partakes of Dion's anguish. The unaccountable suffering of his tortured Christian soul finds relief at last when Cybel suddenly appears. Having ventured out of her parlor to discover why Brown has never come to her again, she enters his home now — a fairy earth mother, a *dea ex machina*. Startling creature, *she is dressed in a black kimono robe and wears slippers over her bare feet. Her yellow hair hangs down in a great mane over her shoulders. She has grown stouter, has more of the deep objective calm of an idol.* Brown is at once comforted by her presence. *Boyishly and naively* he announces, "I am Billy." Cybel *with a motherly solicitude* urges:

Then run, Billy, run! They are hunting for someone! They came to my place, hunting for a murderer, Dion! They must find a victim! They've got to quiet their fears, to cast out their devils, or they'll never sleep soundly again! They've got to absolve themselves by finding a guilty one! They've got to kill someone now, to live! You're naked! You must be Satan! Run, Billy, run! They'll come here! I ran here to warn — someone! So run away if you want to live!

Cybel perceives that the world which condemns Dion does so because it fears and hates him, that its unnatural laws and self-righteousness are merely disguises for its hostile impulses. However, Brown is now behaving *like a sulky child* and is too tired to be impressed by Cybel's psychological insight. He does not want to run away. Indeed, he does not want to live. *With motherly calm* Cybel says, "All right, you needn't, Billy. Don't sulk. Anyway, it's too late. I hear them in the garden now." Putting on the mask of Dion, Brown gains strength. *He makes a gesture as if flinging French windows open.* Then *gayly mocking:* "Welcome, dumb worshippers! I am your Great God Brown! I have been advised to run from you but it is my almighty whim to dance into escape over your prostrate souls!" A volley of shots, and he falls mortally wounded. Whereupon the Earth Mother comforts him as she had Dion.

Brown. (*snuggling against her — gratefully*) The earth is warm.
Cybel. (*soothingly, looking before her like an idol*) Ssssh! Go to sleep, Billy.
Brown. Yes, Mother. (*Then explainingly*) It was dark and I couldn't see where I was going and they all picked on me.
Cybel. I know. You're tired.
Brown. And when I wake up . . . ?
Cybel. The sun will be rising again.
Brown. To judge the living and the dead. (*Frightenedly*) I don't want justice. I want love.
Cybel. There is only love.

For justice is merely the guilty rationalization of those who deny life — masochists who torture themselves with unnatural laws. Where there is creative pagan acceptance of life there can be only love, whose eternal symbols are Dionysus and Cybele. Reassured,

Brown says, "Thank you, Mother." Then, like a child about to go
to sleep, he asks, as Dion had, for the prayer. Cybel responds: "Our
Father Who Art!" Whereupon the dying Brown, the child, is given
a glimpse of the Kingdom of Heaven. If Dion entered the Mother's
domain, Brown is to enter that of the Father — not of the stern and
wrathful God the Father, but of the God who had "become disgusted and moved away to some far ecstatic star where life is a
dancing flame!" It is God conceived, ironically, in the image of
Zarathustra "the godless," he who beseeched the "higher men" to
learn how to laugh. Brown, *taking Cybel's tone — exultantly* repeats, "Who art! Who art!" Then *suddenly — with ecstasy:*

I know! I have found Him! I hear Him speak! 'Blessed are they that weep,
for they shall laugh'! Only he that has wept can laugh! The laughter of
Heaven sows earth with a rain of tears, and out of earth's transfigured birth-
pain the laughter of Man returns to bless and play again in innumerable
dancing gales of flame upon the knees of God! (*He dies.*)

Having gone beyond good and evil, O'Neill outdid the Beatitudes.
He promised not only the kingdom of heaven, but a heaven that
resounds with laughter. Before he brought the play to an end he
reiterated his faith in the doctrine of Eternal Recurrence, "the highest formula of affirmation," according to Nietzsche, "that can ever
be attained." Thus, the Earth Mother, standing over Brown's body,
looks into space and intones *with a profound pain:*

Always spring comes again bearing life! Always again! Always, always forever again! — Spring again! — life again! summer and fall and death and
peace again! — (*With agonized sorrow*) — but always, always, love and
conception and birth and pain again — spring bearing the intolerable chalice
of life again! — (*Then with agonized exultance*) — bearing the glorious,
blazing crown of life again! (*She stands like an idol of Earth, her eyes
staring out over the world*)

The Epilogue, like the final scene of *The Fountain,* exemplifies
and confirms the doctrine that has just been annunciated. The stage
is set as it was in the Prologue: *on another moonlight night in
June.* Margaret, wearing *her mask of the proud, indulgent Mother,*
enters with her three sons. When the boys leave, she *slowly removes her mask, laying it on the bench and stares up at the moon
with a wistful resigned sweetness* — looking, presumably, like
Dion's mother. The "eternal girl-woman with a virtuous simplicity

of instinct," she illustrates what Kublai Kaan had in mind when he spoke of the "eternal life of life." So long as Margaret lives, the Dions — lovers, husbands, boys — shall live, sleeping under her heart, in the womb.

The Great God Pan is dead, and dead too is all hope for the creative life. But if Pan is dead, so is Brown. Only Man remains; and he, faced with the equally distasteful alternatives of satanic skepticism and masochistic faith, may find comfort at last in the eternity of the womb — in birth, suffering, recrudescent childishness, death, and rebirth. Failing to solve the artist's dilemma, O'Neill was nevertheless reconciled to the tragedy of existence.

Dionysus or Death

"*Lazarus Laughed,*" said O'Neill at one time, "is *far* the best play I've ever written." This in despite of Nathan who called it "an unsuccessful attempt at what seems to be operatic Biblical fantasy. Less a theatre play than a libretto." Among scholars and critics who have come to O'Neill's support none has been more bountiful in his praise than Oscar Cargill. "With utter contempt for the nay-sayers," Cargill has written,

we may pronounce *Lazarus Laughed* as much superior to all other dramatic conceptions in its day as were *Faust, Hamlet,* and *Oedipus Rex* to the contemporary drama of their times. . . . Who has ever seen *Hamlet, Faust,* and *Oedipus Rex* performed wholly to his satisfaction? *Lazarus Laughed,* like these other plays, is so stimulating to the imagination, the lines offer such a wide variety of possibilities in interpretation, there is so great an opportunity to develop in a new way almost every situation that this drama will never be played wholly to any one's liking, that is, to the satisfaction of any one possessing imagination of the mimetic kind . . . Americans who are so deferential to the work of the writers of other nations, may rejoice in *Lazarus Laughed,* one of the touchstones in dramatic art.

It is difficult to argue with Cargill's assertion that *Lazarus Laughed* will never be played wholly to any one's liking, since it has been produced only twice; the first time, in 1928, at the Pasadena Com-

munity Playhouse, the second at an Eastern university. If it is not
the greatest play of its day, or even the playwright's best, it is the
crucial work of O'Neill's career and the nearest he came to realizing
Macgowan's conception of the "drama of tomorrow."

Waldo Frank included *Lazarus Laughed* among those works of
art which contained what he called the "apocalyptic vision." He
was heartened to observe by 1929 that T. S. Eliot's "older romantic
pessimism" was being superseded by the attitude of our tragic
artists who employ the *apocalyptic method,* who "literally make,"
as he explained, "the plastic form of their vision from the plasmic
substance of their experience — without obedience to conceptual
heritage or aesthetic tradition." Elements of this method are to be
found, said Frank, in the dance of Isadora Duncan,

the sculpture of Gaston Lachaise, the paintings of Arthur Dove, Georgia
O'Keefe, and Marsden Hartley, the music of Leo Ornstein, the writings of
William Carlos Williams, the mystical verse of Hart Crane, the 'Lazarus
Laughed' of Eugene O'Neill, the photographic studies of Alfred Stieg-
litz . . .

Although Frank discerned in *Lazarus Laughed* "a deliberate programme of prophecy," he found that "the texture of the play is
a thin, effete lyricism. O'Neill [he continued] is intellectually
aware of the apocalyptic need in his art; and aesthetically unable to
transfigure his perceptions so as to make his images the organic
stuff of such creation."

In 1927, the year in which O'Neill completed *Lazarus Laughed,*
Eliot exhibited that pessimistic, "reflective temper." Uncongenial
though Eliot's temper was to Frank, it inadvertently served our
critical purpose by illuminating the actual nature of O'Neill's aesthetic-religious striving. In his essay on *Shakespeare and the Stoicism of Seneca* Eliot described an attitude which, deriving from
Seneca, is nevertheless modern and "culminates, if there is ever any
culmination, in the attitude of Nietzsche." The original stoicism,
declared Eliot,

and especially the Roman stoicism, was of course a philosophy suited to
slaves: hence its absorption into early Christianity.

> *A man to join himself with the Universe*
> *In his main sway, and make in all things fit*

A man does not join himself with the Universe so long as he has anything else to join himself with; men who could take part in the life of a thriving Greek city-state had something better to join themselves to; and Christians have had something better. Stoicism is the refuge for the individual in an indifferent or hostile world too big for him; it is the permanent substratum of a number of versions of cheering oneself up. Nietzsche is the most conspicuous modern instance of cheering oneself up. The stoical attitude is the reverse of Christian humility.

Indeed, Nietzsche's attitude Eliot found to be "a kind of stoicism upside-down: for there is not much difference between identifying oneself with the Universe and identifying the Universe with oneself." The foregoing remarks apply equally to O'Neill who, in the apocalyptic *Lazarus Laughed,* proved more conclusively than ever that he was a disciple of Nietzsche.

In *Desire Under the Elms* O'Neill exposed the substratum of paganism in the New England consciousness, revealing the Satyr in Jehovah and suggesting the pervasive presence of the Earth Mother. In *Marco Millions* he depicted the destructive effects of Western Civilization upon the tranquil pagan life of the Eastern World. In *The Great God Brown* he demonstrated how the principal two forces of our civilization, Christianity and Philistinism, have transformed Pan, respectively, into Satan — bitter skepticism, mocking irony, life-weariness — and into Goat — indiscriminate, tasteless ingestion of all objects into the "moral belly." But contemplation of eternity not only quieted the recurrent spasms of hysteria, but transmuted them into paroxysms of spiritual exaltation. The concept of cyclic eternal recurrence of life, introduced as early as *The Fountain,* became the stock solution to the problem of existence. Regarded as mere segments in the great cycle, the anguish of life and the torment of death were rapturously accepted.

The Great God Brown ended with the return of the divine son Dionysus to the womb of the Great Mother. *Lazarus Laughed,* completed the following year, is concerned with the rebirth of Dionysus, its theme being affirmation of life, denial of death. Declared O'Neill:

> The fear of death is the root of all evil, the cause of all man's blundering unhappiness. Lazarus knows there is no death, there is only change. He is reborn without that fear. Therefore he is the first and only man who is

able to laugh affirmatively. His laughter is a triumphant Yes to life in its entirety and its eternity. His laughter affirms God, it is too noble to desire personal immortality, it wills its own extinction, it gives its life for the sake of Eternal Life (patriotism carried to its logical ultimate). His laughter is the direct expression of joy in the Dionysian sense, the joy of a celebrant who is at the same time a sacrifice in the eternal process of change and growth and transmutation which is life, of which his life is an insignificant manifestation, soon to be reabsorbed. And life itself is the self-affirmative joyous laughter of God.

In *The Fountain* Juan announced categorically that "Death is no more!" He died, and his soul was reabsorbed by the "Fountain of Eternity." There were patent evils in the play none of which, however, stemmed from the fear of death. They were concomitants, rather, of imperialism and Christianity, phenomena whose source O'Neill did not probe. In *Marco Millions* the tendency to brood about death appeared as early as the prologue, after which it shared the stage with the impulsion to castigate stupidity, human and divine. In *The Great God Brown* denial of life was the root of all evil. But even the life-affirming Cybel, whose principal function was to quiet the fear of death, was dispirited by the thought of it. Comforted by the Earth Mother, Dion Anthony died, to be followed two acts later by William Brown who enjoyed the additional benefit of a Nietzschean revision of the Sermon on the Mount: "Blessed are they that weep, for they shall laugh!" This is also the gospel according to Lazarus.

The brief episode in St. John: 11 of Lazarus' return from death had served since the Middle Ages as material for homilies on the divinity and power of Christ and on the horrors of death. Although the Biblical incident was utilized during the past century by such writers as Tennyson, Browning, Edwin Arlington Robinson, Andreyev, and Pirandello, it remained for the neo-pagans to give a fresh interpretation to the miracle of death and resurrection. Yeats, in his short play *Calvary* (1920), conceived Lazarus as one who was indignant with Christ for presuming to raise him from the dead; for giving him life when death was what he had asked that he might escape Christ's love. In *The Resurrection* (1931), Yeats depicted the crucial moment in history after "holy Dionysus died," and after Christ "In pity for man's darkening thought . . . issued thence in Galilean turbulence." Following Christ's resurrection, God and man began to "die each other's life, live each other's death." And D. H. Lawrence, in *The Man Who Died* (1928), related how Christ, newly arisen from death, returned to a world in which men were maddened by the "ultimate fear of death," with the "egoistic fear of their own nothingness." From the priestess of Isis he learned "a soft strange courage of life, so different from [his] courage of death."

In *Lazarus Laughed,* O'Neill's contribution to the myth of death and rebirth, Christ plays a minor role. The Gospels may have excited spiritual conflict in *The Great God Brown,* but now they are ignored entirely. The savior is not Christ but Dionysus, whose major prophet was Zarathustra. With Zarathustra O'Neill had emerged from the cave in the mountains to begin his "downgoing", to "bestow and distribute." Together they had encountered the two-fold problem of Christianity and Darwinism, the Saint and the Ape, and found the solution in paganism. "God is dead!" they chorused as they continued their down-going. Arriving at a town, they addressed the people:

I teach you the Superman. Man is something that is to be surpassed. What have ye done to surpass man?

All beings hitherto have created something beyond themselves: and ye want to be the ebb of that great tide, and would rather go back to the beast than surpass man?

What is the ape to man? A laughing-stock, a thing of shame. And just the same shall man be to the Superman: a laughing-stock, a thing of shame.

Ye have made your way from the worm to man, and much within you is still worm. Once were ye apes, and even yet man is more of an ape than any of the apes.

Even the wisest among you is only a disharmony and hybrid of plant and phantom. But do I bid you become phantoms or plants?

Lo, I teach you the Superman!

The Superman is the meaning of the earth. Let your will say: The Superman shall be the meaning of the earth!

I conjure you, my brethren, *remain true to the earth,* and believe not those who speak unto you of superearthly hopes! Poisoners are they, whether they know it or not.

The Dionysian Superman, Lazarus is the "everlasting Yea to all things" — to Life, to woe as well as to joy. A Yea-sayer, he is also a laugher, and with Zarathustra he cries, "Laughing have I con-secrated! Ye higher men, *learn,* I pray you — to laugh!" Thus Lazarus exclaims to his people:

You forget! You forget the God in you! You wish to forget! Remembrance would imply the high duty to live as a son of God — generously! — with love! — with pride! — with laughter! This is too glorious a victory for you, too terrible a loneliness! Easier to forget, to become only a man, the son of a woman, to hide from life against her breast, to whimper your fear to her resigned heart and be comforted by her resignation! To live by denying life!

In O'Neill's fusion of dramaturgy and thaumaturgy former dis-harmonies vanish wherever death, the root of all evil, is eradicated. Thinker and skeptic are replaced by the laughing redeemer, divine hero with a firm faith and a strong will; Christ, Saint, Satan by immortal Dionysus. For Lazarus is indeed Dionysus, and if his own people do not recognize him the Greeks do. Arriving in Athens on his way to Rome, in Act Two–Scene One, he is greeted by a Chorus of Greeks *clad in goat skins, their tanned bodies and masks daubed and stained with wine lees, in imitation of the old followers of Dionysus. Rumor has led them to hope and believe that* Lazarus *may be the reincarnation of this deity.* Appearing with Followers and Chorus, who wear masks representing a variety of "races" — Egyptian, Syrian, Cappadocian, Lydian, Phrygian, Cilician, Parthian — Lazarus is attired like a Greek God. He is

dressed in a tunic of white and gold, his bronzed face and limbs radiant in the halo of his own glowing light . . . His countenance now might well be that of the positive masculine Dionysus, closest to the soil of the Grecian gods, a Son of Man, born of a mortal. Not the coarse, drunken Dionysus, nor the effeminate god, but Dionysus in his middle period, more compre-hensive in his symbolism, the soul of the recurring seasons, of living and dying as processes in eternal growth, of the wine of life stirring forever in the sap and blood and loam of things.

Again, here is Nietzsche's Dionysus with a difference. Yea-sayer, laugher, lover of eternity, exemplar of eternal recurrence, Lazarus is the savage deity tamed by tender love. If he is more temperate than the Nietzschean Dionysus, it is because the "wine of life" intoxicates him less. One is impressed with his almost maternal tenderness, his saintliness, his rapturous other-worldiness. If he is

the masculine counterpart of that other divinity of earth, Cybel —
the Great Mother —, he is also the pagan counterpart of Christ —
for whom, indeed, he is O'Neill's substitute. Son of woman, not
of God, the reborn Lazarus moves through the life cycle of the
typical savior, converting many as he preaches his gospel, only to
be put to "death" at last by the unbelievers.

Divine though he be, Lazarus shares certain characteristics of
O'Neill's mortal heroes — Robert Mayo, Juan, Michael Cape, Dion
Anthony — who, in turn, displayed a kinship with O'Neill himself. Thus Lazarus is an "impractical dreamer," inept in the world
of affairs. We are told that "the neighbors all get the best of
[him]," that "money slips through his fingers." Mildly distressed
on one occasion by his awareness of this trait, he is comforted by
his wife:

But dearest husband, why do you take it so to heart? Why do you feel
guilty because you are not like other men? That is why I love you so much.
Is it a sin to be born a dreamer? But God, He must be a dreamer, too, or
how would we be on earth? Do not keep saying to yourself so bitterly, you
are a failure in life! Do not sit brooding on the hill-top in the evening like
a black figure of Job against the sky!

Lazarus' wife loves him, but she never fully understands him.
For, like the other heroes who are given to God-like dreaming,
Lazarus is subtle, profound, and visionary beyond the comprehension of woman, who is possessed of a more practical, simple, instinctual nature.

Throughout the play, in a series of Zarathustran discourses,
Lazarus expounds his religious philosophy, the theme of which is
the non-existence of death, the "eternal life of life." Speaking with
the authority of one who has been dead, he illustrates what William
James meant when he referred to those who have experienced
"well-pronounced and emphatic" mystical states. "They have been
'there,' and know," said James. When Lazarus is asked "What is
beyond?" he can reply with exaltation as well as authority, "Life!
Eternity! Stars and dust! God's Eternal Laughter!" His first discourse on the oneness and eternity of life is delivered in Act One-
Scene Two. Chiding his people for living "by denying life," he
exclaims exhortingly:

Why are your eyes always either fixed on the ground in weariness of thought, or watching one another with suspicion? Throw your gaze upward! To Eternal Life! To the fearless and deathless! The everlasting! To the stars! (*He stretches out his arms to the sky — then suddenly points*) See! A new star has appeared! It is the one that shone over Bethlehem! (*His voice becomes a little bitter and mocking*) The Master of Peace and Love has departed this earth. Let all stars be for you henceforth symbols of Saviors — Sons of God who appeared on worlds like ours to tell the saving truth to ears like yours, inexorably deaf! (*Then exaltedly*) But the greatness of Saviors is that they may not save! The greatness of Man is that no god can save him — until he becomes a god!

The stars — of which the star of Bethlehem is only one — are symbols of eternity. Exemplars of self-dependence, they are a part of the eternal cosmic whole of which Man, too, is a part. If men refuse to be saved, the fault is in themselves; for they deny and fear life, forgetting the God that is in them, failing to recognize their kinship with the stars. This note of optimism and self-reliance is further developed in Act Two–Scene One when, in a second discourse, Lazarus exhorts the Romans to become conscious of the cosmos rather than of themselves. "But what do you matter, O Deathly-Important One?" he asks Caligula. "Put yourself that question — as a jester."

(*Exultantly*) Are you a speck of dust danced in the wind? Then laugh, dancing! Laugh yes to your insignificance! Thereby will be born your new greatness! As Man, Petty Tyrant of Earth, you are a bubble pricked by death into a void and a mocking silence! But as dust, you are eternal change, and everlasting growth, and a high note of laughter soaring through chaos from the deep heart of God! Be proud, O Dust! Then you may love the stars as equals! (*Then mockingly . . .*) And then perhaps you may be brave enough to love even your fellow men without fear of their vengeance!

Like Emerson, Lazarus preaches an idealism which recognizes eternal change, eternal growth within the blessed Whole. God *is;* he is in man, in the stars. And man and stars alike are emanations of God. Evil — death, sorrow, fear — is not absolute, but exists "in the minds of men." It is an invention of man, explains Lazarus. Then he continues:

Tragic is the plight of the tragedian whose only audience is himself! Life is for each man a solitary cell whose walls are mirrors! Terrified is Caligula by the face he makes! But I tell you to laugh in the mirror, that seeing your life gay, you may begin to live as a guest, and not as a condemned one!

. . . Listen! In the dark peace of the grave the man called Lazarus rested. He was still weak, as one who recovers from a long illness — for, living, he had believed his life a sad one! (*He laughs softly, and softly they all echo his laughter*) He lay dreaming to the croon of silence, feeling as the flow of blood in his own veins the past re-enter the heart of God to be renewed by faith into the future. He thought: 'Men call this death' — for he had been dead only a little while and he still remembered. Then, of a sudden, a strange gay laughter trembled from his heart as though his life, so long repressed in him by fear, had found at last its voice and a song for singing. 'Men call this death,' it sang. 'Men call life death and fear it. They hide from it in horror. Their lives are spent in hiding. Their fear becomes their living. They worship life as death!'

Since reality is subjective, men can will a joyful life in place of one of sorrow and fear. "Men must learn to live. Before their fear invented death they knew, but now they have forgotten. They must be taught to laugh again!" If men are fallen yet "nature is erect." They may seek, therefore, its "medicinal enchantments" to sober and heal themselves. Lazarus continues, *as to a crowd of children — laughingly:*

Out with you! Out into the woods! Upon the hills! Cities are prisons wherein man locks himself from life. Out with you under the sky! Are the stars too pure for your sick passions? Is the warm earth smelling of night too desirous of love for your pale introspective lusts? Out! Let laughter be your new clean lust and sanity! So far man has only learned to snicker meanly at his neighbor! Let a laughing away of self be your new right to live forever! Cry in your pride, 'I am laughter, which is Life, which is the Child of God!'

The egoistic concept of personal immortality must surrender to the recognition that all matter is immortal, that all things eternally recur. The universe has no goal, no final state. Nor is there a creating and directing deity — only a God who laughs. When his followers die, in Act Two–Scene Two, Lazarus defends his laughter:

(*exultingly*) Did they not laugh? That was their victory and glory! (*With more and more of a passionate, proud exultation*) Eye to eye with the Fear of Death, did they not laugh with scorn? 'Death to old Death,' they laughed! 'Once as squirming specks we crept from the tides of the sea! Now we return to the sea! Once as quivering flecks of rhythm we beat down from the sun. Now we re-enter the sun. Cast aside is our pitiable pretense, our immortal egohood, the holy lantern behind which cringed our Fear of the Dark! Flung off is that impudent insult to life's nobility which gibbers:

'I, this Jew, this Roman, this noble or this slave, must survive in my pettiness
forever!' Away with such cowardice of spirit! We will to die! We will to
change! Laughing we lived with our gift, now with laughter give we back
that gift to become again the Essence of the Giver! Dying we laugh with
the Infinite. We are the Giver and the Gift! Laughing, we will our own
annihilation! Laughing, we give our lives for Life's sake!' (*He laughs up to
heaven ecstatically*) This must Man will as his end and his new beginning!
He must conceive and desire his own passing as a mood of eternal laughter
and cry with pride, 'Take back, O God, and accept in turn a gift from me,
my grateful blessing for Your gift — and see, O God, now I am laughing
with You! I am Your laughter — and You are mine!'

Apart from the non-existence of death there are a number of
advantages to be gained by accepting Lazarus' religious philosophy.
Man need no longer be lonely, for he has the companionship of
"millions of laughing stars" and the knowledge that new stars are
being "born of dust eternally" — of "laughing dust," like himself.
Thus "there is no death, nor fear, nor loneliness! There is only
God's Eternal Laughter!" which "flows into the lonely heart!" Not
only does loneliness vanish, but hope appears, as man becomes less
obsessed with the idea of personal immortality:

Love is Man's hope — love for his life on earth, a noble love above suspicion and distrust! Hitherto Man has always suspected his life, and in
revenge and self-torture his love has been faithless! He has even betrayed
Eternity, his mother, with his slave he calls Immortal Soul!

Hitherto the fear of death had been quieted by resignation, the
attitude of men "whose lives are long dyings."

They evade their fear of death by becoming so sick of life that by the time
death comes they are too lifeless to fear it! Their disease triumphs over death
— a noble victory called resignation! 'We are sick,' they say, 'therefore there
is no God in us, therefore there is no God!'

A third advantage derives from the realization that life is eternal.
No longer need man yearn for youth and dread old age. In short,
no longer need he be dispirited by the passage of time. For "age
and time are but timidities of thought," "meaningless in infinity."
Having vanquished death, fear, loneliness, and despair, Lazarus,
inspired by Nietzsche, presents a final attraction: there is no evil.
There "are only health and sickness." He exhorts Caligula, personification of "evil," to "believe in the healthy god called Man
in you! Laugh at Caligula, the funny clown who beats the back-

side of his shadow with a bladder and thinks thereby he is Evil, the Enemy of God!" Evil, like death, is merely man's invention and as transitory as men themselves, of whom only the essence endures — the symbol, Man. With stars and dust he shares eternity, being a creation of God's Eternal Laughter. "Believe!" Lazarus charges Caligula.

What if you are a man and men are despicable? Men are also unimportant! Men pass! Like rain into the sea! The sea remains! Man slowly arises from the past of the race of men that was his tomb of death! For Man death is not! Man, Son of God's laughter, *is!* (*He begins to laugh triumphantly, staring into Caligula's eyes*) *Is,* Caligula! Believe in the laughing god within you!

Serenely confident in his optimistic-pantheistic faith, Lazarus, unlike those heroes who were possessed of two souls, avoids the afflictions which the tortured spirit is heir to: dissociation of personality, skepticism, frustration, self-pity, life-weariness, even fixation on the mother. In short, Lazarus is a hero without a tragic flaw, one whom fate cannot intimidate. Dramatic action in *Lazarus Laughed* is achieved by revealing the hostility to Lazarus of the unbelievers among the bigoted Jews, the fanatical Christians, the decadent Romans. Dramatic suspense occurs when conversions hang in the balance; the crisis, where Lazarus falters, only to be vindicated. The play begins in Bethany some time after the miracle of Lazarus' resurrection and ends in Rome four acts and eight scenes later when Lazarus is burned at the stake. Appearing in the first scene in the House of Laughter, he is readily distinguished from his fellow Jews not only by his face which is Greek rather than Semitic, but also by his halo and his "illumined" body. About *fifty years* of age at his rebirth, Lazarus grows younger as the play progresses. A variation of the familiar rapid regression to childhood, the phenomenon in *Lazarus Laughed* provides palpable testimony to the truth of the assertion that "age and time are but timidities of thought." The sad old Lazarus had died of self-pity. Having "known [his] fill of life and the sorrow of living," he had longed for peace and had therefore "wished for death." Now since his return, although his Dionysian spirit permeates his people, a note of uncertainty may be discerned in their laughter. For while it is *dominated and inspired by the high, free, aspiring, exulting laughter of Lazarus,* it is also *harsh, discordant, frenzied, desperate and drunken.* Scene One ends on this suggestion of discord and uncertainty.

In the second scene, which occurs some months later, two groups hostile to each other have formed: *The adherents of Jesus, the Nazarenes, among whom may be noted* Martha *and* Mary, sisters of Lazarus; on the other side *the Orthodox, among whom are* Lazarus' Father *and* Mother *and a* Priest . . . Contemptuous of both parties, imbued equally as they are with hatred and fanaticism, O'Neill demonstrated in this scene the manifest superiority of pagan affirmation over life-denying Judaism and Christianity. The Priest, a religious fanatic, embodiment of Old Testament anger and preoccupation with sin, tears his beard and stamps with rage when Mary defends her loyalty to Jesus. "It is a foul sin in the sight of Jehovah!" he cries . . . "The Lord God will punish you!" Mary, *echoing him,* replies, "Jesus will never forgive you!" And shortly after with *fanatic fervor* she exclaims, "He is a king! Whenever He chooses He will gather a great army and He will seize His kingdom and all who deny Him will be crucified!" As she becomes increasingly hysterical, as the Priest becomes more enraged, news of Christ's crucifixion arrives. Whereupon the Priest *with fierce triumph* shouts, "Jehovah is avenged! Hosannah!" And Mary, *insane with rage,* screams, "They have murdered Him!" Her Old Testament impulses coming to the surface, she calls *to her followers — savagely,* "An eye for an eye! Avenge the Master!" *With cries of rage the two groups rush on one another,* and the destruction is intensified by the arrival of a Roman Centurion with a squad of soldiers who use their swords to strike down everyone in their way. Miriam, Lazarus' wife, cries to the Romans for mercy, but, *as they pay no attention to her, in desperation she embraces* Lazarus *beseechingly, forcing his attention back to earth.* Looking *down upon the struggling mass* he *cries in a ringing voice,* "Hold!"

Each person stands transfixed, frozen in the last movement, even the Roman Soldiers *and the* Centurion *himself. Ten dead and mortally wounded lie on the ground, trampled by the feet of friend and foe alike.* Lazarus *looks at the* Crowd. *To each he seems to look at him or her alone. His eyes are accusing and stern. As one head, the heads of all are averted. Even the* Centurion *stares at the ground humbly, in spite of himself. Finally* Lazarus *speaks in a voice of infinite disdain:*

"Sometimes it is hard to laugh — even *at* men!" Killed in the affray are Lazarus' father, mother, and sisters Martha and Mary. As he kneels beside their bodies and *kisses each in turn on the forehead,* his struggle with grief is perceptible. But he overcomes it. He *looks up to the stars and, as if answering a question, again says simply and acceptingly,* "Yes!" *Then exultantly,* "Yes!!" *And begins to laugh from the depths of his exalted spirit.*

Lazarus' conversions come hard. Even Miriam resists. For as the counterpart of Margaret, Dion Anthony's wife-mother, she is "oblivious to everything but the means to her end of maintaining the race." Miriam's *mask is the pure pallor of marble,*

the expression that of a statue of Woman, of her eternal acceptance of the compulsion of motherhood, the inevitable cycle of love into pain into joy and new love into separation and pain again and the loneliness of age. The eyes of the mask are almost closed. Their gaze turns within, oblivious to the life outside, as they dream down on the child forever in memory at her breast.

The eternal mother, she is distressed by any harm that befalls her creatures. The source of life, she agonizes over their death. Thus in the second scene, when the death of Jesus is announced, unlike the Nazarenes who mourn His death because He is the Son of God, she grieves because a Son of Man has died. When, in Act Two–Scene Two, Caligula threatens to kill Lazarus' followers, Miriam implores him to spare them. "And why should you plead for them, Jewess?" asks Caligula. "There are few Jews among them. They are mostly those whom your people call idolaters and would gladly see murdered." *With deep grief,* she replies, "I am a mother of dead children. I plead for the mothers of those who are about to die." After Caligula fulfills his threat, Miriam *kneels bowed with grief* and says *brokenly* to her husband, "Those who have just died were like your children, Lazarus. They believed in you and loved you." Even after he explains to her the facts of death she can only *sigh* and *meekly* reply, "I cannot understand, Lazarus. (*Sadly*) They were like your children — and they have died. Must you not mourn for them? . . . They are gone from us. And their mothers weep." Lazarus is patient with this maternal obtuseness, for he not only loves Miriam, he also has faith in his new religion. What is more, he is patient and loving even though the Mother permits the Sons "to hide from life against her breast, to whimper [their] fear to her resigned heart and be comforted by her resignation!" But if the Mother encourages denial of life, Miriam redeems herself after she dies by confirming Lazarus' faith at the crucial moment of the play. Once dead, she says, "Yes." A symbol in *Lazarus Laughed* of only secondary magnitude, the Mother still contributes a desirable quality to the faith which Lazarus preaches. "Now your love has become Eternal Love," says Lazarus to the dead Miriam. "Now, since your life passed, I feel Eternal Life made nobler by your selflessness! Love has grown purer! The laughter of God is more profoundly tender!"

From Mother Miriam flow such blessings as Eternal Love, a benefit which compensates for her encouragement of the un-Dionysian tendency of resignation. Her antithesis is Livia, mother of Tiberius, who instigates denial of life in its more virulent aspects. Embodiment of a sinister maternity, Livia is the source of hatred and cruelty. Owing to her, Tiberius has become the "most swinish and contemptible of men." He is about the same age as Ephraim Cabot, but he is less fortunate in every respect. He is an "old buck goat" rather than a satyr, and he wants youth again because he loathes lust and longs for purity. A sophisticated misanthropist, he "can deal with men," for, as he says, "I know them well. Too well. Therefore I hate them." And if he knows and hates men, he also understands and loathes himself. He fears "the long nights now in which [he] lie[s] awake and listen[s] to Death dancing round [him] in the darkness." Turning, like Dion Anthony, to vocalized self-analysis, Tiberius does O'Neill the disservice of contradicting the theme of the play. For it becomes evident as the old man reveals "the thing one has always kept hidden," that fear of death is merely one of the branches of evil, that in his case the root of all evil is the mother. In a monologue of self-confession unexceeded in length until *The Iceman Cometh,* Tiberius relates how his mother,

Livia, that strong woman, giving birth to me, desired not a child, but a Caesar — just as, married to Augustus, she loved him not but loved herself as Caesar's wife. She made me feel, in the proud questioning of her scornful eyes, that to win her mother love I must become Caesar. She poisoned Prince Marcellus and young Gaius and Lucius that the way might be clear for me. I used to see their blood dance in red specks before my eyes when I looked at the sky. Now — (*He brushes his hand before his eyes*) it is all a red blot! . . . My mother — her blood is in that blot, for I revenged myself on her. I did not kill her, it is true, but I deprived her of her power and she died, as I knew she must, that powerful woman who bore me as a weapon! The murder was subtle and cruel — how cruel only that passionate, deep-breasted woman unslaked by eighty years of devoured desires could know! Too cruel! I did not go to her funeral. I was afraid her closed eyes might open and look at me! (*Then with almost a cry*) I want youth, Lazarus, that I may play again about her feet with the love I felt for her before I learned to read her eyes! (*He half sobs, bowing his head.*)

Still hating his mother, he explains that she is responsible for his envy of "those who are loved," for his compulsion to "kill love." It is "for retribution's sake," he insists. He had been married; whereupon "that proud woman," his mother, seeing his happiness, jealous perhaps of his love, "condemned [his] happiness to death" by forcing him to divorce his wife and marry a whore, Caesar's daughter. The mother's motive, he feels, was "to keep [him] tortured that [he] might love her alone and long to be Caesar!" After which the scheming of "that subtle and crafty woman" prospered —

and many years passed in being here and there, in doing this and that, in growing full of hate and revengeful ambition, to be Caesar. At last, Augustus died. I was Caesar. Then I killed that whore, my wife, and I starved my mother's strength to death until she died, and I began to take pleasure in vengeance upon men, and pleasure in taking vengeance on myself.

Deprived of tender-maternal love, Dion Anthony wore a satanic mask in self-protection. For the same reason Tiberius has become the most contemptible of men. Loathing himself, he yearns for the innocence and love of early childhood before he had learned to read his mother's eyes. And now he asks the ultimate stock questions which O'Neill's heroes invariably ask, questions to which O'Neill frenziedly strove to supply answers. "How must we live?" implores Tiberius. "Wherein lies happiness? Why are we born? To what end must we die?" Willing to settle for peace, he is promised precisely that by Lazarus. "There is peace!" cries Lazarus, and the *words are like a benediction. Soothed in a mysterious child-like way,* Tiberius repeats the *word after him, wonderingly,* and then proclaims his conversion by shouting:

I have lived long enough! . . . I no longer fear death! I laugh! I laugh at Caesar! I advise you, my brothers, fear not Caesars! Seek man in the brotherhood of the dust! Caesar is your fear of Man! I counsel you, laugh away your Caesars!

If Miriam and Livia together embody the totality of eternal-maternal female qualities, Pompeia, Tiberius' paramour, personifies the eternal mistress — sexual love, passion. Miriam being dead, Pompeia tries to arouse Lazarus' passion. "I love you, Lazarus!" she cries, and gasps with delight when he responds, "And I love you, woman." But to her dismay, she discovers that he loves Woman, not women. Like other females, her "simplicity of instinct," her capacity to comprehend only the practical and the concrete, have made her oblivious to spiritual, abstract reality. Nevertheless she, too, is one of the elect. As Lazarus is being burned alive, crying "Yes" from the flames *in a triumphant assertion of the victory of life over pain and death,* Pompeia finds the situation irresistible.

rising to her feet like one in a trance, staring toward Lazarus . . . *she moves to the top of the steps leading to the arena. Suddenly the flames waver, die down, then shoot up again and* Pompeia's *laughter is heard for a moment, rising clear and passionately with that of* Lazarus, *then dying quickly out.*

Although men are neither evil nor important, they *are* despicable. Accordingly Lazarus encounters those who are immune to salvation — none other than our old friends the brutes. Appearing collectively as the Crowd, individually as Caligula, in either aspect they are apes. Christian, Jewish, Roman, "mob is the same everywhere," with one exception. O'Neill differentiates, as we shall see, between the bestial Crowd on the one hand, the faithful Followers on the other. In *Lazarus Laughed* he was interested, as he explained in his *Memoranda on Masks,* in the artistic effects of stage crowds and mobs, of impersonal, collective mob psychology: "When the Crowd speaks I wanted an audience to hear the voice of Crowd mind, Crowd emotion, as one voice of a body composed of, but quite distinct from, its parts." Kenneth Macgowan was deeply impressed when, in 1922, he watched the performance in Berlin of Toller's *Masse Mensch,* a play which the Theatre Guild produced in 1924. Toller's attitude towards the mob was as realistic as O'Neill's but more benevolent and sanguine. "The Masses are not holy," his heroine exclaims.

> Force made the Masses
> Injustice of possession made the Masses.
> The Masses are instinct, necessity,
> Are credulous humility,
> Revenge and cruelty,
> The Masses are blind slaves
> And holy aspiration.
> The Masses are a trampled field,
> A buried people.

Robert Edmond Jones, as we have seen, was interested in "group-beings"; and Macgowan envisioned a drama in which such beings would be masked in order to attain what he described as "a certain strange and enthralling sense of the mystic quality of the theatre." O'Neill appears to have striven for a similar effect in *Lazarus Laughed*. Whereas in Greek tragedy the mask was used to represent allegorical figures such as Justice, Persuasion, Deceit, Jealousy, Death, Frenzy, O'Neill gave the device a psychological as well as an allegorical emphasis. His crowd, consisting of 49 individuals, are masked according to age and personality type.

There are seven periods of life shown: Boyhood (or Girlhood), Youth, Young Manhood (or Womanhood), Manhood or (Womanhood), Middle Age, Maturity and Old Age; and each of these periods is represented by seven different masks of general types of character as follows: The Simple, Ignorant; the Happy, Eager; the Self-Tortured, Introspective; the Proud, Self-Reliant; the Servile, Hypocritical; the Revengeful, Cruel; the Sorrowful, Resigned.

This proliferation of types out of the earlier "romantic dreamer-ambitious thinker" combination of opposites followed by three years, and was probably suggested by, Jung's elaboration of his own theory of introversion and extraversion. The elaborate process of fragmentizing and classifying may have a psychological relevancy, but its dramatic value is difficult to discover. Nor does it alter O'Neill's obvious contempt for the crowd whose behavior he could never reconcile with human dignity and virtue.

Nietzsche referred to the masses as "buffoons," as "consumptive populace dogs," as an "ill-constituted sullen brood." Yet under certain circumstances the crowd elicited from him the greatest respect: when its Dionysian emotions have been aroused, when it is intoxicated with Dionysian joy. Thus he admired the singing and dancing crowds of the German Middle Ages which

ever-increasing in number, were whirled from place to place under this same
Dionysian impulse. In these dancers of St. John and St. Vitus, we rediscover
the Bacchic choruses of the Greeks, with their early history in Asia Minor,
as far back as Babylon and the orgiastic Sacaea. There are some, who, from
obtuseness or lack of experience, will deprecate such phenomena as 'folk-
diseases,' with contempt or pity born of the consciousness of their own
'healthy-mindedness.' But, of course, such poor wretches can not imagine
how anemic and ghastly their so-called 'healthy-mindedness' seems in contrast
to the glowing life of the Dionysian revelers rushing past them.

In *Lazarus Laughed* the contrast between the "ill-constituted sullen
brood" and the Dionysian revelers is apparent as early as the second
scene of the first act, when Nazarenes and Orthodox *immediately
forget their differences and form into one mob on the appearance of
the* Followers. Led by their Chorus of Old Men, the mob is pervaded
by *a queer excitement.*

*They begin to weave in and out, clasping each other's hands now and then,
moving mechanically in jerky steps to the music in a grotesque sort of
marionettes' country dance. At first this is slow but it momentarily becomes
more hectic and peculiar. They raise clenched fists or hands distended into
threatening talons. Their voices sound thick and harsh and animal-like with
anger as they mutter and growl, each one aloud to himself or herself.*

The behavior of this crowd resembles that of the stokers, the
Neanderthal Men, of *The Hairy Ape.* They *never cease to hop up
and down, to mill around, to twist their bodies toward and away
from each other in bestial parody of the dance of the* Followers of
Lazarus who had previously appeared, *forty-nine in number,*

*composed about equally of both sexes, [wearing] a mask that, while recog-
nizably Jewish is a* Lazarus *mask, resembling him in its expression of fearless
faith in life, the mouth shaped by laughter . . . The music continues to come
from within. Laughing, the* Followers *dance to it in weaving patterns on the
terrace. They are dressed in bright-colored diaphanous robes. Their chorused
laughter, now high and clear, now dying to a humming murmur, stresses
the rhythmic flow of the dance.*

Expressing themselves in song and in dance, the Followers of
Dionysus are members of a "higher community," their gospel being
"universal harmony." Their superiority over the bestial mob is
maintained to their "death," which comes in Act Two–Scene Two.
Crassus, a Roman general, describes the death scene wherein Laz-

arus' converts, true to their faith, die laughing. "Have you killed all his followers?" inquires Caligula *harshly*. And Crassus replies:

No. They died. They did not wait for our attack. They charged upon us, laughing! They tore our swords away from us, laughing, and we laughed with them! They stabbed themselves, dancing as though it were a festival! They died, laughing, in one another's arms! We laughed, too, with joy because it seemed it was not they who died but death itself they killed! (*He stops uncertainly, bowing to* Lazarus, *awkwardly*) I do not understand this. I am a soldier. But there is a god in it somewhere! For I know they were drunk, and so were we, with a happiness no mortal ever felt on earth before! And death was dead!

It is Caligula who *disdainfully* observes that "mob is the same everywhere"; and it is ironical that he should be the one to say so, being its individual counterpart. Caligula's personality is an aggregate of disharmonious crowd characteristics; he is grotesque ape, cruel boy, brutal soldier, decadent Roman, innocent child. With the crowd, he is the embodiment and the amplification of man's faults — despicable, capricious, obscene. Together they represented O'Neill's conception of the nature and destiny of man; tragically incapable of participating in the love, peace, primordial harmony which Lazarus is prepared to offer them. Whereas the innocence and love of Tiberius' childhood had been corrupted by a possessive and power-obsessed mother, the early days of Caligula had been perverted by the *coarse brutality of camps*. Why O'Neill neglected to account for Caligula's early relationship with the mother, as he did at such great length in the case of Tiberius and of Dion Anthony, remains a mystery. Throughout the three acts of the play in which Caligula appears as a figure rivaling Lazarus in importance, he exhibits the conflicting aspects of his personality. Alternately absurd and pathetic, he is overwhelmed at times as the irreconcilable selves become locked in irresolvable struggle. Thus, at the opening of Act Three–Scene One, having come under Lazarus' influence, *he is in a state of queer conflicting emotion, seeming to be filled with a nervous dread and terror of everything about him, while at the same time perversely excited and elated by his own morbid tension.* On other occasions the antithetical aspects of his nature are revealed separately. He is given to *squatting on his hams, monkey-wise;* to crouching *on his haunches;* to whimpering and slinking; and he refers to himself as "a trained ape." The spoiled child in Caligula is apparent when he announces, "I like to watch men die," — exhibiting the sadism of a little boy torturing insects or cats. The same quality appears as he asks Lazarus, *with a childish, mischievous curiosity,* "Then if there is no death, O Teacher, tell me why I love to kill?" Torn between bestiality and innocence, he can never quite bring himself into spiritual accord with Lazarus, however strong the attraction. Thus, after he comes to love Lazarus — love being an emotion that is foreign to him — he tries to protect him from Tiberius. In Act Three–Scene Two after Caligula slays Flavius, whom he has mistaken for the emperor, he laughs for the first time *a clear laughter of selfless joy.* Coming from him, it sounds *startlingly incongruous.* Childishly he cries, "I have saved you, Lazarus — at the risk of my own life — and now, hear me, I can laugh!" But as he *stands with upraised sword by the chair of Caesar, suddenly his laughter cracks, changes, becomes full of his old fear and bloodlust.* That his motive in killing Flavius is a mixed one is evident as he exclaims, "See, Lazarus! (*He points to the body of Flavius with his sword*) Welcome in the name of Caesar, now Caesar is slain and I am Caesar! (*He assumes the absurd grandiose posture of his imperial posing. . . .*)" Slow-witted, like his prototype, the Hairy Ape, he is within reach of the blessedness for which he yearns, but he cannot "get *in* it." In Act Four–Scene One, as Lazarus stares deep into his eyes and urges him to "believe in the laughing god within [himself]," Caligula bursts *suddenly into choking, joyful laughter, and like a visionary,* declares,

I believe! I believe there is love even for Caligula! I can laugh — now — Lazarus! Free laughter! Clean! No sickness! No lust for death! My corpse no longer rots in my heart! The tomb is full of sunlight! I am alive! I who love Man, I who can love and laugh! Listen, Lazarus! I dream! When I am Caesar, I will devote my power to your truth. I will decree that there must be kindness and love! I will make the Empire one great Blessed Isle! Rome shall know happiness, it shall believe in life, it shall learn to laugh your laughter, Lazarus, or I — (*He raises his hand in an imperial autocratic gesture.*)

Whereupon, to this counterpart of Mussolini Lazarus responds, "Or you will cut off its head?" "Yes! I will — !" Caligula *fiercely* cries.

Then meeting Lazarus' *eyes, he beats his head with his fists crazily* and pleads, "Forgive me! I forget! I forget!"

The child in Caligula, craving love, attaches himself to Lazarus, who is Dionysus and Cybel combined. His attitude towards Lazarus is that of a *spoiled, petulant and self-obsessed* child who is uncertain of his mother's affections. "Oh, no, you cannot love me!" he protests to Lazarus. And then in guilty abnegation: "There is nothing in me at bottom but a despising and an evil eye! You cannot! You are only being kind!" Whereupon he struggles unsuccessfully to ignore and to surmount his deep need: "(*Hysterically*) I do not want your kindness! I hate your pity! I am too proud! I am too strong! (*He collapses weepingly, kneeling and clutching* Lazarus' *hand in both of his*)." When, at last, he kills Tiberius, in the final scene of the play — as Lazarus burns at the stake — his principal motive is jealousy. Observing Tiberius' conversion, Caligula screams with *resentful jealousy and rage:* "What do I hear, Lazarus? You laugh with your murderer? You give him your laughter? You have forgotten me — my love — you make him love you — you make him laugh at Caesars — at me!" Having choked Tiberius, he screams, "You have betrayed me, dog of a Jew! You have betrayed Caesar!" He snatches a spear and "kills" Lazarus. This accomplished, he *suddenly* [throws] *his spear away and* [sinks] *on his knees, his face toward* Lazarus, *and says supplicatingly,* "Lazarus! Forgive me! Help me! Fear kills me! Save me from death! (*He is groveling in a paroxysm of terror, grinding his face in his fists as if to hide it.*)" Lazarus' voice is then heard

in a gentle, expiring sigh of compassion, followed by a faint dying note of laughter that rises and is lost in the sky like the flight of his soul back into the womb of Infinity. Fear not, Caligula! There is no death!

Caligula. (*lifts his head at the first sound and rises with the laughter to his feet, until, as it is finally lost, he is on tip-toes, his arms straining upward to the sky, a tender, childish laughter of love on his lips*) I laugh, Lazarus! I laugh with you!

But then, before the final curtain falls, there is a resurgence in Caligula of the ape.

(*He hides his face in his hands, weeping*) No more! (*Then beats his head with his fists*) I will remember! I will! (*Then suddenly, with a return to grotesqueness — harshly*) All the same, I killed him and I proved there is

death! (*Immediately overcome by remorse, groveling and beating himself*)
Fool! Madman! Forgive me, Lazarus! Men forget!

Symbol of man, of man's fear of death, Caligula is not yet ready
for Lazarus' message of comfort and faith. Like the generality of
men, he still needs his sword "to slash at ghosts in the dark. Men,
those haunted heroes!" For mob man there is even less to be said.
As Caligula waves his bloody spear after killing Lazarus and
shouts, "I have killed God! I am Death! Death is Caesar!" the
Crowd turns and scurries away — *huddled in fleeing groups,
crouching close to the ground like a multitude of terrified rats, their
voices squeaky now with fright.*

After *Lazarus Laughed* O'Neill ceased to be aware of the "apocalyptic need in his art" and abruptly terminated his "programme
of prophecy" — not, to be sure, out of deference to Eliot. Having at
last succeeded in regenerating Dionysus, having traced evil to its
source, having identified Man with the Universe, the Universe with
Man, he found nothing more to do along that line. Forswearing
Dionysian drunkenness, he began with dour sobriety to explore the
matter of dream and death. With the dissolution of the triumvirate
—Macgowan, Jones, O'Neill — an incident which coincided with
the completion of *Lazarus Laughed,* O'Neill abandoned the "drama
of tomorrow" for the drama of today.

PART THREE

Death

Everywoman

But whatever one brings to 'Strange Interlude' out of the fulness of one's life and whatever one takes from it, it will be found to be one of the most distinguished pieces of dramatic writing that our American stage has known.

Nathan, who had scorned *Lazarus Laughed,* concluded his long preview of *Strange Interlude* with the foregoing sentence. Writing nearly a decade and a half later, Cargill, who had eulogized *Lazarus,* was disdainful of *Interlude.* "If ever a play were designed to tickle the bourgeois palate," remarked Cargill, "this one was." "*Strange Interlude* is not an original dramatic composition, but a case history." Whereas the former play has never been produced in the commercial theatre, the latter, staged by the Theatre Guild, was O'Neill's most popular success. Performances of O'Neill's longest play began at 5:30, were interrupted by a dinner intermission of an hour after Act V, and continued till 11:00. Having produced Shaw's *Back to Methuselah* in 1922, a play which required three evenings to perform, the Guild undertook the production of *Strange Interlude* fortified by prior experience with the over-size play. The Guild lost $20,000 on the Shaw venture, but O'Neill's show "played six performances a week for one and one half years without a vacant seat at any performance even in hottest weather."

Lazarus Laughed exhibited O'Neill's "propensity to the grandiose and the lavish"; *Strange Interlude* reveals his "ambition to achieve size." A realistic play, *Interlude* exemplifies that "special sort of Naturalism which develops into the mythical." The pagan myth has been abandoned; the new myth is more conspicuously permeated by the psychological tendency. According to his friend Nathan, O'Neill aimed "at an elaborate clinical psychological study of his characters and an automatic commentary upon and analysis of them," an intention which gave to the play a quality of the novel. Indeed, he had "long been pondering," Nathan informs us, "a technical innovation," namely, "a combination of the method of the novel and that of the drama." Such an innovation as it is employed in *Strange Interlude* was justified, pragmatically at least, by the play's popular success both in the theatre and in book form. Its amplitude and its great length deterred neither spectator nor reader. If it is a case history, it is also a drama — a psychological drama, to be sure — and a novel. For it has artistic form. If it tickled the bourgeois palate, it did so not by design. Having exhausted the possibilities of the tendencies which culminated in *Lazarus Laughed,* having long since renounced all faith in social reform, having retained his interest in religion and drama, in myth and psychology, O'Neill resumed his probing of the problem of existence. In *The Great God Brown* and in *Lazarus Laughed* he occupied himself with the agony of Everyman; in *Strange Interlude* he is concerned with the anguish of Everywoman. In the former his aversion was bourgeois Christianity; in the latter it is principally science. The faults of *Strange Interlude* stem neither from its innovations nor from a failure to be dramatic. Its faults are those that have inhered in many of O'Neill's plays: a rhetorical and turgid style; an intensity of feeling "that is in excess of the facts"; a content that is frequently closer to bathos than to tragedy.

In *Strange Interlude* O'Neill returned once again to New England, where the Cabots, because they lived on intimate terms with Nature, were rewarded as few O'Neill characters have been, with integrated personalities. "Unrestrained as beasts of the field" — untouched by the shams of convention, undivided by moral or religious scruples, free, in short, of the conflicts and the repressions which civilization brings — the New England farmer of 1850 could satisfy directly and unhesitatingly the demands of his instincts. Neurosis, a legacy of civilized society, was therefore nonexistent. A true child of Nature, he intuitively practised the salutary thing. Thus, Ephraim found that he could attain peace of mind by going down to the barn and talking out his emotional disturbances with the cows, who offered an understanding ear. And Eben, who revealed a potentially destructive Oedipus complex, dis-

covered that it promptly yielded to Abbie's effective treatment. We
have already observed the pernicious effects of modern civilization
upon the soul and character of the Hairy Ape and Mildred Douglas, Jim Harris and Ella Downey, Marco Polo, Kukachin, Kublai
Kaan, Dion Anthony, William Brown. We have seen in *The Great
God Brown* how O'Neill applied to modern man that aspect of
familial relationship which obtained among the primordial New
Englanders: the attraction of the son to the Mother whereby the
tortured soul of Dion Anthony found solace. In *Strange Interlude*
O'Neill developed not only the Mother motif, but also that of the
Father. It is Nina Leeds's relationship to the Father which enables
her soul finally "to bleach in peace."

It is evident that seventy years of civilized convention and repression have failed to extirpate the original nature of the New
Englander. His animalism has simply been encrusted with fear
and gentility, with introspective and rationalistic habits of mind —
all resulting in a denial of life; his movements, therefore, have
become awkward and painful, producing festering sores which postwar Americans instantly recognized as neuroses. Where once the
Cabot brothers, *their bodies bumping and rubbing together,* hur-
ried clumsily to their food *like two friendly oxen toward their
evening meal,* in modern New England "decorous bodies move
with circumspection through the afternoons." Where, despite his
seventy-five years, the hard, elemental Ephraim rode off in the
spring to go "whorin'," the effete and piteous Professor Leeds, at
fifty-five, takes refuge in his New England study, his "unique
haven," where he can tolerate and understand the *manners and
morals of Greece and Imperial Rome* while fleeing from life about
him. Where the simple-minded Eben, in whom thought was directly converted into deed, overtly revealed his hatred for his father
and readily committed incest with his step-mother, Marsden, Darrell, and Evans place psychic barriers between their ignoble impulses and the satisfaction thereof. Where Abbie, like her modern
counterpart, Nina, was lustful, possessive, calculating, cruel, and
maternal, she, unlike Nina, was never wistful, philosophical, or
neurotic. Where the antitheses of pagan and Puritan, Solomon and
Jehovah, elm and stone, mother and father were synthesized by an
all-powerful life force, duality now leads to insoluble emotional

conflicts, to frustration, to fatigue and decay. In short, where, in *Desire Under the Elms,* it was possible to worship the divinity of earth, in *Strange Interlude* there is nothing to worship: the earth, indeed, is a sterile promontory, and God is "deaf and dumb and blind."

Ephraim, image of authority and power, father of the primal horde, prototype of Jehovah and of Professor Leeds, differed from the latter in many conspicuous respects, among which was the fact that he was the father of sons only. For although the Professor's daughter is embittered by her father's meddling, her relationship with him continues to be the single reality of her life. If the warmth of her affections for him is somewhat dispelled when, upon analysis, they are revealed to consist merely of comfort, security, and peace, she finally is to be resigned to the fact that such love is enough. The distressing experiences which befall her between adolescence and menopause are part of a dream-like strange interlude whose intrusion temporarily disturbs the reality which once again restores her peace of mind and reintegrates her personality. Thus the father is to Nina what the mother is to Eben and to William Brown; but God the Father, far from being an idol of earth, is just a plain male parent. Regression to a childhood relationship with the father produces none of the triumphant exultation which had accompanied a return to the mother; its advantages are, rather, those of peace, and decay, of the tomb rather than the womb.

When Nina was a child the Professor had been stern and protective:

little Nina was never allowed to touch anything . . . she used to sit on his lap . . . cuddle against him . . . dreaming into the dark beyond the windows . . . warm in his arms before the fireplace . . . dreams like sparks soaring up to die in the cold dark . . . warm in his love, safe-drifting into sleep . . . 'Daddy's girl, aren't you?'

His professorial personality was carried into the home, so that Nina was a "loving-attentive, pupil-daughter." *Temperamentally timid, his defense is an assumption of his complacent, superior manner of the classroom toward the world at large. . . . This classroom poise of his, however, he cannot quite carry off outside the classroom;* and if Nina had once been intimidated by it, she is so no longer. For she has perceived that his motive in preventing her marriage to Gordon Shaw was a selfish one, and, outside the class-room now, he confesses that it was:

Let us say then that I *persuaded* myself it was for your sake. That may be true. You are young. You think one can live with truth. Very well. It is also true I was jealous of Gordon. I was alone and I wanted to keep your love. I hated him as one hates a thief one may not accuse nor punish. I did my best to prevent your marriage. I was glad when he died. There. Is that what you wished me to say? . . . I wanted to live comforted by your love until the end. In short, I am a man who happens to be your father. (*He hides his face in his hands and weeps softly*) Forgive that man!

And Nina does, but she cannot forgive herself for refusing to con-summate her love with Gordon. Feeling that she must find some way to give herself to him still in order to pay her debt to him, she leaves her father and serves in a sanitarium for crippled soldiers. When she returns home more than a year later the professor is dead. Bitter and resentful still, she cannot bring herself to weep for him:

I'm sorry, Father! . . . you see you've been dead for me for a long time . . . when Gordon died, all men died . . . What did you feel for me then? . . . nothing . . . and now I feel nothing . . .

But she is not vindictive. She is disillusioned and cynical about the cosmos itself. "Life," she feels, "is just a long drawn out lie with a sniffling sigh at the end." Her search for God has been unreward-ing:

I tried hard to pray to the modern science God. I thought of a million light years to a spiral nebula — one other universe among innumerable others. But how could that God care about our trifling misery of death-born-of-birth? I couldn't believe in Him, and I wouldn't if I could! I'd rather imi-tate His indifference and prove I had that one trait at least in common!

She "wanted to believe in any God at any price — a heap of stones, a mud image, a drawing on a wall, a bird, a fish, a snake, a baboon — or even a good man preaching the simple platitudes of truth," but neither science, nor animism, nor the Gospels could satisfy her craving for faith. The mistake began, she concludes,

when God was created in a male image. Of course, women would see Him that way, but men should have been gentlemen enough, remembering their mothers, to make God a woman! But the God of Gods — the Boss — has always been a man. That makes life so perverted, and death so unnatural.

We should have imagined life as created in the birthpain of God the Mother. Then we would understand why we, Her children, have inherited pain, for we would know that our life's rhythm beats from Her great heart, torn with the agony of love and birth. And we would feel that death meant reunion with Her, a passing back into Her substance, blood of Her blood again, peace of Her peace. Now wouldn't that be more logical and satisfying than having God a male whose chest thunders with egotism and is too hard for tired heads and thoroughly comfortless?

Nina's position is that of a backsliding member of the cult of Cybele, for she has abandoned the principle of rebirth and retained only that portion of the divine cycle that is concerned with death and peace. The "intolerable chalice of life," the "glorious, blazing crown of life" have been omitted from the ritual. Since "life is just a long drawn out lie," ecstatic affirmation is impossible. The question which Cybel had asked and finally answered with *agonized exultance,* "What's the use of bearing children? What's the use of giving birth to death?" Nina also asks, but her most comforting answer comes in the middle of the play, and is, therefore, not conclusive. Nor is it ecstatic. Pregnant with Darrell's child, she sits and *stares dreamily before her,* more nearly like Cybel than at any other point in the play. The latter had been described as a *strong, calm, sensual blonde girl of twenty or so, her complexion fresh and healthy, her figure full-breasted and wide-hipped, her movements slow and solidly languorous like an animal's, her large eyes dreamy with the reflected stirring of profound instincts.* Nina, in Act Five, reveals a great change *in her face and bearing . . . there is a triumphant strength about her expression, a ruthless self-confidence in her eyes. She has grown stouter, her face has filled out. One gets no impression of neurotic strain from her now, she seems nerveless and deeply calm.* Her perplexing question of Act Two, "How could that God [the modern science God] care about our trifling misery of death-born-of-birth?" she now answers:

There . . . again . . . his child! . . . my child moving in my life . . . my life moving in my child . . . the world is whole and perfect . . . all things are each other's . . . life is . . . and this is beyond reason . . . questions die in the silence of this peace . . . I am living a dream within the great dream of the tide . . . breathing in the tide I dream and breathe back my dream into the tide . . . suspended in the movement of the tide, I feel life in me, suspended in me . . . no whys matter . . . there is no why . . . I am a mother . . . God is a Mother . . .

It is evident that she has no answer, that there is not even a question; for "questions die in the silence of this peace." Where Cybel had assured us that death-born-of-birth is nothing to fear because of eternal recurrence of life, and where Lazarus had proclaimed that "there is no death," Nina is temporarily satisfied with the sensation of dreaming and merging, a voluptuous peacefulness. Unfortunately, gestation is of limited duration; the inscrutable returns to torment her. But she continues her perfunctory appeals to God the Mother: "Oh, Mother God, grant my prayer . . ." and "Oh, Mother God, grant that I may some day tell this fool the truth!" she exclaims at the close of Act Seven. "O Mother God, protect my son!" she pleads in Act Eight. That she is still obsessed with the notion that God is a Mother is apparent when, also in Act Eight, in response to Darrell's observation that "Life is something in one cell that doesn't need to think!" she replies (*strangely*), "I know! God the Mother."

Despite the lip-service that she gives to God the Mother, Nina is to kneel at the shrine of God the Father, for hard though He may be she finds after all that He is not "thoroughly comfortless." Peace, the *summum bonum,* provisionally granted by a reunion with the Mother, is permanently attained only after a return to the Father, for whom her feeling has been ambivalent. He represents on the one hand, authority, punishment, the "super-ego"; but on the other, he stands for the warm comfort of childhood. If sexuality plays a part in the relationship with the Father, it is a tacit one. The context of the play reveals that Nina is neither Electra nor Cybele.

Professor Leeds, who dies before the beginning of Act Two, is replaced in his daughter's consciousness by Marsden, who is fifteen years older than Nina and who resembles the Professor most conspicuously in his timidity and primness. She associates the two personalities as early as Act One when, during a tense moment, the men force a nervous laugh; whereupon Nina thinks, "The fathers laugh at little daughter Nina." Throughout the play Marsden hovers over the daughter as a kind of reincarnation of the dead father and fulfills for her the function of the parent. Evans asks him for Nina's hand in marriage: "Father Charlie now, eh?" Marsden says to himself. And shortly thereafter *he unconsciously takes the* Professor's *place behind the table.* Where, in Act Six, Nina thinks ". . . is it possible he loves me? . . . like that? . . . what a sickening idea! . . . it seems incestuous somehow! . . . ," in the following act, eleven years later, she recalls that the idea of giving herself to Marsden had once been "revolting," but now it appears to her that he would make "a perfect love" for "one's old age," "when one was past passion." During her recurrent dreamy states, when she drifts back to childhood, Marsden serves as substitute for her father, and it is on such occasions that God the Mother plays a secondary role. In the second act, Marsden is once again *in her father's place* as she speaks (*in a queer flat voice*), "Yes, he's dead — my father — whose passion created me — who began me — he is ended. There is only his end living — his death." Then, having finished her speech in which she expressed a preference for a female God, she suddenly jumps to her feet and goes to Marsden, exclaiming *with a horrible moaning desolation,*

Oh, God, Charlie, I want to believe in something! I want to believe so I can feel! I want to feel that he is dead — my father! And I can't feel anything, Charlie! I can't feel anything at all! (*She throws herself on her knees beside him and hides her face in her hands on his knees and begins to sob — stifled torn sounds.*)

Then

(*His hands grasping her arms he half raises her to her feet, but, her face still hidden in her hands, sobbing, she slips on to his lap like a little girl and hides her face on his shoulder. His expression becomes transported with a great happiness — in an ecstatic whisper* [he says] *to himself*)
As I dreamed . . . with a deeper sweetness . . .
(*He kisses her hair with a great reverence*)
There . . . this is all my desire . . . I am this kind of lover . . . this is my love . . . she is my girl . . . not woman . . . my little girl . . .

Nina, cuddling up against him — presumably as she did in her father's arms before the fireplace — speaks in a young girl's voice:

I've been so homesick. I've wanted to run home and 'fess up, tell how bad I've been, and be punished! Oh, I've got to be punished, Charlie, out of mercy for me, so I can forgive myself! And now Father dead, there's only you. You will, won't you — or tell me how to punish myself? You've simply got to, if you love me!

Having listened to her story about her compulsive sexual promiscuity in the sanitarium, misbehavior which causes her now to seek
punishment, Marsden thinks (*With intense bitterness*)

> Dear old Father Charlie now! . . .
> ha! . . . that's how she wants me! . . .
> (*Then suddenly in a matter-of-fact tone that is mockingly like her father's*)
> Then, under the circumstances, having weighed the pros and cons, so to
> speak, I should say that decidedly the most desirable course —
> Nina. (*drowsily — her eyes shut*) You sound so like Father, Charlie.
> Marsden. (*in the tone like her father's*) — is for you to marry that young
> Evans. He is a splendid chap, clean and boyish, with real stuff in him, too,
> to make a career for himself if he finds a help-meet who will inspire him to
> his best efforts and bring his latent ability to the surface.
> Nina. (*drowsily*) Sam is a nice boy. Yes, it would be a career for me to
> bring a career to his surface. I would be busy — surface life — no more
> depths, please God! But I don't love him, Father.
> Marsden. (*blandly — in the tone like her father's*) But you like him,
> Nina. And he loves you devotedly . . . Then it's all settled?
> Nina. (*drowsily*) Yes. (*Very sleepily*) Thank you, Father. You've been so
> kind. You've let me off too easily. I don't feel as if you'd punished me
> hardly at all. But I'll never do it again, I promise — never, never! — (*She falls
> asleep and gives a soft little snore.*)
> Marsden. (*Still in her father's tones — very paternally — looking down*)
> She's had a hard day of it, poor child! I'll carry her up to her room. (*He
> rises to his feet with Nina sleeping peacefully in his arms . . .*)

In Act Eight, frustrated in her attempt to win her son away from
Madeline, she again turns to Marsden, who *sits on the deck by her
chair and takes her hand. Staring before her as if she were in a
trance — simply, like a young girl*, she says, "Yes, Charlie. *Yes,
Father*," and having told of the insanity in her husband's family
and revealed her son's paternity, she asks, *childishly*, "So I haven't
been such an awfully wicked girl, have I, Father?" She now loves
only Marsden, her father's surrogate, and Gordon, her son; for
her love for Darrell has faded, and she had never loved Evans. As
the latter lies on the deck, the victim of a stroke, Marsden thinks
exultantly, "I will not have long to wait now!" And he is quite
right. With Evans dead, Darrell departing, the son flying off with
his bride, the interlude terminates, and she returns to her past.

> Nina. (*finally lowering her eyes — confusedly*) Gone. My eyes are growing
> dim. Where is Ned? Gone, too. And Sam is gone. They're all dead. Where

are Father and Charlie? (*With a shiver of fear she hurries over and sits on the bench beside* Marsden, *huddling against him*) Gordon is dead, Father. I've just had a cable. What I mean is, he flew away to another life — my son, Gordon, Charlie. So we're alone again — just as we used to be.

Marsden. (*putting his arm around her — affectionately*) Just as we used to be, dear Nina Cara Nina, before Gordon came.

And, resting her head on his shoulder, she says to Marsden:

You're so restful, Charlie. I feel as if I were a girl again and you were my father and the Charlie of those days made into one. I wonder is our old garden the same? We'll pick flowers together in the aging afternoons of spring and summer, won't we? It will be a comfort to get home — to be old and to be home again at last — to be in love with peace together — to love each other's peace — to sleep with peace together — ! (*She kisses him — then shuts her eyes with a deep sigh of requited weariness*) — to die in peace! I'm so contentedly weary with life!

Marsden. (*with a serene peace*) Rest, dear Nina. (*Then tenderly*) It has been a long day. Why don't you sleep now — as you used to, remember? — for a little while.

Nina. (*murmurs with drowsy gratitude*) Thank you, Father —have I been wicked — you're so good — dear old Charlie!

Nina has come to terms with her father and has made her peace with God, who was created in a male image, that of her father, presumably. The play ends with a "long deep sigh" of resignation; regression is without exaltation, death without transfiguration. To her father she had said, in Act Eight, "It was all your fault in the beginning, wasn't it? You mustn't ever meddle with human lives again!" He had destroyed her happiness, caused her to be self-conscious regarding her wickedness, made her aware of a need to be punished, and had become for her a symbol of death. Thus Professor Leeds, despite his tenderness, was more Jehovah-like than Ephraim had been; and he, rather than Nature or Nature's priestess, the Mother, emerges victorious. Nina surrenders, but not without a struggle. She is fearful, furtive, and antagonistic nearly to the end. As early as Act One her father had become an abstraction:

Nina. (*thinking with weary scorn*)
The Professor of Dead Languages is talking again . . . a dead man lectures on the past of living . . . since I was born I have been in his class, loving-attentive, pupil-daughter Nina . . . my ears numb with spiritless messages from the dead . . . dead words droning on . . . listening be-

cause he is my cultured father . . . a little more inclined to deafness than
the rest (let me be just) because he is my father . . . father! . . . what
is father? . . .

Scornful and bitter as she is, she forgives him; but he remains a
symbol of destructive meddling and of death. In Act Five, free from
neurotic strain, pregnant, and in love with Darrell, she has a terrifying moment when Marsden enters, dressed in deep mourning for
the death of his mother, as she and Darrell are expressing mutual
love:

Nina. (*thinking — in a strange superstitious panic*)
  Black . . . in the midst of happiness . . . black comes . . . again . . .
  death . . . my father . . . comes between me and happiness.
(*Then recovering herself, scornfully*)
  You silly coward! . . . it's only Charlie! . . .
(*Then with furious resentment*)
  The old fool! . . . what does he mean coming in on us without warn-
  ing? . . .

Symbolical of her transformation, Marsden's identical costume in
Act Nine, worn on the occasion of the death of Evans, is now perfectly acceptable. What is more, she is to marry him. In so doing,
she shall be wedded to her father, to death. But during the preceding twenty-five years the father and God the Father are her unrelenting adversaries, equally destructive of happiness. In Act Three
Nina discovers that her mother-in-law shares her attitude:

Mrs. Evans. (*sadly*) . . . And then I used to wish I'd gone out deliberate
in our first year, without my husband knowing, and picked a man, a healthy
male to breed by, same's we do with stock, to give the man I loved a
healthy child. And if I didn't love that other man nor him me where would
be the harm? Then God would whisper: 'It'd be a sin, adultery, the worst
sin!' But after He'd gone I'd argue back again to myself, then we'd have a
healthy child, I needn't be afraid! . . . (*Then scornfully*) But I was too
afraid of God then to have ever done it!

Nina replies (*as from a distance — strangely*) . . . "But I'm not
the same as you. (*Defiantly*) I don't believe in God the Father!"
To which Mrs. Evans responds, also, *strangely*:

Then it'd be easy for you. (*With a grim smile*) And I don't believe in Him,
neither, not any more. I used to be a great one for worrying about what's
God and what's devil, but I got richly over it living here with poor folks
that was being punished for no sins of their own, and me being punished

with them for no sin but loving much. (*With decision*) Being happy, that's
the nearest we can ever come to knowing what's good! Being happy, that's
good! The rest is just talk!

Influenced by this utilitarian philosophy, Nina puts it into practice; but the Father principle is too potent. Having "picked a man
to breed by," Darrell, she persuades him to become her accomplice.
"And, after all," she argues, "you aided and abetted God the
Father in making this mess." Four acts and more than twenty
years later, her breeding experiment having produced unforeseen
results, Nina looks at Darrell and thinks *sadly:*

> My old lover . . . how well and young he looks . . . now we no longer
> love each other at all . . . our account with God the Father is settled . . .
> afternoons of happiness paid for with years of pain . . . love, passion, ecstasy
> . . . in what a far-off life were they alive! . . .

Apparently Nina has made an error in book-keeping, for God's
record of indebtedness shows something owing still. In the next
act, the final one, Darrell's son slaps his father's face:

Nina. (*thinking in desperate hysterical anguish*)
> Oh, I wish Ned would go away and stay away forever! . . . I can't bear
> to watch him suffer any more! . . . It's too frightful! . . . yes, God the
> Father, I hear you laughing . . . you see the joke . . . I'm laughing too
> . . . it's all so crazy, isn't it? . . .

Even at the climax of the play, at the end of Act Six, when Nina
exults in the presence of her four men, saying to herself, "I should
be the happiest woman in the world!" and, *suppressing an outbreak
of hysterical triumphant laughter only by a tremendous effort,* she
still is haunted by the threat to her happiness of God the Father.
She knocks wood before He "hears my happiness." Nina finally
perceives in Act Eight, that love is a threat to happiness, that it is
a weapon devised by the Father:

Nina. (*getting up — thinking with a strange, strident, wild passion*)
> I hear the Father laughing! . . . O Mother God, protect my son! . . . Let
> Gordon fly to you in heaven! . . . quick, Gordon! . . . love is the Father's
> lightning! . . . Madeline will bring you down in flames! . . . I hear his
> screaming laughter! . . . fly back to me! . . .
> (*She is looking desperately up into the sky as if some race of life and death
> were happening there for her.*)

At the end of the play Gordon does fly off, and as Nina looks up at the sky again she says *strangely:*

> My having a son was a failure, wasn't it? He couldn't give me happiness. Sons are always their fathers. They pass through the mother to become their father again. The Sons of the Father have all been failures! Failing they died for us, they flew away to other lives, they could not stay with us, they could not give us happiness!

Like Ella Downey in *All God's Chillun Got Wings,* Nina reverts to childhood, but only an empty kingdom of heaven awaits her conversion; the Gospels are ineffective since the Sons of the Father are failures. "Our lives," she concludes reproachfully, "are merely strange dark interludes in the electrical display of God the Father!" Darrell, even more sardonic, says in mock supplication: "Oh, God, so deaf and dumb and blind! . . . teach me to be resigned to be an atom! . . ." Marsden, earlier, had revealed that he shared the rancorous attitude expressed by Nina and by Darrell. Picking up a newspaper, he had glanced at it *sneeringly:*

> It's in every headline of this daily newer testament . . . going . . . going . . . never mind the gone . . . we won't live to see it . . . and we'll be so rich, we can buy off the deluge anyway! . . . even our new God has His price! . . . must have! . . . aren't we made in His image? . . . or vice-versa? . . .

God today is not only cruelly indifferent, but in pulling the camel through the needle's eye He is guilty of betraying the Gospels. O'Neill at this point discarded the New Testament as well as the Old, Christ as well as Jehovah. "Ripeness is all," and even Cybele is helpless to do anything about it.

Disbelief has been a primary source of anguish for Nina, as it is for her masculine counterparts: Dion Anthony and William Brown, Reuben Light, John Loving. O'Neill perceived the soul-mending quality of unquestioning faith, but his skeptical temperament, even in his early works, had thwarted its attainment: the "religionist" — Catholic and Protestant alike — had invariably been ridiculous or fanatical, the pretensions of the scientist hollow. Pantheism, although it has never been discredited, is abandoned. The roots of anguish, which has spread itself like a green bay tree, tap the destructive element and are two in number, obsession and duality, each with its ramifications.

When Abbie had confidently reminded Eben that Nature would beat him sooner or later, she was referring to the futility of trying to resist seduction. The fate that might have awaited him had he been more recalcitrant had been exemplified by the case of Emma Crosby who had gone "agen an act of Nature" when she refused to marry Caleb; and now it is exemplified once again by the strange interlude in Nina's life during which she is haunted by a single incident of unconsummated love. Pursued by the Furies, she leaps from fulfillment to fulfillment, and falls repeatedly into the turbid waters of neurosis. Her twenty-five years of mental malaise stem, in large part, from the shock of the last night that she had spent with her lover and from the reception of word of his death. Fulfillment had been inhibited by conceptions of chivalry and morality and by a conscience that was permeated with her father's censoriousness. The ambivalent relationship with her father suggests a Freudian influence, an influence which becomes much more apparent as Nina's disturbance is examined more closely. Freud had pointed out how hystericals and neurotics continue to be strongly affected by painful experiences of the distant past, neglecting present reality in favor of the inescapable past. "This fixation of the mental life," he had said in his Clark lectures, "on the pathogenic traumata is an essential, and practically a most significant characteristic of the neurosis." In the first act Nina remorsefully recalls her experience:

That last night before he sailed — in his arms until my body ached — kisses until my lips were numb — knowing all that night — something in me knowing he would die, that he would never kiss me again — knowing this so surely yet with my cowardly brain lying, no he'll come back and marry you! (*Then violently*) But Gordon never possessed me! I'm still Gordon's silly virgin! And Gordon is muddy ashes! And I've lost my happiness forever! All that last night I knew he wanted me. I knew it was only the honorable code-bound Gordon, who kept commanding from his brain, no, you mustn't, you must respect her, you must wait till you have a marriage license! (*She gives a mocking laugh.*)

Her agony is composed of mingled guilt and frustration, for she feels that she is as responsible as her lover for failure to consummate the act. She had "wanted Gordon" but had refused "to make him take" her because "something cowardly" in her had cried "no, you mustn't, what would your father say?" More than a year spent

in expiating her guilt by giving herself to crippled soldiers fails
to improve her mental health. At the end of that period she feels
more guilty and frustrated than ever. That procedure, as Darrell
explains, had led only to the piling on of "too many destructive
experiences. A few more and she'll dive for the gutter just to get
the security that comes from knowing she's touched bottom and
there's no farther to go!" Continuing his diagnosis:

Nina has been giving way more and more to a morbid longing for martyr-
dom. The reason for it is obvious. Gordon went away without — well, let's
say marrying her. The war killed him. She was left suspended. Then she
began to blame herself and at the same time give happiness to various fellow
war victims by pretending to love them. It's a pretty idea but it hasn't
worked out. Nina's a bad actress. She hasn't convinced the men of her love
— or herself of her good intentions. And each experience of this kind has
only left her more a prey to a guilty conscience than before and more determined to punish herself!

What she needs now, according to Darrell's prescription, is "to
find normal outlets for her craving for sacrifice. She needs normal
love objects for the emotional life Gordon's death blocked up in
her." Doctor Darrell, who is a neurologist and not a psychoanalyst,
evidently was sufficiently acquainted with Freudian assumptions to
recognize the dynamic nature of the so-called "libido," attributing
Nina's illness to its frustration. On the basis of this diagnosis he
recommends that she marry Sam Evans, because Evans's "unselfish
love, combined with her real liking for him, will gradually give
her back a sense of security and a feeling of being worth something
to life again . . ." In the following act, having heeded the doctor's
advice, Nina gives every indication of flourishing, until an unforeseen and extraneous matter disrupts her progress: the revelation of
insanity in her husband's family, an act of fate which does not
discredit the validity of Darrell's theory. Its intrusion, however, sup-
ports O'Neill's reiterated moral that it is unwise to meddle in
human lives, an argument which would apply, presumably, to the
psychoanalyst's efforts to cure mental illness. Darrell is to pay
dearly for his meddling. Its intrusion suggests also that O'Neill did
not intend to make of *Strange Interlude* a Freudian tract. Careful
to avoid commitments in that regard, he made Darrell a neurologist
instead of a psychoanalyst (and, significantly, Nina had been sent
by the Professor to a "nerve-specialist"). As a neurologist Darrell

could display a credible familiarity with psychoanalytic theory without injecting into the play immoderate emphasis upon such matters. Meeting the doctor for the first time, Marsden, the victim of an Oedipus complex, is disparaging of psychoanalysis:

> . . . What is his specialty? . . . neurologist, I think . . . I hope not psychoanalyst . . . a lot to account for, Herr Freud! . . . punishment to fit his crimes, be forced to listen eternally during breakfast while innumerable plain ones tell him dreams about snakes . . . pah, what an easy cure-all! . . . sex the philosopher's stone . . . O Oedipus, O my king! The world is adopting you!

It is conceivable that one who spends "his sex life among the phantoms" should be contemptuous of a system that is based upon a boldly unreticent sexuality. Yet it would be erroneous to assume that Marsden's disdain is O'Neill's praise. In short, O'Neill's position with respect to psychoanalysis is an equivocal one. On the one hand it enriched his knowledge of psychopathology and confirmed his earlier conclusions regarding man's irrational and primitive nature. It has become an organic part of *Strange Interlude* where the father complex provides a fresh approach to determining man's relationship to God, and where it shapes the plot structure by suggesting the final mildly incestuous regression. It contributes a pat but superficial tone to the play in the references to neurosis, in Darrell's jargon, in Marsden's Oedipus complex, and in the doubtfully Freudian interior monologues. On the other hand, O'Neill shut the door in the analyst's face, preferring to let the character wage his own struggle with blind fate; for if psychoanalysis is not a "cure-all," it is undeniably a "cure-some." Doctor Darrell, having served O'Neill's pseudo-Freudian purposes as a neurologist, is transformed into a biologist — a "pure" scientist — that O'Neill might avail himself of the opportunity to make frequent deprecatory observations concerning the value of science in matters of religion, the search for truth, and life generally. Insofar as psychoanalysis may be considered a science (its method, at least, is claimed to be empirical) it shares with biology O'Neill's contempt. All of which suggests that Nina is, like Smitty in *The Moon of the Caribbees,* a "poor little lamb that has lost his way," that was "damned from here to eternity"; and that her suffering is the consequence less of the frustration and guilt which followed her traumatic experience with Gordon than it is the product of O'Neill's steady and, by this time, familiar world-view. Cherishing the inscrutable, he is willing to yield only to fate. He was reluctant, therefore, to acknowledge that some mysteries can be resolved, or that science and free-will occasionally can be effective in short-term projects.

Nina's reaction, during the first two acts, to her painful experience with Gordon Shaw may be an accurate clinical picture of a traumatic neurosis, but from the specific event O'Neill developed a universal statement. Although she continues to be obsessed by the memory of her lover — "fixated to the moment of the traumatic occurrence" — he becomes increasingly a symbol, she a typification of the American woman of today, the play itself a modern allegory representing the "predicament of a generation." If the play at first resembles the case history of an individual — the daughter of a New England college professor — it gradually becomes a morality of Everywoman. Where Abbie had been the type of the primitive female, rapacious and maternal, the heroine of *Strange Interlude* is the type of the civilized woman who is neurotic in consequence not only of the shock of a particular event but as a result of a general unfulfillment. Thus, Nina futilely pursues an unattainable romantic ideal, that into which Gordon Shaw had been abstracted; she fails in her quest for personal happiness; she is unable to worship God in any form; she broods over old age and death, recalling with sentimental retrospection the irrecoverable afternoons of passion; and she is tormented by the confusion of truth and reality. In short, Nina's anguish is substantially the same old anguish that had afflicted O'Neill's pre-Freudian, and less obviously Freudian, characters; and its roots spread under all of *Strange Interlude*.

The obsession motif had been a favorite one of O'Neill's ever since he wrote *Ile* in 1917. In that play he had recognized the presence in his protagonist of a mysterious, irrational, compulsive force — a monomania similar to Ahab's. Helpless to understand its nature or to fight against it, Captain Keeney was driven to destroy the person whom he loved. Captain Bartlett, in *Where the Cross Is Made* and in *Gold,* was the victim of a similar aberration. He, too, was driven, against his conscience, to fulfill a compulsive need. Most of O'Neill's heroes have been haunted by one fixed idea or another; but those whose suffering in this respect most nearly approximated Nina's were Emma Crosby of *Diff'rent* and Michael Cape of *Welded,* both of whom were tormented by an irresistible need to fulfill an inhuman, unattainable ideal. Emma was swept to disaster, never realizing what had pushed her. But Michael, and his wife, too, were aware of his "morbid obsession," his "Grand Ideal" for their marriage; and they attributed the urge to possess each other absolutely to the impulsions of the two halves of the cell to rejoin after its splitting a "hundred million years ago into you and me." Nina's "idiotic obsession" is equally perplexing. Even Darrell, who had been trained to treat such mental phenomena, is puzzled by the persistent presence of Gordon Shaw's ghost. Professor Leeds had explained to Marsden, even before Nina had made her first entrance, that "It isn't Gordon, . . . It's his memory, his ghost, you might call it, haunting Nina . . ." But having "had it out" with his daughter, he was confident, at the end of Act One, that Gordon's "ghost will be gone now . . ." In the second act, Darrell says to Marsden: "In my mind she always belongs to Gordon. It's probably a reflection of her own silly fixed idea about him. (*Suddenly, dryly and harshly*) And I couldn't share a woman — even with a ghost!" To which Marsden replies (*In a strange mocking ironic tone*) "I can quite appreciate your feeling about Gordon. I wouldn't care to share with a ghost-lover myself. That species of dead is so invulnerably alive! Even a doctor couldn't kill one, eh? (*He forces a laugh — then in a friendly confidential tone*) Gordon is too egregious for a ghost." In the next act, Gordon's influence is felt not at all, for Nina is pregnant and happy as she spends a delayed honeymoon in the Evans's house, which itself appeared to her to be "obviously haunted" when she had arrived there. Her obsession with Gordon returns in Act Four where she decides to "stick to" her husband as a "point of honor," "to play the game," since that is what Gordon would have done. In her letters to Marsden she writes of Gordon "as if he had been a demi-god" and engages herself in the task of writing his biography. The "Gordon myth as strong as ever," thinks Darrell. "These heroes die hard . . . but perhaps she can write him out of her system." This Freudian supposition evidently has little to recommend it, for Nina, in telling Darrell about her aborted child, reveals her hero's continued presence:

(*with a strange intensity*) Oh, Ned, I loved it more than I've ever loved anything in my life — even Gordon! I loved it so it seemed at times that Gordon must be its real father, that Gordon must have come to me in a dream while I was lying asleep beside Sam! And I was happy! I almost loved Sam then! I felt he was a good husband!

Darrell, *instantly repelled,* thinks *with scornful jealousy:* "Ha! . . . the hero again! . . . comes to her bed! . . . puts horns on poor Sam! . . . becomes the father of his child! . . . I'll be damned if hers isn't the most idiotic obsession I ever . . ." Then Gordon ceases to haunt her while, in the fifth act, she loses herself in her passion for Darrell. The latter, however, is moved to revive the hero's memory when, in struggling against Nina's possessiveness and his own passion, he rebukingly tells her that she does not love him. "You're simply letting your romantic imagination run away with you —," he explains, "as you did once before with Gordon Shaw! . . . Romantic imagination! It has ruined more lives than all the diseases! Other diseases, I should say! It's a form of insanity!" "He is jealous of Gordon," Nina thinks, ". . . how wonderful that is! . . ." Losing Darrell, for the time being, she is at first savagely vindictive; and then she mourns his departure. The sixth act finds her still in love with Darrell, but his earlier estimate of Gordon Shaw's effect upon her is validated when she names Darrell's son for the hero. Meanwhile Darrell's love has drawn him back to Nina. Hearing about his son, he thinks, "little Gordon! . . . Nina called my son after Gordon . . . romantic imagination! . . . Gordon is still her lover! . . . Gordon, Sam and Nina! . . . and my son! . . . closed corporation! . . . I'm forced out! . . ." As the act ends, as Nina feels the desires of her men converge in her, Gordon Shaw is excluded; but it becomes evident that, hereafter, he is to be embodied in young Gordon, one of Nina's four men. Eleven years later, in Act Seven, her love for Darrell has faded; more than this, she hates him, and Marsden and Evans as well. She is thankful that she is only a mother now: "Gordon is my little man, my only man! . . ." Young Gordon's physical appearance is presumably that of Gordon Shaw, for *He does not noticeably re-*

*semble his mother. He looks nothing at all like his father. He seems
to have sprung from a line distinct from any of the people we have
seen.* Spiritually, too, he is to be identified with his predecessor.
Having sensed Darrell's jealousy of Gordon Shaw, and because he
has an instinctive aversion for his mother's lover — his own father
— he determines to "be just like Gordon was and Mother'll
love me better'n him! . . ." He requests Sam to relate again the
story of Gordon Shaw's victory in the shell race, of how Shaw had
fainted at its finish. Ten years later, in the next act, he himself
faints as he strokes his crew to victory. In this turbulent act, the
eighth, the circular movement of the plot becomes apparent as
personalities recur, as early situations are repeated. Nina's *general
manner recalls instantly the* Nina *of Act Four, neurotic, passionately embittered and torn,* for she is in a frenzy over the imminent
loss once again of Gordon, who now is declared to "be a dead
ringer for Gordon Shaw at his best." Gordon's fiancée, Madeline
Arnold, to whom Nina will lose her "lover," resembles, as one
might expect, Nina herself. Nina, hating her successor, frantically
attempting to avoid a repetition of the disturbing incident of her
early womanhood, resorts to savage stratagems. Her unconscious
wishes, rising to the surface, are converted into diabolical deed.
Determined that Madeline shall never possess her son (she *winces*
even at the thought of his "indulging in a passing physical affair"),
she makes two efforts, successively, to separate them. First she
attempts to tell Sam that Gordon is not his son, expecting then that
he will "find some excuse to break their engagement." The shock
to Sam of this revelation would be disastrous, but she has come to
loathe him for his effect upon her son's character and his encouragement of her son's affair with Madeline. "If he'd only die! . . ."
she thinks. Darrell, upon whom she has tried her blandishments,
refuses to help her, declining to meddle in human lives again.
Whereupon, frustrated in her first effort, she turns to a second.
She is about to tell Madeline of the strain of insanity in the Evans
family — as Mrs. Evans had, with considerably more veracity, told
her — when Darrell again thwarts her. Defeated, her inner turmoil
still impels her to think *with a strange, strident, wild passion, to
beseech* the Mother God to protect her son from Madeline's love,
"the Father's lightning." Informed by Evans of Gordon's victory

in the race, she torturedly tries to force out a last despairing protest: "Gordon is Gordon's! — he was my Gordon! — his Gordon is
mine!" As the act ends she concedes her loss to Madeline. In the
final act, she and Darrell wave to their son as he flies off in his
plane. "Good-bye, Gordon's son!" says Darrell. And Nina, *with
tortured exultance* exclaims: "Fly up to heaven, Gordon! Fly with
your love to heaven! Fly always! Never crash to earth like my old
Gordon! Be happy, dear! You've got to be happy!"

On the level of psychological naturalism Gordon is to be taken
as the cause for much of Nina's emotional disturbance. Even her
immoderate affection for her son is motivated by her continued obsession with the memory of her dead lover — a modification of the
Oedipus complex. But Gordon has a second signficance. He had
become for Nina a mythical hero, the product of her romantic imagination, which, as Darrell observed, has ruined more lives than
all other diseases, and which, he added, is "a form of insanity."
Gordon, himself, "for all his good looks and prowess in sport and
his courses, really came of common people and had no money of
his own except as he made a career for himself," Professor Leeds
had told Marsden. Gordon's "proud spot," both had agreed, was
"fairness and honor," attributes of the playing field that appealed
to callow girls like Nina and to the arrested adolescence of the
simple-minded business man, Sam Evans, who also worshiped
Gordon. Together, Nina and Sam strove to make young Gordon
into the image of their hero. The finished product in Act Nine
had attained the age of his prototype at the time of Nina's infatuation. He

*is over six feet tall with the figure of a trained athlete. His sun-bronzed
face is extremely handsome after the fashion of the magazine cover American collegian. It is a strong face but of a strength wholly material in quality.
He has been too thoroughly trained to progress along a certain groove to
success ever to question it or be dissatisfied with its rewards. At the same
time, although entirely an unimaginative code-bound gentleman of his
groove, he is boyish and likable, of an even, modest, sporting disposition.*

Like his thirteenth century counterpart, Marco Polo, he possesses
no spiritual side to throw him into internal conflict. O'Neill illustrated the character by letting us overhear his thoughts:

... think of Madeline ... we'll be married ... then two months' honeymoon in Europe ... God, that'll be great! ... then back and dive into the
business ... Dad relied on me to carry on where he left off ... I'll have
to start at the bottom but I'll get to the top in a hurry, I promise you that,
Dad! ...

The handsome, shallow, quixotic, extraverted Gordon Shaw, the
quintessence of all that the American woman desires for a lover, is
transformed into the obtuse businessman whose only faith is that
of the myth of progress. "The Gordon Shaw ideal passed on
through Sam has made young Gordon an insensitive clod." Nina's
"romantic imagination" is the "romantic imagination" of the typical
woman, and it is as pernicious and inescapable as the pathological
obsession which effected the catastrophe of *Ile,* of *Diff'rent,* of
Welded. The intelligent and perceptive Darrell, who personifies a
worthier ideal — but a false one, since he is a scientist — and the
timorous, equally perceptive Marsden, who is the personification
of still another ideal, that of the literary artist, who unfortunately
is afraid of life, are the antitheses of the Gordons. They know that
"Gordon is always meant — meant to win! ... It's fate!" Their
fate, on the other hand, is to suffer. But suffering, as usual in
O'Neill's plays, has its rewards. In Darrell's case it is that of a
bitter wisdom: he had heeded the cry for happiness once, and had
even cried for it himself, but he finally returns to his cells — "sensi-
ble unicellular life that floats in the sea and has never learned the
cry for happiness!" In Marsden's the rewards are richer. "Passed
beyond desire," he feels that "he has all the luck at last!" Not only
has he acquired Nina after more than twenty-five years of wistful
waiting but, like Darrell, he has become a wiser man; and he
perceives, finally, what is wrong with his writing:

Listen, Nina! After we're married I'm going to write a novel — my first real
novel! All the twenty odd books I've written have been long-winded fairy
tales for grown-ups — about dear old ladies and witty, cynical bachelors and
quaint characters with dialects, and married folk who always admire and
respect each other, and lovers who avoid love in hushed whispers! That's
what I've been, Nina — a hush-hush whisperer of lies! Now I'm going to
give an honest healthy yell — turn on the sun into the shadows of lies —
shout 'This is life and this is sex, and here are passion and hatred and
regret and joy and pain and ecstasy, and these are men and women and sons
and daughters whose hearts are weak and strong, whose blood is blood and
not a soothing syrup!' Oh, I can do it, Nina! I can write the truth! I've

seen it in you, your father, my mother, sister, Gordon, Sam, Darrell and myself. I'll write the book of us!

In effect, he would become what an author should be: he would do precisely what O'Neill himself had done in writing *Strange Interlude*. But Marsden's exalted words were uttered while he was drunk. Sober, he remains "dear old Charlie."

By turning "on the sun into the shadows of lies" O'Neill has shed light upon the causes of the "sickness of today." Six years earlier Yank, the Hairy Ape, had experienced the agony of one who could not "belong," but Paddy's panacea was yet to be tried. Now, in 1927, having exhausted all of the possibilities of the reunion with benevolent Nature, O'Neill had retreated to a position where he once again was confronted with the implications of literary naturalism. The animal cravings and impulses have triumphed over the spiritual part of man's nature as they had in *All God's Chillun* and in *Desire Under the Elms,* but this time O'Neill avoided the *non sequitur* which converted psychopathology into a manifestation of God's holy plan and the sexual urges of beasts of the field into sublime love. If his "honest healthy yell," his shout that "This is life and this is sex, and here are passion and hatred and regret and joy and pain and ecstasy" faded into a weary whisper, he still contrived after some irresolution, to conclude the play in a fashion that is reasonably consistent with his assumptions. Obsessed by obsessions, he not only invoked the aid of Freud to make more probable Nina's monomania, but he expanded the motif into a commentary upon the source of the sickness of today: that the romantic imagination is a disease became his latest diagnosis and a major theme of the play.

Unfortunately, the force of O'Neill's theme was vitiated when he himself revealed symptoms of the disease which he was studying. Although the play ends where the beginning anticipated it might, it follows a devious and irresolute course before it arrives there. Much of the fault is to be traced to the Nina-Darrell relationship, which, to be sure, is an integral part of the plot — love being one of the four elements which complete a woman's life — but which was handled in sentimental and romantic fashion. Of Nina's four men, Darrell is the least probable figure. One suspects that O'Neill's scorn for the scientist caused him to over-compensate when he por-

trayed Nina's lover. Within the framework of the larger drama
Darrell enacts his personal tragedy, wherein the protagonist, a
foolish and proud man of science, is defeated by an ironical fate
which makes love his nemesis. Having deluded himself into thinking that he was engaging in a scientific experiment when he sired
Nina's child (artificial insemination, no alternative as yet, would
have been disastrous to O'Neill's plot), it soon becomes abundantly
evident that love is an overwhelming and mysterious power against
which neither science nor the human will can prevail. When "love
came" to them they enjoyed their "wonderful afternoons of happiness," and in their ecstasy they were ready to abandon family and
career. Struggling against his love, Darrell fled to Europe, from
whence he returned looking *pale, thin, nervous, unhealthy. There
are lines of desperation in his face, puffy shadows of dissipation and
sleeplessness under his restless harried eyes.* "God, I'm licked!" he
confesses to himself. ". . . no use fighting it . . . I've done my
damnedest . . . work . . . booze . . . other women . . . no use
. . . I love her! . . . always! . . . to hell with pride! . . ." Like
Antony, "the triple pillar of the world," he has been "transformed
into a strumpet's fool." Eleven years later, the lovers sit and hear
each other groan, for "those interludes of passion" "occur so very
rarely now." The "life work" of Darrell, who might have been "the
world's greatest neurologist," "is to rust — nicely and unobtru-
sively." And Nina sadly discerns that "To rot away in peace" is "all
he wants now, too! . . . and this is what love has done to us! . . ."
Darrell wonders why he continues "to hang around . . . ," for
"each time after a few months [his] love changes to bitterness." He
blames Nina for the mess he's made of life. Yet he remains grateful
to her for having given him "the only happiness he's ever known."
That love is superseded, after eleven years, by faded passion should
have come as little surprise to a man trained in biology, yet the
revelation produces in him, and in Nina, a gloomy pathos of disenchantment and self-pity. The elegiac tone of the early sea plays
is revived, not only when the cool lovers recall the "afternoons of
happiness," but also when they contemplate the transitory nature of
life. For if custom cannot stale Nina's infinite variety, it is certain
that age can wither her. Accordingly, she sadly broods over the fact
that she is now thirty-five (which again should come as little sur-

prise, since fifteen years earlier she had been twenty). Five years more, "at forty a woman has finished living . . . life passes by her . . . she rots away in peace! . . ." She expresses the pathos of her existence to Darrell when he complains that she no longer loves him:

Oh, Ned, do shut up! I can't stand hearing those same old reproaches I've heard a thousand times before. I can't bear to hear myself making the same old bitter counteraccusations. And then there'll be the same old terrible scene of hate and you'll run away — it used to be drink and women, now it's to the Station. Or I'll send you away, and then after a time I'll call you back, because I'll have gotten so lonely again living this lonely lie of my life, with no one to speak to except Sam's business friends and their deadly wives. (*She laughs helplessly*) Or else you'll get lonely in your lie a little before I do and come back again of your own desire! And then we'll kiss and cry and love each other again!

Environmental and psychological factors accounted for the slow deterioration of Robert and Ruth Mayo, of Jim Harris and Ella Downey, but O'Neill offered no sufficient cause for Nina's increasingly sad condition nor for Darrell's protracted suffering. The purpose of all this is, presumably, to exemplify the destructive quality of the romantic ideal, but it fails to rise to the occasion because of its immersion in a tenacious sensibility. To be sure, O'Neill returned to a naturalistic position at the end of the play when he had Marsden refer to love as "biological preparation" and declare that one's "duty is to love that life may keep on living." But such observations, too feeble and too late, are an inadequate solvent for the sensibility which pervades so much of the play.

Nor is the theme strengthened by the revelation of the ephemeral and illusory nature of happiness. Nina's quest for happiness throughout the play, and Darrell's throughout a large portion of it, their inability to retain it once they have experienced it, is a component of the atmosphere of futility, disillusionment, exhaustion, and impotence which pervades the last act. But, like the discoveries that passion diminishes, that one grows old, the realization that happiness is a product of the imagination is of neither philosophical nor of tragic significance. What is more, the triteness of such observations is enhanced by the turgid and ponderous fashion in which they are revealed.

Nina's suffering, as we have tried to demonstrate, is to be attributed to her vain yearning "to believe in any God at any price," and to her obsession, which is both traumatic and thematic. That her anguish has still another source is apparent in her complaint to Marsden in Act Two:

Do I seem queer? It's because I've suddenly seen the lies in the sounds called words. You know — grief, sorrow, love, father — those sounds our lips make and our hands write. You ought to know what I mean. You work with them. Have you written another novel lately? But, stop to think, you're just the one who couldn't know what I mean. With you the lies have become the only truthful things. And I suppose that's the logical conclusion to the whole evasive mess, isn't it? Do you understand me, Charlie? Say lie — (*She says it, drawing it out*) L-i-i-e! Now say life. L-i-i-f-e! You see! Life is just a long drawn out lie with a sniffling sigh at the end!

What disturbs Nina is her consciousness of the failure of the symbol to correspond to its object: the word to its meaning, the mask to its face. This discrepancy between appearance and reality never ceases to torment her; as late as Act Seven she still laments having to "live this lonely lie of my life." Marsden, the writer of genteel novels, may not have have been conscious of the problem; but O'Neill, the playwright, had been acutely so almost from the start of his playwriting career — a fact to which the inarticulateness of his early protagonists and a continued suggestion of ineffableness bear witness. When he treated essentially primitive characters, like Brutus Jones, in whom appearance — the civilized surface personality — contrasted with and concealed the real personality, O'Neill solved the problem by projecting for the character his true self. In *Desire Under the Elms* the matter was simpler still. For the primitive Cabots, having remained in their pristine state, were never victims of the ravages of duality. Mask corresponded to face, expression and deed to thought. But sophisticated, supersensitive, and articulate figures such as Michael Cape and Dion Anthony, who moved throughout their plays in a world of appearances, presented a fresh problem to which O'Neill found the solution in the device of the mask which he employed in *The Great God Brown* and in *Lazarus Laughed,* but which he abandoned in *Strange Interlude* in favor of a vocal device. Thus, *Strange Interlude* he declared to be "an attempt at the new masked psychological drama . . . without masks." The play itself becomes one extended exemplification of Nina's painful perception that the "sounds called words" are lies as the contradiction of thought and spoken word is made apparent. Less dramatic than the mask, the interior monologue had, by 1927, become a common feature of the novel. Joyce's *Ulysses* (1922) was perhaps the most conspicuous example of the method, but it also appeared in the novels of Dorothy Richardson, of Waldo Frank, of Sherwood Anderson, and of Conrad Aiken. In the theatre Alice Gerstenberg's popular one-act play, *Overtones* (1913), might be said to have used the technique without its long stream of consciousness aspect. The respective overtones of the two characters expressed the interior, true thoughts to develop the theme of hypocrisy and duplicity. In *The Adding Machine* (1923), Elmer Rice adopted the stream of consciousness method. His play opened with a two thousand word monologue, spoken by Mrs. Zero, which recalls the forty-five pages of Molly Bloom's reverie at the close of *Ulysses*. And in the second scene Mr. Zero and Daisy sit at their desks and speak alternately their private erotic thoughts. In *Strange Interlude,* O'Neill appears to have combined the technique of *Overtones* with that of *The Adding Machine,* for he presented at times the contradiction of thought and spoken word, and at other times he pushed his character off into long reverie. Thus, Marsden thinks *with scornful pity* of Darrell: "His work! . . . what a pretense! . . . a scientific dilettante! . . . could anything be more pitiable? . . . poor chap! . . ." But he says to Darrell: "Biology must be an interesting study. I wish I knew more about it." In the opening scene of the play the stream of Marsden's consciousness — a flow of some six hundred words — moves slowly past, laden with recollections of early boyhood; commentary upon the recent war; thoughts about his profession; plans for future work; observations upon the Professor, the Professor's late wife, and Nina; analysis of his own feelings about Nina; revelation of his attitude toward sex; criticism of the sexual life of our time; recollection of his revolting adolescent experience with a prostitute; suggestion of his "mother-fixation." Thus, the long monologue serves admirably the dramatic requirement of exposition both of story and of character, and it is put to similar use in each of the other first seven acts. Reserved for the monologues are matters which are censored by decorum, by pity, by prearranged agreement to remain silent, and such stuff of which the day-dream is made. Never does the stream become subterranean, never is it a stream of the unconscious as, for example, in *Finnegans Wake;* nor even of the subconscious as in the novels of Virginia Woolf, of William Faulkner. As often as not, the concealed truth is exposed in conventional dialogue form. By a Freudian slip of the tongue Darrell reveals his wish that Evans might die. Conscious of his revelation he exclaims to Nina: "God damn it, why did you make me say hope?" She *calmly* replies: "It may have been in your mind, too, mayn't it?" The repressed characters — Professor Leeds and Marsden — are more inclined to conceal from others what they have been honest enough to admit to themselves. Yet the Professor does both when he reluctantly confesses to himself the shocking truth that he had wished for Gordon Shaw's death and then, shortly thereafter, makes the same confession to Nina. But Marsden, upon realizing that the tears which he has been shedding, ostensibly for the dead Professor, were, in fact, stimulated by Nina's coolness toward himself, fails to transmit the true fact to anybody else. And as his thoughts drift off into recollections of "ugly and disgusting" matters at the very time that he felt called upon to mourn for the dead, his sense of propriety causes him to suppress his ignoble real self.

By revealing the discrepancy between thought and the "sounds called words" O'Neill provided Nina with a basis for her conviction that life is a lie. He reinforced the pervasive sense of dissociation by using once again his familiar conception of the disintegrated personality, by exposing the complexity of conflicting selves beneath the smooth mask of appearances. In Abbie the two powerful drives of possessiveness and sexual desire merged into a single force which integrated her personality, but Nina's personality is divided, to flow in separate channels. Yet at one point in the play — at the climax, in Act Six — she enjoys a sensation of unity and well-being as her "strange devious intuitions . . . tap the hidden currents of life . . . and dark intermingling currents . . . become the one stream of desire." By a process of merging and absorbing, complex woman-wife-mistress-daughter-mother temporarily contains in harmony the divergent desires of the simple man: of the husband, the lover, the father, the son. Then, after ten years, it is apparent that disintegration has set in again. As the end of the play is anticipated three streams of desire evaporate successively, and the fourth — that of the daughter — trickles into a quiet pool of peace. With her single, simple, original personality remaining alone at last, conflict disappears, and the mask of appearances may be lowered, since it is identical with the face. Unity is attained in the end by elimination rather than by integration.

It is reasonable that Nina should regard life as a lie, inasmuch as it is obviously so agonizing. Frustration and disenchantment are only apparent realities, however, as Marsden suggests to her a few lines before the final curtain:

> (*paternally — in her father's tone*) You had best forget the whole affair of your association with the Gordons. After all, dear Nina, there was something unreal in all that has happened since you first met Gordon Shaw, something extravagant and fantastic, the sort of thing that isn't done, really, in our afternoons. So let's you and me forget the whole distressing episode, regard it as an interlude, of trial and preparation, say, in which our souls have been scraped clean of impure flesh and made worthy to bleach in peace.

Thus Marsden would resolve the duality of inner spirit and outer impure flesh by scorning the latter. His position, that of spiritual monism, is in direct contrast with Darrell's materialistic monism. Of the two points of view, it is obvious that O'Neill preferred the former. Bitter and sardonic to the end, Darrell stubbornly deludes himself, maintaining that a scientist shouldn't believe in ghosts (implying that there is something after all to be said for immaterial entities) and credulously accepts a concept that is equally mysterious. As he departs *he laughs up at the sky* and cries: "Oh, God, so deaf and dumb and blind! . . . teach me to be resigned to be an atom! . . ." He returns to his laboratory to live a cold and comfortless existence; whereas Marsden, together with Nina, will enjoy a cozier fate. About them O'Neill spins a drowsy, dream-like, protective covering, inside of which they contentedly contemplate the unreality of the rigorous exterior world. After beating their wings helplessly against unrelenting fate for the past twenty-five years, the weary pair are extended the unusual privilege of becoming chrysalises again and returning to the cocoon.

Marsden refers *with a strange ecstasy* to the "russet-golden afternoon . . . a mellow fruit of happiness ripely falling." Because they are "in love with evening," he and Nina will be married "in the hour before sunset when the earth dreams in afterthoughts and mystic premonitions of life's beauty" — a statement which, if it is syntactically ambiguous and inconsistent with the splenetic mood of the nine acts which have led up to it, illustrates once again O'Neill's alchemical urge to find a golden generalization in the oppressive facts which he had hitherto presented. He discovered the road away from duality, and it is marked by weariness, impotence, ripeness, decay, and renunciation of the flesh. His characters arrive at last in a passive twilight world of introspection and reverie wherein the anguish of the feverish world of appearances is dulled and forgotten. Reality is identified with that period, now revived, when Nina cuddled in her Daddy's arms before the fireplace, "warm in his love, safe-drifting into sleep," when "dreams like sparks soared up to die in the cold dark." This condition of suspended animation, of quietism, of anesthesia is not without precedent in his other plays. As early as 1917, in *The Moon of the Caribbees,* and as late as 1939, in *The Iceman Cometh,* the protagonist found refuge in drink. Similarly, the "sustaining lie" is a means of taking the sharp edge off insufferable reality in *The Straw* and in *Gold*. But the favorite nepenthean device is the dream: the wistful romantic one of *Beyond the Horizon* and of *The Fountain,* the pipe-dream of *The Hairy Ape* and of *The Iceman Cometh,* the weary reverie of *Strange Interlude.* From the sea-weary sailors of the Glencairn plays to the derelicts of Harry Hope's saloon, from the hypersensitive introvert to the hulking man of action, from the ruminating female personification of fecundity and maternity to the earth itself in the hour before sunset, the virtues of dreaming were proclaimed. Never excruciating like Strindberg's dreams, never an eruption from the depths of the psyche like those which concerned the Freudians, O'Neill's dreams served the function of making life endurable. Except for the interlude, life is a dream, as many poets have observed. Like the Buddhist, O'Neill regarded the world as purely subjective. If dear old Charlie "has all the luck at last" it is because he has eliminated the cause of suffering — he has "passed beyond desire." No longer wish-fulfillments, his dreams are undisturbed.

Rather than immerse himself in the "destructive element," O'Neill fled into the fog of virtual non-existence. And poignantly aware as he was of the face behind the mask, of reality behind appearance, he had, ever since *Bound East for Cardiff,* been loath to give more than a furtive glance at the "skull beneath the skin." In 1927, "much possessed by death," he wrote *Lazarus Laughed,* wherein he evaded the inevitable and terrifying eventuality by perfervidly denying its existence, followed, in the same year by *Strange Interlude,* wherein he resumed once again his digging "at the roots of the sickness of today" — indicating not only that science and materialism failed "to give any satisfying new God for the surviving primitive religious instinct to find a meaning for life in," but that, after all, "its fears of death" had not been comforted. Where he had denied death, he came to deny life as well. Caught between a contempt for life and a dread of death, he found a *modus operandi* in anesthesia.

The Dynamo and the Mother

Strange Interlude was produced in January 1928. In the spring and summer of that year O'Neill worked upon *Dynamo,* "A symbolical and factual biography of what is happening in a large section of the American (and not only American) soul right now." Ambitious still "to achieve size," he had planned to write a trilogy of which *Dynamo* was to have been the first unit — a group of plays that would, as he told Nathan in another connection, "dig at the roots of the sickness of today." But he abandoned his project after completing the single work and was not to satisfy his trilogic ambition until 1931 when he brought *Mourning Becomes Electra* to a conclusion.

Dynamo "maybe wasn't all it should have been," O'Neill eventually confided to Nathan, "because I was going through a lot of trouble in family matters when I was writing it . . ." There is little doubt that the urgency of his domestic affairs temporarily impaired his analytical and creative faculties, distracted to such a degree that he was incapable of scrutinizing "the American (and not only American) soul" with the penetration and thoroughness that he had exhibited in *Strange Interlude*. Lacking in *Dynamo* is the customary profusion — the consequence in previous plays of labyrinthine psychological introspection and of a piling up of assorted grievances against the conditions of life. Wooden, comparatively simple, devoid of sensibility, its characters resemble those of the pre-pagan plays. A blur of pathos and satire, its tone is indeterminate. Its professed theme, the search for a God to replace the old God, the failure of science and materialism to help in this matter, had indeed been the major theme of every play since *The Hairy Ape*. The truth is, in short, that the "trouble in family matters" may have been an important contributing factor in the failure of *Dynamo;* but the play owes its sterility also to the fact that O'Neill no longer had much to say about the question of faith. Both religiously and aesthetically he was rapidly coming full circle, approaching the point where in *The Hairy Ape* he had commenced to "dig at the roots of the sickness of today." Reaching the pagan substratum, he had unearthed not only Dionysus but also the tree of life, the Elm, the Mother, by whom immortal Dionysus, defunct since 1927, was survived. All that was left from the rhapsodic pagan period, the Mother remained on the scene — except for a brief interval in 1932–33 — to the end of O'Neill's playwriting career. Her function in both *Dynamo* and *Mourning Becomes Electra* was to comfort the fear of death. For life-sickness, she offered no remedy.

Although Nina said that she wanted "to believe in any God at any price," she proved to be more discriminating than that. For she rejected two concepts of God which obtained in her time. She tried hard to pray to the "modern science God," but found that she couldn't believe in Him, and wouldn't if she could. He was "deaf and dumb and blind," and she scorned an indifferent deity. But for the contrary reason, she could not believe in God the Father either. Meddling too much in human lives, "perverting" them by His preoccupation with sin, He haunted her throughout the play. This God of Gods — The Boss — Nina was convinced, was motivated less by righteousness and by wrath, than by the pleasure that He found in destroying human happiness. The thought of Him flashed into her consciousness at the height of her triumph and exultation when at the end of Act Six she achieved her only complete fulfillment; and she quickly knocked wood before He heard her happiness. She heard Him laugh when Gordon slapped Darrell's face. And once again she heard Him laugh — a screaming laughter — as He threatened to bring Gordon down in flames with His lightning, love. Tragic heroine that she was, Nina found a solution to the problem of existence in a universe that is ruled jointly by the modern God of science and the Father God who kills us for his sport. Resigned to her fate, comforted by oblivion, she finally became reconciled to a tragic universe of cosmic positive and negative electric charges in which "our lives are merely strange dark interludes in the electrical display of God the Father." As for God the Mother, in whom Nina wanted to believe — She eluded Nina altogether.

In *Strange Interlude,* Lucifer and Jehovah opposed the accession of the Mother God. But in *Dynamo,* the playwright intervened in favor of the Mother. After hurling God the Father headlong from the ethereal sky, he permitted the God of Electricity to share suzerainty briefly with the Mother. But at the end he saw to it that She was the sole ruler of the mysterious and very disagreeable universe. The deposition of Jehovah, which is accomplished in Act One, consists of a family rebellion — of the mother and the son — against the patriarch, followed by conversion to a new religion, that of the neighbor. The Reverend Hutchins Light, stiff-necked sermonizer, one of the "Bible-punching breed," counterpart of such fanatics as Abraham Bentley, Mrs. Bartlett, Ephraim Cabot, worships a God who is made in his own unprepossessing image. Because God is a projection of his own ego, the obstinate, wrathful, vengeful Light is always sure of what God wills. "I have decided," he says when he informs his son Reuben that he shall follow in his footsteps. "It is God's manifest will." But Mrs. Light, scornful of her husband's omniscience, is equally determined that Rueben shall never be a minister, for she wishes to shield him from the poverty and humiliation which she has had to face. She is the personification of the American middle-class maternal virtues. Submitting to a barren and restrictive religious practice in which she clearly has no faith, she can conceive of nothing better in its place than the "comforts of life," the "sinful sloth of the flesh." It is her ambition that Reuben shall "go to college . . . then into business . . . marry a nice girl with money" (although she is thankful that he doesn't care anything about girls yet). Mrs. Light's love for her son transcends solicitude, for she is frantically possessive of him, fiercely jealous and vindictive, when he exhibits an interest in the neighbors' daughter. Reuben is likewise a personification. He represents the American of today who has outgrown the Old Testament religion of his ancestors, who casts about for a substitute and finds only what science and materialism have to offer. Mother-ridden, sex-ridden, he attempts to incorporate into his new faith these incongruous phenomena. Like his bovine prototype, Eben Cabot, Reuben is antagonistic towards his father, deeply attached to his mother. After she is dead his longing for her activates his worship of the dynamo. It is her betrayal of him, in the first act, that causes a disillusionment of sufficient intensity to make the violent break with his family. Furiously jealous, the mother conceals the father in Reuben's bedroom that he might overhear the son's confession of love for the neighbor girl. Her motive being sadistic vengeance, she wishes to see him beaten, to hear him yell. Upon discovering his mother's treachery, his eyes turn to her vindictive face and he thinks in a tortured *agony of spirit*. "He was hiding in the closet! . . . she knew it! . . . she cheated me! . . . when I trusted her! . . . when I loved her better than any one in the world!" *He cries out in a passion of reproach*. "Oh, Mother! Mother!" Not only has she been deceitful, she has betrayed him to his rival, his father. "I thought you loved me better'n any one," he wails, "and you'd never squeal on me to him!" Suddenly afraid no longer of his father or of his father's God, he defies them both. As the lightning flashes, Light *gives a gasp of superstitious fright*. Reuben, *with a hard, mocking laugh,* says to his mother, "Do you still believe in his fool God?" After which he *addresses the sky with insulting insolence*. "If there is his God let Him strike me dead this second! I dare Him!" *His father squeals with terror . . . His mother screams. He laughs triumphantly*. Turning *his back on his home determinedly* [he] *starts walking off left — with bitter defiance:* "There is no God! No God but Electricity! I'll never be scared again! I'm through with the lot of you!" What he is through with is his father and the "old God." His mother still remains a vital part of his soul.

Reuben Light's situation at the close of the first act recalls that of Henry Adams who, forlorn and disillusioned, "drifted in the dead waters of the *fin de siècle*," deploring on the one hand his Puritan heritage and on the other the chaos of modern science. Having dismissed Jehovah, Adams sought to explain the riddle of the universe in terms of force, and embarked upon the task of reducing revelations of mysterious energy — whether of physics or of the Cross — to a common value. "He would risk translating rays into faith." Whereupon he visited the great hall of dynamos at the Paris Exposition of 1900 accompanied by Langley who proceeded to reveal how little the scientist knows "about electricity or force of any kind." "To Adams the dynamo became a symbol of infinity."

As he grew accustomed to the great gallery of machines, he began to feel the forty-foot dynamos as a moral force, much as the early Christians felt the Cross. The planet itself seemed less impressive, in its old-fashioned, deliberate, annual or daily revolution, than this huge wheel, revolving within arm's-length at some vertiginous speed, and barely murmuring — scarcely humming an audible warning to stand a hair's-breadth further for respect of power — while it would not wake the baby lying close against its frame. Before the end, one began to pray to it; inherited instinct taught the natural expression of man before silent and infinite force.

Continuing his effort to reduce all forces to a common value, he was ready to feel the force of all — whether of rays, or of sex as manifested in the conception of Venus and of the Virgin. Thus, at the Louvre and at Chartres there was evident "the record of work actually done and still before his eyes . . . the highest energy ever known to man, the creator of four-fifths of his noblest art, exercising vastly more attraction over the human mind than all the steam-engines and dynamos ever dreamed of." In the Middle Ages, Adams explained, the Virgin had "conceived herself and her family as the centre and flower of an ordered universe which she knew to be unity because she had made it after the image of her own fecundity." The twelfth and thirteenth centuries passionately flung themselves at the feet of the Woman rather than of the Man, loving and adoring Mary "with a passion such as no other deity has ever inspired"; for in her man had found a door of escape from his prisonhouse. "She was imposed unanimously by all classes," observed Adams, "because what man wanted most in the Middle Ages was not merely law or equity, but also and particularly favour. Strict justice, either on earth or in heaven, was the last thing that society cared to face. All men were sinners, and had, at

least, the merit of feeling that, if they got their deserts, not one
would escape worse than whipping." But, as the embodiment of
a mysterious, independent, potent force — "illogical, unreasonable,
and feminine" — Mary offended and threatened the theocratic masculine order. Her disregard for conventional morality eventually
got her into trouble with respectable middle class society. The
"Puritan reformers, . . . not satisfied with abolishing her . . .
sought to abolish the woman altogether as the cause of all evil in
heaven and on earth."

O'Neill's hero, having cut himself loose from the "theocratic masculine order," begins his frenzied quest for faith. Returning home
after fifteen months of travel, study, and thought, Reuben convinces
himself that the only God he believes in now is electricity. But if
his speculations lead him to this conclusion, his instincts bring him
to another, that of sex. Henceforth nearly all of his relationships are
with women, with Ada Fife, Mrs. Fife, and with his mother, who
died while he was away. Not only has he abolished the Puritan,
he has restored the woman as the source of all goodness in heaven
and on earth. She is to become, finally, like the Virgin, a door of
escape.

Ramsey Fife, *a good-natured man except where the religious
bigotry of his atheism is concerned,* exemplifies how little the
scientist knows "about electricity or force of any kind," but his
wife, in the stirring of her "profound instincts," penetrates deeper
into the mystery of life. When Reuben explains the conclusions
which he has reached after "studying a lot of science,"

It all comes down to electricity in the end. What fool preachers call God
is in electricity somewhere. (*He breaks off — then strangely*) Did you ever
watch dynamos? What I mean is in them — somehow.

Mrs. Fife is the only person who understands what he means. She
responds (*dreamily*):

I love dynamos. I love to hear them sing. They're singing all the time about
everything in the world! (*She hums her imitation of a dynamo's whirring
purr.*)
    Reuben. (*startled — looks at her with growing interest*) 'Singing all the
    time about everything in the world.' . . . she gets them all right . . . listen
    to her . . . she's caught the sound . . . (*Abruptly he puts down his books
    and walks up to Mrs. Fife*) Say, you're all right!

Like Reuben's mother, Mrs. Fife is a symbol of maternity and fecundity. She stands not only for maternal love but for sexual love as well, encouraging as she does Reuben's illicit passion for her own daughter. Given to "dope-dreaming," to "mooning up at the moon," to sitting and blinking "placidly in the sun," this cow-like, sentimental, unmoral, languorous creature, who weighs well over two hundred pounds, is the counterpart of Cybel, the stout and voluptuous idol of Mother Earth. Cybel, at the age of forty, her divinity faded, has degenerated from exalted goddess into a "damn funny woman." The decline of the Earth Mother after the *Great God Brown* is indicative of O'Neill's increasing pessimism. There is a steady progression in this direction, from the fervor of that play to the sardonic, wooden quality of *Dynamo,* to the death-laden *Mourning Becomes Electra.*

Although he no longer was to glorify the Mother, he was far from ready to dispense with her. Mrs. Fife, living, and his mother, dead, together inspire Reuben to worship the dynamo. At his mother's grave he starts "to do a prayer act," when it suddenly occurs to him that there is nothing to pray to. Yet, the inherited instinct of man or the recurrent patterns of childhood — the memory of his mother's tenderness as well as the habit of praying at her side — make it difficult to resist the impulse to pray. Once again he involuntarily slips to his knees — at the bedside — and tells his mother that he is sorry that she is dead. Chiding himself again for trying to pray "when there's nothing," the thought of praying to electricity occurs to him. Before she died his mother had repeated the words which he had written to her: "We have electrocuted your God. Don't be a fool." Convinced that the "dying see things beyond," he wonders now whether the impulsion to pray to electricity may not have come from his mother. Whereupon, he goes down to the hydro-electric plant "to take a look in at the dynamos." The dynamo is *huge and black, with something of a massive female idol about it, the exciter set on the main structure like a head with blank, oblong eyes above a gross rounded torso.* Reuben observes that "below it is like a body . . . not a man's . . . round like a woman's . . . as if it had breasts . . . but not like a girl . . . not like Ada . . . no, like a woman . . . like her mother . . . or mine . . . a great dark mother! . . . that's what life is! . . ." Once again he feels an impulse to pray, and after *arguing tormentedly with himself, he gets down on his knees and prays aloud to the dynamo:* "Oh, Mother of Life, my mother is dead, she has passed back into you, tell her to forgive me, and to help me find your truth! (*He pauses on his knees for a moment, then gets slowly to his feet. There is a look of calm and relief on his face now. He thinks reverentially*) Yes, that did it . . . I feel I'm forgiven . . . Mother will help me . . . I can sleep . . . I'll go home . . ."

Henry Adams neglected to indicate how he felt after he prayed to the dynamo at the Paris Exposition in 1900. Electricity he recognized as a silent and infinite force, but yet nothing to worship. Sex, another and distinct force, had, to be sure, been the object of worship for thousands of years. It was the principal, if not, the only, component of art, beauty, and religion; and until the Puritans insisted that sex was sin, every previous age knew that it was strength:

Every one, even among Puritans, knew that neither Diana of the Ephesians, nor any of the Oriental goddesses was worshipped for her beauty. She was a goddess because of her force; she was the animated dynamo; she was reproduction — the greatest and most mysterious of all energies; all she needed was to be fecund.

Regretfully, we presume, Adams turned from the Virgin to the dynamo; for, unlike Reuben Light, he had failed to perceive that they were expressions of a single force. The heat of Reuben's febrile speculations produce the synthesis for which he has been groping. In the third act he explains the ultimate mystery of life to Mrs. Fife:

Yes. You're like her — Dynamo — the Great Mother — big and warm — (*With a sudden renewal of his unnatural excitement, breaks away from her*) But I've got to finish telling you all I've come to know about her — how all things end up in her. Did I tell you that our blood plasm is the same right now as the sea was when life came out of it? We've got the sea in our blood still! It's what makes our hearts live! And it's the sea rising up in the clouds, falling on the earth in rain, made that river that drives the turbines that drive Dynamo! The sea makes her heart beat, too! — but the sea is only the hydrogen and oxygen and minerals, and they're only atoms, and atoms are only protons and electrons — even our blood and the sea are only electricity in the end! And think of the stars! Driving through space, round and round, just like the electrons in the atom. But there must be a center around which all this moves, mustn't there? There is in everything else! And that center must be the Great Mother of Eternal Life, Electricity, and

Dynamo is her Divine Image on earth! Her power houses are the new churches! She wants us to realize the secret dwells in her! She wants some one man to love her purely and when she finds him worthy she will love him and give him the secret of truth and he will become the new saviour who will bring happiness and peace to men! And I'm going to be that saviour — That's why I asked you to come — I want you to be a witness! I know the miracle will happen to me tonight because I had a message from my mother last night. I woke up and saw her standing beside my bed — just as she used to when she came in to kiss me good night — and she smiled and held out her arms to me. I know she came from the spirit of the Great Mother into which she passed when she died to tell me she had at last found me worthy of her love.

Ingenious as Reuben's conclusions are, it is evident that they are only a wish-fulfillment. Wanting, like Nina Leeds, "to believe in any God at any price," what he really longs for is the mother. Nina, too, repudiated God the Father and wished to fling herself "at the feet of the Woman."

We should have imagined [she wistfully explained] life as created in the birth-pain of God the Mother. Then we would understand why we, Her children, have inherited pain, for we would know that our life's rhythm beats from Her great heart, torn with the agony of love and birth. And we would feel that death meant reunion with Her, a passing back into Her substance, blood of Her blood again, peace of Her peace!

In Act Three, Reuben, his body grown very thin, his face gaunt and pale, his eyes deeply sunken, is in hot pursuit of the Mother. His suffering is the consequence on the one hand of a sense of guilt — of having been unfaithful to his mother — and, on the other of his intense longing for her. Placating a Puritan conscience has become easy enough for one who has read up on biology: "What we did," he explains to Ada Fife, "was just plain sex — an act of nature," and "what people call love is just sex — and there's no sin about it." But to soothe a deeper disturbance, that attendant upon the violation of his love for the mother, is far more difficult. He himself becomes distressed even upon imagining her in a similar situation: "Did Mother really love the old man?" he asks himself ". . . she must have or how could she stand him? . . . and she made me with him . . . act of Nature . . . like me and Ada . . . (*He jumps to his feet distractedly*)." Increasingly he feels that his sins of the flesh stand in the way of a return to the mother, prevent a whole-hearted worship of the animated dynamo. What he desires above all is forgiveness and peace. As he listens with Mrs. Fife to the sounds of the dynamo, he says:

It's as if that sound was cool water washing over my body! — washing all dirt and sin away! Like some one singing me to sleep — my mother — when I was a kid — calling me back to somewhere far off where I'd been once long ago and known peace!

His mother has appeared every night to warn him that he is living in sin, that Dynamo will never find him worthy of her secret until he has given up the flesh and purified himself. Although the joys of the flesh are almost irresistible, his love for his mother — for Dynamo — takes precedence. He has even become a flagellant that he might purify himself. As he awaits the miracle, kneeling before the dynamo, *his arms stretched out to it supplicatingly,* and *cries out* with a note of despair: "Mother! Don't you hear me? Can't you give me some sign? O Dynamo, who gives life to things, hear my prayer! Grant me the miracle of your love!" — Ada, the temptress, appears. Seizing upon this coincidence, he decides that "Dynamo sent her here" to prove that he has conquered the flesh. And he determines not only to resist temptation but to convert Ada, to make her pray to the Mother. Certain now that the miracle will happen this night, that "then there will be only the kingdom of happiness on earth," he takes the girl by the hand and leads her, as they climb precariously from the dam to the dynamo-room roof, to different levels within the building where the oil switches, *their six cupped arms stretching upward, seem like queer Hindu idols tortured into scientific supplications.* Here, the hysterical hero, torn between sexual love for the girl and loyalty to his mother succumbs to the former; then, having desecrated the church and betrayed the mother, he is *hounded by remorse.* He shoots the harlot — "that's what Mother called her!" — and clambers frenziedly up the rungs on the dynamo's side. *Up on the platform, he stops for a moment, gasping for breath, stretching out his arms to the exciter-head of his Dynamo-Mother with its whirling metal brain and its blank, oblong eyes.* Here he pleads to the dynamo *like a little boy:*

I don't want any miracle, Mother! I don't want to know the truth! I only want you to hide me, Mother! Never let me go from you again! Please, Mother! (*He throws his arms out over the exciter, his hands grasp the carbon brushes. There is a flash of bluish light about him and all the lights*

*in the plant dim down until they are almost out and the noise of the
dynamo dies until it is the faintest purring hum. Simultaneously, Reuben's
voice rises in a moan that is a mingling of pain and loving consummation,
and this cry dies into a sound that is like the crooning of a baby and merges
and is lost in the dynamo's hum. . . .)*

Down below, the absurd Cybel, Mrs. Fife, utters a startled cry as
she runs to the fallen body. "Reuben! Are you hurt bad?" she
foolishly inquires of the boy who has just immolated himself.

(She turns with childish bewildered resentment and hurt to the dynamo)
What are you singing for? I should think you'd be ashamed! And I thought
you was nice and loved us! (. . . Mrs. Fife *pounds the steel body of the
generator in a fit of childish anger)* You hateful old thing, you! (*Then she
leaves off, having hurt her hands, and begins to cry softly)*

The final curtain falls.

Reuben's search for strange gods has ended in the Mother. He has
rejected the meddlesome Jehovah and also the indifferent Lucifer.
If Cybel, the earth goddess, with her rhythm of the seasons, her
cycle of death and rebirth, has become a ridiculous, childlike
woman, he still may enjoy the comfort and peace of the mother's
womb. At least, he "belongs." Where the Hairy Ape went to the
animal house only to be crushed to death in the arms of the gorilla,
Reuben goes to the power house to die in the bosom of his Mother.
The Mother, indeed, is the new God who replaces the old One
who has died, and who compensates for the "failure of science and
materialism to give any satisfying new One for the surviving religious instinct to find a meaning for life in." But the annunciation is
uttered without conviction, without the exaltation that accompanied
similar insights in the pagan plays.

Everymannon

THERE WAS not much to choose between the animal house
and the power house. The extent of O'Neill's precipitous spiritual
decline since *Lazarus Laughed* becomes more impressive in *Mourning Becomes Electra*. Having evacuated the House of Laughter,

O'Neill now moved into the House of Death, the ancestral home of Everymannon. Here he remained, to dream on two occasions — in *Days Without End* and in *Ah, Wilderness!* — of an unreality that lay beyond the horizon in the past, and then to shut the doors to all but the Iceman of Death. The antithesis of the messianic *Lazarus Laughed, Mourning Becomes Electra* presents something more nearly akin to a pessimistic *Weltanschauung* than to a religion. And as tragedy *Electra* was not intended to be Dionysian. Bearing aspects of Aeschylus and Euripides, it approximates neither.

Within the framework of classical tragedy O'Neill repeated the familiar background pattern — the yearning for mother love, the longing for the "death-birth-peace" of the womb — a repetition which one tolerates for the sake of the outer structure. When Reuben Light died he returned to the Mother who, as *Mourning Becomes Electra* now emphasizes, is also the ultimate source of the supreme living human needs once presumably supplied by religion: love and peace. Love is mother love, peace is in the womb. O'Neill's other characters, although they were unaware of the origin, had frequently felt the attraction of these two prime values. We have seen them reject those ways of life that are dominated by indifference, hate, cruelty, acquisitiveness. Attracted by the Gospels, they repudiated modern Christianity for failing to fulfill them. Sexual passion never remained mere animal urge. It became human desire, spiritual need, and transfigured such animal-like characters as Eben and Abbie. Darrell, who insisted that "desire is a natural male reaction to the beauty of the female," was forced to pay dearly for his irreverence. Similarly, Reuben's twisted life was reflected in the cynicism which he acquired after reading up on love in biology textbooks. The benefits of tender love were exemplified in *The Straw*, wherein it was recommended as the way to conquer disease and death. "There is no God but love," cried Juan Ponce de Leon, hero of *The Fountain*. Where love was unrequited death ensued: Kukachin, who "loved love," "died for love of a fool." Love and life were synonymous and ends in themselves, as *Welded* illustrated. Thus, Cape finally learned the supreme lesson: "to love life — to accept it and be exalted." That, he explained, "is the one faith left to us." And his wife discovered the same truth. "Perhaps I'm praying," said she. "I don't know. I love." For Dion Anthony, too, who, indeed, was the personification of love, love was the only faith. He, like Kukachin, "loved love," and his chief virtue was that he had "the strength to love in this world." William Brown wanted love, not justice. The secret of Lazarus' victory over death resided in his love for Man and Woman. His example moved Caligula at one time to announce that the Empire must become "one great Blessed Isle of kindness and love." And Nina loved Darrell's love for her.

Lazarus tried to soothe the tormented Caesars, who yearned for peace. "Peace! . . . yes . . . that is all I desire . . . ," exclaimed Nina as her interlude neared its end. With *intense longing,* the hero of *Days Without End* was to speak of love that "will go on forever within the eternal peace and love of God." Nina found peace in anesthesia; Larry Slade in alcohol and pipe-dream; James Tyrone, Jr. in alcohol and death. Meanwhile we are to hear Lavinia in *Mourning Becomes Electra* express her agonized wish: "Nothing matters but love, does it? That must come first! No price is too great, is it? Or for peace! One must have peace —."

In reiterating the two foregoing demands, O'Neill used motifs which appeared in his earliest plays: the vision of death in *Bound East for Cardiff,* the ubiquitous prostitute who, in *Welded* and in *Marco Millions,* was abstracted into a symbol; the joining of that symbol with the conception of maternal love in *Desire Under the Elms;* — all leading to the presentation of the divine prostitute, the Earth Mother, in *The Great God Brown,* who embodied the "harmony of womb and grave," the miracle of death and rebirth. In *Strange Interlude* the myth took clearer shape when Nina, mourning man's misery of death-born-of-birth, explained that the mistake began when God was created in a male image and pointed out the advantage of worshiping instead a God made in the image of the Mother. It then remained for Reuben Light to rectify the error — to repudiate both the male God and the science God, and to fulfill Nina's yearning for reunion with God the Mother, "passing back into Her substance, [becoming] blood of Her blood again, peace of Her peace!" The theme of *Mourning Becomes Electra* is man's yearning throughout his "death-in-life" — a life perverted by the worship of God the Father — for "death-birth-peace" — the reward for worshiping God the Mother.

In *Electra,* the Mother is a primordial image, an archetypal experience shared by all of the Mannons. Thus, Lavinia is identified with her mother, Christine, and both are the image of Marie Brantôme. Adam Brant has fallen in love with Christine because he associates her with his mother, Marie. For the same reason, he is attracted to Lavinia, to whom he says:

You're so like your mother in some ways. Your face is the dead image of hers. And look at your hair. You won't meet hair like yours and hers again in a month of Sundays. I only know of one other woman who had it. You'll think it strange when I tell you. It was my mother . . . (*dropping his voice to a reverent hushed tone*) Yes, she had beautiful hair like your mother's, that hung down to her knees, and big, deep, sad eyes that were blue as the Caribbean Sea!

Ezra Mannon, returned from war, is similarly attracted to Christine, his wife:

(*Leans toward her, his voice trembling with desire and a feeling of eagerness and awe — touching her hair with an awkward caress*) You're *beautiful!* [he exclaims] You look more beautiful than ever — and strange to me. I don't know you. You're younger. I feel like an old man beside you. Only your hair is the same — your strange beautiful hair . . .

Likewise tapping the "collective unconscious," Orin says to his mother, "you're my only girl." Then he asks, "And do you remember how you used to let me brush your hair and how I loved to? . . . You've still got the same beautiful hair, Mother. That hasn't changed." (*He reaches up and touches her hair caressingly*) To his sister, Lavinia, he says: "What a paradise the Islands were for you, eh? All those handsome men staring at you and your strange beautiful hair! It was then you finally became pretty — like Mother!" Again he says to Lavinia:

There are times now when you don't seem to be my sister, nor Mother, but some stranger with the same beautiful hair — (*He touches her hair caressingly. She pulls violently away. He laughs wildly.*) Perhaps you're Marie Brantôme, eh? And you say there are no ghosts in this house?

By means of a visual symbol the mothers are tied together.

By means of a second symbol they express the fulfillment of Mannon longing for love and peace. The Blessed Isle is also the Mother, the counterpart of Cybel, of Lazarus, of God the Mother, of the Great Mother. Speaking to Adam *in a dry brittle tone,* Lavinia says:

I remember your admiration for the naked native women. You said they had found the secret of happiness because they had never heard that love can be a sin.

Brant. (*surprised — sizing her up puzzledly*) replies: So you remember that, do you? (Then romantically) Aye! And they live in as near the Garden of Paradise before sin was discovered as you'll find on this earth! Unless you've seen it, you can't picture the green beauty of their land set in the blue of the sea! The clouds like down on the mountain tops, the sun drowsing in your blood, and always the surf on the barrier reef singing a croon in your ears like a lullaby! The Blessed Isles, I'd call them! You can forget there all men's dirty dreams of greed and power!

Adam's wistful revelation is followed by Ezra's hopeful suggestion to Christine that they "leave the children and go off on a voyage together — to the other side of the world — find some island where [they] could be alone a while." Orin's wish follows the same pattern. "If you only knew how I longed to be here with you — " he says to his mother. As *his voice becomes dreamy and low and caressing,* he tells her of the "wonderful dreams" that he had had about her. Then he asks, "Have you ever read a book called 'Typee' — about the South Sea Islands?" Christine, startled by the question, says strangely, "Islands! Where there is peace?" Orin continues:

Someone loaned me the book. I read it and reread it until finally those Islands came to mean everything that wasn't war, everything that was peace and warmth and security. I used to dream I was there. And later on all the time I was out of my head I seemed really to be there. There was no one there but you and me. And yet I never saw you, that's the funny part. I only felt you all around me. The breaking of the waves was your voice. The sky was the same color as your eyes. The warm sand was like your skin. The whole island was you. (*He smiles with a dreamy tenderness*) A strange notion, wasn't it? But you needn't be provoked at being an island because this was the most beautiful island in the world — as beautiful as you, Mother!

When Orin decides to kill himself, he declares: "It's the way to peace — to find her again — my lost island — Death is an Island of Peace, too — Mother will be waiting for me there —" He escapes from death-in-life, from the "tomb" which Abe Mannon had built, to death-birth-peace, to the womb.

Christine and Lavinia also yearned to escape, but they were

anatomically precluded from following Orin. The former plotted
with Adam to sail to the Blessed Islands where they would be
"happy." And Lavinia actually realized her wish, voyaging there
with Orin, much as if Adam and Eve had been readmitted to the
Garden of Eden after their eviction. To Lavinia, the Islands were
"Paradise enow."

I loved those Islands [she says *dreamily*] They finished setting me free.
There was something there mysterious and beautiful — a good spirit — of
love — coming out of the land and sea. It made me forget death. There was
no hereafter. There was only this world — the warm earth in the moonlight — the trade wind in the coco palms — the surf on the reef — the fires
at night and the drum throbbing in my heart — the natives dancing naked
and innocent — without knowledge of sin.

But she returned to New England with Orin who was "too much
of a Mannon, after all, to turn into a pagan" and enjoy Lavinia's
islands. Home once again, she is filled with love for Peter who is
"simple and fine" like the natives. Throwing her arms around him,
she exclaims:

Oh, Peter, hold me close to you! I want to feel love! Love is all beautiful!
I never used to know that! I was a fool! (*She kisses him passionately. He
returns it, aroused and at the same time a little shocked by her boldness. She
goes on lovingly*) We'll be married soon, won't we, and settle out in the
country away from folks and their evil talk. We'll make an island for ourselves on land, and we'll have children and love them and teach them to
love life so that they can never be possessed by hate and death!

Lavinia's instincts, once she has replaced her mother, are directed
towards love and life and are the antithesis of all that her Mannon
heritage represents.

With *bitter longing* Christine asks, "Why can't all of us remain
innocent and loving and trusting?" and then answers her own
question: "But God won't leave us alone. He twists and wrings
and tortures our lives with others' lives until — we poison each
other to death!" She is referring to the Mannon God, who is made
in the male image, the sadistic and meddlesome deity the worship
of whom had made "life so perverted, death so unnatural." Consequently, the tortured and desperate Orin rejects God entirely, insisting that man must exist by his own light as he strives feebly to
understand himself during his existence in "the darkness of death

in life." But such philosophy is cold comfort; and shortly after uttering it Orin consummates his yearning for death-birth-peace, preferring warmth to light. All of the Mannons, in the stirring of their profound instincts, display the emotional behavior pattern that we have observed in Adam, Orin, and Lavinia. Possessed by hate and death, they "cannot be trusted with love." Even Lavinia's exogamous impulse is revealed at the end of the last play to be an incestuous love after all. Yet her effort to break the Mannon chain of destiny is the most vigorous one in the entire trilogy.

The destiny against which the Mannons struggle is that of death itself. Ezra looks like a "statue of an eminent dead man"; his son, his cousin, his daughter, too, much of the time, resemble him; and he himself is the image of his ancestors whose portraits hang in the study. The pictures, objectifications of the family destiny, symbolize an evil influence much as did the portrait of Colonel Pyncheon in Hawthorne's novel of family guilt; and are similar also to the portraits of the heroine's ancestors in Moody's *The Great Divide* who, obsessed with sin, tried to cleanse themselves with wretchedness, self-torture, and pain. To the Mannons "Life was a dying. Being born was starting to die. Death was being born." That one need not be a Puritan to be possessed by death is evidenced by the anguish which so many other of O'Neill's life-weary characters suffer, from *Bound East for Cardiff* to his latest plays. It is an element that was incongruously introduced into the satirical *Marco Millions*. The consciousness of death haunted Dion Anthony. It formed the theme of *Lazarus Laughed*. The thought of it dulled the edge of Nina's few happy moments. John Loving, after a miserable period of time, triumphantly proclaimed that "death is dead!" But it was reborn to haunt the broken men who languished in Harry Hope's saloon. And it awaited the wretched Tyrone who searched for it throughout *A Moon for the Misbegotten*. Freud had explained in 1922 the "riddle of life" in terms of the striving of the life and the death instincts and affirmed that the "goal of all life is death," a theory which Santayana, for one, believed was "calculated to enlighten and to chasten us enormously about ourselves." But if it had any influence upon O'Neill—who was acquainted with it—it served to enlighten and chasten him to the point of moribundity. For, ever since *Desire Under the Elms,* the life instinct in his plays appears to have exhausted itself. In *Strange Interlude,* O'Neill denied both life and death; but now, in *Electra,* he sought to evade life that, from birth, is subject to death. He therefore faced the inevitable and strove to make a virtue of necessity. This he did by meeting destiny on his own terms — of love and peace — and comforting his fears of death in the bargain.

Having fashioned a religious myth that payed proper respect to the two human values that he cherished most, O'Neill wove it into the texture of the Electra story. His recreation of that legend is, in effect, the artistic counterpart of Freud's interpretation of another Greek legend. In fulfilling his intention to write a "modern psychological drama using one of the old legend plots of Greek tragedy," O'Neill drew heavily upon the theories of both Freud and Jung, hoping to get a "modern psychological approximation of the Greek sense of fate into such a play, which an intelligent audience of today, possessed of no belief in gods or supernatural retribution, could accept and be moved by." Thus, at last, he found it possible once again to bring together the religious and the artistic aims towards which he had been striving. In 1926, the year in which he made the first entry in his notebook concerning the adaptation of "an old legend plot of Greek tragedy," he expressed elsewhere the conviction "that it is possible . . . to develop a tragic expression in terms of transfigured modern values and symbols in the theatre which may to some degree bring home to members of a modern audience their ennobling identity with the tragic figures on the stage." "Of course," he added, "This is very much of a dream, but where the theatre is concerned, one must have a dream, and the Greek dream in tragedy is the noblest ever!" Thus he was less cynical than Ezra Pound, who had declared in *Mauberley* (1920):

> The age demanded an image
> Of its accelerated grimace,
> Something for the modern stage,
> Not, at any rate, an Attic grace;
>
> Not, not certainly, the obscure reveries
> Of the inward gaze,
> Better mendacities
> Than the classics in paraphrase!

And more sanguine than Joseph Wood Krutch, who, as the decade drew to a close, observed that "we read but we do not write tragedies," that "The tragic solution of the problem of existence, the reconciliation to life by means of the tragic spirit is, that is to say, now only a fiction surviving in art."

There appeared in the twentieth century a number of versions of the Electra story, to say nothing of other adaptations of classical legends. In Spain, Galdós wrote a modern allegory, *Electra,* that was first produced in 1901 and which attacked the Church. In Austria, von Hofmannsthal wrote a savage, Dionysian version of *Electra* in 1904. In *The Tower Beyond Tragedy* (1925) Robinson Jeffers adapted *The Agamemnon* and *The Libation Bearers* to present his theme of "racial introversion — man regarding man exclusively —." Robert Turney, in 1936, emphasized the tragedy of warfare in his *Daughters of Atreus.* And Jean-Paul Sartre wrote *The Flies* in 1943 to exemplify the philosophy of Existentialism. These "classics in paraphrase" — including O'Neill's — may have reflected an image of the age's "accelerated grimace," and they may have wanted an "Attic grace"; but they were, nevertheless, designed for the modern stage, and there was nothing mendacious about them. And what playwright has ever been more preoccupied than O'Neill with the "obscure reveries of the inward gaze"? As for Joseph Wood Krutch — he was to reverse his opinion after seeing *Mourning Becomes Electra.*

O'Neill's version of the Electra story follows the broad outlines of Aeschylus' trilogy. Three "storms spend their strength against the walls" of the house of Mannon: Abe Mannon's "act of guile," Christine's murder of Ezra, Orin's "murder" of Christine. These occur in the order in which they appeared in Aeschylus: the first before the trilogy begins, the second at the close of the first play, the third at the end of the second play. In the last play, the Furies, assuming the shape of a guilty conscience, make their assault and are finally appeased. With respect to plot, O'Neill's most conspicuous departure from Aeschylus was his giving the central role to Lavinia rather than to Orin. In so doing he appears to have followed Euripides' *Electra,* not only diverging from Aeschylus, but also disregarding *The Electra* of Sophocles wherein brother and sister divided the part of protagonist.

The counterparts of O'Neill's characters are to be discovered not in any of the three Greek tragedies, but in other plays of O'Neill. If his female figures — Christine and Lavinia — display at times an obstinate strength, a calculating intelligence, and a streak of wantonness suggestive of Clytemnestra, one should be reminded of such characters as Abbie, Pompeia, Nina, and Josie Hogan. As for the men, they resemble their classical prototypes not at all. Ezra, a pitiful, pleading creature, returns from war, as Agamemnon did, seeking to love his wife and asking only that she love him. Far from dallying at Appomattox, returning home with a mistress, or killing his daughter, Ezra's only manifest guilt — apart from his indifference to the request of Marie Brantôme — consists of possessing a characteristic Mannon ineptitude where love is concerned. But because he is the father, he is guilty by implication. In *Strange Interlude* the male parent became the personification of death itself. "Death . . . my father . . . comes between me and happiness!" Nina exclaimed. And now, in *Electra,* Ezra is the image of death, the personification of "death in life." If Lavinia loves him, it is because she is the jealous rival of her mother; but she is quite ready to transfer her affections to other men — to Orin and to Adam — just as Christine does. Adam Brant, although he, too, is a Mannon, is "gentle and tender," everything that Ezra has never been to Christine and what she has "longed for all these years . . . — a lover." That he should possess these commendable attributes is comprehensible, for he bears none of the infamy of being a father or of being a full-blooded Mannon. Yet his hybrid heritage — pagan and Puritan — produces a regrettable disharmony in his personality. Thus, his *mouth is sensual and moody, strong and weak by turns.* And *he gives the impression of being always on the offensive or defensive, always fighting life.* Like Aegisthus, he is constant in love, but less to his cousin's wife than to his own mother. Orin, who is also half-pagan, is dominated by the unwholesome other half — two circumstances having contributed to this unfortunate imbalance. He has been wounded in the head and he has suffered from overexposure to war and death. On the whole, however, apart from his act of violence against Adam, he shows himself to be less vengeful than wistful. If Lavinia, Christine, and Marie Brantôme share a common identity, so also do Orin, Brant, Ezra, Abe, and Dave.

These Mannon men belong in O'Neill's long line of life-weary characters which extends from Smitty to Tyrone, Jr.

"To develop a tragic expression in terms of transfigured modern values and symbols," O'Neill had first to discover, if not to create, such values and symbols. Having passed beyond traditional good and evil, he had now to establish a reasonably fixed moral position if he was to fulfill his purpose of writing an approximation of Greek tragedy which depended for its effect upon the concept of crime and retribution, upon the equivalent of the "Puritan conviction of man born to sin and punishment." To be sure, he had always been "acutely conscious of the Force behind — (Fate, God, our biological past creating our present, whatever one calls it — Mystery certainly) —," but it swept the protagonist to his doom irrespective of moral choice or tragic flaw. For there are no moral choices and nothing so trifling as a flaw: "Man is born broken," as the Great God Brown observed. "There is nothing to lay hold on," Jeffers had his Cassandra declare,

No crime is a crime, the slaying of the King was a meeting of two bubbles
   on the lip of the cataract,
One winked . . .

But with the Mother myth O'Neill tried to find "something to lay hold on," to fill up the moral void, to discover a rationale for his tragedy of family guilt. If Freud could trace the beginning of religion and morality to the slaying by the sons of the primordial father, O'Neill could seek it in the murder of the primordial mother. He contrived to make his male characters, at least, have sharp feelings of guilt as a result of their transgressions and expiate their "sins" for violating the moral order which he had created. Neither traditional nor transcendent, it is a moral order which takes no heed of impersonal justice or of objective truth. It is founded, rather, upon the only two values which O'Neill would recognize.

The calamities that haunt the house of Mannon stem from a central primal offense, the crime against Marie Brantôme. The sons, who are made in the image of the father, not only suffer for his sin but repeat it. In this way, O'Neill conveyed a sense of fate, of family guilt. Yet, in other plays the mother-son motif imparted the same quality of guilt without, to be sure, involving the family.

Eben Cabot was haunted by his dead "Maw" and hesitated to love Abbie without the mother's permission. Abbie then became not only the object of his passion but the instrument by which he avenged the wrongs which the father had committed against the mother. Deeply attached to his mother, Marsden suffered for years from the "ugly and disgusting" memory of his experience with a prostitute during his prep school days — a symbol of disloyalty to the mother. Reuben Light, whose religious and sexual instincts converged in his mother, felt that he had betrayed her when he performed the sexual act with Ada; whereupon he killed both Ada and himself. Ten years after *Electra* the motif reappeared in *The Iceman Cometh,* when Parritt, a "mad tortured bastard," was driven to kill himself because he felt that he had betrayed his mother. And in *A Moon for the Misbegotten,* the tragic situation was based upon Tyrone's remorse and guilt, the source of which was his drunken, sexual debauch in a drawing-room of the train which carried his dead mother to the East for burial.

In *Mourning Becomes Electra* the counterpart of the horrible banquet which Atreus had prepared for his brother Thyestes is the harsh treatment of Marie. To be sure, Abe Mannon put his brother Dave out of the house, disowned him, cheated him out of his share of the business; but the "act of guile" against the brother is in itself of no significance. What was important is the disastrous consequence of the deed upon Dave's wife, Adam Brant's mother. Indeed, Adam felt that his father was as guilty as his uncle:

He was a coward — like all Mannons — once he felt the world look down on him. He skulked and avoided people. He grew ashamed of my mother — and me. He sank down and down and my mother worked and supported him . . . One night when I was seven he came home crazy drunk and hit my mother in the face. It was the first time he'd ever struck her. I hit at him with the poker and cut his head. My mother pulled me back and gave me a hiding. Then she cried over him. She'd never stopped loving him.

Hating his father, Adam refused to forgive him; whereupon Dave went out in the barn and hanged himself. "The only decent thing he ever did," commented Adam *savagely.* Ezra, too — not because of his father's crime, but because of his personal sin — is involved in the crime against Adam's mother. Dying of sickness and starvation while Adam was away at sea, Marie wrote to Ezra asking for a loan. "He never answered her," Adam explains. "And I came too late. She died in my arms." Then, with *vindictive passion,* he exclaims, "He could have saved her — and he deliberately let her die! He's as guilty of murder as anyone he ever sent to the rope when he was a judge." When Adam first met Christine he hated her for being Ezra's. "I thought, by God, I'll take her away from him and that'll be part of my revenge! And out of that hatred my love came!" Revenge has turned to rivalry for the possession of Christine, the mother.

And rivalry is the motive for Orin's murder of Adam Brant. Far from mourning the death of his father, Orin quietly rejoices in it, feeling at last that he has his mother for himself. But he has not reckoned with Christine's new love. Once Lavinia proves the mother's disloyalty, Orin remains in a *murderous rage,* his face *distorted with jealous fury,* until he can kill Adam. Having done so, he stoops *over the body and stares into* Brant's *face, a queer fascinated expression in his eyes,* and observes the resemblance between Adam and Ezra. "Do you remember," he asks Lavinia, "me telling you how the faces of the men I killed came back and changed to Father's face and finally became my own? (*He smiles grimly*) He looks like me, too! Maybe I've committed suicide!" O'Neill was exploiting here Freud's Oedipus complex, according to which the son, in his guilty wish to destroy the father that he might gain the mother, identifies himself with the father. Seeing his new rival accomplishing what he himself has always wished to achieve — the removal of the father, possession of the mother — he once again sees his own image in the rival's face. How ingeniously this theory may be applied was demonstrated by Ernest Jones, who explained the mystery of Hamlet's delay in terms of struggle for the mother. Hamlet, like Orin, had unconsciously sought his father's death, but seeing his uncle achieving what he himself had always unconsciously hoped to achieve, he identified himself so completely with Claudius that to kill him was to kill himself.

To be sure, there was no delay in Orin's murder of Adam after Lavinia proved herself to be an honest sister, just as Orestes unhesitatingly killed Aegisthus. What dark wishes had been present in Orestes' unconscious mind we can easily surmise if we accept the Freudian premises; but on the surface, the Greek hero, savagely destroying his cousin, fulfilled his duty to avenge Agamemnon and to remove the man who had usurped the kingship. When the time came for the Orestes of Aeschylus to slay Clytemnestra, he hesitated briefly to ask whether he ought to let mercy blunt his sword against his mother. Then, abiding immediately by Pylades' advice, he turned to his mother and exclaimed:

I will slay thee by the man thou lovest! / Thou didst account him better than my sire / In life: then in his death thou shalt lie with him, / Since here thou hast loved, hating where love was due.

Inquiring whether Clytemnestra was at Aegisthus' side, Euripides' hero also criticized his mother's behavior. Upon being informed that she was waiting for the country-folk to disperse before joining her husband, Orestes declared,

Enough! She knows what eyes are turned upon / Her passings in this land!

What the Freudian psychologist detects in Orestes' disapproval of Clytemnestra's affair with Aegisthus, O'Neill made blatantly explicit in his play. Preoccupied with the revelation of the impulsions of instinct, he seldom let his characters express the demands of civilized convention. But when Orin cries, "You say Brant is her lover. If that's true, I'll hate her! I'll help you punish her!" he reveals the ambivalent nature of human behavior, the mask-like quality of society's moral code. Like the Hamlet whom Jones has analyzed, Orin is aware of his duty to avenge the death of a father whom he wanted to be dead, to punish a mother whom he dearly loved. Punishing the mother is a painful task, and Aeschylus and Euripides — if not Sophocles — recognized this. In the tragedy of the former, Orestes was pursued by the mother's Furies and, after purging himself for a long time, appeared at the shrine of Athena where his fate rested in the hands of the gods. In Euripides' *Electra,* Orestes was exiled — "impure, a murderer in a stranger's land." In O'Neill's trilogy, although Orin never lays hand upon his mother, he suffers the deepest anguish of guilt, and eventually shoots himself. For by killing Christine's lover he has directly caused her death, and he feels as responsible as if he had murdered her himself. Seeking vainly for forgiveness while she is yet alive —

Mother! Don't you hear me? Why won't you speak to me? Will you always love him? Do you hate me now? (*He sinks on his knees before her*) Mother! Answer me! Say you forgive me!

— he is rewarded by absolution after a year of expiation which culminated in the supreme act of forbearance:

I'll get on my knees [he says with *excited eagerness* to his dead mother] and ask your forgiveness — and say — (*His mouth grows convulsed, as if he were retching up poison*) I'll say I'm glad you found love, Mother! I'll wish you happiness — you and Adam!

She hears him, and her maternal heart responds. She forgives and summons him to her. Thus, the Furies are appeased not by gods who engage in dialectic and balloting, but by the mother's bestowal of grace.

Such are the transfigured modern values and symbols which the "Greek dream in tragedy" is made on. If O'Neill's premises were diametrically opposite to those of Aeschylus, he still contrived to find an approximation of the Greek conception of crime and retribution and of the Puritan conviction of man born to guilt and punishment. Where Aeschylus took the father's side — arguing that "he that sows is author of the shoot," that she who is called the mother of the child is not its parent, but "the nurse of seed implanted in begetting" — O'Neill, with the support of modern psychology, took the mother's side. But so unconditionally that no issue is present. The nurse of the seed, Aeschylus acknowledged to be almost as indispensable as the sower, thereby creating a situation which demanded of the hero a tragic choice, and which produced a conflict that had to be reconciled. O'Neill, recognizing no conflict, resolved Orin's tragedy in death.

Unfortunately, being so absolute for the mother has its disadvantages. Infallible creature that she is, her crimes must always be justified. She is tortured not by guilt, but by the old bugbear, unfulfillment. Christine's murder of Ezra — accomplished by enticing him to bed, ensnaring him with the promise of sexual satisfaction, cleaving his weak heart with taunts of her disgust and revelations of her infidelity, and stopping it with the poison which Adam procured — is motivated by hate and revenge whose source is frustrated love. Her hate and disgust for Ezra began on their wedding night, and her desire for revenge came when she was deprived of Orin's love. Orin was born, she explains to Lavinia, while Ezra was with the army in Mexico:

> He seemed my child, only mine, and I loved him for that! (*Bitterly*) I loved him until he let you and your father nag him into the war, in spite of my begging him not to leave me alone . . . When he had gone there was nothing left — but hate and a desire to be revenged — and a longing for love!

Bitterness over the loss of the son's love is the counterpart of Clytemnestra's fury over the sacrifice of Iphigenia, but O'Neill found it well to ignore that part of the legend wherein the mother displays a strong attachment for the daughter. That Christine's killing of her husband is adequately motivated, no Freudian would deny. Unlike Nina Leeds, her counterpart of the 1920's, she fulfills her primitive wish in overt action instead of drifting in the endless anguish of repressions, regressions, neuroses, and daydreams. Yet, her character is essentially that of Nina, for she too is unfulfilled, wistful, fearful of approaching old age, dissatisfied with God the Father. What impels her to satisfy her desire for Ezra's death, we may surmise, is the example set by her prototype of the Greek legend which O'Neill was committed to follow. But in contrast with the "man-souled" Clytemnestra, who was driven by elemental passions, Christine is a frail, feminine, effete creature. And if Ezra's offenses earn for him the retribution that he receives, they are trifling when set beside those of Agamemnon. For Ezra is simply the tired businessman masquerading as a Civil War general, and Christine is his dissatisfied and unhappy wife. Although her urge to kill him is comprehensible, he has done nothing to deserve such a fate. Whereas Agamemnon carried with him not only his father's crime, but also his own wrongs, which stemmed from the folly and evil of the ten year war that had been fought over the "infatuate Helen," Menelaus' beauteous wife. When Clytemnestra murdered him, the memory of all his sins was awakened — from Atreus' cruel banquet to the slaying "with iniquitous sword" of Iphigenia. He not only earned his fate, but Clytemnestra's determination to see that he met it was well motivated on all levels. At the same time, however, it was just as evident that her deed was tragically criminal. In killing Ezra, Christine simply destroys the "statue of an eminent dead man." We appreciate her wish to remove obstacles that frustrate her desire for love and life, and we approve of cruelty inflicted upon the father. We are therefore moved less by her crime than by her improvidence, by the redundancy of killing what is already dead. O'Neill developed his allegory at the expense of his tragedy, for Christine's deed is an incident which arouses neither pity nor fear. Whatever qualms the spectator feels, as he watches the scene, derive from the Gothic atmosphere and the dramatic suspense.

As for his heroine, Lavinia, O'Neill succeeded a little better in involving her in the Mannon evil destiny, the "crime and retribution chain of fate"; for she is half Mannon. But, being a woman and, what is more, a "mother," Lavinia resists O'Neill's attempts to punish her as he felt that he should. Euripides, he thought, had permitted Electra to escape with a relatively light penalty — compared with Orestes — by giving her in marriage to Pylades, the brother's friend. He was convinced that this was an unworthy ending for such a tragic figure. "In Greek story," he wrote in his notes (without specifying Euripides' *Electra*), "she peters out into undramatic married banality. Such a character contained too much tragic fate in her soul to permit this — why should Furies have let Electra escape unpunished?" To be sure, Aeschylus dropped his Electra entirely before the final play of his trilogy, and Sophocles had her share equally with Orestes in the vindication and affirmation of law and order. But neither version was acceptable to O'Neill. For he preferred to let Lavinia be his central character rather than Orin; and his ethos, consisting exclusively of love and peace, precluded a resolution to his tragedy that would proclaim the triumph of justice. Indeed, justice is one of the "sounds called words," a hollow voice produced by the mask which society has constructed for Lavinia as it has for Orin. She speaks of Brant as having "paid the just penalty for his crime," insisting that his death was an act of justice — "the only way true justice could be done." Yet it was patently an act of revenge — against Brant and against Christine. When the mother shoots herself, Lavinia again declares, "It is justice! It is your justice, Father!" Finally perceiving his sister's real motive, Orin cries, "You know damned well that behind all your pretense about Mother's murder being an act of justice was your jealous hatred! . . . You wanted Brant for yourself!" When

O'Neill refused to permit Lavinia to marry Peter, he was correcting what he felt to be a fault in the *Electra* of Euripides. More than that, he was working out a plan according to which the tragic pattern which ended with Christine's death, at the close of the second play, is repeated in the third play — a plan which emphasized the existence of a Mannon evil destiny. Orin has become the father and, like Ezra, seeks to consummate his love for Lavinia, his sister-mother-wife. Since Lavinia has replaced Christine, she is repelled by Orin as Christine was by Ezra. Except for their voyage to the Blessed Isle, a journey which, to be sure, Ezra wanted to make with Christine, the brother and sister follow the course which their parents took. Like her mother, Lavinia wishes for the death of the Mannon to whom she is bound and sees that it is fulfilled. Then, as she is hopeful of escaping the Mannon destiny by creating an island of her own, her slip of the tongue makes evident to her that she is doomed to follow her mother's path to the end. Her "love" choices have been precisely the same as Christine's, whose place she has always wanted to steal: Ezra, Orin, and Adam-called-Peter. Thus, the third play of the trilogy is a replica of the first two, and yet O'Neill achieved a sense of finality. For when the cycle is completed a second time, there is no possibility of its beginning again; because Lavinia, the unmated, is the last Mannon, and she is determined to pay out the family curse by retiring into the ancestral home. Knowing when she is defeated, she chooses to yield to fate, a decision motivated not by a wish to expiate her sins, but by an impulsion towards masochism. Retribution, like justice, is not what it seems. *With a strange cruel smile of gloating over the years of self-torture,* Lavinia says, "I know they [the Mannons] will see to it I live for a long time! It takes the Mannons to punish themselves for being born!" Puritans that they are, the willful, aberrant Mannons deny themselves the consummation for which they yearn: reunion with God the Mother, embodiment of "death-birth-peace." Life is the curse which Lavinia is resolved to pay out; living is its expiation, death its redemption.

In *Mourning Becomes Electra,* O'Neill exemplified what Schopenhauer declared to be the "true sense of tragedy," "that it is not his own individual sins the hero atones for, but original sin, i.e., the crime of existence itself." So devoted was he to this conception, that he permitted it to inform the entire trilogy. The pessimism of the Greeks may have been equally black, their tragedies just as aware of the crime of existence, still "they would have despised," as William James observed, "a life set wholly in a minor key, and summoned it to keep within the proper bounds of lachrymosity." The unfulfillment, exhaustion, and apathy which O'Neill's tragedies increasingly reflected were conditions completely foreign to Greek tragedy. The Greeks were never so contemptuous of life as to seek consolation in death, nor so afraid of death as to calm their fears by promising themselves the fulfillment after death of all that they had vainly yearned for in life. O'Neill is not to be censured for the predicament in which he found himself, or for the fashion in which he chose to extricate himself, but rather for misinterpreting his dream. For however ingeniously he substituted the premises of a rationalistic psychology, however adeptly he interpolated his allegory, however glibly he spoke of fate and destiny, crime and retribution, guilt and atonement, his dream in tragedy was not the Greek dream.

The appearance of *Mourning Becomes Electra* subsequent to Krutch's estimate in 1929 of modern tragedy gave Krutch no cause to revise his assertion that the "tragic solution of the problem of existence, the reconciliation to life by means of the tragic spirit is . . . only a fiction surviving in art." Indeed, O'Neill's play bears out the statement by achieving precisely the opposite results: *Electra* offers a solution not to the problem of existence but to that of nonexistence; it reconciles not to life, but to death. Nor did O'Neill invoke that Tragic Spirit which Krutch regarded as the product either of a religious faith in the greatness of God" or of "faith in the greatness of man," although by 1932 it seemed to Krutch that he had satisfied this demand, that he had, in short, succeeded in investing man "once more with the dignity he has lost." "The greatness of the plays," he insisted, begging the question, "lies in the fact that they achieve a grandeur which their rational framework is impotent even to suggest." In *Mourning Becomes Electra,* he was convinced that

once more we have a great play which does not 'mean' anything in the sense that the plays of Ibsen or Shaw mean something, but one which does, on the contrary, mean the same thing that 'Oedipus' and 'Hamlet' and 'Macbeth' mean — namely, that human beings are great and terrible creatures when they are in the grip of great passions, and that the spectacle of them is not only absorbing but also and at once horrible and cleansing.

Here, it seems Krutch is entirely wrong. Not only has he missed the "meaning" of O'Neill's trilogy, he has discerned in O'Neill's characters qualities that are mostly nonexistent. They are characters, moreover, whose passions, infantile rather than great, are a spectacle that is horrible but scarcely cleansing. Catharsis is a condition which O'Neill seldom achieved, preferring, as he did, narcosis or necrosis. That the deficiencies of *Mourning Becomes Electra,* when it is compared "with the very greatest works of dramatic literature," are limited only to its language, is an opinion which, if our judgments have been even moderately sound, has little to be said in its support. There is equally little to be said for Krutch's contrast of Ibsen and O'Neill, wherein he finds that O'Neill avoided the central fault of Ibsen's tragedies, namely, that they are "too thoroughly pervaded by a sense of human littleness to be other than melancholy and dispiriting."

Having defined "true tragedy . . . as a dramatic work in which the outward failure of the principal personage is compensated for by the dignity and greatness of his character," Krutch concludes that "O'Neill is almost alone among modern dramatic writers in possessing what appears to be an instinctive perception of what a modern tragedy would have to be." Yet one has only to strip *Mourning Becomes Electra* of its spiritual malaise, its Freudian machinery, its selfconscious symbolism, its Gothic properties, its turgid style, to see how little better O'Neill has succeeded than Ibsen in satisfying Krutch's definition of "true tragedy." *Ghosts,* too, was a tragedy of family guilt in which the original sin is traced to the life-denying impulse. On one side is happiness, on the other is "the source of all the misery in the world": law, order, duty. Living in the house polluted by her husband's profligacy, Mrs. Alving, the counterpart of Christine, revolts against the restrictive virtues which society has imposed upon her and which prevented Alving from finding "any outlet for the overmastering joy of life that was in him." Oswald, haunted by his father's sin, suffers not only physical consequences thereof, but repeats — like Orin — the parent's behavior. Where Orin is afflicted with a stubborn case of

Weltschmerz, and complications induced by a wound in the head — the dowry of the Mannons in general, Ezra in particular — Oswald suffers from congenital syphilis — the indirect inheritance of the Manders way of life, but the direct consequence of his father's dissolute actions. When, at the conclusion of the tragedy, Oswald locks himself and his mother inside their haunted house, he is paying out the family curse much as Lavinia is. Surely the madness of a paretic is not more melancholy and dispiriting than the masochism of a woman who denies herself the pleasure of dying.

More restrained than Krutch, George Jean Nathan never compared *Mourning Becomes Electra* "with the very greatest works of dramatic literature," but he did declare it to be "indubitably one of the finest plays that the American theatre has known." Like Krutch, he mistook *Weltschmerz* for tragedy and ascribed purgative powers to hyper-emotionalism and to the manifestations of a neurotic sensibility. But Nathan came closer to the truth when he observed that O'Neill's "passionate inspiration," "the sweep and size of his emotional equipment and emotional dynamics" transcended the characters and the play. This is a euphemistic way of saying that *Mourning Becomes Electra* contains no adequate equivalent for the playwright's excess of feeling. It is a fault that is present in most of O'Neill's plays, and O'Neill himself was apparently aware of it when in *Electra* he consciously shunned "the many opportunities for effusions of personal writing anent life and fate." If the trilogy is less effusive than some of the preceding plays, its grandiosity is threefold greater than most. If it contains less "personal writing," it is far from reticent concerning the author's conception of life and fate, a conception which suggests that the glow felt by Nathan to be spreading over all — "the glow that is O'Neill" — is less "luminous and radiant" than feverish.

Remembrance of Things Past

PART FOUR

Remembrance of Things Past
Passive Adsorption

Tentative Atonement

UNABLE SINCE 1927 to cheer himself up, O'Neill sank, as he told Nathan in the early 1930's, into "a bog of tedium and life-sickness." Destitute of faith and terrified with skepticism, he experienced the corollary predicament — a contempt for life and a dread of death. Aggravating this double dilemma — inducing it, too, in part — was the "trouble in family matters." Having long since dissociated himself from society, O'Neill began to dissociate himself from his painful past — first to repudiate it in *Days Without End* and then to relive a portion of it in *Ah, Wilderness!* in a form closer to the heart's desire. Instead of a Temple where he might communicate the "religion of a poetical and symbolical celebration of life," the theatre became for him a sanctuary — a place of refuge — its stage a confessional. Indeed, this tendency had been evident as early as *Welded* and had been more conspicuously manifested in *The Great God Brown*. In *Days Without End* the theatre assumed a virtual identity with the Church itself. A temporary peace of soul ensued, of which *Days Without End* appears to have been partly cause, partly effect. Following the hiatus in the progress of his life-sickness, O'Neill continued to use the stage as a confessional in the retrospective play *The Iceman Cometh,* wherein he not only affirmed the repudiations that he had made in *Days Without End* but renounced everything that he had tried to affirm both in that play and in *Ah, Wilderness!*

"They were an interlude," declared O'Neill, referring to *Days Without End* and *Ah, Wilderness!* less than five years after he had written them. Strange, almost miraculous, the interlude was joyfully welcomed by O'Neill. "Life has certainly changed for me," he reported to Nathan,

> and for the first time in God knows how long I feel as if it had something to give me as a living being quite outside of the life in my work . . . I feel as if I'd tapped a new life and could rush up all the reserves of energy in the world to back up my work. Honestly, it's a sort of miracle to me, I'd become so resigned to the worst. So be a little indulgent and don't mind my unloading a little of the pop-eyed wonder of it at you!

Nathan attributed the transformation in his friend, this onset of a cheerfulness which, paradoxically, coincided with the beginning of the economic depression, to the easing of O'Neill's personal life "with solicitude and affection and faith." Resembling the state of euphoria which accompanies the completion of a successful psychoanalysis, the "mood of optimism and faith that . . . supplanted his old, indurated pessimism and disillusion," followed, for one thing, the dissolution of the marital trouble. O'Neill's remarriage, following divorce in 1928 from his second wife, was, ostensibly, a happy one. Another factor which conceivably influenced his new state of mind was the financial security that accrued to him from the success of *Strange Interlude,* a security which was not alarmingly diminished by the depression. Finally, although we rejected the claim that *Mourning Becomes Electra* could have had a cathartic effect upon its audience, we shall not deny that the passing of the trilogy at this time could have had salubrious consequences for O'Neill himself. And if *Electra* cleansed his emotions, it also depleted the psychological and mythical possibilities of the universal drama of life and death.

Dramatic testimony to his apparent spiritual rejuvenation, *Days Without End* and *Ah, Wilderness!* celebrate orthodoxy in religion, fidelity in marriage, stability in family life, and, once again, the death of death. After finishing two drafts of *Days Without End,* O'Neill was suddenly inspired to put aside the manuscript and to write in its entirety *Ah, Wilderness!,* his comedy of conventional American family life — after which he completed the unfinished piece. Although the comedy was first to be produced, it was, in a sense, a sequel to the serious play, the product and exemplification of the peace of mind that seemed to be achieved in the latter through reconsideration, renunciation, and atonement. If O'Neill never seriously considered reconversion to Catholicism for himself, *Days Without End* was apparently a deeply felt imitation of the act, a dramatic-religious ritual sufficiently moving as to induce a temporary feeling of complete spiritual well-being. *Ah, Wilderness!* is a monument to that fleeting moment.

Professionally as well as personally *Days Without End* was a backward glance o'er travel'd roads, a belated impulse to detour. The play is primarily concerned with the conflict of skepticism and faith, secondarily with love and marriage, and scarcely at all with the depression, despite the topical allusions. Having joined Man to the Universe, having returned him to the womb, O'Neill now brought him back to God. By resurrecting the "Old God" — the "Old Graybeard" who had been accused of crimes to His children ranging from neglect to downright cruelty — O'Neill enabled his hero to cure the "sickness of today" and comfort his fear of death, to re-acquire in a spiritual way the harmony that he used to have as a child. John Loving gets what he wants, which is what O'Neill wanted him to have; but the example is meretricious as religion, tedious as drama. Although John confesses his sins of adultery and pride, renounces his blasphemous ways, ceases his pursuit of strange gods, and expiates all through suffering, he remains still the extreme individualist, the sentimental, self-obsessed character, concerned ultimately only with his own salvation. Early and late he displays neither pity nor understanding as he refers to the "stupid cowardice," the "blind greed" of the depression's victims. Purged of hate, he is still not actually prepared to love. For he demands love only for himself. He loves his wife because he finds, as he says, peace and security in her love, because she revives for him the happy days of his childhood when "life *was* love." And God serves the same purpose. John Loving makes his peace with Him privately in a secluded old church — a transaction whereby he receives tender, forgiving love in exchange for his atonement. There is no suggestion of the vast hierarchy of the Church, of its austerity, dignity, authority. Nor is there any evidence that John is likely to affirm the Catholic notion that the individual is less important than society. Although he conquers the mocking, skeptical part of himself, what remains of his personality gives little promise of willingness or ability to submit to the routine discipline of the Church, to accept the duties that it would impose, or to regard it as a place of worship as well as a refuge.

Had O'Neill himself re-embraced Catholicism he might have done so with the foregoing reservations. The fact that he did not suggests that he was aware of his limitations. For *Days Without End,* even more emphatically than *Welded* and *The Great God Brown,* is an autobiographical play, indicating how close O'Neill came to reconversion by the fact that he confessed his sins not in the customary form of the agonized soliloquy but in the presence of a priest. Up to the last scene John Loving not only typifies the twentieth-century renegade, he is the composite O'Neill hero, resembling Michael Cape and Dion Anthony, as well as O'Neill himself. Roughly the same age as the playwright, John even resembles him in certain physical characteristics: straight nose, square jaw, broad forehead, blue eyes. Although the hero is a businessman, O'Neill never felt the fact important enough to indicate the nature of the business or to refer to it at all after the first act. John is also a writer, if only by avocation, and is at work upon an autobiographical novel, whose unfinished plot he relates to his uncle-priest by way of confession. This occupies much of the play, but in the course of it we soon realize that John is stricken with the life-sickness from which O'Neill had been suffering. Brought on by the skeptical tendency, the disease is characterized by impulses to self-destruction, by hatred of life, by obsession with death.

Thus *Days Without End* is another episode in the ordeal of Eugene O'Neill, in his sustained effort to attain spiritual wholeness and health, a condition that would ensure the love and peace for which he craved. As he saw it now, the only thing standing in his way was his unfortunate predisposition to ironical skepticism, the tendency that he had deplored in *The Great God Brown.* In *Days Without End* he confessed that he had been a devil's advocate and dedicated the play to the exorcism of the devil. To achieve this end he provided his hero with a childhood that contrasted sharply with that of Dion Anthony and other protagonists, a childhood of love and faith. Thus John Loving had a past in which he could dream, to which he could return. Although his Mephistophelean self sneered at this "cowardly yearning to go back," back he went as usual. But before John could return he had first to confess the

sinful ways of those years which intervened between childhood and
the present — thoughts and deeds which, for the most part, he
shared with other O'Neill heroes and with O'Neill himself.

John Loving was "an only child." His father "was a fine man.
The boy adored him." And "he adored his mother even more. She
was a wonderful woman, a perfect type of our old beautiful ideal
of wife and mother." Both parents were "devout Catholics." "But,"
adds John,

not the ignorant, bigoted sort, please understand. No, their piety had a
genuine, gentle, mystic quality to it. Their faith was the great comforting
inspiration of their lives. And their God was One of Infinite Love — not a
stern, self-righteous Being Who condemned sinners to torment, but a very
human, lovable God Who became man for love of men and gave His life
that they might be saved from themselves. And the boy had every reason
to believe in such a Divinity of Love as the Creator of Life. His home
atmosphere was one of love. Life was love for him then. And he was happy,
happier than he ever afterward — (*He checks himself abruptly*)

So confident was he in his faith that "the God of Punishment,"
about Whom he had learned at school, made little impression upon
him. "He grew up as devout as his parents. He even dreamed of
becoming a priest. He used to love to kneel in the church before
the Cross." Then at age fifteen John experienced the trauma that
twisted his life, and God fell from the hero's grace. John's parents
died in quick succession — this despite the boy's fervent prayers.
"His God of Love" began "to show Himself as a God of Vengeance," as "deaf and blind and merciless — a Deity Who returned
hate for love and revenged Himself upon those who trusted Him!"

In his grief and bitterness John took to a life of sin: to social
radicalism, to pagan religions — mystical, Oriental — to rational-
ism, even to adultery. He indirectly describes his state of mind to
Father Baird as he tells about the "period of black despair" that
he has the hero of his novel undergo. The fictional character

was seized by fits of terror, in which he felt he really had given his soul
to some evil power. He would feel a tortured longing to pray and beg for
forgiveness. It seemed to him that he had forsworn all love forever — and
was cursed. At these times he wanted only to die. Once he even took his
father's revolver —

But he was afraid to face death [sneers the Mephistophelean aspect of
John]. He was still too religious-minded you see, to accept the one beautiful,

comforting truth of life: that death is final release, the warm, dark peace of annihilation.

Father Baird *quietly* comments: "I cannot see the beauty and comfort." And John's diabolical self continues: "He often regretted afterwards he had not had the courage to die then. It would have saved him so much silly romantic pursuit of meaningless illusions." After this "period of black despair," John's hero, although he took "a rationalistic attitude," "read all sorts of scientific books," and "ended up by becoming an atheist," still could not remove the "indelible scar" that his traumatic experience had left "on his spirit." He

never could explain away a horror of death — and a strange fascination it had for him. And coupled with this was a dread of life — as if he constantly sensed a malignant Spirit hiding behind life, waiting to catch men at its mercy, in their hour of secure happiness — Something that hated life! — Something that laughed with mocking scorn! . . .

A credulous, religious-minded fool, as I've pointed out! And he carried his credulity into the next period of his life, where he believed in one social or philosophical Ism after another, always on the trail of Truth! He was never courageous enough to face what he really knew was true, that human life is unimportant and meaningless. No! He was always grasping at some absurd new faith to find an excuse for going on!

An example of such a faith was *Lazarus Laughed*. And John is still moved by the apocalyptic fervor that possessed O'Neill when he had worked on the play a half dozen years earlier. *An idealistic exaltation coming into his voice,* John declares:

We need a new leader who will teach us that ideal [". . . to measure the value of our lives by"], who by his life will exemplify it and make it a living truth for us — a man who will prove that man's fleeting life in time and space can be noble. We need, above all, to learn again to believe in ourselves! A new savior must be born who will reveal to us how we can be saved from ourselves, so that we can be free of the past and inherit the future and not perish by it!

The priest reminds John that he is forgetting "that men have such a Savior," that "all they need is to remember Him." Whereupon, in an excess of skepticism John Loving denies both Christ and Dionysus. "No! We have passed beyond gods!" he cries. "There can be no going back!" Having answered the priest, he replies to his own brief plea for a superman:

But, on the other hand, I'll grant you the pseudo-Nietzschean savior I just evoked out of my past is an equally futile ghost. Even if he came, we'd only send him to the insane asylum for teaching that we should have a nobler aim for our lives than getting all four feet in a trough of swill! (*He laughs sardonically*)

Renouncing all of his "absurd" faiths, John "did go on" and "found his truth at last — in love, where he least expected he ever would find it. For he had always been afraid of love." Like Michael Cape, he believed that love could make his marriage into "a true sacrament . . . a sacrament of faith in which [he and his wife] would find the completest self-expression in making [their] union a beautiful thing." Although John is "happy again for the first time since his parents' death," he is haunted by a "malignant Spirit," a "mocking Something," "a recurrent dread" that his wife "might die and he would be left alone again, without love." Possessed by this "spirit of evil," he has tried deliberately to destroy his happiness by committing adultery with a woman for whom "he had not the slightest desire." Thus, like Michael Cape, he has wished "to murder love." John's wish is almost realized when his wife contracts pneumonia following a walk in the rain which she took in response to John's hypnotic persuasion. Having learned of her husband's infidelity, she does not wish to recover. The crisis of the illness and the crisis of the play coincide. Father Baird informs John that "Human science has done all it can to save her. Her life is in the hands of God now." Loving insists that "there is no God," but the impulse to pray has remained alive within him. Torn between faith and skepticism, he even contemplates suicide. Then recalling "the old church not far from where he now lives, in which he used to pray as a boy," *he suddenly gets to his feet as if impelled by some force outside him. He stares before him with obsessed eyes. Moving like one in a trance,* he exits, to be discovered in the final scene struggling with his Mephistophelean self inside the church before a life-size figure of Christ. He overcomes evil skepticism and, with *an expression of mystic exaltation on his face,* stands before the Cross and prays. For the first time since *Desire Under the Elms* the "light of the dawn" appears at a play's end. Now, like those defiant New England pagans, Eben and Abbie, John's attitude is "aloof and devout." As Father Baird enters to report the miracle of the wife's recovery, John cries *exaltedly* out of his *ecstatic mystic vision:* "I know! Love lives forever! Death is dead! . . . Life laughs with God's love again! Life laughs with love!"

Marking the stages in O'Neill's "pilgrimage from turmoil to peace," Richard Dana Skinner was gratified to see the playwright in *Days Without End* enter the third stage — that of Emergence, following the periods of Turmoil and of Regression. Skinner felt that the play, "like 'Dynamo,' suffers somewhat from over-intensity and from a certain sense of strangeness," but these qualities he attributed to the fact that O'Neill was "like a wanderer finding himself in a new and unfamiliar land." The critic found the play to be one "of splendid affirmation instead of death . . . of a man's problem in the full surge of real life . . . of victory through the great mystical paradox of surrender." Actually these characteristics are scarcely discernible in *Days Without End.* There is little splendor in its affirmation, and death was denied with equal vigor in the plays of the so-called Regression stage. Far from surging, the life which it depicts is more appropriately described as commonplace than as "real." And both "victory" and "surrender" are contrived. George Jean Nathan, a more reliable dramatic critic than Skinner, more reliable because he did not permit his devotion to the theatre to be diverted by religious considerations, declared that *Days Without End* is "not only, along with 'Welded' and 'Dynamo,' one of the poorest things [O'Neill] has written but . . . one of the dullest that has come to the more ambitious stage in some time." "It may be a testimonial," he added, "to O'Neill's newly found optimism, but it is hardly one to his older gift for sound dramatic writing."

The Jolly Millers

O'NEILL IS SAID to have awakened one morning "with the story, characters, plot scheme and practically all the details of *Ah,*

Wilderness! in his mind clamoring to be put down on paper."
Having enjoyed his beatific wish-fulfillment dream, he converted
it into a play within a month. Still under the influence of the
dream he declared that his

purpose was to write a play true to the spirit of the American large small-
town at the turn of the century. Its quality depended upon atmosphere, sentiment, an exact evocation of the mood of a dead past. To me the America
which was (and is) the real America found its unique expression in such
middle-class families as the Millers among whom so many of my own generation passed from adolescence into manhood.

Fully awake, he described *Ah, Wilderness!* not only as "a comedy
of recollection," but as "a dream walking." At no other time in his
playwriting career did O'Neill respond to the pleasant, harmonious
simplicity of the "real America" or regard "such middle-class families as the Millers" with anything more affectionate than disdain.
Indeed, it is unlikely that reality had ever before seemed so agreeable to him. For even as a young man, a cub reporter, he displayed
the quality of mind that manifested itself in the tragedies that he
was to write, a mind that was unable "to dwell on a group of
happily placed characters . . . without reaching out further and
discovering the inevitable underlying submerged group that . . .
contributed to the happy placement." Himself a member of the submerged group prior to his newspaper days, a vagrant and an inebriate, he must have viewed the world during that time through
jaundiced eyes. Nor were his first marriage, which he called a
mistake, or the situation which led him to attempt suicide, conducive to any but a tragic apprehension of reality. And if O'Neill's
adolescence, which coincided with that of the hero of *Ah, Wilderness!,* was not so wretched as his early manhood, it was still not
a time when he could have felt that "life *was* love." The only permanent home that O'Neill had known was the family summer
place in New London. Throughout most of the year he was away
at prep school, his father on the road. As for middle-class stability,
one would not expect to find it in the family of an actor. For a
more accurate family portrait one should probably turn to *The
Great God Brown* wherein the young Dion Anthony, deprived of
love and protection, approached maturity in spite and bitterness.
Years later, referring to *Ah, Wilderness!* O'Neill confirmed the

wish-fulfillment character of the play. "That's the way I would have liked my boyhood to have been," he said. "It was a sort of wishing out loud." Although O'Neill's dream reflected and contributed to his temporary calm repose, it was Apollonian only in the blandest sense. Revealing his innermost being at a time when it was never less turbulent, the dream arrived at a truth that was about as high as that achieved by a Norman Rockwell cover for *The Saturday Evening Post.*

If *Ah, Wilderness!* disregards the religious aspect of *Days Without End,* it compensates by sharing the moral attitude expressed in that play. Precisely as John Loving's interlude of foolish radicalism, atheism, and paganism was treated with gentle ridicule and forgiving censoriousness by Father Baird, similar experiments of Richard Miller are regarded with mingled mirth and mild concern by the loving father of the family in *Ah, Wilderness!* Having renounced in *Days Without End* his own follies of the preceding couple of decades, O'Neill now looked upon them as amusing aberrations of a sensitive, earnest adolescent. If the hero were born with ghosts in his eyes, they have long since been exorcised, and with them the "spirit of evil." Freed of rationalistic skepticism, O'Neill was not inclined to burden Richard with ambiguities and masks. Liberated from incertitude, he was driven neither to mocking irony nor to pathos and "black despair." In *Ah, Wilderness!* there is no problem of existence; no fighting of life or fear of death; no probing of hidden motives; no unfulfilled longings, neuroses, or obsessions; no father-son hostility, mother fixation, or marital difficulty. Here, without its piety, is John Loving's blissful youth, secure and happy in the bosom of the family.

Even the stage directions reflect O'Neill's currently cheerful mood. Thus, the *sitting room of the Miller home in a large small-town in Connecticut* — New London, presumably — is *homely looking and cheerful in the morning sunlight, furnished with scrupulous medium-priced tastelessness of the period.* In the bookcases are *books the family really have read. A medium-priced inoffensive rug covers most of the floor. The walls are papered with a cheerful, ugly blue design.* One is reminded of the sitting-room of another middle-class home, one which O'Neill described when he was in a less expansive state of mind. Having indicated that

Mrs. Dion Anthony's house was located in *one of those one-design districts that daze the eye with multiplied ugliness,* O'Neill explained that the *background is a backdrop on which the rear wall is painted with the intolerable lifeless realistic detail of the stereotyped paintings which usually adorn the sitting rooms of such houses.*

Tolerant in *Ah, Wilderness!* of bourgeois tastelessness and ugliness, he was more than forbearing with the perpetrators of such offenses. Even the father — indeed, *especially* the father — is treated with uncommon affection. If Richard is the hero, he divides the role with Nat Miller, as did Eben Cabot with Ephraim. Nat, to be sure, resembles Ephraim not at all. For, like the late Mr. Loving, he is "a fine man" and the antithesis of all the other fathers in O'Neill's plays. Nat

is in his late fifties, a tall, dark, spare man, a little stoop-shouldered, more than a little bald, dressed with an awkward attempt at sober respectability imposed upon an innate heedlessness of clothes. His long face has large, irregular, undistinguished features, but he has fine, shrewd, humorous gray eyes.

Shrewd and humorous, he is also tolerant, relaxed, tender, loving. The *pater familias,* he is also Mrs. Miller's little boy. Mrs. Miller is a "perfect type of our old beautiful ideal of wife and mother" and the exact counterpart of no other O'Neill mother. She

is around fifty, a short, stout woman with fading light-brown hair sprinkled with gray, who must have been decidedly pretty as a girl in a round-faced, cute, small-featured, wide-eyed fashion. She has big brown eyes, soft and maternal — a bustling, mother-of-a-family manner.

Her maternity is not possessive, not even obtrusive. Since her husband is no ogre, she is not, like Dion's mother, thin, frail, faded, nervous, distraught; or, like Mrs. Light, stubborn and rebellious. Nor is she bovine and dreamy like Mrs. Fife, for there is nothing of the Earth Mother in her. If anything, Mrs. Miller is the type of middle-class mother, the Mother's Day Mother.

It is not surprising that the off-spring of this harmonious pair — of the fine father and the ideal mother — should be a son who reflects their harmony, their perfection of character. Richard Miller

is going on seventeen, just out of high school. In appearance he is a perfect blend of father and mother, so much so that each is convinced he is the image of the other. He has his mother's light-brown hair, his father's gray eyes; his features are neither large nor small; he is of medium height, neither fat nor thin. One would not call him a handsome boy; neither is he homely. But he is definitely different from both of his parents, too . . . There is something of extreme sensitiveness added — a restless, apprehensive, defiant, shy, dreamy, self-conscious intelligence about him. In manner he is alternately plain simple boy and a posey actor playing a role.

Although his personality is potential for tragedy, Richard is the comic counterpart of such characters as Jim Harris, Dion Anthony, Charlie Marsden, Reuben Light, John Loving — all of whom had passed through painful adolescence into the agonies of adulthood. His prototype is the young Marco Polo. Whereas Marco, increasingly dominated by his acquisitive instinct, twisted by the influence of his father and of his uncle, passed into vicious manhood, Richard, living in the "real America" of 1906, a member of the middle-class Miller family, remains untouched by evil impulses, free of corruptive influences. For *Ah, Wilderness!* is indeed a blissful dream in which characters out of the tragic reality of the other plays make their appearance divested of all their former significance: Thus Sid Davis is a drunk, but he is described as *short and fat, bald-headed, with the Puckish face of a Peck's Bad Boy who has never grown up.* In his drunken state, far from stupefied, he radiates happiness. Indolent, and at odds with his middle-class family, he is happily tolerated by them. Muriel's father, the cause of Richard's innocent orgy, is the counterpart of the dark fathers of the tragedies. But the part he plays is a slight one; his baleful presence cannot dim the bright atmosphere of the play. The prostitute, for the first time since *Anna Christie,* has no symbolic significance, no permanent effect upon the character or destiny of the hero. Far from being haunted by his memory of the tart, Richard boastfully confesses the incident to Muriel the following evening. Like Marsden's, his is a fugitive virtue; but he is not given, as was dear old Charlie, to guilty introspection about sinful acts unconsummated. In *Ah, Wilderness!* O'Neill does not follow his usual practice of completing the life cycle of his hero. Yet he assures us that Richard's future will be secure and happy. At the end of the play Nat Miller says of him: "And I don't think we'll ever have to worry about his being safe — from himself — again. And I guess no matter what life will do to him, he can take care of it now."

Indeed, the boy may look forward to the enjoyment of that state of harmony, fulfillment, and contentment which the parents experience at the final curtain when, standing in the moonlight with his arm around his wife, Nat recites from the *Rubaiyat* with a *gentle nostalgic memory:*

> 'Yet Ah, that Spring should vanish with the Rose!
> That Youth's sweet-scented manuscript should close!'

Then throwing off his melancholy he says *with a loving smile,* "Well, Spring isn't everything, is it, Essie? There's a lot to be said for Autumn. That's got beauty, too. And Winter — if you're together." With Essie beside him singing in the Wilderness, Nat finds that Wilderness is Paradise enow. Death being dead, life laughs with love. Nat appears to be enjoying the benefits of that revelation. Less fortunate than he, the tragic heroes have had to face the terrors of the wilderness alone, lost without love, shrinking fearfully from both life and death. Perplexed by both the problems of existence and of non-existence, some sought comfort in the concept of the renewal of life, in the pagan Earth Mother's annunciation that "spring comes again bearing life! Always again!" Craving love and peace, others returned to childhood or to the source of life and love, the Mother. But Nat Miller has no need of either myth or psychology. Wistful at first about the passing of Spring, he quietly renounces its glories, proclaims the beauty of Autumn, anticipates without displeasure the approach of Winter — provided that his wife be with him.

Although Spring is pleasant, it "isn't everything." This, the theme of *Ah, Wilderness!* is developed by juxtaposing Spring and Autumn, adolescence and maturity, son and father. Formerly the season of Dionysian intoxication, of the eruption of the creative life force, Spring and Youth in other O'Neill plays have never passed without regret. Now, Autumn is Spring improved with age, and Nat is the callow Richard nourished by long years of peace and love. Attractive though it is, Spring is the time of minor hazards: of harmless impulses, naive notions, innocuous indiscretions. Richard, as his father explains,

is only a fool kid who's just at the stage when he's out to rebel against all authority, and so he grabs at everything radical to read and wants to pass it on to his elders and his girl and boy friends to show off what a young hellion he is!

The father, having passed through a similar period, understands the son. Urged by Mrs. Miller to give Richard "a good talking to" about "those awful books" he is reading, Nat says *with a grin,* "I know there's nothing to it anyway. When I think of the books I used to sneak off and read when I was a kid." With Richard upon the carpet, Nat's demeanor is one of ill-concealed delight. There is *a twinkle* in his eye when the son, *frowning portentously,* declares, "I don't believe in this silly celebrating the Fourth of July — all this lying talk about liberty — when there is no liberty!" He puts his *hand to his mouth to conceal a grin* when Richard, *getting warmed up,* adds.

The land of the free and the home of the brave! Home of the slave is what they ought to call it — the wage slave ground under the heel of the capitalist class, starving, crying for bread for his children, and all he gets is a stone! The Fourth of July is a stupid farce!

And, he is *greatly amused* when Richard *adds grimly,* "No, you can celebrate your Fourth of July. I'll celebrate the day the people bring out the guillotine again and I see Pierpont Morgan being driven by in a tumbril!" An "advanced thinker" — like John Loving — Richard has been reading the pagan poetry of Wilde, of Swinburne, and of Omar Khayyam. " 'The Rubaiyat . . .' That's the best of all!" In 1906 everybody is reading *the Rubaiyat,* Nat Miller explains to his scandalized wife, "and it don't seem to do them any harm. There's fine things in it, it seems to me — true things," a judgment which, as we have seen, he bears out as the play ends. Indeed, the *Rubaiyat* was being read as late as 1919 when, in *The Straw,* O'Neill had his hero parody one of its verses:

'A glass of milk, and thou
    Coughing beside me in the wilderness —
Ah — wilderness were Paradise enow!'

Nat continues to be amused even with the sexual aspects of his son's advanced thought. He defends Richard against McComber's angry charge that the boy is "dissolute and blasphemous" and is trying "to corrupt the morals" of his young daughter, Muriel. But then as Nat reads Richard's transcriptions of voluptuous love poems by Swinburne, the *irrepressible boyish grin* leaves his face. With *a trace of shocked reproof showing in his voice* he says to his brother-in-law, Sid,

But it's no joking matter. That stuff *is* warm, if you ask me! I don't like this a damned bit, Sid. That's no kind of thing to be sending a decent girl. (*More worriedly*) I thought he was really stuck on her — as one gets stuck on a decent girl at his age — all moonshine and holding hands and a kiss now and again. But this looks — I wonder if he is hanging around her to see what he can get? (*Angrily*) By God, if that's true, he deserves that licking McComber says it's my duty to give him! I've got to draw the line somewhere!

Whereupon he asks Richard whether he has "been trying to have something to do with Muriel — something you shouldn't — you know what I mean." Richard *stares at him for a moment as if he couldn't comprehend — then, as he does, a look of shocked indignation comes over his face.* "No!" he exclaims. "What do you think I am, Pa? I never would! She's not that kind! Why, I — I love her! I'm going to marry her — after I get out of college! She's said she would! We're engaged!" *With great relief* the father says, "All right. That's all I wanted to know. We won't talk any more about it." Vindicated, the son, we may be sure, will follow in his father's footsteps. If the Awakening of Spring has been marked by an impulse to rebel against all authority, it remains, in the case of Richard Miller, singularly free of all other irresistible, fateful forces. Although for a seventeen year old Richard is precocious in certain respects, his sexual development is obviously arrested. But the rewards of sexual anesthesia, of purity, are apparent. They are those which Nat is now enjoying. And they exist only in the sentimental pipe-dream.

Dream, Drunkenness, and Death

DURING THE TWELVE YEARS that intervened between the production of *Days Without End* in 1934 and the appearance of *The Iceman Cometh* both further fame and fresh misfortune came to

O'Neill. In 1936 he was awarded the Nobel Prize. In 1937 he fell chronically ill. The surprising turn that his playwriting had taken in *Days Without End* and *Ah, Wilderness!* was the occasion during his long silence for speculation about the nature of the work which he had in progress. Before 1946 only O'Neill's friends knew that his respite in faith and euphoria had ended long since. They also knew that in 1935 he had begun to work, not on a trilogy but, as in 1920, towards the realization of "a scheme quite on a grand scale" — a Cycle of nine plays dealing with the story of an American family and of America itself over a period of 150 years. O'Neill announced that in the Cycle he was returning to his "old vein of ironic tragedy." Evidence of a reactivated inclination towards rationalistic skepticism was contained in a letter that he wrote to Barrett Clark in 1937. "God with a change of whiskers becomes the State," observed O'Neill,

> — and then there's always a Holy Book — dogmas — heresy trials — an infallible Pope — etc. — etc., until you become sick. It appears we apes always climb trees — and fall out of them — with a boringly identical behavior pattern! . . . the above sounds pessimistic — whereas I feel full of hope these days. For, noting the way the world wags, I am sure that Man has definitely decided to destroy himself, and this seems to me the only truly wise decision he has ever made!

At about the time that he supplied the foregoing sample of his irony he reported to Clark the result of two years labor upon his ambitious playwriting project. One play in the Cycle was "in good shape, needing only revising"; another was "in a first draft as long as *Interlude,* needing complete rewriting"; the others were "well thought out and scenarioed with much detail." Although once again O'Neill was "determined to grow," he was no longer young. If he still had "prospects," he was approaching the end of his career more rapidly than he probably cared to realize. By 1941 it was apparent that desire had many years outlived performance. Work upon the Cycle had begun to languish, had become sporadic. He claimed to be waiting "a return of sanity and future to our groggy world." Insisting that the Cycle was "still very much alive," he explained that the "stories of the separate plays [weren't] affected much, but the vision of life that binds them into a whole [had] bogged down in shifting uncertainties." But if his state of mind had been influenced by current world catastrophe, it had also been affected by personal factors. During the winter of 1940–1941 his health had been the worst "since [his] crack-up in '37." Equally important, he had reverted spiritually to the condition that had prevailed when he wrote *Mourning Becomes Electra,* a condition that was conducive to the writing of better plays than those that he had turned out during his period of cheerful optimism, but scarcely one to revitalize his creative powers. By 1946 it was evident that there was to be no resurgence of the spirit which had inspired and dominated the plays of the 1920's. In that year O'Neill reported that he had not only "made lots of changes in the scheme" of the Cycle, but that he had destroyed two of the plays. And by 1948 he was said to have destroyed every play in the Cycle but one.

Meanwhile, however, he had completed some non-Cycle plays, two of which have been produced: *The Iceman Cometh,* "most of which was written after war started in '39," and *A Moon for the Misbegotten.* The former, produced by the Theatre Guild in October 1946, ran in New York for 136 performances and then went on the road. The latter, performed by the Guild early the following year, played for a short period only in the provinces. Neither the company's financial position nor O'Neill's reputation would have been enhanced by bringing *A Moon for the Misbegotten* to New York.

While *The Iceman Cometh* was still in rehearsal O'Neill received a group of reporters in a mass interview. Answering questions about *The Iceman,* about his other plays, written and unwritten, he spoke at greatest length about the nation and the world. In so doing he revealed to the public at last that state of mind of which his acquaintances had been aware for nearly a decade and which permeated the play whose opening was expectantly awaited. After pointing out that America, in trying to gain the whole world, had lost its soul, he turned his attention to mankind:

> If the human race is so damned stupid that in 2000 years it hasn't had brains enough to appreciate that the secret of happiness is contained in one simple sentence which you'd think any grammar school kid could understand and apply, then it's time we dumped it down the nearest drain and let the ants have a chance. That simple sentence is: 'What shall it profit a man?'

The theatregoer was forewarned. There was to be no sweetness and love in *The Iceman Cometh.*

Having atoned for his earlier sinful paganism and radicalism, O'Neill rejected the faith for whose sake he had atoned. And in place of the jolly Millers of *Ah, Wilderness!* he presented their antitheses: derelicts without faith or family. Adrift between heaven and hell, like the Hairy Ape they are neither angel nor gorilla, and "belong" to nothing: neither to Pan nor Christ, the cell nor the universe, the womb nor the hearth. Adrift, they are sodden, virtually submerged. Some have already settled to the bottom of the sea where they have accommodated themselves to its silence, its twilight, its peace. In *The Iceman Cometh* there is neither poignant yearning nor feverish quest. In this painless purgatory, not love and peace, but peace alone is the central human need. And it is being satisfied for most of the derelicts from the opening curtain. O'Neill proposed three ways in which men can find peace: through dream, drunkenness, or death. Life is endured only with the aid of the pipe dream and the bottle. Deprived of these, men begin to die. But once they are reconciled to death, it, too, brings peace.

These three roads to peace are familiar, for O'Neill had set foot on them before. Back in 1920 he had the old sea-captain of *Gold* cry, "The truth! It's a lie!" Having dreamed of gold all his life, the old man could not relinquish the illusion that the treasure which he had found was gold and not brass and junk. Responsible for the murder of two men, he evaded his guilt by lying to himself. For a long time he was sustained by his two lies, and died forthwith when he confessed the truth to himself. In subsequent plays there was expressed a maddening uncertainty about the nature and existence of truth, of external reality, of justice, faith, even love. One thing was certain about facts and reality: they were harsh. One sought protection from them in mothers and masks, in dream — reverie, vision, trance — in drunkenness — alcohol or ecstasy. While a drunken orgy raged about him Smitty secluded himself and tried to forget that he was "damned from here to eternity," obliterating painful memories by swallowing quantities of liquor. Indeed, his "old friend in the bottle" had driven him to sea in the first place. The father and the lover in *Anna Christie* were driven to a two day souse by Anna and the Davil Sea. Unable to heed the advice of his mates to drink, not think, incapable of following the example of Paddy, Yank rushed headlong to violent death. Paddy meanwhile sat at his ease drinking and thinking and dreaming dreams. He fortified himself against both the spectacle of Yank's frenzy and the metallic roar of machinery by *taking one gulp after another from his bottle, at first frightenedly, as if he were afraid to listen, then desperately, as if to drown his senses.* He achieved thereby *complete, indifferent, even amused drunkenness.* After *The Hairy Ape* O'Neill, as we have seen, continued to celebrate the virtue of dream. But, abjuring alcohol, he supplanted it with mystic ecstasy and exaltation. "No. I'm not drunk," exclaimed Michael Cape when he looked as if he had "been lappin' up some bum hooch." "I thought of that—but it's evasion." Although Dion Anthony had taken to "hard drinking and gambling," he renounced those vices after he came under the soothing influence of the dreamy-eyed Cybel. Lazarus, O'Neill pointed out, represented not the coarse, drunken Dionysus, but Dionysus in his middle period. In *Strange Interlude,* although dream predominated, there was some drinking. *Dynamo* and *Mourning Becomes Electra* were completely abstemious. Mystic ecstasy was briefly revived ·in *Days Without End.* And although liquor flowed once again in *Ah, Wilderness!* it served not as a refuge but as a stimulant—the inspiration for two of the most hilarious scenes in the play.

Dream was not always a means of enduring reality. In *Mourning Becomes Electra,* where there was no drunkenness, O'Neill introduced the tortured dream, thereby anticipating a motif that appeared in *The Iceman Cometh.* Afflicted with this type of dream, Orin Mannon escaped into death, death being "an Island of Peace" where Mother would be waiting for him. With the exception of Lavinia, the Mannons fulfilled their longing for death-birth-peace, and were released from the "darkness of death in life." Dying, they satisfied their need for both love and peace—for the Mother. But in *The Iceman Cometh* such consolation is no longer provided. Although most of the characters have recourse to dream and drunkenness, to some such sustenance is denied. For when the dream is excruciating, alcohol is powerless; and only death remains. Death is still peace but not a return to the Mother. That notion would be regarded now as a pipe dream.

John Loving, dominated by his Mephisthophelean tendency, confessed that he had never been "courageous enough to face what he really knew was true, that there is no truth for men, that human life is unimportant and meaningless." O'Neill generally shared this conviction. Hating men, he comforted himself with the thought that they are "unimportant," that anyway, "Man remains," and paradoxically insisted that "love is man's hope." The vanity of that hope seemed to be acknowledged when even maternal love — love in its purest, most durable form — yielded only cold, grim comfort; when the attractiveness of the womb no longer compensated for the menace of the tomb. It occurred to John Loving that perhaps, in his soul, he hated love. And he felt at times that were he not damned by a fear of the truth hiding behind the mask of lies he might concur with "what the dead know" — that death is merely "the warm, dark womb of Nothingness." In Christ and in the bourgeois family love flickered briefly and then died out, after which O'Neill found the courage at last "to face what he really knew was true": not only that men are "despicable" — stupid, cowardly, deceitful, treacherous, selfish, greedy — ; that truth, justice, faith are untenable; but that love is non-existent. Waking from his pipe dreams, peering behind the mask of lies and illusions, he discovered only hate and death. For himself, as he approached the winter of life, he preferred death to death-in-life. For the other apes — let them continue to climb trees and fall out of them. Those who have ceased to climb but continue to live — let them lie where they last fell, broken, but oblivious to their condition. This is the vision of life that O'Neill dramatized in *The Iceman Cometh*.

When he recalled the destitute days which he had spent nearly three decades before on the waterfront of New York's downtown West Side, he was clearly not motivated by "his old secret weakness" — "the cowardly yearning to go back." It was not the kind of past to dream in. And he returned not as one who had recently passed from adolescence into manhood, but as a desolate man of sixty — as Larry Slade, a misanthropic derelict who acknowledges and finally relinquishes his last illusion: that he is not afraid to die. O'Neill described Larry as

tall, raw-boned, with coarse straight white hair, worn long and raggedly cut. He has a gaunt Irish face with a big nose, high cheekbones, a lantern jaw with a week's stubble of beard, a mystic's meditative pale-blue eyes with a gleam of sharp sardonic humor in them . . . He stares in front of him, an expression of tired tolerance giving his face the quality of a pitying but weary old priest's.

The protagonist, Larry, also serves a choral function as he comments upon the action and interprets the motives of the numerous other characters. Remaining somewhat aloof from his Neanderthal mates, he is like Paddy in his weariness and wisdom, but without the brogue. He has taken a seat, as he says, "in the grandstand of philosophical detachment to fall asleep observing the cannibals do their death dance." As the curtain rises Larry is sitting at a table in the back room of Harry Hope's saloon. The time is early morning in summer, 1912. Distributed about the room at other tables are the pipe dreamers — most of them in a drunken stupor. This is the No Chance Saloon, Larry explains *with a sardonic grin.*

It's Bedrock Bar. The End of the Line Café, The Bottom of the Sea Rathskeller! Don't you notice the beautiful calm in the atmosphere? That's because it's the last harbor. No one here has to worry about where they're going next, because there is no farther they can go. It's a great comfort to them. Although even here they keep up the appearances of life with a few harmless pipe dreams about their yesterdays and tomorrows, as you'll see for yourself if you're here long.

The derelicts have found peace, for not only are they spared the "worry about where they're going next," they "manage to get drunk, by hook or crook, and keep their pipe dreams, and that's all they ask of life." "I've never known more contented men," observes Larry. "It isn't often that men attain the true goal of their heart's desire." Although he is aware that "the lie of a pipe dream is what gives life to the whole misbegotten mad lot . . . ," he refuses to "fall for no pipe dream." Convinced that his dreams "are all dead and buried," he finds provisional peace in looking ahead, in contemplating "the comforting fact that death is a fine long sleep." He is "damned tired, and it can't come too soon . . ."

It soon becomes evident that Larry's philosophical detachment has not produced a philosophical calm, for he is confronted with O'Neill's perennial predicament. By his own admission Larry is "afraid to live" and "even more afraid to die." "So I sit here," he confesses in Act Three, with my pride drowned on the bottom of a bottle, keeping drunk so I won't see myself shaking in my britches with fright, or hear myself whining and praying: Beloved Christ, let me live a little longer at any price! If it's only for a few days more, or a few hours even, have mercy, Almighty God, and let me still clutch greedily to my yellow heart this sweet treasure, this jewel beyond price, the dirty, stinking bit of withered old flesh which is my beautiful little life! (*He laughs with a sneering, vindictive self-loathing, staring inward at himself with contempt and hatred.*)

It is characteristic of Larry that he has never been able to make a choice, even a less crucial one than that which he now faces. His indecision, as he sees it, has stemmed not from sinful skepticism but from a more virtuous source: from tolerance and compassion. "Life is too much for me," he wails. "I'll be a weak fool looking with pity at the two sides of everything till the day I die!" Here, it seems that Larry is merely trying to cheer himself up. For most of the time there is less virtue in his incertitude than obfuscation. Thus he complains that he "was born condemned to see all sides of a question. When you're born like that," he points out, "the questions multiply for you until in the end it's all question and no answer." Although O'Neill created Larry in the midst of world catastrophe — between 1939 and 1946 — he endowed his wise old character with a singular lack of perspicacity, with a curious deficiency of moral sense. Obsessed with his own problems the playwright was unable to immerse himself in the contemplation of external disaster. Consequently Larry's vision of evil is as narrow, his insight as shallow as John Loving's. Like the hero of *Days Without End,* he bitterly denounces a suffering, foundering mankind for its stupidity and greed, and announces his secession:

All I know is I'm sick of life! I'm through! I've forgotten myself! I'm drowned and contented on the bottom of a bottle. Honor or dishonor, faith or treachery are nothing to me but the opposites of the same stupidity which is ruler and king of life, and in the end they rot into dust in the same grave. All things are the same meaningless joke to me, for they grin at me from the one skull of death.

Having witnessed the "stupid greed of the human circus," Larry has concluded that

men didn't want to be saved from themselves, for that would mean they'd have to give up greed, and they'll never pay that price for liberty. So I said to the world, God bless all here, and may the best man win and die of gluttony!

In the matter of truth Larry again concurs with the pre-regenerate John Loving: "To hell with the truth!" he exclaims. "As the history of the world proves, the truth has no bearing on anything. It's irrelevant and immaterial, as the lawyers say."

Larry's bitterness is intensified as the play progresses, and the disparity between that emotion and the facts which O'Neill gave to account for it is widened. Larry continues to be a mysterious figure even after we supplement the inadequate facts with inferences. Never completely divulged, the content of his pipe dreams is insufficient motive and cue to his acrimonious expressions of self-loathing, misanthropy, nihilism. Larry is increasingly distressed as certain other characters in the play try to disinter his "dead and buried" dreams. During these attempts, although their outline is dim, we can discern that they were pipe dreams of faith and love. In one instance were it not for the author's interpolation the significance of a remark would go unnoticed. For when, near the end of the play, Larry, moved by horrified pity mumbles, "God rest his soul in peace," O'Neill informed the reader of the play that *a long-forgotten faith* [has returned to Larry] *for a moment* . . . Having called attention to the phenomenon, O'Neill never again referred to it. What spiritual trauma was responsible for the disaffection remains hidden. We are left to deduce that the cause lay in Larry's innate weakness, his compulsion "to see all sides of a question." And it was that weakness in part which led Larry to withdraw from another faith, the Syndicalist-Anarchist Movement. But we infer from information slowly, obliquely conveyed that the situation was complicated by another factor, that of love.

In the course of two days Larry completes a cycle which begins with dubious peace, moves through emotional turmoil, and returns to a peace that is more genuine, the kind which death alone can bring. The turmoil is precipitated by the arrival of two characters: Hickey, a hardware salesman, and Don Parritt, until recently a member of the Movement and son of the woman with whom Larry seems to have been in love. The mission of the former is to sell the derelicts the idea that they can find peace only if they rid themselves of their "lying pipe-dreams." Larry alone has perceived that this is the peace of death. Hickey succeeds in persuading some fifteen of the vagrants to make an effort to abandon their dreams, to accept reality and adapt themselves to it. The ensuing commotion of confession, self-revelation, resolution, action provides a spectacle so ridiculous, pitiful, horrifying, and sordid as to justify Larry's denial of love and life, and affirmation of hate and death. Out of the unmasking, one truth, together with its corollary, emerges above all others: love is an illusion, and all women are bitches or whores. Palpable and undisguised symbols of this truth are the three prostitutes, the only women to appear on stage. Yet the presence of four others is felt: Hickey's wife, Evelyn; Parritt's mother, Rosa; Hope's wife, Bessie; Jimmy Cameron's wife, Marjorie. And their stories form the main substance of a weird and discordant symphony. Throughout most of the long piece the tales of Hickey and of Parritt are counterpointed, those of Hope and of Jimmy serving as variations on the main theme. Meanwhile the revelations of the numerous other characters furnish minor background melodies. It is the lesser figures who, as the fourth movement draws to a close, bring the composition to its conclusion in a cacophony of noisy song, laughter, howls, and jeers.

Hickey's wife and Parritt's mother represent antithetical aspects of love — the former an excess of love and forgiveness, the latter a deficiency. Both generate hate in the men who are closely associated with them. The first to appear in Harry Hope's saloon, Parritt has fled from the Coast where his mother is awaiting trial following a bombing in which "several people got killed." Deprived of her freedom, she is as good as dead. Lonely, haunted, guilt-ridden, young Parritt is the recurrent type of O'Neillian son of a dead mother, recalling Eben Cabot, Dion Anthony, Charlie Marsden, Reuben Light, Orin Mannon. Among these Orin incurred the deepest guilt by being responsible for his mother's death. Yet he loved his mother, whereas Parritt hates his, a fact which intensifies his feeling of guilt. And as the destructive quality of Rosa Parritt's character is revealed by her tortured son we are reminded also of the mother of the cruel and death-haunted Tiberius — Livia, "that strong woman" who had denied her son the love which he had craved and driven him to take vengeance on her. "There's nothing soft or sentimental about Mother," remarks Parritt.

When she's finished with anyone, she's finished. She's always been proud of that. And you know how she feels about the Movement. Like a revivalist preacher about religion. Anyone who loses faith in it is more than dead to her; he's a Judas who ought to be boiled in oil.

And later he adds: "To hear her go on sometimes, you'd think she was the Movement." Then, feeling *confused and guilty,* he says, "I keep forgetting she's in jail. It doesn't seem real. I can't believe it about her. She's always been so free." Jealous of her devotion to the Movement, Parritt is equally bitter about that aspect of his mother's freedom which took the form of sexual promiscuity. According to Parritt, Larry too had resented this and left the Movement because of it.

I remember her putting on her high-and-mighty free-woman stuff, saying you were still a slave to bourgeois morality and jealousy and you thought a woman you loved was a piece of private property you owned. I remember that you got mad and you told her, 'I don't like living with a whore, if that's what you mean!'

Larry denies that he ever "called her that," but Parritt continues until, with a *bitter repulsion,* he exclaims, "It made home a lousy place . . . I'd get feeling it was like living in a whorehouse — only worse, because she didn't have to make her living — "

Whereas Tiberius suffered no remorse for the revenge he had taken against his mother, Parritt, like Orin, rapidly disintegrates under the destructive power of guilt. Nothing short of death can save him. But in desperation he seeks the protection of the pipe dream. He tries first to persuade himself and Larry that his mother interfered with his freedom, that, far from being indifferent, she was jealous of him: "She bawled me out because I was going around with tarts." Then, resentful of her preoccupation with the Cause, he abandons for the time being his tale of the tarts to pursue a pipe dream about his defection for the Movement. "I got wise it was all a crazy pipe dream!" he explains. "I couldn't go on believing forever that gang was going to change the world by shooting off their loud traps on soapboxes and sneaking around blowing up a lousy building or a bridge!" Elaborating upon this pipe dream within a pipe dream Parritt confesses what is true — that he is the one who sold out after the recent bombing — and then constructs a false motive for the defection that was actually a treacherous betrayal. Thus he finds temporary refuge in the pipe dream of patriotism:

I didn't want this country to be destroyed for a damned foreign pipe dream. After all, I'm from old American pioneer stock. I began to feel I was a traitor for helping a lot of cranks and bums and free women plot to overthrow our government. And then I saw it was my duty to my country —

Hounded by Larry who is revolted by "such hypocrite's cant," Parritt admits that this story is false and scurries back to the previous one. He seeks again to persuade himself that he had enjoyed a sexual life apart from his mother, feeling that this would have justified his betrayal. "I got stuck on a whore," he lies, "and wanted dough to blow in on her and have a good time! That's all I did it for! Just money!" Indeed, Larry has observed Parritt's revulsion for the three prostitutes in Hope's saloon. When he first sees them in Act One he cries, "I never want to see a whore again!" When, near the end of that act, Larry remarks that he seems "down on the ladies," Parritt replies, "I hate every bitch that ever lived! They're all alike!" Not till Act Four do we realize that "whore" and "mother" are synonymous. "I'm through with whores," he declares *vindictively*. "I wish they were all in jail — or dead!" By this time his pipe dream has begun to collapse and death begins to haunt him. Having expressed indirectly the wish for his mother's death Parritt feels that she wishes the same to him. At last he *suddenly gives up and relaxes limply in his chair — in a low voice in which there is a strange exhausted relief,* he relinquishes, as did Captain Bartlett, his "sustaining lie": "I may as well confess, Larry. There's no use lying any more. You know, anyway. I didn't give a damn about the money. It was because I hated her." Parritt reveals now that his motives were those of a son scorned. And he concludes his confessional tirade with:

And I'm not putting up any bluff, either, that I was crazy afterwards when I laughed to myself and thought, 'You know what you can do with your freedom pipe dream now, don't you, you damned old bitch!'

Clearly, no pipe dream can support the weight of such guilt. Sizing up the situation, Larry makes the decision which Parritt is incapable of making for himself — to jump off the fire escape. Larry's face is convulsed with detestation and *his quivering voice has a condemning pity in it* as he cries, "Go! Get the hell out of life, God damn you, before I choke it out of you! Go up — !" Whereupon

Parritt's *manner is at once transformed. He seems suddenly at peace with himself. He speaks simply and gratefully:*

Thanks, Larry. I just wanted to be sure. I can see now it's the only possible way I can ever get free from her. I guess I've really known that all my life. (*He pauses — then with a derisive smile*) It ought to comfort Mother a little, too. It'll give her the chance to play the great incorruptible Mother of the Revolution, whose only child is the Proletariat. She'll be able to say: 'Justice is done! So may all traitors die!' She'll be able to say: 'I am glad he's dead! Long live the Revolution!' (*He adds with a final implacable jeer*) You know her, Larry! Always a ham!

Larry *pleads distractedly:* "Go, for the love of Christ, you mad tortured bastard, for your own sake!" Before he can *break down and sob,* Parritt goes.

Whereas Parritt is a familiar tragic figure in O'Neill's drama, Hickey is a fresh and novel creation. If he has any counterparts in the other plays they are Marco Polo and Reuben Light. Like Marco he is glib and brash; and he acquired the knack of salesmanship from his father. For the old man, a hell-fire "preacher in the sticks of Indiana," was adept at selling "the Hoosier hayseeds building lots along the Golden Street." Like Reuben, Hickey rebelled against the father and left home, which was "like a jail." But having no mother to lure him back, he never returned. Hickey is a more engaging and sympathetic figure than either the Venetian merchant or the bewildered New Englander. Indeed, on former visits to the saloon he is said to have "brought kindness and laughter." This time, however, "there's something not human behind his damned grinning and kidding." Upon his arrival he is almost immediately suspect, for he refuses to drink, after which he announces that he has also thrown overboard "the damned lying pipe dream" that had been making him miserable. Having discarded his dream he is at peace with himself and therefore doesn't "need booze any more." And now he urges his friends to follow his example — to "stop lying to [themselves] and kidding [themselves] about tomorrows." They are suspicious and resentful, but he is persuasive. Larry alone recognizes that Hickey has "started a movement that'll blow up the world."

When the motives behind Hickey's revolutionary views about dreams and drunkenness are finally disclosed we see that Hickey has deceived himself as well as the others. He is afraid to get drunk because he might tell his secret, namely, that he has killed his wife. But he has found peace, and he has found it by destroying a pipe dream — Evelyn's, not his own. A salesman, Hickey had long had a cynical contempt for pipe dreamers. For he had the knack of "sizing people up quick, spotting what their pet pipe dreams were, and then kidding 'em along that line, pretending you believed what they wanted to believe about themselves." As a boy he had never fallen for his father's "religious bunk." "Listening to [his] old man whooping up hell fire and scaring those Hoosier suckers into shelling out their dough only handed [him] a laugh." Then to his dismay, married to Evelyn, he discovered that she, too, "was a sucker for a pipe dream," for "nothing on earth could shake her faith in [him]," "or her dreams about the future." In the "damned hick town" of his boyhood everybody had said that he "was a no-good tramp." But he "didn't give a damn what they said" for he "hated everybody in the place. That is, except Evelyn. [He] loved Evelyn. Even as a kid. And Evelyn loved [him]." The truth is that he had been "a no-good tramp," and he continued to be one. He insists that he wanted to reform, that he promised Evelyn and believed it himself. "That's what made it so hard," he explains. "That's what made me feel such a rotten skunk — her always forgiving me." And she always forgave even when she "knew about the tarts [he'd] been with," the venereal disease he had contracted, even after he had lain in the gutter like "something they threw out of the D.T. ward in Bellevue along with the garbage, something that ought to be dead and isn't!" On such occasions he "could see disgust having a battle in her eyes with love. Love always won." He wished that she hadn't "been so damned good," that she, too, would be unfaithful. "Go on, why don't you, Evelyn?" he would say. "Of course, I'd pretend I was kidding — the same way I used to joke here about her being in the hay with the iceman. She'd have been hurt if I'd said it seriously." She continued to forgive and at last he shot her so that "she wouldn't have to forgive [him] again." Had he "just run away from her, she'd have died of grief and humiliation." Had he killed himself, "she'd have died of a broken heart." "You see," he explains, "Evelyn loved me. And I loved her. That was the trouble. It would have been easy to find a way out if she hadn't loved me so much. Or if I hadn't loved her. But as it was, there was only one possible way."

Thus Hickey insists that when he killed his wife "there was love in [his] heart, not hate." And this is his pipe dream, for the contrary is true. He hated Evelyn's pipe dreams and he hated "her for making [him] hate [himself] so much." Having shot her he heard himself "speaking to her as if it was something [he'd] wanted to say: 'Well, you know what you can do with your pipe dream now, you damned bitch!'" Evelyn's love and forgiveness were as destructive as Rosa Parritt's selfishness for they generated shame, guilt, hate, death. "Any tart" would have been better for Hickey than Evelyn. What he wanted "was some tramp [he] could be [himself] with without being ashamed — someone he could tell a dirty joke to and she'd laugh." He longed, not for his home where Evelyn "kept everything so spotless and clean," but for Harry Hope's saloon, where it is "peaceful . . . sitting around with the old gang, getting drunk and forgetting love, joking and laughing and swapping lies." He yearned to settle into an agreeable, natural depravity; to follow his inclinations, however vicious, without feeling haunted by love and virtue. What Hickey wanted, in short, was peace without love.

And so does Harry Hope whose wife, however, died a natural death. The model for Hope was Jimmy the Priest, the saloon proprietor whom O'Neill had known in his vagrant days and whom he had introduced in *Anna Christie*. Yet in the twenty years which elapsed between that play and *The Iceman Cometh* O'Neill's conception of the character underwent a complete change. In *Anna Christie* the man's priest-like exterior, the illusion which he gave of softness, blandness, mildness, concealed the real character who was *cynical, callous, hard as nails.* Harry Hope, on the other hand, tries to present a tough exterior. *He attempts to hide his defenselessness behind a testy truculent manner, but this,* observed O'Neill, *has never fooled anyone.* For Hope *is one of those men whom everyone likes on sight, a softhearted slob, without malice, feeling superior to no one, a sinner among sinners, a born easy mark for every appeal.* The play, to be sure, requires a saloon-keeper who tolerates all sorts of indigent patrons. Yet in choosing his man, O'Neill went back to *Ah, Wilderness!* and resurrected Nat Miller.

Older and whiter than Nat, like him, Hope is thin and of an engaging personality: gentle, generous, tolerant. Whereas Nat was the father of four children, the husband of a woman named Essie, the brother-in-law of a ne'er-do-well, Sid Davis; Hope had a wife called Bessie and still has a brother-in-law, Ed Mosher, whose identity with Nat's relative is striking. As if O'Neill were repenting his earlier cheerful optimism, he did away with the bourgeois mother-wife and brought the husband into the winter of life without her. Mosher has no illusions about his late sister. "Dear Bessie wasn't a bitch," he declares. "She was a God-damned bitch!" Hope is more tender and wistful, but it soon becomes evident that he is using her death as a pretext for complete inactivity, for withdrawal from a world which he fears and hates. With Bessie's help and prodding he had been a ward politician and now in response to Hickey's incitement he is about to take a walk around the ward. Putting *a reluctant hand on the swinging door,* Hope recalls *with sentimental melancholy* that "the last time [he] went out was to Bessie's funeral." *His voice breaks on a sob,* whereupon the *amused* Hickey says,

It's a great act, Governor. But I know better, and so do you. You never did want to go to church or any place else with her. She was always on your neck, making you have ambition and go out and do things, when all you wanted was to get drunk in peace.

Furious, Hope *pushes the door open and strides blindly out into the street,* reaches the middle, and turns back panic-stricken. His self-protective, sentimental pipe dream has been shattered and with it the peace that he has enjoyed. *Spiritlessly* he says, "Close that big clam of yours, Hickey. Bejees, you're a worse gabber than that nagging bitch, Bessie, was."

Jimmy Cameron also mourns the loss of a wife, of whom he *speaks with muzzy, self-pitying melancholy out of a sentimental dream,* declaring that "there are more bitter sorrows than losing the woman one loves by the hand of death." Again Hickey remarks:

Now listen, Jimmy, you needn't go on. We've heard all that story about how you came back to Cape Town and found her in the hay with a staff officer. We know you like to believe that was what started you on the booze and ruined your life.

When Jimmy protests that his life is not ruined, Hickey adds, "But I'll bet when you admit the truth to yourself, you'll confess you were pretty sick of her hating you for getting drunk. I'll bet you were really damned relieved when she gave you such a good excuse." To be sure, Jimmy confesses, in the last act, that all this is true:

> . . . it was absurd of me to excuse my drunkenness by pretending it was my wife's adultery that ruined my life. As Hickey guessed, I was a drunkard before that. Long before. I discovered early in life that living frightened me when I was sober. I have forgotten why I married Marjorie. I can't even remember now if she was pretty. She was a blonde, I think, but I couldn't swear to it. I had some idea of wanting a home, perhaps. But, of course, I much preferred the nearest pub. Why Marjorie married me, God knows. It's impossible to believe she loved me. She soon found I much preferred drinking all night with my pals to being in bed with her. So, naturally, she was unfaithful. I didn't blame her. I really didn't care. I was glad to be free — even grateful to her, I think, for giving me such a good tragic excuse to drink as much as I damned well pleased. (*He stops like a mechanical doll that has run down.*)

In an inspired bit of playwriting, O'Neill, having unmasked love by means of recollection and recognition, showed the pipe dream forming while we watch. He further fortified his repudiation of love by presenting an ironical travesty on romantic love and middle-class blissful domesticity. Cora, one of the three prostitutes, and Chuck, the day bartender, her pimp, have been "kiddin' demselves wid dat old pipe dream about gettin' married and settlin' down on a farm." "Yeah, of all de pipe dreams in dis dump," comments Rocky, the other bartender, "dey got de nuttiest!" "Jees," says Rocky, "can yuh picture a good barkeep like Chuck diggin' spuds? And imagine a whore hustlin' de cows home!" Although both lovers have reservations about their affair, these, together with their typical lovers' disagreements, are resolved in an access of incongruous tenderness. In Act Three they go off to get married to prove that they have not been pipe dreaming. In Act Four we see that they were dreaming, that the dream has exploded. By the time they return to the saloon they have already resumed their original realistic relationship. "Jees, imagine me kiddin' myself I wanted to marry a drunken pimp," Cora declares. And Chuck replies, "Dat's nuttin', Baby. Imagine de sap I'da been, when I can get your dough just as easy widout it!"

That the unmasking of love is the main intention of the play is borne out not only by the fact that the individual tragedies of all the principal characters achieve that end, but also by the title of the drama itself. Its irony is apparent, as was that of an earlier title, *The Great God Brown,* even to one who is unfamiliar with the play's content: the substitution of iceman for Scriptural bridegroom being of a piece with the substitution of bourgeois Brown for Pan. But having seen the play we discover that love, illicit or otherwise, has been converted into its contrary, death. It is Larry who perceives this for us when, *with a sardonic laugh,* he observes, "Death was the Iceman Hickey called to his home."

Yet so possessed was O'Neill with disgust and contempt that he was driven to wholesale unmasking of existence in general. Sharing Swift's low opinion "of human wisdom and integrity," he found irresistible the opportunity to reveal how the world is dominated not only by whores and pimps but also by parasites and buffoons. With Swiftian irony he showed that "the springs and motives" of man's actions are "roguery" and "ignorance," "cowardice" and "ill-conduct." Thus O'Neill revealed the aristocratic and tyrannical tendencies of the "one-time editor of Anarchist periodicals," the man's essential contempt for the proletariat whom he professed to love. Behind the mask of the truculent, proud and boastful Negro, O'Neill revealed the humble, servile man. He disclosed the dishonesty of the urbane officer and gentleman and, what is not astonishing, of the police lieutenant. The boastful, once powerful Boer soldier is discovered to have been a coward. And he ridiculed the pretensions of the streetwalkers — who insist that they are tarts, not whores — and of their pimp who regards himself as a benevolent bartender looking out for the girls' best interests. That creatures such as these should be the most contented of people, having attained "the true goal of their heart's desire," is the ultimate irony of the play. O'Neill's hero, unable to reconcile himself to misbegotten mad humanity, overwhelmed by the concentrated display of self-deception, sordidness and evil, prefers to die. "Be God," declares Larry as the play nears its end, "I'm the only real convert to death

Hickey made here. From the bottom of my coward's heart I mean that now!"

The Iceman Cometh is O'Neill's valediction. It brings to a climactic conclusion the death-peace theme of *Mourning Becomes Electra,* its actual predecessor; and it is followed only by the feeble, pale *Moon for the Misbegotten.* An anti-climactic play, *A Moon for the Misbegotten* suggests the onset of rigor mortis following the visit of the iceman of death. Afflicted with incurable life sickness — the ills of body and soul — O'Neill, like a dying man, reviewed his past in *The Iceman Cometh* and renounced every aspect of it. In so doing, he repudiated not only love, faith and truth but also, by implication, that to which he had dedicated his life: the theatre itself dependent as it is upon the willing acceptance of illusion.

Despite the personal writing, the incongruous mingling of pathos and irony, the over-explicit statement and re-statement of theme, the substitution for dramatic action of almost interminable narrative passages, *The Iceman Cometh* is a better play than *Mourning Becomes Electra.* For it is less confused than the trilogy, less turgid and less encumbered with theatrical and psychological claptrap. It has been compared most frequently with Gorky's *The Lower Depths,* a play to which it bears a striking resemblance. Obviously, there is no question of influence, for *The Iceman Cometh* follows the drift of O'Neill's personal emotional and intellectual experiences and convictions; its characters and plot were deeply rooted in memory and consciousness. George Jean Nathan categorically declared *The Iceman Cometh* to be "an immeasurably better play" than *The Lower Depths;* but apart from asserting that the former "explores the confused and agonized souls of mankind with rare understanding and with powerful dramatic result," the critic failed to defend his statement. If he implied that Gorky's play was deficient in these respects, he was quite wrong. On the other hand, the faults which Nathan found in *The Iceman* are trifling. "There are repetitions in the middle sections," he felt. "There is also an excess of profanity," a surprising and irrelevant observation. As for the great length of the play, Nathan pointed out that *Hamlet,* "which is a good play too," runs nearly as long. Except for the profanity, the Russian play has none of these defects. Nor does it display any of those to which we referred at the beginning of this paragraph. Above all, *The Lower Depths* pursues no such central theme as that which O'Neill developed in *The Iceman Cometh*. Gorky was under no compulsion to deny life and affirm death. To direct all the tragic incidents, all the human suffering, to a single untragic end, the purgation of the protagonist's (and the author's?) fear of death would, we surmise, have been a conception beyond the comprehension of any playwright blessed with physical and mental health.

Conclusion

AS "A BIT OF A POET" O'Neill sought "to transmute his personal and private agonies into something rich and strange, something universal and impersonal." He often achieved the strange, occasionally the rich, seldom the impersonal. As for the universal, he saw especially to that: the abiding theme of his plays was the struggle between life and death. Varied and modified by other themes — the conflict of love and hate, the clash of faith and skepticism, the confusion of illusion and reality — the major theme was metamorphosed into a compulsive preoccupation: the maintenance of an equilibrium between life-sickness and death-fear. Attributing the sickness to loss of faith, O'Neill was convinced that capitulation to disbelief could result only in death, that immersion in the "destructive element" would be suicidal. Accordingly he wrote plays of conversion wherein the ecstatic religiosity was contrived, histrionic in fervor, tentative in finality. In an effort to recover spiritual comfort, that of his early childhood or that of the race, he continued the "backward tendency" that had been revealed in the naturalistic dramas as an aspect of primitivism; for he never truly believed that religion was an illusion with a future.

Love O'Neill identified as the prime component of faith and found it equally elusive and illusory. He had his characters plead for love, profess it, pursue it, but seldom experience it in any but the most elemental way. Human relationships, individual as well as social, were almost invariably discordant. Suffering, among other things, from excessive self-consciousness, O'Neill's heroes, at odds with society, sought the remoteness of the cosmos, the privacy of the womb, the anonymity of the grave. In their neurotic self-obsession they remained indifferent to the suffering of other men while bravely avowing their love for Man. They strove to love much as they struggled to believe, reproaching themselves for their failure, exhausting themselves by their effort. The situation was always one in which both the intellect and the will were powerless; overwhelmed, the victim passed into a state of torpor from which he emerged only in the conversion plays. O'Neill's impotence in these matters caused him to overcompensate, to produce the strained effects which characterized so much of his work — the turgid style, the hysterical intensity.

Although he began his career at the start of the First World War and ended it at the conclusion of the Second, O'Neill paid little heed in his plays either to specific circumstances of world catastrophe or to significant occurrences of two intervening decades of turbulent peace. Sequestering himself, he distilled from modern life the futility, the emptiness, the chaos, and left out the particulars of external events. Yet, preoccupied though he was with the universal and the abstract, he continually revealed the thinly disguised particular and concrete facts of his personal history. A consideration of the details of his private life is far more illuminating than a study of contemporary political and social history. Even a moderately penetrating biography would reveal the extent to which O'Neill's early years — the religious apostasy, the resentment of the father, the deep devotion to the mother — conditioned his personality and motivated his experiences: the troubled conscience, the neurotic sensibility, the emotional and intellectual instability, the antithetical toughness and tenderness; and then the youthful self-imposed period of destitution, the drunkenness, the early sickness, the unhappy marriages, the pervasive life-sickness, the virtually medieval dread of death.

Frequently when the transmutation of personal and private agonies failed to result in something rich and strange it produced something crude and familiar. Such failure was most conspicuous, perhaps, after the attempted synthesis of religion and theatre had begun to disintegrate and as O'Neill attempted "to do big work" by digging "at the roots of the sickness of today." Then he appeared to display something more than a "backward tendency" — as if he were not merely drawn to his early past, but as if he had never really left it. For he seemed somehow under compulsion to repeat, to fulfill, the vapid philosophical and prophetic observation that he had made back in 1912 in the verse called "The Lay of the Singer's Fall":

> *'When Truth and Love and God are dead*
> *It is time, full time, to die!'*

Thus, while O'Neill advanced along technical lines, while he sharpened certain perceptions, while he probed more deeply into some conditions, he failed generally to move intellectually and emotionally beyond early manhood. What is more, language and imagery, appropriate to the content of 1912, continued to be appropriate one, two, and three decades later. O'Neill's style remained not only strained and turgid, but awkward, inarticulate, banal.

Whereas O'Neill thought that he was digging at the roots of the sickness of today, much of the time he was really digging at his own roots. Having conceived Man in his own image, he took for his tragic theme Man suffering, and sought the source of the suffering in such dark areas as existence itself, the ill-conceived universe, the stupidity of the human race. Yet, while keeping himself private he was, without knowing it, in the stream and, like the other great writers of the age, a victim of time out-of-joint. He reacted in his own way not only to the disjunction but to the dehumanization, the inwardness, the spiritual vacuity, the self-destructiveness of the world in which he lived and united with the others in presenting variations of the archetypal waste land image — with men dwelling in oases which they have themselves constructed out of mirages. For anyone dedicated to the writing of tragedy the implications of this world view have been especially disquieting. Faced with what has been called the dilemma of modern tragedy, he has been forced to choose honesty and reject sublimity. Unable to accept the assumption that God, Nature, a Moral Order confirm man "in his feeling that his passions and his opinions are important," the tragic writer has had to deny the Tragic Fallacy, one of the "mighty illusions by means of which human life has been given a value." O'Neill tried to supply what dramatic tragedy seems to demand: sublimity as well as honesty; struggle, triumph, and illumination to balance the suffering. But his conception of reality made transfiguration untenable, impelling him to seek release rather than reconciliation. And that outside the bounds of agonized living — in embryo or corpse. Himself a victim of the time, O'Neill struggled more heroically — with greater courage, strength, determination — than did most of his own protagonists. His example, his best plays, his powerful influence are a measure of his triumph.

Beside most of his fellow American playwrights he was uncommonly gifted, exciting, original, prolific. The most competent of them lacked his stature; his intensity, his power, his grandeur both true and false. None was so inordinately ambitious as he; none strove so prodigiously, displayed such firm integrity; none was so uncompromising; none exerted so much influence. For O'Neill imparted to a large American audience an awareness of problems — psychological, philosophical, religious — with which the commercial theatre had never dared concern itself. He incited and inspired other playwrights with examples, good and bad, of dramaturgy by which to guide their course. He discomfited the multitude of hacks in the American theatre, thereby doing a significant service for the serious dramatist. Greater than the sum of its parts, his total achievement was an impressive triumph and made him, in an important sense, the master as well as the victim of the time.

In one respect the untragic tragic age was a propitious one for O'Neill. He came upon the scene at the most opportune time for the full utilization of his talent and for the widespread recognition of his achievement. A generation earlier he might conceivably have written variations of *The Count of Monte Cristo* and won acclaim only after the star actor had enjoyed his. Arriving when he did, O'Neill benefited from the changes that had occurred in the theatre itself during the preceding half-century, first abroad and then at home; he was inspired and instructed by modern European playwrights the greatest of whom had already died or were about to pass their heyday and whose literary successors were inclined toward fiction and poetry rather than drama; he enjoyed a reputation that had been built up, not only through his own efforts, but through those of George Jean Nathan who shared the generally favorable attitude toward O'Neill's work, and as America's foremost dramatic critic, was in a position profoundly to influence critical opinion.

Thus, for thirty years, from his entrance at Provincetown to his exit in the provinces, O'Neill played the leading role in American drama. In 1920, when he won the Pulitzer Prize for *Beyond the*

Horizon, his play was impressive indeed beside such successes of the same season as *Déclassée* and *The Famous Mrs. Fair.* Nathan was among those who were impressed, and he remained impressed even after rival contestants for O'Neill's role began to turn up upon the hitherto tawdry stage — Elmer Rice, Sidney Howard, John Howard Lawson, Paul Green, Maxwell Anderson, Philip Barry — all between 1923 and 1930; all interesting, serious, competent; all lesser men than O'Neill. When, in the thirties, such playwrights as Clifford Odets and Thornton Wilder were added to the list, Nathan remained firm in his conviction — and justifiably so. For while O'Neill had temporarily withdrawn from the theatre, his potential successors, for some reason or other, were impotent to fulfill their early promise. O'Neill's winning of the Nobel Prize was confirmation of his opinion should Nathan have needed any. In the forties, immobilized by his afflictions, O'Neill was forced to surrender his role to whoever could fill it, Tennessee Williams and Arthur Miller being the principal aspirants. To their predecessor, as we have seen, their debt is incalculable.

Coincident with the improvement of the American product, the European drama began to fade. Between 1920 and 1924 the Theatre Guild alone had produced three extraordinary plays of Shaw, works new or recent enough to demonstrate the author's current creative vitality: *Heartbreak House, Back to Methuselah, Saint Joan.* Also during this period there had appeared on Broadway productions of plays by Andreyev, Capek, Kaiser, Lenormand, Pirandello, Toller. These, among the "first dramatists of present-day Europe," overshadowed O'Neill; and Nathan had refused to rank him with them. But by 1924 the trend shifted, and with it Nathan's attitude. Henceforth, apart from revivals of Shaw's earlier plays, an occasional showing of Pirandello's, the introduction of Sean O'Casey's drama, the work of the "first dramatists" of Europe was to be less and less in evidence, a loss which Nathan seemed now to mourn but little. Still sharply critical of O'Neill, by 1924 he regarded most of the Europeans with disapprobation. Shaw he declared to have been "slipping during the past decade." The others he viewed with mixed feelings, preponderantly unsympathetic. Strindberg, O'Neill's acknowledged master, and long since dead, had been rediscovered, three of his plays being performed in New York: *The Dance of Death,* by the Guild in 1920; *The Spook Sonata* by the Provincetown in 1924; and a year later, *The Dream Play,* by the same group. Strindberg, too, now met with Nathan's disapproval: he had been, wrote Nathan, "occasionally a genius . . . occasionally an absurdly unconscious quack."

No longer in competition with the dramatists of Europe, O'Neill could now be confident of retaining the high regard of his critic-friend. With the exception of *Lazarus Laughed* Nathan was pleased with most of the plays that O'Neill wrote after 1924, and enthusiastic about *Strange Interlude* in 1928. Indeed, the dramas that moved him most profoundly were the outsize ones: *Interlude, Electra, The Iceman.* After he had seen *Mourning Becomes Electra* he was willing to honor O'Neill with a position among the foremost "present-day English-speaking dramatists," Shaw and O'Casey being the only others worthy of consideration. After he had seen *The Iceman Cometh* he elevated O'Neill still further, making him "one of the three really distinguished among the world's living." Again, Shaw and O'Casey were the other two. By that time Shaw was nearly ninety, and O'Casey had yet to write a better play than *Juno and the Paycock* of the mid-Twenties.

The big plays seemed even more impressive at the time they were produced than had the more modest ones. It seems now to have been ambition verging on presumptuousness which drove O'Neill, after about 1925, to overestimate his capabilities, assuming powers bordering upon the messianic; to display an extraordinary disregard for the ideas and insights of his gifted contemporaries, as if he were determined to keep inviolate his own, which were nonetheless derivative; to attempt works whose magnitude was out of proportion to what he had to say. For a number of reasons these pretentious efforts were thought to have transcended the previous dramas. Like the latter they not only benefited from O'Neill's never-failing knowledge of the stage, but also from the intelligent and expensive productions given them by the Theatre Guild and, in the case of *Electra* and of *The Iceman,* from the contribution of Robert Edmond Jones, O'Neill's Provincetown associate and foremost scene designer in America. Like the more modest pieces no play was without some resourceful and daring innovation, some legitimate gimmick, some startling motif: the mask, the aside, the audaciously long performance, adultery, incest, wholesale alcoholism. Above all, the big plays appealed for the illusion which they gave of profundity: their bold psychological penetration, with its sexual and religious ramifications; their prolonged probing of problems of existence, which often titillated as much as it disturbed. Finally, by virtue both of the foregoing and of the author's redoubtable reputation, the audience felt that they were watching dramatic history in the making: the performance of a new O'Neill play had increasingly become a notable theatrical event.

But in critical retrospect the unpretentious earlier pieces are more striking than the bigger works: three of the four Glencairn plays, *The Dreamy Kid, The Emperor Jones, Desire Under the Elms.* These, not only expertly but effortlessly written, clear in their conception, firm and powerful in their effect, displayed more beauty and truth than their ponderous successors. Both *The Emperor Jones* and *Desire Under the Elms* remain unsurpassed in the entire range of American drama and deserve to be ranked with the finest anywhere since Ibsen. Here was the "sweep and size" which Nathan thought he saw in *Electra;* and no *Weltschmerz,* no personal writing, no obfuscation. What is more, the monolithic figures, Brutus Jones and Ephraim — not Eben — Cabot, in their crude grandeur appear more likely than any other of O'Neill's characters to withstand the erosions of time. Bigger than life, they gave the illusion of life — before both life and illusion had come to be regarded as lies. They typified that aspect of their creator the development of which was numbed by circumstances — internal and external — and were frozen eventually into mere statues of eminent dead men. The Mannons, Larry Slade and company, Tyrone Jr. may more accurately have embodied the spirit of the death-ridden world of the past quarter century; they surely reflected faithfully O'Neill's forlorn outlook. Perhaps as much as the rest of us he would have liked to continue with life as it seemed in the days of *The Emperor Jones* and *Desire Under the Elms.* But O'Neill would have been the last person in the world to falsify reality as he saw it — even at the expense of the theatre, through which his life blood had flowed long before he was born.

Index